owl

Critical Perspectives
on **Pat Barker**

Critical Perspectives
on **Pat Barker**

edited by
Sharon Monteith
Margaretta Jolly
Nahem Yousaf
Ronald Paul

UNIVERSITY OF SOUTH CAROLINA PRESS

Published in Columbia, South Carolina, by the
University of South Carolina Press

Manufactured in the United States of America

09 08 07 06 05   5 4 3 2 1

Library of Congress Cataloging-in-Publication Data

Critical perspectives on Pat Barker / edited by Sharon Monteith . . . [et al.].
    p. cm.
    Includes bibliographical references and index.
    ISBN 1-57003-570-9 (cloth : alk. paper)
    1. Barker, Pat—Criticism and interpretation. 2. Women and literature—Great Britain—
History—20th century. I. Monteith, Sharon.
    PR6052.A6488Z63 2005
    823'.914—dc22

                                                              2004021842

A version of Ann Ardis's essay originally appeared as "Political 'Correctness' vs. Attentiveness: Teaching Pat Barker's *Blow Your House Down*," *College Literature* 18, no. 3 (1991):
44–54. Sarah Daniels's play *Blow Your House Down* (©2004 by Sarah Daniels) is an adaptation of Pat Barker's *Blow Your House Down* (©1984 by Pat Barker). All rights whatsoever in
this play are strictly reserved and application for performance, etc., must be made before
rehearsal to Casarotto Ramsay & Associates Ltd., National House, 60–66 Wardour Street,
London W1V 4ND. No performance may be given unless a license has been obtained. Jenny
Newman's essay originally appeared as "Souls and Arseholes: The Double Vision of *The Century's Daughter*," *Critical Survey* 13, no. 1 (2001): 18–36. Anne Whitehead's essay originally
appeared as "Open to Suggestion: Hypnosis and History in the *Regeneration* Trilogy," *Modern Fiction Studies* 44, no. 3 (1998): 674–94.

Contents

Introduction

Reading Pat Barker

Pat Barker's fiction always stands in critical and imaginative relation to the society she describes: she captures, exposes, and debunks social and political anxieties that have characterized twentieth-century Britain in novels that are ambitious in terms of the range of topics they explore and hugely popular with the reading public. Reading Barker one is stretched from the 1890s to the 1990s, a time frame that in his essay "England Your England" (1953) George Orwell imagined could encompass English civilization as a continuous thread: "It stretches into the future and the past, there is something in it that persists, as in a living creature. What can the England of 1940 have in common with the England of 1840? But then, what have you in common with the child of five whose photograph your mother keeps on the mantelpiece? Nothing except that you happen to be the same person."[1]

While Orwell cast back to the nineteenth century as he grappled with the nation's imperial agenda and the changing class formations that derived from two world wars, Barker's kaleidoscopic vision inevitably accelerates away into postmodern anxieties at the end of the twentieth century. Orwell argues that personal values should undergird public life but Barker's anxious fictions give the lie to any moral framework, or, indeed, what D. J. Taylor calls the "ancient standbys": the uncluttered values of liberalism.[2] Barker's literary landscape is more closely illuminated when compared to Eric Hobsbawm's "short" twentieth century in which "a rising curve of barbarism" from 1914 to the end of the epoch reflects an "age of extremes."[3] For Barker, apprehensiveness over what she calls living in the "shadow of monstrosities"—or Hobsbawm's "growing barbarisation"—pollutes even the most entrenched of social exchanges: client and prostitute in *Blow Your House Down;* the giving up of one's soldier-son to war in *Liza's England;* psychotherapeutic conversations between characters in the *Regeneration* trilogy and in *Border Crossing;* the artist and his or her subject in *Double Vision.*[4]

In Barker's fiction, history is a vast and encircling pressure on the lives of her characters. She engages with what one of her earliest and most perceptive critics, Peter Hitchcock, calls "community memory." Hitchcock draws on Mikhail Bakhtin's idea of the "chronotope," a semantic field in which time and space are interdependent that operates as a kind of literary x-ray to reveal the "organizing center" of the text.[5] In *Liza's England,* for example, eighty-four-year-old Liza is preparing for death.

Looking back over her life, she strokes memories as she might the faces of loved ones by touching the items in her "memory box." The items are props that evoke past moments for Liza, a gifted storyteller reconstructing a socially conscious trajectory through twentieth-century, working-class life on the eve of the miners' strike of 1984–85. For Liza vicissitudes extend beyond members of her immediate family for their experiences are inevitably bound up with the nation's changing fortunes. She remembers her own and others' experiences as munitions workers in wartime and as steelworkers in peacetime, workers whose lives are decimated by redundancy and truncated by poverty. Liza's personal history is deepened by its location in specific historical contexts: the First World War, the depression of the 1930s, and, finally, the recession of the postindustrial 1980s. Liza's stories, as told to her social worker, Stephen, are prompted by her age but also by her need to bear witness to the historical texture of the everyday. In Martin Heidegger's major work *Being and Time* awareness of one's own death is the grounds for one's "authentic existence"; in other words what it has meant to be alive is centrally related to what it may mean not to be. Liza prepares for her death as one might prepare for writing a novel, singling out key episodes and looping back and forth to test the parallels between periods and across lives. But her stories are cut short by a grotesque and tragic end at the hands of others. At the very moment of her death, Liza is truly "within time," and as she ruminates on the past, memory overwhelms the violent and ugly situation in which she finds herself and gives her peace.

The first edition of *Liza's England* was retitled *The Century's Daughter* by Barker's publisher in an effort to reinforce the interdependence of the private life with public history. But Barker's preferred title, in privileging Liza over the century she describes, is the more reflective of both subject and method: her fictions are character-driven, and it is *in* the characters themselves, each holding a precarious place in the changing social landscape, that Barker's mapping of memory and historical forces begins, and via which the determinants of space and time are explored. In *The Ghost Road* W. H. R. Rivers calls on his memories of Melanesia because his anthropological study of a society dying through the lack of war and haunted by the ghosts of its warriors has an eerie resonance when revisited amidst the carnage of the First World War. In *Another World* centenarian Geordie Lucas is subject to the adumbration of a past event he can never forget and compulsively repeats in his nightmares. The battleground over which his inner conflict is waged is no-man's-land where his brother died in 1918. For Danny in *Border Crossing* an aberrant moment in childhood becomes the pivot on which his adult life turns: murdering an elderly lady for no apparent motive leaves him locked in the defining moment of his life—her death.

Barker's uncompromising depiction of male violence against women in *Blow Your House Down,* and of working-class women making do in *Union Street* and *Liza's England,* propelled her into feminist circles. In the 1970s and 1980s feminist publishers, like Carmen Calill at Virago, broke new ground, strategically separating women's writing from men's to fulfill a feminist need to rediscover writing for and about women. Not only were women's stories discovered on dusty shelves where neglected authors had lain for decades, but new voices like Pat Barker's (named one of the

Twenty Best Young British Novelists in 1982) came to the fore. Indeed, some of the contributors to this collection assess the impact of her earliest writing in terms that play out the tensions inherent in what Margaretta Jolly terms Barker's "double status as feminist and mainstream writer." Although as Beatrix Campbell and others have noted, the 1970s was "a women's decade," a period in which women's political and personal lives coalesced in activism, Barker makes it very clear in *Union Street* and *Blow Your House Down* that for many working-class and poor women the second wave of feminism changed nothing at all. She buries telling examples in her prose. When his teenage daughter becomes pregnant in *Union Street*, Ted King remains silent, leaving his wife Iris to cope alone: "He never mentioned it. Worrying about that was her job." Iris is all too aware that since it is too late for her daughter to have a legal termination, the choice remains a difficult one: teenage motherhood ("a man can put his cap on, you can't, you're stuck with it") or the same dangerous risk women have taken for decades (a backstreet abortionist who "didn't know what an ovary was but she wasn't going to admit ignorance").[6] When a prostitute is attacked by a client in *Blow Your House Down*, a police inspector who questions her about the attack is dismissive: "Well look, *dearie*, we want him behind bars even if you don't. The next girl he attacks might be somebody decent."[7] Feminist rhetoric let alone praxis has failed to permeate the brittle lives of women characters in the novels Barker sets in the Northeast of England in the 1970s and 1980s.

Tough and phlegmatic, Barker's early novels play out psychological dramas that begin inside her characters' heads but seep into a variety of British settings, most notably the urban Northeast and in *Double Vision* the rural Northeast. This is not to say that Barker is an uncomplicatedly "regional" writer if only because the term, like "local color" in the American literary tradition, has often been used pejoratively to diminish the effect or achievement of the writer in question. T. S. Eliot, an expatriate American whose study of British culture had encompassed three decades in England by 1948, pointed out that, in the postwar era, Britishness is inherently fused with notions of regionalism and that regions *form* national culture rather than exist in liminal relation to it.[8] Barker's settings function metonymically to signal shifts in the nation's social history. Barker often explores urban life in the wake of industrialism; the effects of a crumbling economy are funneled through individuals to greater and lesser degrees in *Union Street*, *Blow Your House Down*, *Another World*, and *Border Crossing*. Eric Hobsbawm notes how often streets and public places are named after public figures and events, and Barker plots her novels similarly, mapping people onto locations and intermeshing the public and the private at every turn.

In *Another World*, for example, a car journey maps a cityscape, Newcastle-upon-Tyne in postindustrial decline. Driving home from the railway station Nick skirts an inner-city area where "streets run in parallel lines down to the river, to the boarded-up armaments factory, like a row of piglets suckling a dead sow. Before the First World War 25,000 local men worked in that factory. Now it employs a few thousand who drive in from estates on the outskirts of the city."[9] Continuing his drive across Newcastle, Nick passes through a housing estate where burned-out cars and charred houses proliferate, motorists dare not slow down, and fast food shops refuse to deliver.

It is the same kind of estate in which social worker Stephen supports unemployed youths in *Liza's England,* becoming the target of their disaffection as Liza becomes a target of their violence. Leaving the estate behind, as Nick climbs the hill in Newcastle, Victorian houses come into view; once the family homes of local magnates, they are divided into flats. Except one—Lob's Hill, "one of the few houses left that's still a family home"—his own. Characters and locations are woven into a fabric that is very British in design.

Newcastle's docklands, bleak and derelict when Liza visits them in 1984 in *Liza's England,* are still run down at the beginning of *Border Crossing,* a novel set in the last years of the twentieth century. But by the close of that novel the docks are being regenerated into a paragon of postindustrial town planning: "Shops, streets and restaurants were springing up. Even the river changed. The crumbling jetties and quays were demolished, paths laid, trees planted." Like the *Angel of the North,* the sculpture that stands at the head of the Great North Road as one enters Newcastle, built of reclaimed shipbuilders' steel, the city's renaissance is also aesthetically grounded in its past. But, as Barker sagely implies, the loft conversions in Newcastle's docklands are beyond the pockets of the indigenous population.[10] Reading Barker sometimes means one needs to read beyond the "ending." As *Border Crossing,* a psychological thriller, closes, Tom quietly watches Danny in a new incarnation—the postgraduate student amidst other successful students—hopeful, following a master's degree in creative writing. Denying comfortable closure, Barker nods to the reader's assumption that Danny's evil but seminal experience will become a fiction and that his notoriety may even secure his success. The taste of cruelty remains bitter and will not go away. She returns to this idea in *Double Vision* when in his new incarnation of Peter Wingrave Danny begins to publish gruesome short stories set in prison and after prison in which recidivists feature.

The philosopher Hannah Arendt provides readers with a very pertinent metaphor for training the imagination, "thinking without a banister."[11] As one ascends a flight of stairs, the banisters are intended to provide solid support and to facilitate movement forward. Reading Barker's fiction one becomes very aware of a writer whose facility for fictionalizing taboo subjects and confusing times remains intriguingly disorienting in a variety of the situations described across the text. In *Another World,* at his grandfather's funeral Nick dismisses the idea that time "is like a rolling stream." The hymn that is played, "O God, Our Help in Ages Past," does not help him to grieve or create a sense of release; his suffering is "something altogether more viscous and unpredictable, like blood. Suppose it coagulates around terrible events, clots over them, stops the flow." And in the graveyard Nick finds wisdom in letting "the innocent and the guilty, the murderers and the victims, lie together beneath their half-erased names, side by side."[12] Barker is unafraid of disorienting her readers as part of a process in which the reader "sees" around and between and even beyond the textual world so that the familiar is made strangely resonant. For example, although the emphasis in the *Regeneration* trilogy is on the precise ways in which combatants suppress unspeakably traumatic experiences at the front, key figures Sassoon and Owen, while suppressing their own trauma, also seek to reveal what is concealed and to recapture those very experiences in words that elude the mute and stammering soldiers. Owen's "Anthem for Doomed Youth" is drafted and redrafted and drawn into intertextual relationship with Sassoon's "The Troops," the prelude to *Counter-Attack and Other Poems* (1918). In *Another World,* young Gareth inhabits a postliterate world. Rather than communicate with others, he spends all his time in front of a computer screen playing games or watching action movies on the television in a sad parody of Marshall McLuhan's "the medium is the message." Locked into an alternative world of violent computer games, Gareth's thinning faith in wider social interaction (within the family or at school) is an indictment of the family's ability to synthesize this new technology with wider skills like the facility to sustain an ongoing conversation between parent and child. The family is a metonym for a community under pressure, most notably in this novel where the death of Geordie is "like the side of a house going," but also in *Union Street* and *Blow Your House Down* where the draconian ideal of the nuclear family is ripped open to reveal the inner sexual and cross-generational tensions that give rise to anger and resentment and that often dominate Barker's fiction.

While the BBC's 1964 series *The Great War* and Thames TV's 1974 series *The World at War* were landmarks in television history, reviewers have cited Barker's *Regeneration* trilogy, speculating on the broader meanings of war, as a landmark in British fiction and in her writing career. Barker is not, of course, the first British woman writer to write effectively about war. Susan Hill's *Strange Meeting* (1971) and Jennifer Johnston's *How Many Miles to Babylon* (1974) follow in a tradition of women writing about war and the effects of war as epitomized by Rose Macauley (*Non-Combatants and Others,* 1916) and A. T. Fitzroy (*Despised and Rejected,* 1918) and popularized in fiction by Rebecca West's *Return of the Soldier* (1918), Virginia Woolf's *Jacob's Room* (1922) and *Mrs. Dalloway* (1925), and the American writer H.D.'s *Bid Me to Live* (1960), set in London during the Blitz.[13] But Barker's sustained evocation of the warrior as well as wartime extends the way in which the soldier-combatant has been examined in fiction. Figures like Woolf's Jacob Flanders are clearly representative of a generation decimated in the killing fields but Barker also reveals warfare as an aphrodisiac whereby the intense fear men feel becomes a charged sensuality, a sexual frisson in Billy Prior's case, "racing blood, risk, physical exposure, a kind of awful . . . *daring.*"[14] Prior's war involves sexual adventure, the trying on of different sexual roles while for others the root of their neurasthenia lies partly in sexual anxiety or in nightmares, like those war correspondent Stephen suffers in *Double Vision,* in which sex and death become interchangeable.

Barker's soldiers are men whose drives and desires are as much a part of the war story as their soldiering. The conflation of sex with war in the social imaginary underpins the trilogy, as reflected in the Venereal Diseases Act of 1917, for example, a response to fears that returning soldiers would initiate an epidemic of sexually transmitted diseases. Similarly, the Pemberton Billing affair—whereby the MP claimed to know of the existence of a list of forty-seven thousand eminent people whose private lives singled them out as disloyal to the nation—fueled the kind of anxiety experienced by Charles Manning and others in the trilogy: Manning's carefully closeted homosexuality is tested in wars when he spends more time apart from his family, and Robert Graves's seemingly homophobic anxieties are revealed when a soldier friend is caught soliciting outside a barracks. In Barker's soldiers feelings of emasculation become tangled with sexual fears, as in the case of Anderson who dreams he has returned home to his family naked and that his punishment is to be straitjacketed in a pair of women's corsets. As he tells Rivers, "that's what you Freudian Johnnies are on about all the time."[15] Across the trilogy soldiers display a heightened sexuality as physical awareness or as disability, as in the case of Moffet, an officer who is suffering from hysterical paralysis. A cure is found by drawing stocking tops on his legs and lowering them each day until Moffet is convinced that his legs have been released from torpor. Moffet contemplates suicide once "his whole defence against the unbearable" is taken away, just as Prior does on discovering that his nightmares about the war get "muddled up with sex."[16] Barker defamiliarizes some of the effects of war in order to illuminate a neglected facet of war neuroses: sexual anxiety.

The reader's desire for a sequel is usually a desire to return to the familiar, familiar characters and settings, in a cycle of novels comfortably recognizable via a market-driven assurance that a successful formula endures. However, the novels that follow *Regeneration* are animated rather by what Freud in *The Interpretation of Dreams* famously called "secondary revision." Barker extrapolates on her own thesis of regeneration: she returns to the arena of war to animate the scene via different perspectives, making meaning out of the war by amplification. The therapy that takes place in the safe environment of Craiglockhart War Hospital takes up most of *Regeneration*. But it is on the battlefields in France that its success has to be tested in *The Ghost Road*. Her character Billy Prior is the mobilizing force in the trilogy; not only does he experience the war in phases, his chameleonlike character also facilitates shifts in perspective. In *The Eye in the Door* Prior is stationed in London working as a government spy with the War Department, but he becomes caught up in the anti-war movement. The plight of conscientious objectors explored in this novel sheds light on the historical support for Sassoon's Declaration of 1917 in which he protested to the War Office about casualties increasing dramatically as politicians perpetuate the conflict. Again, Barker opens up a corner of war history that is only beginning to be explored by writers of fiction: the tensions inherent in patriotic pacifism or the plain speaking exemplified by Sassoon's controversial intervention. Although Barker's fictions turn on similar preoccupations, they address very different contexts.

From *Blow Your House Down* to *Border Crossing*, Barker has explored many of the dangers for a society that projects evil onto the nation's "enemy" in war, or the specter of the monster killer or criminal individual, without recognizing their humanity. The psychopath is a cautionary figure she situates firmly within the realms of the everyday rather than an avatar of an evil "other" world. Barker's fictional world is punctuated by random acts of violence that break out in what have traditionally been the safest corners of people's lives: their homes, neighborhoods, and minds. Eschewing simplistic dichotomies of good versus evil, Barker critiques media paparazzi and vigilantism in *Border Crossing*. The images she creates in one particular scene of this novel are disturbingly close to those readers recognize from the James Bulger case and the controversy over whether his killers should be granted anonymity on their release back into the community. In fact, topicality is something Barker backs away from, she has said that she did not intend *Border Crossing* to echo quite so uncannily the controversy over the release from prison of two-year-old James Bulger's killers in 2001.[17] Nor was she to know that the controversy would echo a second time when Mary Bell, who aged eleven murdered two young children in Newcastle in 1968, sought a permanent court order in 2002 to hide her identity once it had been uncovered by paparazzi. Barker's work reflects a consciousness of British politics and of the issues that color contemporary society. *Liza's England*, for example, is a darkly acerbic assault on Margaret Thatcher's policies in Britain from her election in 1979, though it includes comic touches and wry exchanges. In the very first pages of the novel, eighty-four-year-old Liza tells Stephen that a doctor testing her faculties asked "such bloody stupid questions: who was the prime minister. I told him I was trying to forget."[18] There is a clear historicized sense of when and where each novel takes place precisely because Barker takes arterial routes through the British social landscape. In *Double Vision* she takes another route, privileging the rural over the urban but drawing in other settings—New York, Bosnia, Afghanistan—as a foreign correspondent returns from "other people's wars" to the English countryside. The novel is unusual for Barker—while she often crosses the borders she sets up between characters, it is rare for them to stray far across national borders. Yet she is also merciless in her critique of English parochialism. This collection will tease out some of these tantalizing tensions and complexities in her work.

The essays in this collection represent scholarly interest worldwide. The collection is varied in approach and methodology, espousing no single way of "reading Barker" over any other. It is divided into sections that although they may appear discrete, operate merely as an organizing principle: the ideas unpacked overlap with issues discussed in other sections, and novels are subject to multiple and sometimes conflicting interpretations. This collection does not aim for consensus of any kind beyond the general agreement between critics from different nations and backgrounds that Pat Barker's is a very significant voice in contemporary fiction. The size and breadth of the volume represents something of the critical interest devoted to Barker's work over the last two decades. Each novel has stimulated commentary and criticism from a variety of disciplines: theologians (Michael Bochenski), other writers and novelists (Michèle Roberts and Blake Morrison), playwrights and filmmakers (Sarah Daniels, Martin Ritt, and Gilles Mackinnon), as well as the preponderance of literary critics gathered here.[19]

The volume begins with a section devoted to Barker's early work and specifically to her representations of working-class women and their communities. In "The Small

World of Kelly Brown: Home and Dereliction in *Union Street*" John Brannigan reads Barker as a revisionist who undermines the ideology of continuity in British working-class relations. He draws on Shelagh Delaney's *A Taste of Honey* (1958), Nell Dunn's *Up the Junction* (1963), and Beryl Bainbridge's *An English Journey* (1984) to begin to set up some of the overarching coordinates of his approach, and Brannigan pursues Kelly Brown's "small world" beyond the confines of literary realism. Clearly Barker's own working-class background contrasts with that of Dunn, who endeavors to demythologize a class she observes, and Brannigan shows how Barker reorients "given" working-class voices and the literary contexts they espouse (the street, the community, and notions of social realism) in his close reading. Most specifically Richard Hoggart's working-class "small worlds, each homogenous and well-defined as a village" are rent asunder. For example, wandering the steel town where she lives, young Kelly Brown finds herself drawn late at night to the edge of town and the Victorian houses that "have preserved their air of smug assurance into a more violent and chaotic age."[20] She breaks into one of them in an effort to release pent-up feelings of rage she feels at the "mucky bloody" adult world in which she has been raped. Brannigan considers Barker at her most "thoroughly feminist" in redefining her home, and he reads *Union Street* as a revisionist, feminist critique of the "small world" of community. The "small world" is a theme Barker returns to twenty years later in *Double Vision* and her disruption of a village community is the subject of the final essay in this collection.

In a review in the *Washington Post*, one critic described *Blow Your House Down* as "a world as remote from the civilized habitats of most modern novel-readers as the dark side of the moon."[21] Ann Ardis engages directly with this overarching assumption in "Political Attentiveness vs. Political Correctness: Teaching Pat Barker's *Blow Your House Down*." Ardis discusses the strategies she has employed when teaching Barker's novel about working-class prostitutes to a predominantly middle-class student body in two universities in the United States. She believes the novel works to call attention to all the differences in students' class backgrounds, economic status, and life experience that "usually remain politely beyond the scope of classroom discussion." She shows how applying feminist theory in order to debate women's lack of autonomy within the context of the novel opens up a closed classroom and she discusses how students' readings and misreadings of the novel are revealing: they sometimes try to use the "foreignness" of the novel as a means to displace and disassociate from the situations it describes. However, Ardis scrutinizes the way in which *Blow Your House Down* affords middle-class readers scant emotional relief from its "raw and painful insights." The social divisions that Ardis describes are also a starting point for Sarah Brophy, as is the idea of women as the alienated products of their labor. In her essay she homes in on the socioeconomic local landscape of two of Barker's novels centered on women's lives and labor. She focuses on Barker's refusal to idealize matrifocal communities or, indeed, working-class neighborhoods. Most specifically Brophy believes the exploitation of labor creates divisions between women. Women's reproductive work is represented interchangeably with other forms of labor in *Union Street* and *Liza's England,* like factory work and domestic service, so that motherhood is "implicated" with other modes of production. In her essay, Brophy details the kinds of "protective mechanisms" that many women characters, and girls like Kelly Brown, adopt and she reveals that entrenched assumptions about femininity inhibit individual women and, by extension, their communities.

Critical Perspectives on Pat Barker combines an interest in pedagogy with an interest in the analysis of genres and forms, and the collection is especially unusual in the fact that it includes the first publication of a work that operates in specific intertextual relation with Barker's own. Readers may compare Sarah Daniels's *Blow Your House Down* with Barker's original text. Daniels is an award-winning British dramatist whose first works were performed at the Royal Court Theatre in London in the early 1980s. Like Barker, Daniels has proved a controversial writer: *Masterpieces* (1983) examines a woman who feels driven to murder a man after being exposed to pornography and *Neaptide* (1986) was the first play by a living woman playwright to be produced by the Royal National Theatre.[22] In *Blow Your House Down,* Sarah Daniels is involved in a complex negotiation between pastiche and extrapolation when she intervenes creatively in a novel she clearly identifies as an originary feminist, working-class model to be redescribed and interpreted. In this way her play is in performative dialogue with Barker. Daniels assumes that the interpretative community for her work is similar to that which values Barker's fiction because her text resonates with Barker's literary preoccupations and a "Barkeresque" tone. For example, *Blow Your House Down* opens in a spiritualist church, which, as Jenny Newman demonstrates in her essay for this volume, is a narrative setting to which Barker returns often. Similarly, Sharon Monteith in her discussion of *The Man Who Wasn't There* argues that Barker uses the medium as a metaphor for the artist, and ghosts of the dead parading across Daniels's stage correspond to ghosts that recur across Barker's fiction: in *The Ghost Road* Rivers believes that life's important questions "become more insistent, more powerful, for being projected into the mouths of the dead."[23] In the play, when a locksmith goes bust in a crime-ridden area, it is compared to "an ammunition factory not making a profit in a war," an idea that Daniels picks up from comments and scenes in *Liza's England* and *Another World.* The comic tone also resonates for Barker's readers (standing around "won't buy the baby new shoes").

Daniels deploys Barker's *Blow Your House Down* as a "tracer text," an idea that Sheryl Stevenson also uses to effect in her rereading of *The Strange Case of Dr. Jekyll and Mr. Hyde* with *The Eye in the Door* for this volume. While Barker returns to Robert Louis Stevenson's classic tale of a deeply divided self to textualize her descriptions of Prior's fugue states, Daniels turns to Barker's novel to focalize her feminist critique of misogynist violence. By telling the story of fear, rape, murder, and the moral ambivalence of revenge over again, Daniels demonstrates that a text is always "writerly" as well as "readerly" and the goal of literature, as Roland Barthes has argued, is to make the reader a producer as well as a consumer of the text. Daniels builds a bridge with the earlier text in that by returning to the novel a decade after its publication, she updates Barker's 1984 novel, including references to AIDS, for example, a second killer in the prostitutes' midst; "Was a time none of them wanted to wear a blob, now next to their willies, jonnies are their most treasured possessions." This makes the play an act of "re-vision," defined by Adrienne Rich as the "seeing with fresh eyes, of entering an old text from a new critical direction."[24]

This particular aesthetic is apposite as a way to read Barker's fiction for a number of readers and critics. In this collection Sarah Brophy traces the ways in which in *Liza's England* Barker provides a commentary on *Union Street.* She notes that Barker transposes specific details from one text to the other in order that they be read inter-textually. Daniels makes very specific inroads into Barker's text: she tackles the issue of prostitution that Barker raises in the novel but she uses a technique that Carina Bartleet calls "turnabout." For example, she thwarts the lesbian relationship between Carol and Jean that is the center of Barker's novel, projecting it into the realms of the possible but then treats Carol's homophobia with a telling irony in scene 14. Similarly, what Bartleet reads as Barker's "textual voyeurism" in the representation of Kath's death becomes, in her view, Daniels's "theatrical anti-voyeurism." Carina Bartleet's comparison of Daniels's stage adaptation with the original novel is the first sustained consideration of a "sequel" to Barker's fiction. Bartleet's focus is Daniels's dramatic and feminist dialogue with the novel, and consequently, like Pat Wheeler in this volume, she draws on Mikhail Bakhtin's ideas of dialogism and double-voiced discourse. Clearly, the play reopens the novel to generate not just a secondary narrative but a text in another genre, which involves an analysis of the different technical and structural issues at work to discover what these reveal about both works. Bartleet's theory of "transformation via substitution," her elucidation of comic and symbolic elements in Daniels's playtext, and her feminist dramaturgy demonstrates how pastiche generates a sympathetic critique of the original text. As Ardis and Jolly argue in their essays for this volume, Barker's *Blow Your House Down* does not fit neatly into feminist paradigms about violence against women, and Bartleet's reading of Daniels reading Barker expands on this idea.

Jenny Newman in "Souls and Arseholes: The Double Vision of *Liza's England*" takes an entirely different approach to the idea of dialogue under pressure, the metaphor that links the essays in this section. In *Liza's England,* Walter is made redundant from the local steelworks and, unable to define himself according to his trade, finds nothing in life to substitute for work until cancer, a condition that may well be work-related, overtakes him. He is lost, bereft of work, even though it consisted of "turning the same bloody crank handle forty, fifty, sixty thousand times a day."[25] Barker captures expertly the tension between the shock of change and what remains maddeningly repetitive and pervasive in a way that echoes T. S. Eliot's *Four Quartets.* In "Burnt Norton," for example, Eliot juxtaposes the lines "Ridiculous the waste sad time / Stretching before and after" with the immediacy of "Quick now, here, now, always." A novelist as well as a literary critic, Newman pays close attention to the very specific literary strategies Barker deploys in *Liza's England:* "In the attention paid to the overlooked and the expunged, each of her novels can be seen as part-indictment of what we accept as history, part-meditation on its making." Newman explores this idea as a struggle between language and silence, memory and forgetting, and studies the ways in which many of Barker's characters lose their voices—both figuratively and literally—while others speak for the collective, spiritually or politically.

Sharon Monteith in "Screening *The Man Who Wasn't There*: The Second World War and 1950s Cinema" traces the connection between Barker and film texts, exploring Colin's cinematic daydream. This novel sees Barker at her most experimental, in a way that is partly reminiscent of Dennis Potter's stylistically innovative TV plays like *Pennies from Heaven*, where nostalgia combines with comedy and parody. Interviewed in this volume, Barker cites Potter's *Dreamchild* (a "wonderful screenplay" about Alice Liddell and Lewis Carroll) as an influence on her thinking through particular facets of *The Ghost Road*. Much earlier in *The Man Who Wasn't There*, Barker creates a Potteresque screenplay-in-a-novel in which characters are trapped in performance and fantasy, enmeshed in a network of cinematic images. Attributing himself the nomme de guerre Gaston, Colin plays out the roles he sees on screen in the 1950s in ways that reflect the influence of mass and popular culture in that decade. Monteith argues that Barker taps into fears of the mass deception of impressionable (and often youthful) audiences prevalent in 1950s debates on British cinema and cinemagoing and she draws out possible film intertexts.[26] In so doing she argues for the ideological depth of this often overlooked short novel. Pat Wheeler argues from a different position in "Transgressing Masculinities." She reads *The Man Who Wasn't There* as a pivotal text in terms of class and masculine identity, issues that Barker takes up most overtly in the form of masculine institutions like the army in the trilogy but that also find place in the earliest fictions set in largely domestic contexts. Like Jolly, Wheeler shows that in reading Pat Barker both feminine and masculine identities are exposed and explored for the ways in which class, sexuality, national politics, and local community intersect. Wheeler explores conflicting models of masculinity in *The Man Who Wasn't There* by employing Bakhtin's idea of the "novel of ordeal" to explicate the way in which the bildungsroman form operates to effect in characterizing twelve-year-old Colin Harper's adolescent anxieties. Wheeler tests the extent to which Colin's life turns on his search for male role models with whom to identify. In so doing, Wheeler's reading of the novel alights on very different coordinates from Monteith's: for Wheeler the anxieties of "the scholarship boy" described by Richard Hoggart, Tony Harrison, and others are a salient determinant of the "real" and "fantasy" worlds that structure Colin's life and Bakhtin's theories of language and narrative illuminate Barker's exploration of a developing masculine subject.

The section "Men at War" gathers essays and an interview with Pat Barker that respond to the trilogy and extrapolate on ideas that circle the texts and that exist in dialogue with Barker's descriptions of wartime. In *Regeneration* Barker describes in detail the medical experiment that W. H. R. Rivers and Henry Head undertook in Cambridge before the war whereby they traced the process of regeneration of the nerve endings in Head's arm after severing and suturing them over the course of five years. In the novel this experiment haunts Rivers and becomes a metaphor for his role in preparing officers to return to the fighting, having successfully mapped the psychological pain of the soldiers whose fighting lives are to be "regenerated." For Rivers the situation often feels impossible and even immoral. He muses on Billy Prior's response to treatment: "He seemed to be saying, 'All right. You can make me dredge up the horrors, you can make me remember deaths, but you will never make me feel.'"[27] In responding to Sheryl Stephenson's questions about the trilogy in "With the Listener in Mind," an interview that took place over the summer of 2001, Barker reveals the extent to which research is a creative wellspring for *Regeneration*. But she goes much further too, providing readers with insights as to her strategies in creating male characters and into the issues that preoccupy her over the novels. She is especially elucidatory when discussing the idea of impeded communication between men and the ways in which men speak through their bodies or through their wounds; public and private violence; and the resurgence of buried war memories, which are for Barker "the final insult of war."

In *The Eye in the Door* Barker differentiates between the England in which middle-class officers grew up (a pastoral place) and the wasteland that Billy Prior knew so well before the war, an urban setting with patches of waste ground that come to remind him of the trenches in France. In his essay, Ronald Paul draws on a literary and intellectual history of writing about the First World War in order to contextualize this binary opposition. Paul explores Barker's stated intention to "humanise the experience of men by thinking of it in terms of what women do." He assesses her statement in an extended critical comparison with classic First World War narratives. Where Dennis Brown in an essay that follows, foregrounds what he sees as the postmodern turn in Barker's fiction, Paul stresses a "basically naturalistic, semidocumentary approach." He outlines this approach by revisiting William Empson's classic *Some Versions of the Pastoral* (1935) but also finds in Barker's break with the pastoral form the images and ideas that lift her trilogy away from the expectations inherent in classic war stories.

Realistic and nonrealistic approaches to texts are also significant when discussing the cinematic adaptation of a novel. *Regeneration* is not the first film to be adapted from a novel by Pat Barker. However, Martin Ritt's *Stanley and Iris* (1991) bears only superficial resemblance to *Union Street*. While some of the issues that concern Barker in the novel remain apparent in the movie,[28] once Hollywood bought the rights to the novel only the barest of novelistic bones were left: character, plot, and setting are all sacrificed. Iris King, one of Barker's ensemble of characters, becomes the heroine, and when casting began for Iris, who is "built like the side of a house" with "dull eyes and the permanently grey skin of somebody who keeps going on cups of tea, cigarettes and adrenaline," bizarrely Barbra Streisand and Mary Tyler Moore were in the running for the part that finally went to Jane Fonda. The casting of Robert de Niro as Stanley, the love interest for Iris, seals the estrangement of the movie from the novel and the setting in Detroit exacerbates it.

Gillies MacKinnon's *Regeneration* (1997), on the other hand, is impeccably cast with Jonny Lee Miller as Prior and Jonathan Pryce as Rivers. The trenches and bleak windswept battlefields were recreated on scrubland outside Glasgow and filming

there began on November 11, 1996. Amidst the filming of scenes of mass destruction
in rain and mud that day, actors and crew stopped at eleven in the morning to mark
the Armistice with two minutes silence. One member of the film crew recalls the
commemoration as "the most eerie experience I've ever known" and in MacKinnon's
words, "We caught a glimpse of the reality of that war in a way that few people have
ever had."[29] Uncannily, in the simulacrum of war as cinema the detachment of director and crew is cracked open to reveal a level of "reality" that could not have been
intentionally created. A further historical irony enters the frame when one remembers that Wilfred Owen's family received the news of his death on the day the war
ended. As bells rang to celebrate Armistice, the telegram arrived at the Owen family
home and Owen plays a much more significant role in the film than in Barker's novel.
His poetic voice is emphasized over Sassoon's, perhaps reflecting the turn toward war
poetry that occurred during his time at Craiglockhart hospital and his continued
popularity with the British public. Barker once expressed Owen's popularity as that
of "a talented victim, which most adolescents secretly believe themselves to be" and
since he never grew old, Owen has never diminished in the eyes of generations of
schoolchildren who read his poems.[30] There are reasons why Owen as something of a
national treasure might be allowed more space in the film, and for Karin Westman
in her essay for this collection, the success of the film hinges precisely on what it
misses out.

Westman argues that the erasure of the cross-generational relationships that figure in the novel spoils the film's "streamlined narrative," leaving it "bereft" of Barker's
commentary on class and gender, and "both generations powerless to explain fully
why the conflict persists in their culture." Her essay is a lively position piece that tackles the precise areas Barker privileges in the novel as they are obviated in the film. For
example, where Lewis Yealland's electroconvulsive technique for forcing mute soldiers back into speech is powerfully dramatized on the screen by John Neville, and
Rivers's belief in the "talking cure" over any kind of aversion therapy is clear, the
tenets of the "talking cure" are only ever implied in the film through the conversations Rivers has with the men in his care. The theory on which so much is based in
the novel is never explained in the film. Consequently, the dialectical relationship
between the epicritic and the protopathic is also lost. Interestingly, for Westman,
Sarah Lumb is a character who connects many of threads in the novels but her role
is simplified as a by-product of the film's emphasis on heterosexual love as a retreat
from war. Homosexual desire, on the other hand, is erased in what Westman believes
is a "failure of the imagination." As Westman shows, interpersonal relationships have
been focal across Barker's oeuvre and their subordination to other elements in the
cinema only reinforces the reader's recognition of their significance in the novels.

Barker's trilogy contributes to the culture of remembrance that has evolved. The
war poets continue to be the focus of study for generation after generation and Wilfred Owen, Siegfried Sassoon, and Ivor Gurney, for example, are also the subjects
of new biographies and literary studies.[31] In this collection, Dennis Brown examines
the trilogy as a complex representation of interclass male endurance and endeavor

within the context of literary discourse about the Great War. Following the model he constructed in *Intertextual Dynamics* (1990), Brown studies relational/generational dynamics across the novels. For Brown Billy Prior is a fictive foil to Rivers and the crucial linkman in the group dynamics of male bonding. He is a "postmodern hero" and a "canny interpreter" who bridges the cultural transition from Victorian confidence to modernist doubt. And he teases out the coordinates of Rivers's intellectual development positing him as a "modern embodiment" of Hermes, an "apt figure to preside over the phenomenon of postmodernity" and Brown's elucidation of hermeneutics. Brown carefully locates his discussion within a range of psychoanalytic ideas that were given originary impetus in warfare and in their "mirror," the Craiglockhart rehabilitation hospital.

Anne Whitehead, in her essay "Open to Suggestion: Hypnosis and History in the *Regeneration* Trilogy," continues the exploration of therapy, this time as linked to memory. She argues that the act of remembering—or regenerating—the past is character-driven and that the first narrative in which the soldiers figure involves both characters and readers in a negotiation between a haunting past and an uneasy present. Whitehead's focal scene is Rivers's hypnotizing of Billy Prior in *Regeneration* to recover the "forgotten yet active experience" that lies beneath his war neurosis. She provides a detailed reading of the literature while maintaining a strongly contextual line of argument to tease out the history of the symptomatology of warfare and the condition of hysteria, as studied by Freud and most significant in this context, by physicians W. H. R. Rivers and Charles Myers. Whitehead suggests that in reading Barker modernist and postmodernist notions of history are problematized around the single traumatic event and its insistent return, and, consequently, her essay opens up the "project of regeneration" in which Barker is involved.

Like *Regeneration*, Barker's *The Eye in the Door* is a complex and compelling evocation of the personal and political machinations of the home front, but it has very different emphases. In a close textual reading of the novel, "The Uncanny Case of Dr. Rivers and Mr. Prior: Dynamics of Transference in *The Eye in the Door*," Sheryl Stevenson draws our attention to the detailed interlacing of imagery that builds into a novel that is "textually conscious." Stevenson stresses the importance of wordplay (as part of the therapeutic conversation that is countertransferential), and since documents and letters proliferate in the novel, she emphasizes the novel as a "writerly" text. Her essay is a precise and evocative extrapolation on the relation between vision and perception in a novel that turns on ambiguity and a "monstrous" nightmare. In *The Eye in the Door*, there are secrets, doubles, and double agents; there is blackmail and betrayal revolving around the "formidable" Billy Prior, and Stephenson's nuanced reading succeeds in providing a new interpretation of this rich mixture.

"Regeneration" is a mobile metaphor throughout the trilogy and remains a key trope beyond the novel of the same name, so the final section of the volume, "Regenerating the Wasteland" focuses on the novels that follow the trilogy. The metaphor would seem to begin in *Regeneration* where officers suffering from shell shock are described as "wash-outs" and "degenerates" whose fighting lives are to be regenerated, following therapy at military hospitals like Craiglockhart. However, "regeneration" is present in earlier texts where the meaning is less grounded but no less resonant for Barker's themes: in *Union Street*, after suffering the rape that breaks open her childhood to expose the raw emotional places, Kelly Brown tries to understand the act that has ripped her out of the cocoon of childhood and forced her into painful awareness of her sexuality: "She felt her skin tighten as if at any moment it might split open and deposit her, a new seed, on the earth."[32] In her essay for this collection, Margaretta Jolly argues that Barker's interest in birth and regeneration is echoed in the specific narrative structures she employs in *Union Street* and *Liza's England*. Jolly uses the term "masculine maternal" to explore the ways in which the body at once determines and is determined by a wider social life. She demonstrates how women's bodies are sites of social control in the early work, and she extends her analysis to the exploitation and sacrifice of men's bodies in war. For Jolly, Barker's assessment of national crisis is pessimistic (Prior's "logic of sadism" wins out) but at the symbolic level the idea of "male mothering," of "male birth to counter male death," is a narrative principle with which the reader must come to terms.

Anita Biressi and Heather Nunn in their essay for this section detail the ways in which violence circles around *Another World*. They focus on the idea of trauma as located in the "public monstrosity" of the First World War and the private fears lived out in its aftermath, and they link trauma to contemporary anxieties about random violence, an idea that Sharon Monteith discusses in her book *Pat Barker*. Random acts and crimes are the specters that haunt Barker's *Another World*. They read the specific death that haunts war veteran Geordie Lucas as the brutal fulfillment of a childhood fantasy of sibling rivalry and of the violence at the dark center of the family. This is the novel in which Barker really begins her examination of children who murder, the taboo subject that becomes the basis of *Border Crossing*, and the fictional Fanshawe case operates in dialogue with the 1993 James Bulger murder, as well as referring readers to the case of Mary Bell. The authors explore Freudian readings of doubling and repetition to provide a nuanced discussion of the complex relationships between reality and fantasy, and real and fictional violence.

Eluned Summers-Bremner takes up Barker's preoccupation with aberrant children in a psychoanalytic but keenly historicized reading of *Another World* and *Border Crossing*. She argues that the Oedipal is replaced by sibling rivalry as the key context for trauma in the novels that follow the trilogy. She shows how the central traumatic incidents at the heart of each novel are "indigestible" and how in refusing to make clear the connective tissue between characters or events, Barker "disables" readers from easy identification or a comfortable reading experience. Clearly, Barker's use of the supernatural and the gothic contributes to this effect but Summers-Bremner also believes Barker is conservative in her "waylaid realism" and this fuels her excursion into Barker's uncanny "postrealist" fictions.

Finally, Sharon Monteith and Nahem Yousaf turn to Barker's most recent work. When this collection was going to press, Barker published *Double Vision*, her first novel set in a village environment. The friendship between foreign correspondents

Stephen and Ben is the strongest relationship in the book, yet remains largely unspoken instead becoming a Barkeresque example of men failing to communicate their emotions, with Stephen reluctant to address the gap that Ben's death leaves in his life.[33] The basic inarticulacy is reinforced in Stephen's discovering Ben's dead body then subsequently journeying through the English countryside that meant most to his friend. It is emphasized too in the stone bust of Ben that flickers in the firelight as Stephen sits with Ben's widow, Kate: in death Ben is the third corner of a grief-infused, erotically charged triangle. Stephen misses Ben far more than he misses his estranged wife, Nerys; he feels quite simply that he has shared more with Ben. In fact, he sacrificed his marriage to their career partnership. The frisson of sexual attraction that passes between Kate and Stephen on first meeting is partly a transference of Stephen's latent attraction to and admiration for her husband. In her knowledge of their friendship, Kate transfers affection too. The relationship between Ben and Stephen is the pivot for the ethical turn of the novel, especially since Ben is an icon; resilient in photographing the real in all circumstances. It is to debates around representation that Monteith and Yousaf turn and their painterly reading of the novel draws out Barker's references to Goya while opening up the text's emphasis on impressionist and "nonrepresentional" art to literary-critical scrutiny. Barker's oeuvre is an artful work in progress, and this collection will provide readers with cogent criticism to match.

NOTES

1. George Orwell, "England Your England," in *England Your England and Other Essays* (London: Secker and Warburg, 1954), 194. For a discussion of Orwell's ideas of Englishness see, for example, Graham Holderness, Bryan Loughrey, and Nahem Yousaf, *George Orwell* (London: Macmillan, 1998).

2. D. J. Taylor, *After the War: The Novel and England since 1945* (London: Flamingo, 1993), 293.

3. Eric Hobsbawm, "The Age of Total War," in *Age of Extremes: The Short Twentieth Century, 1914–1991* (London: Michael Joseph, 1994), 21–53.

4. "Pat Barker in Conversation with Sharon Monteith," Hay-on-Wye Literary Festival, June 2, 2001.

5. Peter Hitchcock, "Radical Writing" in *Dialogics of the Oppressed* (Minneapolis: University of Minnesota Press, 1993), 55; Mikhail Bakhtin, "Forms of Time and Chronotope in the Novel," in *The Dialogic Imagination,* ed. Michael Holquist and Caryl Emerson, 84–258 (Austin: University of Texas Press, 1981).

6. Pat Barker, *Union Street* (London: Virago, 1982), 201–9.

7. Pat Barker, *Blow Your House Down* (London: Virago, 1984), 109.

8. T. S. Eliot, "Notes toward a Definition of Culture," in *The Selected Essays of T. S. Eliot* (London: Faber, 1979). Although, we should note that debates over Europe and political devolution in the UK have brought regional autonomy and governmental and national agencies into contestation demonstrating that British identity remains under negotiation.

9. Pat Barker, *Another World* (London: Viking, 1998), 11.

10. Pat Barker, *Border Crossing* (London: Viking, 2001), 212.

11. For a discussion of this idea, see Lisa J. Disch, *Hannah Arendt and the Limits of Philosophy* (Ithaca: Cornell University Press, 1994), 143–46.

12. Barker, *Another World*, 271 and 277.

13. For a detailed discussion, see Claire M. Tylee, *The Great War and Women's Consciousness: Images of Militarism and Womanhood in Women's Writing, 1914–1964* (London: Macmillan, 1990).

14. Pat Barker, *The Ghost Road* (London: Viking, 1995), 172.

15. Barker, *Regeneration*, 28–29.

16. Ibid., 100.

17. "Pat Barker in Conversation with Sharon Monteith."

18. Pat Barker, *Liza's England* (London: Virago, 1996), 1.

19. See, for example, Michael I. Bochenski, *Theology from Three Worlds* (Macon, Ga.: Smith and Helways, 1997), 70; Blake Morrison, "War Stories," *New Yorker*, January 22, 1996, 78–80.

20. Barker, *Union Street*, 51.

21. Elizabeth Ward, "The Dark at the End of the Street: *Blow Your House Down*," *Washington Post*, September 9, 1984, section 10.

22. See, for example, Elaine Aston, "Daniels in the Lion's Den: Sarah Daniels and the British Backlash," *Theatre Journal* 47, no. 3 (1995): 393–403; Christine Dymkowski, "Breaking the Rules: The Plays of Sarah Daniels," *Contemporary Theatre Review* 5, no. 1 (1996): 63–75.

23. Barker, *The Ghost Road*, 212.

24. Adrienne Rich, "When We Dead Awaken: Writing as Re-Vision," *College English* 32 (1974): 18.

25. Barker, *Liza's England*, 117.

26. See, for example, Alan O'Shea, "What a Day for a Daydream: Modernity, Cinema, and the Popular Imagination in the Late Twentieth Century," in *Modern Times: Reflections on a Century of English Modernity*, ed. Mica Nava and Alan O'Shea, 243–45 (London: Routledge, 1995).

27. Barker, *Regeneration*, 78–79.

28. See Sharon Monteith, *Pat Barker* (Plymouth: Northcote House, 2002), 75–78; Karin Westman, *Pat Barker's Regeneration; A Reader's Guide* (London: Continuum, 2001), 69–72. See also Sara Martin, "Regenerating the War Movie? Pat Barker's *Regeneration* according to Gillies Mackinnon," *Literature/Film Quarterly* 30, no. 2 (2002): 98–103. Martin argues *Regeneration* is "an over-ambitious adaptation of an already ambitious source respected by the adapter in excess."

29. Liz Hunt, "Fake Blood, Real Mud as Film Relives the Somme," *Independent on Sunday*, February 16, 1997.

30. Pat Barker in conversation with Dominic Hibberd, "Centurions 44: Wilfred Owen's 'Strange Meeting,'" BBC Radio 4, November 8, 1998.

31. See, for example, Stephen MacDonald, *Not About Heroes: The Friendship of Siegfried Sassoon and Wilfred Owen* (London: Faber, 1983); Jean Moorcroft Wilson, *Siegfried Sassoon: The Making of a War Poet* (London: Duckworth, 1998); Dominic Hibberd, *Wilfred Owen: The Last Year* (London: Constable, 1998); and *Wilfred Owen: A New Biography* (London: Weidenfeld, 2002); John Lucas, *Ivor Gurney* (Plymouth: Northcote House, 1996).

32. Barker, *Union Street*, 53.

33. Monteith, *Pat Barker*, 37–38. Barker also discusses the idea in her interview with Sheryl Stevenson in this volume.

Part One ■ Writing Working-Class Women

JOHN BRANNIGAN

The Small World of Kelly Brown
Home and Dereliction in *Union Street*

The title of Pat Barker's first novel, *Union Street* (1982), evokes the familiar topography of working-class community. It seems to promise the intimate neighborliness, shift-work routines, and cheerful endurance common to the popular, often nostalgic, imagination of working-class life. "Street" has obvious significance as the parochial unit of urban, working-class community, and it functions in the classic British soap opera *Coronation Street* (1960–) as a convenient, symbolic container of a knowable, familiar society, the kind of place Richard Hoggart described as "small worlds, each as homogenous and well-defined as a village."[1] "Union" establishes an association with working-class labor, a history of struggle against exploitation, as well as the more suggestive resonances of unity, togetherness, family, and sexual union. "Union Street" is a symbolic space that functions to delineate the imaginative contours of an urban, working-class landscape and social structure. In doing so, it connects with those earlier intrepid cartographers of working-class community, with George Orwell, Hoggart, Raymond Williams, and with the social realism in literature, drama, film, and television of the late 1950s and early 1960s. These connections, I want to argue, provide important contexts for Barker's novel, although my ultimate focus will be the ways in which Barker reorients these contexts, in her construction of the experiences and identities of working-class women, against an emergent condition of postindustrial economic blight.

For Orwell, working-class community is centered on notions of domesticity and interiority. Indeed, community as an idea is best embodied for Orwell in the cozy, familial environment of a working-class home:

> In a working-class home—I am not thinking at the moment of the unemployed, but of comparatively prosperous homes you breathe a warm, decent, deeply human atmosphere which is not so easy to find elsewhere. . . . I have often been struck by the peculiar easy completeness, the perfect symmetry as it were, of a working-class interior at its best. Especially on winter evenings after tea, when the fire glows in the open range and dances mirrored in the steel fender, when Father, in shirt-sleeves, sits in the rocking chair at one side of the fire reading the racing finals, and Mother sits on the other with her sewing, and the children are happy with a pennorth of mint humbugs, and the dog lolls roasting himself on

the rag mat—it is a good place to be in, provided that you can be not only in it
but sufficiently *of* it to be taken for granted.[2]

Orwell's depiction of working-class domesticity is deliberately sentimental. He avoids
thinking of the struggle with debt and disease, and settles instead for a comfortable
image of homeliness and sufficiency. There is a hint of warning in his distinction
between being *in* this home and being *of* it, which remembers that community relies
upon exclusion and suspicion. Its attraction as an idea for Orwell is its rootedness, its
almost mythical connection with the "deeply human."

Hoggart describes the roots and core values of this community in more detail and
with less sentiment in *The Uses of Literacy,* but finds also the deep mythic structures
of working-class life, the "extraordinary changelessness" of working-class culture,
in which men and women have their apparently timeless places at the hearth and
the factory. Such depictions of working-class life represent as natural and fixed the
rhythms and patterns of an industrialized working-class community, which runs to
a daily clock of factory sirens and the weekly cycle of pawnshops and payday. The
temporal rhythm of working-class life is the subject of Alan Sillitoe's novel *Saturday
Night and Sunday Morning* (1958), which figures working-class community as a
solid, timeless culture, with its own mythic figures and rituals:

> Fat Mrs. Bull the gossiper stood with her fat arms folded over her apron at the
> yard-end, watching people pass by on their way to work. With pink face and
> beady eyes, she was a tight-fisted defender of her tribe, queen of the yard because
> she had lived there for twenty-two years, earning names like "The News of the
> World" and the "Loudspeaker" because she watched the factory go in every
> morning and afternoon to glean choice gossip for retail later on.[3]

Community for Sillitoe is figured in the familiar rhythms and routines of daily working life; it revolves around the aggressive, mechanical time of factory and pub, as well
as the seasonal, slow time of home and nature. Arthur Seaton, Sillitoe's hero, is representative in some respects of an emergent class of affluent workers, but the novel
suggests that even the arrival of the "affluent society," symbolized in the novel by television sets, will do nothing to dent the temporal patterns and deep structures of
working-class society. The resilience of working-class culture to change, which is
related to the persistent representation of its deep-rootedness and organicism, is a
recurrent theme in the postwar imagination of the working-class community, and
one that serves to invest symbolic significance in the working class as a repository of
"natural," homely values.

It is against this ideological context that *Union Street* is best read as a novel that pays
considerable attention to demythologizing the homeliness and continuity of working-
class culture and that registers the traumatic impact of the decimation of particular
economic and social structures. *Union Street* comprises the stories of seven working-
class women, ranging from Kelly Brown, who is eleven years old, to Alice Bell, who is
in her seventies. "Home" and "street," the stable anchors of existence in Hoggart's
working-class community, are derelict or dystopian sites in Barker's postindustrial

imagination. The working-class homes of *Union Street* are falling apart, literally and metaphorically. Windows are boarded up, or partially boarded where panes have been smashed. The floors and stairs contain treacherous holes and gaps that disrupt the function of home as sanctuary. Chimney backs are broken, allowing the smoke from neighboring houses to pour in. For Kelly Brown, the streets are filled with "a smell of decay, of life ending."[4] The streets around Union Street are in the process of complete demolition, so that Kelly finds whole landscapes of dereliction, pockmarked with the rubble of disused factories and crumbling houses:

> She liked particularly the decaying, boarded-up houses by the river. There a whole community had been cleared away: the houses waited for the bulldozers and the demolition men to move in, but they never came.
>
> Grass grew between the cobbles, rosebay willowherb thronged the empty spaces, always threatening to encroach, but still the houses stood. Officially empty, but not in reality. You had only to walk down these streets at night to realise that life, life of a kind, still went on. (59–60)

In these abandoned streets, Kelly finds an abandoned throng of homeless, hopeless tramps and drunks, derelict people hidden in a derelict landscape. "Derelict" is a word repeated several times in the course of the novel, and this term serves as a metaphor for the decrepit condition of life in the wastelands of England's industrial communities. It defines the economic, psychological, cultural, and geographical landscape of Barker's fiction, and serves to connect the apparently isolated instances of rape, murder, domestic violence, abandonment, and sickness to the social and cultural structures of this bleak, postindustrial scene.

Barker's novel depicts working-class community, then, through tropes of absence, brokenness, and ruin. This might lead us to suspect that her depiction of the postindustrial plight of the working class is heavily scored by nostalgia for a lost haven of communality and rootedness. This would put the community depicted in *Union Street* in close proximity to the England that Beryl Bainbridge describes in her *English Journey* (1984), as she tours abandoned mines, struggling shipyards, and deserted factories, and mourns the deaths of England's industrial, maritime, and cultural past.[5] The landscapes to which Bainbridge is constantly drawn, two years after the publication of *Union Street,* are ones of erasure, disappearance, and decimation, the rotting, forsaken landscapes that bear the scars of once industrious communities, just as in Barker's *Union Street.* Bainbridge's narrative is structured to resemble the journey undertaken by J. B. Priestley in 1933, narrated in his *English Journey* (1933), but it also converses with Orwell's *The Road to Wigan Pier* (1937), upon which Bainbridge plays a sardonic joke in her subtitle, *The Road to Milton Keynes.* Bainbridge finds much of England to be ghostly, haunted by what it has lost, paralyzed into acts of perpetual remembrance and mourning. Barker's England, and specifically her northeastern corner of England, is as much a site of memory, of loss and paralysis, as the one Bainbridge depicts. But Barker is not so much nostalgic as revisionist in her approach, revisionist in the sense of returning critically to the myth of homeliness and community pervasive in earlier representations of the working class.

This approach is exemplified in the first story of the novel, the story of Kelly Brown, whose home is broken, quite literally, and whose sense of homeliness is severely disrupted in the course of the story. Kelly is eleven, on the cusp of entering an adult world of work and sexuality. The division between childhood and adulthood is conventionally figured in terms of interiority and exteriority, in which childhood is cocooned from the painful knowledge of the world outside by a series of physical, emotional, and moral barriers, and in which home and family represent comfort and safety. For Kelly, however, these barriers are shown to be porous. This is the significance of the story's opening, in which Kelly is awakened by the noise of a square of cardboard flapping against the broken window frame of her bedroom. It is one of a number of images of exposure, of the lack of the protective shell that "home" should represent, which recur throughout the novel. The boundary between home and outside is breached. This is exemplified further when Kelly discovers that her sister, Linda, has discarded a soiled sanitary towel in Kelly's clothes drawer. Kelly rejects the "mucky bloody" adult world that Linda represents: "She looked at the hair in Linda's armpits, at the breasts that shook and wobbled when she ran, and no, she didn't want to get like that. And she certainly didn't want to drip foul-smelling, brown blood out of her fanny every month" (3). Kelly's innocence is marked here by her disgust at what appears to her as the grotesque physicality of adulthood. Later, she will discover that more affluent families shroud their young girls in the cozy, pink world of glossy make-believe to preserve their innocence (52). For her, however, the boundaries between innocence and experience are as thin as the walls through which she hears her mother "on the hump all night" with some new man dragged home from the pub (3). Her mother's latest lover is introduced to Kelly the following morning, almost comically, as *Uncle* Arthur, but the intrusion of a strange man into their home life seems expected, signaling again the permeable boundaries between the homely and the strange. The story of "Kelly Brown" shares in this respect the domestic situation of Shelagh Delaney's *A Taste of Honey* (1958), in which Helen's unstable sexual life leaves her daughter, Jo, in circumstances in which her childhood and the securities afforded by "home" are compromised. Delaney's play provides a significant pretext in this case for Barker's stories about the disjunctive experiences of working-class women caught outside the familial structures of their communities. In Delaney's play, for example, Helen and Jo are not part of a street, but instead inhabit a transient world of defaulting tenants and serial evictions.

Some semblances of home and community do exist for Kelly, and they are perhaps the only indications of a preserved innocence. She chooses to wear one of her mother's sweaters, for example, because "they were warmer, somehow, and she liked the smell" (4). She shows no such signs of familial affection toward her mother, but the gesture is an indication at least of a desire for sentiment, for connection. So too, she feels connected to the local shopkeeper and to Iris King, who embodies some degree of stability and continuity in the street (although Iris's own story in chapter 5 revisits and undermines this reputation as a myth). There is some trace here of the solidity and commonality of Hoggart's and Sillitoe's depictions of working-class community. It is associated in the story, however, with Kelly's childhood fictions of the world around her, and it is shattered when Kelly is raped.

Kelly is raped by an older man, whom she has begun to construct as a substitute father. He shapes this image of himself when they first meet in the park, when he treats her in a gentle, paternal manner, which allows her to begin "telling herself stories again, fantasies whose warmth eased away the last ache of doubt. Her father had come back" (16). Kelly does not entertain this fantasy for long, and she knows that the man is a threat. She is drawn to him, however, because he appears to fill a void in her identity. "Other people—her mother, Linda, the teachers at school—merely glanced at her and then with indifference or haste, passed on. But this man stared at her as if every pore in her skin mattered" (15–16). On their second encounter, after Kelly has been at the fun fair, the man pretends to lead her home, but leads her instead into a deserted industrial wasteland, where he rapes her. Barker here connects the rape symbolically to a powerful matrix of absent centers. Kelly is drawn to the man because he takes the place of her absent father, and because his gaze "creates her," where she has been ignored by her own mother, sister, teachers, and everyone else. His choice of location is also symbolic, for if the community of Kelly's birth once thrived upon the monumental power of industry, the deserted factory yard is now the symbolic core of a deserted, vulnerable community.

Set in such a bleak landscape of loss and dereliction, the rape has obvious allegorical significance for the community as a whole. It destroys any sense of connection, cohesion, or self-validation, so that when Kelly realizes that the rape defines her— "she *was* what had just happened to her" (32)—she also recognizes that she is now made in the image of her surroundings. The man has deprived her of the last tissue of protection between her and the painful, blighted landscape around her. He makes her, "and he was . . . nothing!" (32), and so she becomes nothing too. She has been initiated into the world of dereliction, and thereafter she sees the world around her in all its terrifying mundanity:

> His face remained. And would be there always, trailing behind it, not the card-board terrors of the fairground, those you buy for a few pennies and forget, but the real terror of the adult world, in which grown men open their mouths and howl like babies, where nothing that you feel, whether love or hate, is pure enough to withstand the contamination of pity. (57)

Kelly's newly broken vision of the world around her is suggested in the story by a series of images and metaphors of sight and specularity. She cannot escape seeing the man who has just raped her when she sits with him in a fish and chip shop lined with mirror tiles (33). She cannot avoid the "unadmitted speculation" of neighbors, the prying eyes of the street (47). She sees in her mother's beaten face a mirror of her own (58), and when she encounters her own savage reflection in a mirror in a house she has broken into, she smashes it, "hurling her whole body against the glass" (54).

Kelly's rage at what she has become is the rage of Caliban, born of the recognition of herself as the creation of the man's violent, sadistic desires. "You taught me language;

and my profit on't is, I know how to curse," speaks Caliban in *The Tempest* (1.2.353–67). This lesson is exemplified in Kelly's enraged defacement of her school, in which she daubs her shit all over the headmaster's office,[6] and chalks graffiti on her classroom blackboard:

> She careered down the corridor to her own classroom, the smell of her shit
> hot above the usual smells of gymshoes and custard. She almost ran at the black-
> board, and wrote, sobbing, PISS, SHIT, FUCK. Then, scoring the board so hard
> that the chalk screamed, the worst word she knew: CUNT. (56)

This is the language she has been taught in the derelict, crumbling community of her upbringing. This is the product of the social and economic deprivation of her street. She screeches in chalk the "worst word she knew," the word that sums up her worth in a society in which she has only ever been valued by a man intent on raping her. This is Kelly's exasperated cry at the cruel knowledge of what she will become. It is the fate of her mother, of Linda, and of the characters in later stories, of Iris King, for example, whose husband invites his drunken friends to rape her. In the derelict society symbolized in Union Street, women are frequently reduced to commodities for use and exchange, their value determined in the impoverished system of social and cultural relationships of their ruined community.

Barker is thoroughly feminist not just in pursuing these anguished cries of oppressed women, but also in showing such oppression as the product of a bankrupt social economy. In this context even the rapist is not the victor, but is reduced before Kelly's eyes to a sniveling wreck. Everywhere, in fact, in Barker's landscape are the signs of a failed social system, from Kelly's acts of outrage, to the absence of any authorities or guardians in her community, or the sicknesses paralyzing the few remaining men in the street, or the dead baby that Kelly discovers buried under a heap of rubble near her home. "Barker's main aim," Ian Haywood argues of *Union Street*, "is to show that working-class femininity, as constructed by those largely absent contexts of capitalist and patriarchal power, is a process of almost unremitting gloom and entrapment."[7] In this sense it more than superficially resembles the stories in Nell Dunn's *Up the Junction* (1963), in which working-class women are depicted as trapped in a relentless cycle of poverty and debt, casual underage sex, backstreet abortions, abusive relationships, and early signs of illness. Barker's women, like those in Dunn's stories, or in Margaret Lassell's *Wellington Road* (1962), are as condemned as the slum housing they live in.

This recognition that she is condemned to dereliction seems to enrage Kelly into her acts of destruction. When she wanders bewildered into an affluent Victorian house, one which had "preserved [its] air of smug assurance into a more violent and chaotic age" (51), she marvels at how sheltered and cloistered the house is, with its enclosed garden, and delicately scented and ordered rooms. It is the opposite of her own world, in which everything is fragile, porous, and disordered. Kelly discovers this to be particularly the case in the parent's bedroom, in the depiction of which Barker conjoins the symbolism of a safe, protective home with the image of venerated femininity:

She turned her attention to the bed, rubbing her hands across the flesh-coloured satin until a roughened flap of skin from a healing blister snagged on one of the threads and tore. There was a pile of cushions at the head of the bed: big, soft, delicately scented, plump, pink, flabby cushions, like the breasts and buttocks of the woman who slept in the bed. A man slept there too, of course, but you could not imagine him. It was a woman's room, a temple to femininity. And the altar was the dressing table. (53)

This scene plays out a kind of rape on the protected femininity of this cozy middle-class world, figured in Kelly's easy penetration of its enclosed spaces, and her prurient probing of the woman's dressing table and bed.[8] Kelly desecrates this "temple to femininity" because it appears to be invulnerable to rape, because it is imagined as the antithesis of her own world of violence, neglect, and poverty. She understands that she is excluded from this world, even if she does not comprehend the social structures that create and maintain such exclusions, and hence, in the girl's bedroom, she feels pity or hatred, but "she would not have known how to envy her" (52). There is no more stark comparison than this middle-class domestic interior to her own broken, neglected home and childhood, no more salient reminder of the impermeability of the social and cultural barriers between classes. In contrast, the interiority of working-class culture, which Orwell celebrated as "a good place to be," is explored in Union Street as a postindustrial hell, an abyssal ghetto, from which there is neither respite nor escape.

The course of Kelly's life after this painful awakening is mapped out for her in the lives of the women around her. She begins to see herself, as if for the first time, in the eyes of her mother and sister. She sees herself figured as female monster when she compares herself with the angelic femininity venerated in the middle-class home, a contrast that reflects on the divergent class-bound experiences of femininity. Her mother attempts belatedly to foster an already derelict model of femininity when Kelly is given presents at Christmas that orient themselves around the preparation for adult womanhood: "a doll that wet itself, a hairdressing set, a matching necklace and brooch" (63). But, in a phrase that is repeated frequently throughout Union Street, Kelly is said to be "too far gone" (62). Instead she spends her time drifting around deserted streets at night, encountering the wasted, vagrant women with faces that show "the outward and visible signs of an inner and spiritual collapse" (60), or in the park, where she watches a boy and girl having cold, robotic sex in the bushes. Again, she sees terror in the ordinary, when "something mechanical in his movements, a piston-like power and regularity, began to make it seem not ridiculous, but terrible" (62–63). She identifies with the girl's alienation from this mechanical process, and later Kelly feels that she is "turning into a machine. Her legs, pumping up and down the cold street, had the regularity and power of pistons. And her hands, dangling out of the sleeves of her anorak, were as heavy and lifeless as tools" (64). After this, the whole landscape seems to take on the character of an exhausted, mechanical world, like the former steel town in which the novel is set, with the sun imagined as a "brutal, bloody disc," the sky a "red furnace," and the earth exhibiting a "steely blue radiance" (64–65). Kelly's world is hardening into a predetermining landscape of decay and entrapment, and she sees this not only in the landscape, but also in the assembly-line girls she watches emerging from the cake factory. It is her fate to work there, along with all the other women from Union Street, and to inhabit the same mechanical routines as they do.

It is her fate to live out the lives of all the women depicted in *Union Street*. This is the significance of the end of the story, when Kelly sits hand in hand with Alice Bell, the subject of the final story in the novel. The brief encounter between the two signals a barely formed possibility of communication, humanity, perhaps understanding, as Kelly "stared at the old woman as if she held, and might communicate, the secret of life" (67). Alice Bell sits on a park bench, exposed to the freezing air, waiting to die as a salvation from what she perceives to be the spiritual death of having to go into a "home." Kelly finds in herself a well of compassion and empathy for the old woman, and she comforts Alice in her final moments as she slips into "sleep, or unconsciousness, or death" (68). The story concludes with a chain of symbolic images of women as birds, from Alice, who appears to Kelly to have bird's claws for hands, and a throat "as vulnerable as a bird's" to the association of the women emerging from the cake factory with the "fierce, ecstatic trilling" of the starlings she has heard in the park (68). Barker relieves the painful, miserable knowledge of the stultifying existence of working-class women with this glimpsed, lyrical vision of the women of Union Street as vulnerable but trilling birds.

The final line of the story—"She was going home"—which seems to recover some sense of comfort in her home, suggests that Kelly finds in this vision some way of living with the confining conditions of her social situation. "Home" is not the protective cocoon that it should be, but she resigns herself at least to what it does have to offer. *Union Street* develops this theme through a number of images of broken shells —the split shells of the conkers in "Kelly Brown," for example (14), and the galling image of the man's face cracking open like an egg after he has raped Kelly (33); the breaking waters of Lisa Goddard as she gives birth (127), and in the same story, symbolic images of smashed eggs and a crushed chrysalis (138); the open coffin containing the broken body of John Scaife, whose death leaves his son feeling exposed, "with nobody now to stand between him and the great void" (167). Many more such images in the story suggest the fragility of protective shells such as body and home, and serve to identify the women symbolically with each other. "Home" is equated through these images with figures of the womb, thus indicating the familiar configuration of home, identity, and community with security and interiority. But this configuration is fragile and troubled in Barker's novel, as each story in the novel interrogates and explodes received notions of homeliness and community. Even the provisional, fleeting notions of solidarity between the women are fractured by issues of race ("Joanne Wilson"), and social class ("Iris King"), just as the possibility that some of the characters might form anything resembling Orwell's idyll of a working-class home proves illusory.

The structure of Barker's novel resembles that of James Joyce's *Dubliners* in the sense that it is possible to argue that the characters are really versions of one character's progress through life. Barker indicates this in the recurrent scenes in which characters see their younger or older selves reflected in the other characters; the mutual recognition between Kelly Brown and Alice Bell is perhaps the most obvious example. Like *Dubliners, Union Street* develops a dark, oppressive theme in all of the stories that is both concluded and relieved in the final story. The final story in *Union Street*, "Alice Bell," brings the equation between home and identity to its conclusion, as Alice struggles for a home in which to die. Home, despite the fact that it is cold, damp, broken, and hazardous, is defined positively for Alice in opposition to the "workhouse." That she keeps herself warm with newspapers like a street tramp, is, however, indicative of the thin line distinguishing her from those sleeping on park benches.

Home symbolizes the dignity of defining her own space and determining her own death. As she begins to lose control of her own body, after a fall and a stroke, she increasingly turns to home as an instinctive shell: "She burrowed down into her house, savoring its various textures and smells, an old fox that had reached its earth at last" (248). It is described as "almost an extension of her own body" (234), while her desire for home is experienced as "a physical pain" (246), which is connected symbolically to a desire to return "in spirit to her beginnings. To her first home . . . to her mother" (249). For Alice, home is equated fully with self-identity, so that she conceives the attempt by social services to remove her from her home as equivalent both with rape and death (260). Barker's novel here suggests the ambivalence of the working-class home as a construct, for, in a culture in which the identity of house and self is a potent and pervasive myth, it exhibits at one and the same time the marginal social status of its inhabitants and the stubborn assertion of self-identity. Union Street exists on a social scale that is seldom comforting, but the street still holds itself above the states of dereliction or vagrancy that exist nearby. Alice clings to what her home symbolizes, therefore, long after it has ceased to afford her the comforts of a home, because even the fact of its possession effectively signifies her social elevation above the level of a pauper in the workhouse, which is her anachronistic marker of indignity.

If home is depicted as more comforting and desirable in "Alice Bell" than in the other stories in *Union Street,* it is also shown to be the site of the unhomely, of the return of haunted memories, and the ghostly presence of unfamiliar voices and faces. All of the characters in *Union Street* experience the ghostly in some form, even if it is only in the form of seeing themselves mirrored in the lives of others. It is through such spectral visions of themselves as others that *Union Street* proposes an alternative conception of community, one that can only be imagined through the symbolic and psychic realm of the ghostly. In "Alice Bell," the ghosts accumulate in the course of the story, so that the clamor of ethereal voices builds into the same crescendo of "fierce, ecstatic trilling" that Kelly Brown hears in the park (264). For Alice, these voices are associated with an apparently communal chorus of feminine identity, which begins with indistinguishable sounds like "speech under water" (253), becomes clearer as a "web of voices"—"a child shouting, a young girl laughing, a woman crooning over her child" (263)—until finally the "electric clicks" of women talking commingles with the vision of birds trilling in a "withered and unwithering tree" (265). As Alice Bell fades toward death, she experiences this mythical vision of women as birds in a tree, while at the same time "her white hair and skin took on the colours of blood and fire" (264). Barker presents Alice here as the chimerical embodiment of a mythic symbol of renewal, like the "Lady Lazarus" of Sylvia Plath's poem, at the same time as she serves to bring the disparate, troubled women of Union Street into an imaginary unity.

This is where the story of "Alice Bell" seems most to resemble Joyce's "The Dead," in its lyrical, generous vision of the symbolic unity achieved in the twilight moment of passing toward death. Like Gabriel Conroy in Joyce's story, her identity seems to dissolve as she passes away, so that she experiences a fusion of her memories and consciousness with those of other women. "She had been so many women in her time" (263), Barker writes, and Alice seems ultimately to function as a mythical conduit for the spiritual or symbolic regeneration of all the women. This is symbolized in particular in the final passage of the novel:

> The world dwindled to a park bench and a litter of dead leaves in the grass.
>
> But there was a child there, now, a girl, who, standing with the sun behind her, seemed almost to be a gift of the light. At first she was afraid, the child had come so suddenly. Then—not afraid. They sat beside each other; they talked. The girl held out her hand. The withered hand and the strong young hand met and joined. There was silence. Then it was time for them both to go.
>
> So that in the end there were only the birds, soaring, swooping, gliding, moving in a never-ending spiral about the withered and unwithering tree. (265)

Barker creates in this climactic image what Isobel Armstrong calls, in her discussion of Angela Carter's *Nights at the Circus* (1984), "a dance of possibility,"[9] in which the materialist depiction of social and economic dereliction is intertwined with a sublime vision of flight and rejuvenation. Like Carter's novel, *Union Street* holds these two conflicting modes of representation in parallel, so that while the novel is thematically and formally indebted to social realist writing, it succeeds also in glimpsing the symbolic realm explored more intensively by Carter. Such a formation reproduces the dialogic tension between myth and history, the real and the symbolic, the material and the ideal, not in order to transcend the bleak depiction of dereliction presented throughout the novel, but to signal the possibility of an imaginative transformation of the structures that produce these material conditions. *Union Street* revisits the topography of the "small worlds" of Hoggart's account, in part to offer a revisionist, feminist critique of received notions of working-class community, but, perhaps more importantly, to delineate the grounds upon which we might be compelled to conceive of the functions and forms of "home" and community anew.

NOTES

1. Richard Hoggart, *The Uses of Literacy* (Harmondsworth: Penguin, 1958), 59.
2. George Orwell, *The Road to Wigan Pier* (Harmondsworth: Penguin, 1962), 104.
3. Alan Sillitoe, *Saturday Night and Sunday Morning* (London: Grafton, 1985), 31.

4. Pat Barker, *Union Street* (London: Virago, 1982), 13. All subsequent references will be included in the text.

5. Beryl Bainbridge, *English Journey; or, The Road to Milton Keynes* (London: Flamingo, 1984).

6. This action seems to connect with the "dirty protests" current in Northern Ireland's prisons in the early 1980s, particularly as images of the war in Northern Ireland perforate the novel in several places.

7. Ian Haywood, *Working-Class Fiction: from Chartism to Trainspotting* (Plymouth: Northcote House, 1997), 145–46.

8. See Margaretta Jolly, "After Feminism: Pat Barker, Penelope Lively and the Contemporary Novel," in *British Culture of the Postwar: An Introduction to Literature and Society, 1945–1999,* ed. Alistair Davies and Alan Sinfield, 65 (London: Routledge, 2000).

9. Isobel Armstrong, "Woolf by the Lake, Woolf at the Circus: Carter and Tradition," in *Flesh and the Mirror: Essays on the Art of Angela Carter,* ed. Lorna Sage, 257–78, esp. 273 (London: Virago, 1994).

ANN ARDIS

Political Attentiveness vs. Political Correctness
Teaching Pat Barker's *Blow Your House Down*

The author blurb on the inside back cover of the Ballantine paperback edition of Pat Barker's novel *Blow Your House Down* (1984) reads as follows:

> Pat Barker was born in Thornaby-on-Tees in 1943. She was educated at the local grammar school and at the London School of Economics, where she studied economics, politics, and history. She is married to the Professor of Zoology at the University of Durham, and she has two children.[1]

Why, my students ask, did Barker write this book about working-class prostitutes trying to protect themselves from a serial killer? On what authority does an academic's wife, a mother of two, and a graduate of the London School of Economics describe the experience of working-class women in a decaying inner-city neighborhood who have only two means of employment open to them: walking the streets, and working on the assembly line in a chicken slaughterhouse? On what authority, in other words, does Barker write about women who choose to *be* chickens (an English slang word sometimes used for prostitutes) rather than "shoving chickens' legs up their arses" (44)? And whom does she write this book for?

These are important questions, questions sustained by a tradition of Marxist criticism that values the authenticity of working-class writing—and that often, as Cora Kaplan has noted, alleviates the tension between the literary and the political in the Marxist critical project by advocating essentialism. Because I believe, however, that questioning the authenticity of *Blow Your House Down* as working-class writing can be a defensive distraction on a reader's part, a means of avoiding Barker's very disturbing insights into the way "social divisions and ideologies [are] worked through psychic structures . . . [and] worked into sexual and social identity," I ask my students to bracket such questions temporarily in order to focus first on how this novel challenges us to confront the "powerful symbolic force of class and gender in ordering our social and political imagination."[2]

This essay is about what happens in the classroom when I teach *Blow Your House Down*. It is about teaching feminist theory and literature together: teaching literature as theory, teaching literary and theoretical texts that highlight the politics of the classroom. The charge of "political correctness" (read "academic fascism") has been levied frequently against feminists, multiculturalists, and other advocates of curricular reform at least since the early 1990s. Particularly as this charge has filtered out into the popular press, it has served to contain and curtail curricular debate by caricaturing one side of the argument. Through a discussion of classroom conversations about Barker's novel, I would like to suggest that there is an important distinction to be made between political correctness and political attentiveness. *Blow Your House Down* does invite students to reflect on how cultural categories such as class and gender reciprocally constitute each other—which might be termed a politically correct insight. But Barker's work also points up the radical instability of such categories. Hence it does not exemplify class-based paradigms of analysis. Nor does it fit neatly into feminist arguments about male violence against women. As I hope to show, it is too disturbing to be politically correct. I teach it because it challenges my theoretical paradigms. I teach it because it teaches *me* as well as my students to be attentive to the ways we negotiate difference in the classroom and in the world at large.

TEACHING CLASS AND GENDER

American discourse about class is misleading, insofar as most Americans claim to be middle-class even though their incomes actually give them either a higher or a lower class standing. Moreover, class is inflected differently with issues related to race and ethnicity than in Britain, while also lacking the latter's rich tradition of writing on social class, however skewed by a prevailing focus on male experience.[3] There are all good reasons to ask American university students to read Barker's novel about a North-of-England working-class women's culture they would prefer to treat as "foreign" on multiple levels. More than any other piece of literature I have taught, Barker's novel requires students to position themselves. It challenges them to acknowledge their own class allegiances as they try to talk about this text; it calls attention to all the differences in students' class background, economic status, and life experience that usually remain politely beyond the scope of classroom discussion, thanks to common assumptions about the classroom as an apolitical space and the educational process as a simple transmission of nonideological, universal "truths."

Not more than five minutes into the first day's discussion of this novel in an "Introduction to the Novel" class, for example, one of my students stopped herself in midsentence when she realized that she was taking her own experience to be universal. She was assuming that this subject was equally exotic to all of her classmates, that this was everyone's first up-close-and-personal view of prostitution. Even as she was speaking, something someone else had just said finally registered with her, and when she realized that some of her classmates live in neighborhoods where prostitutes hang out on street corners, she had to go back and qualify what she had just asserted about "normal" households and "normal" occupations.[4]

That process itself—the process of putting quotation marks around such words as "normal," of destandardizing, denaturalizing, bourgeois experience—is something Barker's narrative demands of its readers from its opening pages. Consider the first scene of the novel:

> There were two beds and a wardrobe in the room. To get between them you had to stand sideways and shuffle your way along.
>
> Brenda was in a hurry to get out and grumbled as she bent down to tuck a blanket in. "I don't know, when I was your age I was making me own bed."
>
> Her daughters, getting ready for bed in the corner, turned and looked at her. Lindsey, the elder by two years, said, "I don't see why I have to go to bed the same time as our Sharon."
>
> "Because if I let you stop down you'd only have a carry-on and wake every-bugger up. Besides, you'd start picking on your Uncle Norman, you know you would."
>
> "It's him picks on me."
>
> Brenda pulled back the sheets on the other bed and a powerful smell of urine filled the room. "Sharon, I wish you'd tell me when you're wet. I could've had this changed this morning if you'd told me."
>
> "God, what a stink," said Lindsey.
>
> Brenda rounded on her. "Shut your face, you. You want to think on, she's been ill." (3–4)

As students are quick to note, this scene impresses us with its ordinariness. Even if this bedroom is smaller than those my middle-class and upper-middle-class American students (claim to) remember from their own childhoods, and even if the dialect takes some getting used to, the rituals are nonetheless familiar: an older child complains about having the same bedtime as her younger sister; a mother expresses her exasperation with her children's rivalry, but her rough scolding is well laced with affection.

In "Women on the Market," Luce Irigaray identifies three symbolic positions that women can occupy in a capitalist patriarchy: virgin, mother, and prostitute.[5] Without necessarily requiring them to read Irigaray,[6] I talk with my students about the way Barker collapses these three categories as she introduces her characters. The "respectable" lower-middle-class folks who live on the margins of this decaying inner-city neighborhood continue to assume that the categories are noncontiguous; they employ these classifications to construct reassuringly rigid distinctions between themselves and those who differ from them in various ways. In contrast, Barker's prostitutes are painfully aware of the contradictions fueling this ideological system.

As the entire first section of the novel—not just its opening paragraphs—stresses, Brenda is both a mother and a prostitute. Like Kath and Audrey, in fact, she is a prostitute because she is a mother. After her husband disappears, leaving her with the children and a sheaf of unpaid bills stashed under the seat cushions of the sofa, Brenda tries to make it on her own by applying for child support and then working full-time at the chicken factory. She quickly realizes several things. First, after she goes to the corner store for a pint of milk one evening and is accosted by a man looking for someone to give him a blow job, she is made to understand that in her neighborhood, a woman walking alone at night is assumed to be a prostitute whether she is one or not. But if Brenda is upset by this encounter and others like it, she is even more upset by her social workers' visit, which starkly reveals to her the economic base subtending bourgeois patriarchy's valorization of marriage:

> After they'd gone Brenda sat down and pressed her hands together to stop them shaking. What got her was the hypocrisy of it all. They went on about being married, but when you got right down to it, past the white weddings and the romance and all that, what they *really* thought was: if you're getting on your back for a fella, he ought to pay. *That* was what they really thought. And where did that leave you? You might just as well be standing on a street corner in bloody Northgate—at least it'd be honest. (38)

In fact, that is exactly what Brenda does once she realizes that hooking will give her both more time and more money for her children than will the chicken factory.

If Brenda is alienated from her own body when she puts it on the market; if sexual desire is not a factor in the exchanges she makes with her customers; if, moreover, she cannot control the process of "switching off" (tuning out emotionally with her johns and "switching on" again when she is with her children), she recognizes nonetheless that a "respectable" life would be no different. For the women she worked with on the factory line are equally alienated from the products of their labor; they too "switch off" to get through the day. Moreover, while Edith, Brenda's mother-in-law, certainly claims both the respectability and the class status she refuses to grant Brenda, she is as alienated from her sexuality as are the prostitutes. As indicated by her single act of intimacy with her husband—dusting him off before he leaves the house for the day—desire simply is not part of the heterosexual economy of the patriarchy. Watching this strange daily ritual, Brenda notes: "It was just like scrubbing the front door step. It didn't matter what you thought about the bloke, it was just something you had to do" (27).[7]

Kaplan argues that "without the class and race perspectives that socialist feminist critics bring to the analysis both of literary texts and of their conditions of production, liberal feminist criticism, with its emphasis on the unified female subject, will unintentionally reproduce the ideological values of mass-market romance" because it "tends to represent sexual difference as natural and fixed—a constant, transhistorical femininity in libidinized struggle with an equally 'given' universal masculinity" (148). She goes on to suggest that "a feminist literary criticism that privileges gender in isolation from other forms of social determination offers us a . . . partial reading of the role played by sexual difference in literary discourse, a reading bled dry of its most troubling and contradictory meanings" (148). Thus it is striking that *Blow Your House Down* does not let readers isolate gender from other forms of social determination. You cannot bleed sexual difference dry of its "most troubling and contradictory meanings" in this narrative. Furthermore, there are no unified female subjects in this novel. For every encounter, every "speaking-to another person," in this novel is "fraught with the history of . . . sex and class," to borrow Minnie Bruce Pratt's phrasing (12).[8] Every character experiences the kind of "vertigo" or "homelessness" that Pratt associates so powerfully in "Identity: Skin Blood Heart" with an expanding consciousness of oppression (35).

TEACHING THE "ZERO DEGREE OF SOCIAL CONCEPTUALIZATION"

"I'll never think about these ladies in quite the same way again."

"I used to think that prostitutes were bad . . . that they were just sluts, dirty from the waist down or something like that. But they are mothers too and stuff."

Student comments such as these suggest that the experience of reading Barker's novel "enlightens" students, that is, that it introduces them to a world and a way of life that would otherwise remain foreign to them—and that therefore is the target of the negative stereotyping epitomized by the "dirty from the waist down" remark. But if this novel shows them how class and gender reciprocally constitute each other, I nonetheless consider responses like the above only the point of departure in class discussions.

Virginia Woolf writes in *Three Guineas* that "the number of books written by the educated about the working class would seem to show that the glamour of the working class and the emotional relief afforded by adopting its cause, are today as irresistible to the middle class as the glamour of the aristocracy was twenty years ago."[9] I teach Barker's novel regularly because it challenges students to deal with issues of class. More importantly, however, I teach it because it does not afford my middle-class students the kind of "emotional relief" Woolf discusses in *Three Guineas*. *Blow Your House Down* does not let middle-class academic feminist readers commend ourselves for the correctness of our politics. Instead it calls attention to the voyeurism involved in any reading experience, particularly when reading demands identification across lines of social classification.[10] As her title might suggest, Barker refuses to let us sustain the self-congratulatory attitude reflected in my student's comment, "I'll never think about these ladies in quite the same way again." She refuses to let us construct either "the prostitute" or "the serial killer" as other to ourselves. (This is where students' reactions to the author blurb and the quotations from reviews featured on the back cover of the paperback edition become relevant again, as they can serve to introduce a discussion of the commodification of working-class experience for the "benefit" and pleasure of middle-class readers.)

Besides the title, several other aspects of the novel work to destabilize class and gender categorization by highlighting the psychological construction of otherness. I want now to focus on students' reactions to three distinctive narrative strategies: the use of a first-person narrative in the third section of the novel; the tangential relationship of the final section to the preceding three sections; and the narrator's direct addresses to the reader throughout. I am particularly interested in students' resistance to the realization that they are implicated in the psychological dynamics Barker exposes so relentlessly in this early novel.

Blow Your House Down has four chapters. The first focuses on Brenda, on her socialization as a prostitute, and on her relationship with Kath, an older woman who will be one of the serial killer's victims. The second chapter introduces us to the whole community of women who meet for drinks at a local pub before going out on their "beats." The third is about Jean, the only woman in the group who hooks because, as she herself notes, she likes the life: she enjoys the risk associated with the job. And the fourth deals with Maggie, a "respectable" chicken factory worker whom Brenda rescues after Maggie is knocked unconscious by an unidentified assailant on her way home from work one night. Only Jean's story is narrated in the first person. It opens with the following observation: "You do a lot of walking in this job. More than you might think. In fact, when I get to the end of a busy Saturday night, it's me feet that ache. There, that surprised you, didn't it?" (119). Interestingly enough, students are very uncomfortable with Jean's assumption of intimacy with her readers. "I can identify with Brenda, but I don't want to see the world from Jean's perspective," one of my students in a feminist theory seminar wrote; "I don't like the way she draws me into conversation." The victim of a client's violence, Jean too is capable of violence. And when she kills the man she thinks is one of her murdered lover's "regulars"; that is, when she perpetuates the cycle of violence rather than stopping it by solving the murder mystery, she violates two things: the reader's desire for narrative closure, for resolution of the central conflict in the novel;[11] and the reader's assumption that he or she observes these characters without being observed by them.

For very similar reasons, as Dale Bauer has noted, students are troubled by the fourth section. They want to dissociate Maggie's story from the rest of the novel. For example, even though Brenda is recognizable in this section (her name is not used, but her clothing and speech are familiar), students often do not identify her as the woman who calls the police and the ambulance after Maggie is attacked. "There's no connection between Maggie's story and the rest of the novel," they claim. "She's not a prostitute; why did she get attacked?"

If such misreadings are symptomatic, still more telling are students' responses to Barker's use of direct address in key scenes such as the murder of Kath. I quote at length from this scene in order to give a sense of its impact. First, the murder itself, from the point at which her client's interaction with Kath escalates into violence:

> His cock felt small and worm-like inside her stretched arse. He pulled it out and examined it carefully. At first it looked much the same as usual, purple and glistening in the torchlight. But then a drop of gingery fluid gathered on the knob and dripped down onto her bum. He smelled the thin, sour smell of shit. And looked. Her cleft was full of it. He lashed out at her then, but she wriggled away from him and tried to stand up. She got as far as her knees.
>
> "There's no need for that," she said. "Look, you can have your money back."
>
> Those were the last words she spoke. He hit her again, full on the jaw, and she crumpled up on the floor and lay still. He dragged her back onto the mattress. Then reached into his pocket for the knife.
>
> It was almost soundless. There were only slight grunts of effort and the shadow of an upraised arm coming and going on the wall.
>
> At some point, unnoticed by him, Kath died.
>
> After a few minutes he was able to stop and look down. It wasn't enough that she was dead, he needed more. He gathered handfuls of feathers together and started shoving them inside her cunt. It wasn't easy: as fast as he pushed them

inside they turned red. He had to practically stuff her with them, like stuffing a chicken, before he could get the effect he wanted: a ridiculous little white frill between her legs. (80–81)

Five short paragraphs (less than a page of text) describing the murderer's rituals of self-distancing after he has finished follow the above. The last two paragraphs of the chapter, quoted below, are then set off from the preceding with a line of asterisks:

The sleeping and the dead. Any resemblance between them is a contrivance of undertakers: they do not look alike. Kath's body seems to have shrunk inside its clothes. If you approached the mattress casually you would see nothing but a heap of old rags. You would tread on her before you realized a woman's body lay there.

The window is boarded up, the room dark, except for five thin lines of moonlight that lie across the mattress like bars. One of them has just reached her eyes. They look so alive you wonder she can bear the light shining directly into them. Any moment now, you feel, her eyes will close. (82)

Barker's use of the present tense and the second person in these last two paragraphs is as shocking as the detailed description that precedes them. My students often suggest that the graphic nature of Barker's descriptions makes this novel inappropriate for classroom discussion. (This point in itself constitutes an opportunity to talk about the institutionalization of literary study—both in terms of an English department's curricular commitments to a canon of high art and in terms of students' own expectations about the ways in which the texts they study should differ from the fiction they read on their own time, the language they hear in their own conversation, and the cultural forms they either produce or consume on Saturday nights.) They also note, rightly I think, that Kath's murder is pornographic, in the sense that Barker shows the murderer's association of sex and violence without reassuring us that we are being offered a critique of this behavior.[12] They are, however, much more reluctant to talk about the way Barker catches us peeping: she turns a one-way mirror into a window, and then in effect breaks the glass and draws us into the scene of this horrific crime as she switches from past to present tense and describes *our* approach to Kath's body. This crime is never solved; there is no gratifying resolution to the whodunit plot. Instead the violence keeps spiraling outward, implicating not only this particular serial killer, not only Jean (who murders someone she thinks is the killer), but Barker's readers as well.

This idea is reinforced in the final chapter through one of Maggie's most powerful meditations on evil. On one of her first forays back out into the world after being attacked, Maggie meets a neighbor in the grocery store. As she parries this woman's insinuations about her husband's having been her assailant, Maggie comes to the following realization:

You thought evil was simple. No, more than that, you *made* it simple, you froze it into a single shape, the shape of a man waiting in the shadows. But it wasn't simple. This woman, this wheezy middle-aged woman, with her corrugated-iron hair and her glasses that flashed when she looked sideways to see how you were taking it, she knew what she was doing. And she was enjoying it. You couldn't put evil into a single, recognizable shape. (194–95)

Passages like this one in Barker's novel, together with the other narrative strategies discussed above, challenge our attempts to classify human experience on the basis of binary oppositions. Neat, clean, simple distinctions of whatever sort—between "us" and "them," good and evil, middle and working class, male and female—are misleading, as Maggie acknowledges here. In this respect, *Blow Your House Down* invites us to confront what Hortense Spillers terms the "zero degree of social conceptualization."[13]

In "Mama's Baby, Papa's Maybe," Spillers challenges research in African American history for its reification of gender as a category of analysis, and for the erasure of certain chapters in American history that follows from this reification. Central to her argument is a distinction between "the body" and "the flesh." The "body" is gendered, marked by a "grammar" and an iconography of sexual difference; in contrast, "flesh" is the "zero degree of social conceptualization," "the primary narrative." Given this distinction, Spillers goes on to note what has been left out of revisionary "herstories" of American culture: female slaves were not only raped; they were beaten, lynched, and mutilated as well. That is to say, the violence against them was not gender-specific: their physical beings were not always treated as female. Instead they were treated as "flesh," flesh that could be "lacerated, wounded, torn, scarred [or] ruptured" by anyone who reduced a human being to a thing and denied that being subjectivity. What feminist revisionary historians have either wanted to forget or have failed to realize, according to Spillers, is that the African female subject has been "the topic of specifically externalized acts of torture and prostration that we imagine as the peculiar province of male brutality and torture inflicted by other males." Images of female bodies "strung from a tree limb, or bleeding from the breast on any given day of field work because the 'overseer,' standing the length of the whip [away], has popped her flesh open, add [another] dimension to the narratives of women in culture and society," a "materialized scene of unprotected female flesh—of female flesh 'ungendered.'"[14]

Perhaps this reference to Spillers's research is distracting, a shocking evocation of mutilated black bodies that now competes with Barker's description of Kath's murder for readers' attention. Certainly, as I write this, I feel anxious about being accused of appropriating a point that Spillers makes about black women's experience in order to focus exclusively once again on white women. The criticisms of white feminist theory that women of color voice in *This Bridge Called My Back* and elsewhere cannot be ignored. But perhaps Spillers also offers us a way to explore the relationships among systems of oppression, their interconnectedness—without, however, assuming that one system of oppression is exactly analogous to or subsumed within another. Spillers's distinction between body and flesh makes it possible, I think, to read the "grammar" of Kath's violated form.

As she lies on that pallet in an abandoned row house with her eyes still open, refusing to look like a sleeping body, Kath is "flesh." The crime that her murderer has committed is not merely an act of male violence against a woman. It is a crime against something more primary than a gendered body. For this reason, Barker's narrative does not fit neatly into feminist arguments about male violence against women. Nor does it exemplify class-based paradigms of analysis. As the safe spaces we usually construct to protect ourselves from otherness are blown down in this novel, as our modes of social analysis are exposed as secondary constructs (and inadequate ones at that), a primary narrative of domination becomes painfully, searingly, visible in this text. This narrative is not always or necessarily played out along lines of race, gender, and class. Like the bodies of the black slave women who were lynched in nineteenth-century America, Kath's dead form and her still staring eyes can haunt us into awareness of our capacity to turn subjectivities into property, bodies into flesh.[15] For this reason, I am not satisfied when my students offer politically correct pronouncements on class and gender oppression when we have finished discussing this novel. I want them to say, "This novel upset me." "This novel disturbed me." And, what is even harder, "This novel implicated me."

NOTES

1. Pat Barker, *Blow Your House Down* (New York: Ballantine, 1984). All subsequent references will be included in the text.

2. Cora Kaplan, "Pandora's Box: Subjectivity, Class and Sexuality in Socialist Feminist Criticism," in *Sea Changes: Essays on Culture and Feminism*, 147–76, esp. 163, 169 (London: Verso, 1986).

3. See bell hooks, *Where We Stand: Class Matters* (New York: Routledge, 2000) for further discussion of Americans' racialization of class difference. See Pamela Fox, *Class Fictions: Shame and Resistance in the British Working-Class Novel, 1890–1945* (Durham, N.C.: Duke University Press, 1994) and Julia Swindells, *What's Left? Women in Culture and the Labour Movement* (New York and London: Routledge, 1990) for thoughtful responses to the occlusion of women's experience from British scholarship on social class.

4. I should note here that I have taught this novel at two institutions, Miami University of Ohio and the University of Delaware, with fairly privileged student populations. As was noted in the discussion following the Radical Caucus MLA panel at which I presented an early version of this essay in December 1989, teaching *Blow Your House Down* would be a quite different experience at an institution with predominantly urban and working-class students.

5. Luce Irigaray, "Women on the Market," *This Sex Which Is Not One*, trans. Catherine Porter (Ithaca: Cornell University Press, 1977), 170–91.

6. In the general education course that I teach, "Introduction to the Novel," I do not ask students to read secondary material; instead, I either make handouts of short passages or introduce concepts in lecture. In both an upper-division course for English majors, "British Women Novelists," and a senior seminar in feminist theory, however, we read theory and literature together in order to talk about the ways these have cross-fertilized each other in recent years. See Donna Perry's interview with Barker "Going Home Again: An Interview with Pat Barker," *Literary Review* (Winter 1991): 235–44.

7. The only heterosexual relationship in this novel that encompasses sexual pleasure is Maggie's with Bill in the final section, and this relationship is all but destroyed by the attack on Maggie's life. The ditty Bill used to sing about girls' knickers echoes through Maggie's

long soliloquies as a reminder of their intimacy; but she can no longer think of their relationship as a safe haven from a violent world. I have not always been able to convince my students of my point of view, but I find the final scene of the novel, in which Maggie lets Bill rub her down with a towel after one of her long walks in the rain, extremely poignant. A final gesture of physical intimacy and tenderness replaces the shocking images of male violence we have been bombarded with previously: a scene of genuine, non-romanticized, male-female intimacy answers Edith's ritual of dusting her husband in the first section of the novel. Although Barker's *Border Crossing* (London: Viking, 2001), revisits the topic of male violence against (aging) women, its treatment is much less graphic, and there is nothing comparable to this scene's suggestion of an alternative to an economy of sexual violence and emotional "shutting off" in heterosexual relationships.

8. Minnie Bruce Pratt, "Identity: Skin Blood Heart," in *Yours in Struggle: Three Feminist Perspectives on Anti-Semitism and Racism,* ed. Elly Bulkin, Minnie Bruce Pratt, and Barbara Smith, 11–63 (Ithaca: Firebrand, 1984).

9. Virginia Woolf, *Three Guineas* (New York: Penguin, 1977), 196.

10. Thus, for example, Barker refuses to display lesbian sexuality for the voyeuristic pleasures of the heterosexual reader. She does not titillate us with scenes of Jean and Carol's relationship in the third section. As in the opening scenes of Brenda with her children, what we are offered instead are Jean's memories of their routines: eating Chinese takeout, painting a room in their apartment, "jumping in and out of cars" (140). As Jean notes, she has only one photograph of Carol, "and that isn't a very good one." Which is just fine with Jean, because, as she says, "The pictures in my mind are better than photographs" (151). For Barker on her refusal of a middle-class perspective, see Sharon Monteith, *Pat Barker* (Plymouth: Northcote House, 2002), 14–16.

11. In this regard, as Dale Bauer has noted in "The Other 'F' Word: The Feminist in the Classroom," *College English* 52, no. 4 (1990): 382–96, Barker's novel challenges literary as well as social systems of classification (393). This is a murder mystery that subverts the conventions of the genre in at least two ways: the mystery is never solved, and thus the reader has to relinquish the desire to master the situation intellectually by figuring out the puzzle.

12. Angela Carter's characterization of the "moral pornographer" in *The Sadeian Woman* (London: Virago, 1979), is useful in this context, as she charts the "no-man's-land" between reproduction and italicization of repressive sexual ideologies.

13. Hortense Spillers, "Mama's Baby, Papa's Maybe: An American Grammar Book," *Diacritics* 17, no. 2 (1987): 65–81.

14. Ibid., 68.

15. In the novel itself, however, Jean notes that this haunting is mitigated outside the immediate community of Kath's friends as soon as the huge billboard bearing an image of her face is replaced by a beer advertisement. I feel compelled to note here that *Blow Your House Down* went out of print in the United States (though not elsewhere) in 1990. Overshadowed by the critical acclaim granted to Barker's First World War trilogy—but thankfully back in print now, no doubt because of the critical success of her later work—its raw and painful insights are as yet unmatched, to my mind, by anything she has written subsequently.

SARAH BROPHY

Working-Class Women, Labor, and the Problem of Community in *Union Street* and *Liza's England*

Abuse, violence, poverty, and isolation proliferate at all stages of the female life cycle in the northern industrial working-class neighborhoods Pat Barker explores in *Union Street* (1982) and *Liza's England* (1986). The subsistence of women and their families on the proletarian fringes of capitalist plenty in late twentieth-century Britain (where the employment of men in industrial settings is far from reliable) is scrabbled together from a variety of exhausting labors: factory work, paid cleaning, domestic work, prostitution, and the constant struggle of making ends meet. Barker's novels make the human costs of working-class women's labor perceptible, connecting the labor of "production" with that of social reproduction and exploring the ways in which working-class women's relationships are shaped by the (post)industrial socioeconomic context in which they live and work. *Union Street* is organized synchronically, offering seven chapters documenting the experiences of seven women in one community in ascending order of age over a period of a couple of months. As Alice Bell, the eldest of the women, muses, the women's lives form a web of perceptions, voices, and images: "She had been so many women in her time." She wonders whether her "memories" are her own or the "debris" of "other lives"?[1] Their lives serve as revealing mirrors for one another's, putting into perspective for readers the women's various experiences, choices, and fears. In *Liza's England*, Barker replots working-class maternity and community along diachronic lines: Liza Jarrett, turning eighty-four in 1984, and born on the stroke of midnight, represents both a generation and the twentieth century. Linked to the local landscape, she bears witness, in memory and body, to the working-class community she has been a part of, that she has participated, in a sense, in giving birth to. Accounting for the abandonment and dereliction of the neighborhood in 1984 and trying to come to terms with her losses in the two world wars are the historical burdens borne by Liza's narrative. But the connections between the two novels are more than thematic in a general sense: Barker transposes so many details from *Union Street* to *Liza's England* that they are usefully read together as two connected mappings of working-class mothering and community, with the subsequent novel revising and commenting on the first.

Barker's contemporary Carolyn Steedman has suggested in her groundbreaking autobiographical essay *Landscape for a Good Woman* that "fiction can't" show the "bits and pieces" of working-class women's experiences, that, like history or theory, fiction must always rewrite it either in relation to bourgeois or masculine values.[2] Barker's female-centered fictions of the 1980s demonstrate that Steedman's conclusion is probably too hasty, for they respond in an innovative fashion to the need for alternative stories that speak to the maternal ambivalence Steedman describes, for accounts of "mothers who told you how hard it was to have you, how long they were in labour with you, and who told you to accept the impossible contradiction of being both desired and a burden; and not to complain."[3] Where Steedman's narrative strategy involves interweaving her autobiographical "I" with reflections on the tradition of working-class history as well as on psychoanalytic and Marxist theory to demonstrate the insufficiencies of each, Barker strategically recasts the mundanely painful experiences of working-class women's everyday lives. As critics such as John Kirk have argued, Barker endeavors to reconstruct women's "experience through the production of a feminized class memory," attempting "to create a collective experience and consciousness, rather than the individualistic one associated with the novel of middle-class life."[4]

Neither realist novels nor psychoanalytic case studies, but partaking of and revising both genres, *Union Street* and *Liza's England* render a multifaceted account of the complex structures of feeling inhabited by working-class women, highlighting the gaps that persist between their dreams of fulfillment and their everyday struggles for survival. But *Union Street* and *Liza's England* raise serious doubts about whether the women's communities they depict do in fact model solidarity or work effectively to mitigate exploitation and suffering. Referring to her second novel, *Blow Your House Down* (1984), which focuses on a group of prostitutes facing the threat of a serial killer, Barker described her "ambivalence" about the role of women's friendships in the characters' lives, especially the possibility that their "stoicism" precludes thinking toward other "alternatives," such as political organization.[5] But critics have often tended to stress that the emphasis on sisterhood in *Union Street* and *Liza's England* "encodes," as Kirk summarizes, a shared "struggle against patriarchy, capital, and the state."[6] Peter Hitchcock has even argued that these two novels offer "a lesson in the discourse of resistance," building solidarity among women and across generations out of the "dire social relations of their existence."[7] This essay seeks to extend and to complicate the critical discussion of Barker's feminist fictions by highlighting certain aspects of the novels that have been underplayed in readings of her vision as affirming the existence of collective agency, dissent, and resistance amongst working women: specifically, I think that Barker's investigation of maternal ambivalence and her ironic qualifications of any tendency to idealize female solidarity in the working-class communities she depicts deserve a more thorough consideration.

By first discussing the connections between motherhood and work in the two novels, and then examining Barker's depiction of working-class women as a community, I aim to establish the full extent of her ambivalence about the existence of coherent and sustaining female collectives in the working-class neighborhoods she depicts. Narrating the women's conscious and unconscious thoughts and emotions in terms of dense material detail infused with symbolism and a pervasive irony, and blending subjective and objective perspectives, *Union Street* and *Liza's England* portray women as actively engaged in negotiating the ideological inscriptions of class and gender that shape their experiences. But while she strives to bring hitherto hidden structures of feeling to light and to celebrate women's resilience, Barker does not flinch from exploring the forces that divide working-class women. *Union Street* and *Liza's England* show how alienated and exploited labor creates feelings of fear and shame; these emotional patterns divide the women internally and function to separate them and to pit them against one another. Maternity is implicated in this cycle of alienation, exploitation, and division along with other kinds of work. Both the women themselves and Barker's third-person narrator perceive women's reproductive and domestic labors as a mode of economic production, using them as metaphors for one another. No different, in some ways, from factory labor and domestic service, women's reproductive "work" places them at odds with themselves and with one another; it threatens to sabotage even as it promises to fulfill their desires for security and love. In this profoundly disconnected environment, apparently supportive relationships tend to reinforce stoic endurance of the status quo and to stress the importance of maintaining respectable appearances. At the same time, the most vulnerable members of the community are shown to be at risk of being overlooked, as individuals struggle to cope with and are preoccupied by their private burdens. Although both novels emphasize women's coping strategies, and explore the limitations of the community's ability to offer support and sympathy, certain differences do emerge, however, when the two are compared: the emphasis on the women's entrapment (and complicity) in a cycle of violence and degradation in *Union Street* is modified, to some degree, by the investigation in *Liza's England* of how this cycle may be interrupted, as well as by Liza's turn to historical and economic explanations for her experiences.

Liza Jarrett watches her mother, Louise, work as a domestic for the Wynyards, wealthy steelworks owners. Barker emphasizes the child's awareness of her mother's entrapment. The daughter sees her mother's entry into part-time domestic service, scrubbing floors for her husband's employer, as at first mystifying but increasingly as indicative of her powerlessness. But for Liza, as she looks back in 1984 on her childhood, labor also refers to the processes (the "work") of memory—internal, self-reflexive processes—that prepare the ground, now that she prepares for death, for a retelling of her experiences that might make them mean differently than before. The fire in her hearth and the box of papers she keeps beneath her bed both "stimulated her imagination to enter again and explore the long country of the past."[8] Her role is an active one: the dancers pictured on the box "came to life beneath her hands, and their movements flowed through her" (21); death is, to Liza's surprise, "so much like *work*. Like labour" (76). In exploring the past, Liza's memories of the care her mother's hands were capable of providing, in illness and in labor, alternate with the memory of the vicious blows she rains on her daughter (44). The dancers on the box pass on a gift from one to the other, as the box is passed down the maternal line in Liza's family, but the legacy that Liza's mother passes on confusingly mingles maternal care with violence and the hopelessness she feels working for the Wynyards, scrubbing floors until her hands are "red, like raw meat" (30).

Working at a factory is monetarily advantageous when compared to domestic labor, but it, too, exacts a toll on the minds and spirits of Barker's women. The gendered division of labor spills over from the domestic into the industrial setting, especially on the assembly line: the monotonous, repetitive, minute tasks that the women perform require just enough of their attention to rule out any conversation, which is already almost out of the question in the din of the factory. In fact, in the cake factory, where Joanne Wilson works, "After a while not only speech but thought became impossible":

> The first sponge cake reached Jo. She began the sequence of actions that she
> would perform hundreds of times that day. It took little effort once you were
> used to it and, provided the cakes continued to arrive in a steady stream, it could
> be done almost automatically.
>
> Almost. But not quite. Now that she was alone—for in this roaring cavern of
> sound each woman was alone—she wanted to think about Ken, she wanted to
> plan the evening, to work out exactly how she was going to tell him about the
> baby. She couldn't do it. Each half-formed thought was aborted by the arrival of
> another cake. She was left with a picture of his face floating against a backcloth
> of sponges: dark-haired and sallow-skinned, the rather prominent Adam's apple
> jerking when he laughed. (*Union Street*, 85)

Cast back upon herself, Joanne is unable, nonetheless, to complete the syntax of her thoughts, arriving at an eerily disconnected image of Ken's face that fails to clarify her decision. Her thoughts repeatedly "aborted," in this environment, she cannot quite bring to consciousness the question of "abortion" itself, or weigh it against the options of single parenthood or marriage to Ken. Joanne's difficulty in thinking through her decision suggests the importance of environment in shaping patterns of thought and behavior, contradicting the manager's tendency to dismiss the female factory workers as mere "girls," his belief that they "would never be anything else though some of them were forty, fifty, even sixty years old. You only had to listen to them: nothing but gossip and giggle and rubbish" (*Union Street*, 93).

Disunity among women workers is endemic to the factory environment according to Barker's accounts: anonymous and infantilized, the women turn against one another. For example, defending herself against the racist comments of some of the women, Bertha, the first black woman to be employed in the factory, fights back, once with her fists, but more effectively by creating a slight delay in the rhythm of the factory work that, though it would be "hardly perceptible to a casual observer," creates havoc and pain for the women who stand down the line from her (*Union Street*, 88). Ironically, the manager's inability to see the women as anything but children also means that he fails to anticipate the conflicts and struggles for power that are unfolding on the assembly line, interrupting the productivity of the factory. However, while the women's retaliatory strategies certainly have some disruptive effects for the operation of the factory, the disturbances they create are neither organized nor targeted in a strategic way: rather, the women themselves bear the brunt of one another's boredom, exhaustion, and dissatisfaction.

Barker puts the conditions and conflicts faced by women factory laborers in twentieth-century Britain into a historical perspective in *Liza's England*. When Liza Jarrett goes to work at the local munitions factory during the First World War, she does so not by choice, nor primarily for the war effort, as the wealthy daughter of the steelworks owner does, but because it offers the best income of the options available to her. While Elizabeth Wynyard "plays" at work, for the other women, the physical exhaustion, enervation, and danger of these jobs are experienced as oppressive, despite their relatively high pay: "'Canary girls' they were called, and that was what they looked like. Badly kept canaries. Caged, moulting, songless, much given to the pecking of their own and each other's breasts." This description of the women munitions workers suggests the surreal, inhuman transformation of their appearances by the "sour light" and strong chemical power and dust in the factory, and their embittered turning against one another. Perhaps more importantly, the epithet "canary girls" highlights their status as "canaries in the mine," drawing attention to the high level of personal risk involved in their job of testing fuse springs (*Liza's England*, 51–52). For her part, Elizabeth Wynyard has recourse to a life of ease once she finishes contributing to the cause. Although both she and Liza lose brothers at the front, at the end of the war Miss Wynyard moves with her family to an even more elegant and spacious house in the country, a move facilitated by the already wealthy industrialist's war profits (*Liza's England*, 64). The economic circumstances faced by Liza and her friends once they are no longer needed for the war effort are, by contrast with Elizabeth Wynyard's, extremely tenuous. Released from the "caged" environment of the factory at the end of the war, they have few alternatives from which to choose, all of them, including marriage and motherhood, a step down from the well-remunerated but debilitating munitions work.

Liza's recollection of the consequences for her family of larger economic patterns—the boom-bust cycle of war—emphasizes the fragmenting effects of the war economy on working-class women's domestic lives. She comes to see women's munitions work as an intrinsic part of a cycle of destruction that links the economic to the military: the women's munitions jobs, and the measure of independence they bring with them, are contingent on making "the shells that exploded in France," the machinery that kills their brothers, sons, husbands, and fathers (*Liza's England*, 85). The agency afforded to women by wartime employment in factories is to some extent illusory, for they remain powerless to protect their loved ones or to achieve economic stability. Over the course of her life, Liza is haunted by a feeling of doom: she endures a pattern of loss that threatens to make a mockery of the exhausting labors she performs to provide for her family. Once her husband Frank departs for the life of a vagabond, having given into despair in the face of his war memories and the frustrations of joblessness, Liza is left to the indignity of "scratting" for coal on the slag heap in order to eke out a living for herself and her children (*Liza's England*, 158). And she labors for subsistence aware of the possibility that another war could threaten to alienate her as a mother from the product of her maternal labor, her son Tom. From the time of his birth she is painfully aware of her inability to protect him from destruction:

> Already the cord that had bound him to her was withering away. They could take him away and kill him for no reason she would ever understand. They could fill his head with dreams of adventure and glory and make him want to go. Her son was no different from the rest. (*Liza's England*, 82)

The call of the war is ultimately irresistible to Tom, not only because of dreams of glory, but because of the depressed economic situation (*Liza's England*, 176–77). Liza's maternal solicitude is undermined by the power wielded by an anonymous "they" bent on annihilating what she has worked so hard and sacrificed so much to create. Despite her feelings of powerlessness in the face of seemingly inevitable seduction and destruction of war, she persists in seeing her son's death (a death that recalls her prior loss of brother and husband) as "a wound that wouldn't heal." She vows that "she would never be brought to say that his death"—and the wasting in war of her labor as a mother—"was worthwhile" (*Liza's England*, 199). Thus, while Liza determinedly copes with loss and with material deprivation through these difficult times, inwardly she rages against the cycle of violence that constantly intensifies her struggle to build a liveable life for herself and for her family.

Contextualized, too, by a mechanized world that puts them on a treadmill whereby all of their labors and their determination to resist seems to be useless, Joanne Wilson and Lisa Goddard of *Union Street* struggle, as they face motherhood in the context of the (post)industrial malaise of the 1970s, with feelings of vulnerability, despondency, and entrapment. Joanne, as she becomes aware of her pregnancy, perceives her body as having been taken hostage: it looks "frightening," "like another face, with nipples instead of eyes, a powerful, barely human face," and "by comparison, her real face seemed childish and unformed" (*Union Street*, 72). Despite the difficulty of thinking through her problem in this environment, Joanne's reflections are as complex as they are fractured. Her comparison of the options represented by the women she works with shows Joanne struggling to find ways to think through her crisis: "Everybody she met today she seemed to be seeing for the first time. Perhaps it was because her own life was about to change so radically: every older woman became an image of the future, a reason for hope or fear" (*Union Street*, 94). For the single female worker, the prospect of motherhood may both intensify her drudgery and make her a social outcast. This fate is exemplified by the scorn heaped on "Soppy Lil," mother to two illegitimate children, who haplessly flirts with any man who will pay attention to her, and by the women's avoidance of Maureen Sullivan out of fear they might absorb her bad luck and find themselves also trying to raise a large family on the cake factory wage without a husband's income.

Joanne's concern with making a living and her fears about maintaining her reputation prompt her to marry Ken, who comes from a middle-class family and whose prospects are relatively bright. The price Joanne pays for her claim on respectability and security is leaving the community and making herself dependent on Ken. And she makes the decision despite the looming threat that his resentment of the marriage poses, as becomes evident to her when they have sex in the train tunnel after she has told him about the pregnancy. He thrusts into her "as though he hated her," with "a terrible, monotonous power," an "impersonal machine-like passion"; realizing that "he was trying to screw it [the baby] out of her," she counters his aggression by imposing a rhythm that forces away from her, but one that is itself mechanical, automated, suggesting that her body is disturbingly geared to the mechanical context of her life, limiting her ability to resist others' assertions of power (*Union Street*, 100). For Joanne, there is no promise of pleasure or love on this horizon, only work of a different kind: "Instead [of the cake factory] there'd be a house. Somewhere. Housework. And, eventually, a baby. Well, that was what she wanted. Wasn't it?" (*Union Street*, 106). Forming a counterpoint to Ken's hostility, however, Joanne's friendship with the "midget," Joss, is based on care and compassion, and offers a peaceful refuge from fears about the future. While marriage to Joss is impossible, practically unthought of, because of the stigma it would certainly involve, the differences Joanne observes in the two men suggests a belief that she desires and deserves more than Ken offers.

Lisa Goddard's situation confirms that Joanne's turning toward the protected, private sphere of bourgeois motherhood may be a misleading and even a dangerous fantasy. Lisa is a housewife, but economic circumstances have changed with her husband's redundancy at the steelworks, and she suffers the physical and emotional consequences of her dependency on her husband. Only a few years older than Joanne, she feels herself utterly displaced from "that girl who had worked all day in the cake factory still found the energy to dance at night" (*Union Street*, 113). The phrasing hesitates between the specific and the generic—is "that girl" Lisa herself, or Joanne, or any girl?—suggesting the one life that is lived by the women of Union Street, as well as the profound disconnections experienced by each woman as she moves from one stage and type of labor to the next. Three pregnancies in rapid succession and the stress of her husband's joblessness have deadened Lisa's ability to connect emotionally with her children; the first baby seems a miracle, but the arrival of the third is held in dread. Brian's redundancy at the factory makes him childlike, irresponsible, lost, confused, alcoholic, and prone to hitting her, and Lisa, frustrated with her own lot, hits her son Kevin: "He clung to the deep-freeze counter, and she hit him again and again, stinging, hard slaps, her face distorted by hatred as she looked at him. Yet, inside, another woman was watching, and that woman felt nothing but horror and shame" (*Union Street*, 108). Lisa is internally split and cannot connect her insights with her actions, as though her actions are entirely predetermined. Although Lisa recognizes her responsibility for this violent behavior, her subsequent observation (that in the supermarket "the brightly coloured sweets . . . were placed so temptingly within reach" of children) puts her guilt into a different perspective. Lisa has a nascent insight into the ways in which economic forces, in this case the marketing of commodities in the capitalist system, contribute to the desperation of her situation (*Union Street*, 109).

Entering the newly built hospital to give birth to her baby, Lisa, like Joanne in the cake factory, finds herself, her thoughts and emotions, shaped by mechanization. The hospital, which has replaced the nursing home, which in turn replaced midwife-assisted home birth, parallels factory work's mechanization of labor: the approach to birth is almost entirely instrumental, administered by a faceless doctor with "unsee-ing" eyes (*Union Street*, 124–26). The description of Lisa's artificially induced labor develops the comparison:

> The pains were stronger too. Very strong. There was something mechanical
> about their strength, their remorseless regularity. She felt them as extreme heat,
> as though she were being forced to stand too close to a furnace to watch the door
> open, slowly, knowing that the heat would be strong enough to sear her eyeballs
> and burn her skin. Then as the contraction ebbed, as the door closed, came cold
> and ashen darkness. (*Union Street*, 128)

This account of drug-induced labor resonates quite precisely with Lisa's husband's vision of birds (and men) plunging to a fiery death in the steelworks' furnaces: sea-gulls who seek shelter in the foundry during bad weather often fall into the blast fur-naces after being anaesthetized by the fumes (*Union Street*, 121). Brian tries to be nonchalant about the anecdote, but his silence after telling this story suggests that he sees his own redundancy at the factory in similar terms. He sees himself as the random, anonymous victim of a noxious economic system. The analogy between birthing in the hospital and industrial production suggests that both kinds of work have dehumanizing, potentially destructive effects on the laborer. Lisa is alienated from the baby, the product of her body and labor: "Lying there with the blood flow-ing out of her, she did not feel that she had given birth at all. It might as well have been an operation. There was no baby there. No babies anywhere, though sometimes in the distance she thought she heard one cry" (*Union Street*, 132). Even as she duti-fully nurses the baby, she admits that "there was nothing about this baby she recog-nized as hers. If she had been an animal she would have rejected it, would have sniffed at it and turned away, at once and finally" (*Union Street*, 133). The sight of blood on the baby's diaper makes it possible for Lisa to identify the child as her daughter. The blood is a sign of the baby's femaleness (the release of the blood is caused by separa-tion from hormones in the mother's blood supply), as well as a sign of its existence as a body once connected to her own but now miraculously independent from it. See-ing the blood enables Lisa to break down the "enormous distance" created by her frustration and reinforced by the hospital's impersonality and mechanization of her experience (*Union Street*, 137). This organic image emphasizes the reintegration of bodily processes with emotions and acts, making them an antidote to the severing of the human being by mechanization. A positive reading of Lisa Goddard's recognition of her infant is thus possible, for the reconnection suggests there are aspects of mater-nal experience that cannot be completely systematized or degraded. At the same time, however, this generational bond is shown to be as fragile as it is precious and threatened by the violence of everyday life. Revisiting a childhood memory of going bird-nesting with her brothers, Lisa recalls not just the exhilarating freedom of wandering on the moors, but also how she and her brothers smashed some of the precious eggs they had gathered, in a moment of wanton violence (*Union Street*, 138–39). At the end of her narrative, Lisa returns to her abusive husband, and her "wonder" at the birth is mingled with "fear" about what the future holds.

In an environment where subsistence is so hard-won, where lives are profoundly mechanized, and where relationships between women and men are riven with conflict, each individual woman turns to the community of women for support, advice, and practical help in Barker's narratives. But distance is generated by each woman's fears about her own precarious position; each is aware of the gossip that forms the undercurrent of the community and fears being held in contempt or pitied by the others. The costs of alienated labor, particularly the specters of economic insecurity and loss of face in the community, persist in dividing Barker's female characters, contradicting them internally as well as severing them from one another. Lisa Goddard, for example, in her struggle at the supermarket, feels that she has become a spectacle that other women, especially younger ones, still free from the burdens of pregnancy, childcare, and domestic work, secretly disdain (*Union Street*, 109). While emphasizing the existence of a support system among their female characters, *Union Street* and *Liza's England*, far from idealizing these relationships as representative of class and gender solidarity, highlight their limitations and failures. They criticize not just gossip but the ways in which women's support for one another favors the status quo, reproducing the structures of power that shape their experiences of oppression in the sexual, maternal, domestic, and industrial spheres. As is particularly evident in the discussion of the pivotal matriarch, Iris King, as well as in the depiction of Kelly Brown and Alice Bell, who are each embraced, though conditionally, by the rest of the community, *Union Street* details the subtle violence inflicted by the women on one another, demonstrating the frequency with which aggression is embedded in offers of support. In the later novel, however, Liza Jarrett struggles self-consciously against the cycle of pain and violence initiated by her own mother. Through Liza, Barker sketches out the possibility of some healing of the wounds in relationships between working-class women and between generations.

Union Street provisionally assigns to Iris King the stereotypical role of indomitable working-class mother. The impression that Iris literally holds the community together in her two broad arms is suggested by the following passage:

> There were long spells when she was entirely well. Then she mothered half the street. Kelly Brown and the Scaife children, Lisa Goddard's little lads—they all knew and loved their Iris. Oh, my Iris, Kelly used to say when she was little. Oh, my Iris. And she sat with women in labour. Even laid out the dead, thought there wasn't as much call for that now. . . .

All this was meat and drink to her. She loved life. She loved to feel life bubbling and quickening all around her, and took it for granted that life included old age, suffering, and death. (*Union Street*, 196)

References to Iris's role in promoting order and compassion for her neighbors appear in each of the seven stories, substantiating her presence as a source of support for the other women, and the very embodiment of connectedness in the narrative; she plays the role of "midwife" to the other women's experiences.

As it develops, however, Barker's portrait of Iris rules out reading her as heroic, and compels a more complex view of her powerful role in her family and community. Despite the years that have passed since she grew up in the city's most derelict district, Wharfe Street, where "suicide, mental illness, crime, incest had flourished," Iris is unable to forget its horrors, and, as compensation for these disturbing memories, becomes overwhelmingly concerned with maintaining her reputation as the "cleanest woman in the street" even as she is haunted by the undoing of her hard-won status: "She would look around her at the home she had toiled and sweated to create and it meant nothing. She wanted to destroy something. Anything. Herself if nothing else offered." (*Union Street*, 74, 185). Barker's sketch of Iris's mental state emphasizes her preoccupation with preventing her own and her family's slide back to Wharfe Street and suggests that it even fuels a dangerously manic will to destroy what she has created before someone or something else does. Iris's fear that she will lose her hold on the decent life she has built helps to account, for example, for her comments to Lisa Goddard when Iris notices that Lisa's husband has hit her. While the two women share a moment of camaraderie over the incident, Iris's message emphasizes survival and endurance as the only possible response to feeling powerless. She does not question the status quo, but rather confirms that violence in marriage is entirely to be expected. For Iris, marriage is a war in which the only possible response to abuse is to find some way of becoming dominant, of "fettling" one's husband (*Union Street*, 124). Her advice to Lisa implies that keeping the family unit together is vital to maintaining respectability, and marital conflict, however violent, is to be dealt with and endured without rupturing the public appearance of domestic decency.

The most dramatic instance of Barker's reservations about Iris's power involves her decision to seek an abortion to end her sixteen-year-old daughter Brenda's pregnancy. In a sense, Iris labors to interrupt the cycle of exploitation and dependency that traps the women of Union Street—but at the cost of inflicting violence on both of them. When Iris first learns of Brenda's pregnancy, she becomes so angry that she hits Brenda in the mouth, drags her around the hospital room, and calls her a "whore," expressing her anger without regard for Brenda's distress, and inadvertently revealing to anyone within earshot the source of her outrage and the family's shame (*Union Street*, 184). Aware that the doctor has refused to perform an abortion on the grounds that the pregnancy is too far advanced, Iris decides to procure one in any case. Reflecting on her decision, she admits that, "Her reputation mattered to her more than anything else. It was the measure of her distance from Wharfe Street, the guarantee that the blackness that came from her past would never return. It was this that Brenda threatened to destroy. Well, she wouldn't be allowed to" (*Union Street*, 196). Paradoxically, in order to escape Wharfe Street, Iris literally and metaphorically returns to it when she brings Brenda to the squalid room of the backstreet abortionist, Big Irene, "a woman I wouldn't piss on if I had the choice" (204). Iris's weighing of risks in this scenario makes her more similar to Irene than she admits: like Irene, who is motivated by a mixture of "greed and fear" and "pity," Iris persists in her plan, although "She couldn't justify what she was doing" (*Union Street*, 209, 207). If anything, Iris's calculation is more deliberate than Irene's: she knows she is risking her daughter's life but manages to make herself "sound confident. Confident enough to take Brenda in" (*Union Street*, 205). Even more disturbing is the recognition that the abortion involves a distorted labor, resulting in a stillbirth and Iris's secret, solitary act of "burying her own flesh and blood," thus implying the distortion of Iris's role as matriarch and "midwife," giver of life (*Union Street*, 217). In this episode, Iris's attitude toward motherhood is self-contradictory: she subverts her own maternal principles in order to maintain the community's impression that she is a superior mother. Despite, or perhaps because of, her role as its lynch-pin, she still dreads being "shown up" by her daughter in others' eyes (*Union Street*, 203). Drawing further attention to these contradictions, this section of *Union Street* concludes by emphasizing the next to intolerable juxtaposition in Iris's thoughts of the pride she takes in her living, legitimate grandchild with the memory of the one whose life she chose to end. The psychic dissonance she experiences puts into question whether Iris, already prone to depression, will be able to hold these contradictory memories and feelings together, and whether she will continue her work of "mothering" the rest of the street with the burden of this guilt added to her load.

In a reprise of this scene in *Liza's England*, Barker transforms the outcome: Liza Jarrett takes her teenage daughter, Eileen, out of a sordid backstreet abortionist's and makes a commitment to her grandchild's upbringing. She makes her decision in response to imagining herself as a tree, a source of life and generation (*Liza's England*, 206–7). Having lost her son in the Second World War and her brother in the First World War, and having witnessed her husband's trauma, Liza determines to remedy the discontinuity of generations in her family: responding to Eileen's pregnancy is one sphere in which she possesses authority to act against death, and to influence positively the shape of the future. In connection with the different courses pursued by Liza and Iris, the story and children's rhymes associated with Mary Ann Cotton, a working-class woman convicted and hanged in Durham in 1873 of poisoning her children and stepchildren, functions as an illuminating touchstone: "Mary Ann Cotton, / She's dead and rotten. She lies in the grave with her eyes wide open" (*Liza's England*, 26, 273).⁹ The Victorian murderess—and the spectacle that was made of her—haunts Liza Jarrett from her childhood as a specter of the inability to cope, a failure resulting in a cynical, monstrous turning toward violence as the only kind of agency possible in economically bleak circumstances. Contrasting with Iris's domination by feelings of fear and shame, Liza's struggle against these forces, and her embrace of Eileen's daughter, Kath, can be interpreted as an act of resistance to passing on her own mother's poisonous legacy to the next generation, a breaking of the cycle of displaced aggression and desperation.

In addition to problematizing Iris, *Union Street* explores the limits of community through the depiction of two particularly vulnerable women: the young girl Kelly Brown and the elderly, ailing Alice Bell. After the community learns that Kelly has been raped, she becomes the object of sympathy but also of gossip and avoidance:

> Nobody knew how to react. They all knew and liked Kelly. You couldn't very well ignore it. And yet to come right out with it. . . . In the end they behaved as if the child had been ill. They asked after her, they gave comics and sweets, they clucked, they fussed; they even offered to do the shopping. . . .
> Behind the family's back they talked, grown-ups and children alike. The whispering never stopped. (*Union Street*, 45)

From Kelly's point of view, gossip, support, shame, and violence are inextricably meshed, and the "real terror of the adult world" is the self-deceptive cruelty of adults. More than anything else, Kelly is tormented by the memory of tears in the rapist's eyes, the demand he makes on her pity. She begins to see the community's response to her in a similar light, suspecting that its pity is "contaminated" by motivations that are mysterious and threatening (*Union Street*, 57). The sexual assault is emblematic of class and gender exploitation: the rapist, distinguished by his posh voice and casual "dress" clothes, loathes Kelly, while seeming to need and to expect her forgiveness (*Union Street*, 25, 27–30). Alternately machinelike and animal-like in her behavior after the rape, Kelly adopts protective mechanisms similar to the psychic splitting demonstrated by Lisa Goddard and Iris King. In Kelly's case, however, this splitting becomes more radically antisocial. Angry and defiant, she cuts off her hair and begins to look people in the eye with a gaze that is "Cool. Amused. Hostile. Controlled" (*Union Street*, 47). The community's coping strategies are thrown into crisis by Kelly's increasingly rebellious, unfeminine behavior and are ultimately withdrawn: "They were affronted. They had offered sympathy and been rejected. What they could not know was that in their own eyes when they looked at her she saw not sympathy but an unadmitted speculation. In the end they let her alone" (*Union Street*, 47). Here Barker underlines the limits of the community's ability to address the needs of those who are the most vulnerable and needy: although Kelly is in a sense "accepted" in Union Street, she has "moved beyond the range of its understanding" and, deeply suspicious about connecting with others, lives with "savage pride in her ability to survive alone" (*Union Street*, 47, 45).

Likewise, Alice Bell is in danger of slipping outside the community's support system. Only when Alice is finally bedridden do the other women reach out to approach her with offers of assistance, a detail that suggests that in order to merit help, a person must be defined as ill and totally powerless. Still, the support of women of the community, who "shopped, made tea, lit the fire" and talk with her does sustain Alice;

and, in turn, Alice serves in the role of trusted friend and mother figure (*Union Street*, 236–39). This ad hoc system eventually breaks down, since "it wasn't anybody's job [to light the fire]. She had to rely on people doing it out of kindness" (*Union Street*, 242). In fact, the women who have gathered to help Alice become distracted by political dissension: to Iris, Mrs. Harrison is a "bad-minded old cow"; Mrs. Harrison thinks Iris "vulgar, loud-mouthed and irreligious"; and Alice defends socialism in opposition to Mrs. Harrison's conservative tendencies (*Union Street*, 238–41). The women are divided by their allegiances to various political ideologies, by their assumptions about morality, femininity, and politics, and, as a consequence of these tensions, the two visitors depart hastily, without remembering to light Alice's fire or to replenish her fuel supplies. Her subsequent attempt to search for coal leads to her fall, a stroke, and, ultimately, to her son's decision to place her in a nursing home, which leaves Alice robbed of her dignity by the unseeing face of the social worker, whose assumption of authority makes her feel utterly defenseless. Her stroke has made her alien even to herself, unable to communicate her wishes, but her memory is still alive, and, like Kelly after the assault, she rages against the way in which the "pity" of others (real or pretended) threatens her autonomy (*Union Street*, 249, 260). By emphasizing the mixed results of the support Alice receives, and by paralleling her situation with Kelly's, the final chapter of *Union Street* calls attention to the limitations of the women's community, as well as pointing up the inadequacy of the social safety net in 1970s Britain (with Alice's resistance to the nursing home, which she perceives as the "Workhouse," extending the critique of the medicalization of childbirth I discussed earlier [*Union Street*, 258]).

At the end of the novel, Alice does communicate with Kelly and finds solace as she embraces death in her vision of an illuminated tree, a vision of her body as a "tree in winter," now dormant, but once a source of life and generation (*Union Street*, 261). But to read the encounter between Alice and Kelly in the park as evidence of their "mutual recognition" of each other's oppositional relationship to the "Establishment," and "a strong statement on the sisterhood of class," as Hitchcock does, for instance, is, I think, to overstate the case. The "union" of Alice and Kelly is more emblematic than it is political. Barker links the two of them—and connects them, in turn, to the rest of the women—through a constellation of organic images that take on symbolic significance. Most importantly, the tree is significant *from Alice's point of view*, for it provides the occasion for her to sum up her life by formulating an associative pattern of connections; Kelly, on the other hand, notices the tree but cannot "break out of that room inside her head" where she relives her trauma. While Kelly associates Alice's aged body with the naked vulnerability of a bird (*Union Street*, 68), Alice herself is filled with hope and wonder when she notices a tree that is so thickly covered with birds that the tree itself appears to sing (*Union Street*, 264). Alice sees the tree as spiritually significant, an occasion for existential reflection as she prepares for death. Quoting from the Bible, she asks herself and Kelly "is not the life more than meat and the body more than raiment?" (*Union Street*, 67).[10] Embedded in this question is a quiet refutation of a primarily materialist view of the world, the view embodied in Iris's frantic business and in Alice's own preoccupation with the material conditions of her life; Alice desires to see her life as meaningful in a broader sense. The leaves of the tree are now dead, but it appears to be radiant, full of voice, and suggests to Alice that she belongs to a "web of voices," and that her life is meaningful for being mingled with that of the other women (*Union Street*, 263). In the context of Alice's attempt to work out the meaning of her life, the appearance of Kelly, too, can be called "a gift of the light," part of Alice's final consolation (*Union Street*, 265). Kelly's response to this scene, however, is necessarily more ambivalent. Her reaching out to Alice, taking her hand, and promising not to betray her by informing the authorities that she is sitting in the park, indicates a capacity for "concern" for others that in the aftermath of her rape Kelly seemed to have lost (*Union Street*, 66–68). After sitting with Alice, Kelly's belief that she can survive alone is shaken, and she returns "home" to the community—but home, Barker reminds us, is a place in a community of women who labor in factories, whose reproductive and domestic lives are, in turn, contextualized by this industrial environment, and whose voices are, ominously, described as "discordant" (*Union Street*, 68).

With Liza Jarrett, Barker expands and rewrites Alice Bell's story, placing it in broader historical perspective. Not only is there a close correspondence in the details of Liza's and Alice's childhoods and marriages, but as elderly women each tries to resist the dehumanization that their frailty subjects them to in others' eyes and in the eyes of the state. Liza and Alice persevere in hanging on to a sense of connection between generations, as well as in defending the autonomy and comfort they find in their homes, however dilapidated and unsafe. But while the impact of Alice's wisdom on others is unclear, in *Liza's England* Barker imagines Liza's memories as having a potentially powerful, transformative effect on at least one person. The social worker Stephen, as he struggles to come to terms with his father's death and with their lack of connection due to Stephen's education and his sexual orientation, finds in Liza a point of contact with the past, with the history of working people that is also his history (*Liza's England*, 271). Reciprocally, Stephen performs the role of the empathetic listener—gender notwithstanding, or, rather, complicated by his "feminized" role as a social worker—who receives her testimony, giving it continued life in his memory. In contrast, the gang of boys who mistake her box of keepsakes for money, inadvertently killing her for it, lay waste to the memories that Liza has carefully collected and nurtured, emphasizing her vulnerability and marginality within the community (*Liza's England*, 267–69). Even as she suffers their blows, however, Liza retains a certain dignity, conferred by her memories of what she has loved, suffered, won, and lost.

The tragedy of her death lies in the disconnection between Liza and the community at large, who cannot see any value in her as a representative of the past. But Barker's portrayal of Liza is far from nostalgic or sentimental. Pointing to the role of larger socioeconomic and political structures in creating Liza's violent death, Barker frames intergenerational disconnection in the community in political and governmental terms. Both Liza and Alice remain Labour Party supporters throughout their lives, even when it is unfashionable, and look at the world with a political cast of mind that marks their difference from contemporary trends of apathy. Their fates—both deaths are precipitated by their falling (literally falling) to the wayside in a society that has no use for the aged—indict the failures of the welfare state but emphasize the worse delinquency of neoconservatism and its rhetoric of war, which cynically holds out a solution to suffering and unemployment while continuing to profit from the structural inequities that precipitate the desperation of young people (*Liza's England,* 196).

Union Street and *Liza's England* are significant for their powerful articulation of the complex factors shaping working women's subjectivity and their relationships with one another. *Union Street* tells the story of women living in a particular location, who endure the same economic conditions and who help one another to cope in difficult circumstances. But rather than providing a model of resistance and change, as some critics have implied, this novel is more interested in examining the nature of the women's community in all of its intricacy. Barker's vision goes far beyond a generalizing aim to depict "sisterhood"; instead it includes an awareness of the powerful, destructive, and alienating emotions they experience in the context of work and motherhood. Barker explores how fear, guilt, shame, and the pressure to maintain respectability divide the women internally and from one another, arguing that these emotions are linked to the alienation of the women's labor and to the attendant feeling of powerlessness. The women are certainly portrayed as struggling to find ways of understanding and reshaping their lives. With the exception of Alice, however, the women tend to achieve a sense of power and control by adopting a stance that places the interests of the individual above the community's, and material security above ethical and emotional concerns. Joanne, Lisa, Iris, and Kelly are to a significant extent isolated and individualized, each locked in "that room inside her head" (*Union Street,* 68). In *Liza's England,* Barker not only rewrites specific elements of *Union Street's* content, but offers a notably more affirmative vision of working-class women's lives. The later novel reconsiders the disintegrative, individualizing force of feelings of powerlessness emphasized in the earlier one.

There is no question that Liza Jarrett experiences exploitation, alienation, and despondency commensurate with that of the women of *Union Street,* but she makes a conscious ethical choice not to repeat her mother's legacy of cruelty and violence. She is, moreover, resolute in thinking about her life, not only as an individual and familial entity, but as one shaped by larger political, social, and economic patterns. Looking at the complexities and limitations of the women's communities depicted in *Liza's England* and *Union Street* may be illuminating, too, in a broader sense, for readers of Barker's fiction of the 1990s. In the war trilogy, for instance, Barker continues to question the links between social reproduction, industry, and war, and is deeply circumspect about the possibilities of effective resistance. Psychiatrist W. H. R. Rivers, a surrogate parent figure, whose "maternal" solicitude prepares soldiers to return to the front and who breaks down in the face of his complicity in their destruction, confronts a dilemma that resonates with the ethical problems encountered by Barker's women, whose labor is similarly compromised, and who, powerless to transform the larger determining contexts of their worlds, can, it seems, only shape their immediate lives in a very limited range of ways.

NOTES

1. Pat Barker, *Union Street*, 263. All subsequent references will be included in the text.

2. Carolyn Steedman, *Landscape for a Good Woman: A Story of Two Lives* (London: Virago, 1986), 16, 21.

3. Ibid., 16.

4. John Kirk, "Recovered Perspectives: Gender, Class, and Memory in Pat Barker's Writing." *Contemporary Literature* 40, no. 4 (Winter 1999): 603–26.

5. Donna Perry, "Going Home Again: An Interview with Pat Barker," *Literary Review* 34, no. 2 (Winter 1991): 235–44.

6. Kirk, "Recovered Perspectives." Sharon Monteith writes against this view, and recognizes Barker's critique of sisterhood, in *Pat Barker*, 15–24.

7. Peter Hitchcock, "Radical Writing." in *Dialogics of the Oppressed* (Minneapolis: University of Minnesota Press, 1993), 53–82.

8. Pat Barker, *Liza's England* (London: Virago, 1986), 21. All subsequent references will be included in the text.

9. Mary Ann Cotton is thought to have poisoned fifteen people in total, including her children, stepchildren and husbands. See Arthur Appleton, *Mary Ann Cotton: Her Story and Trial* (London: Michael Joseph, 1973), 101, 135. That she collected insurance on most of their deaths (after having pushed the issue of insurance policies with her husbands, suggests that her motivations were in large part economic (47–59). The relatively high rate of mortality (especially for children) in the nineteenth century allowed the deaths by arsenic poisoning to be interpreted as gastric fever, as the symptoms are remarkably similar (25).

10. Luke 12:23. Christ's lesson continues: "Consider the ravens: for they neither sow nor reap; which neither have storehouse nor barn; and God feedeth them: how much more are ye better than the fowls? / And which of you with taking thought can add to his stature one cubit? / if ye then be not able to do that thing which is least, why take ye thought for the rest? / consider the lilies how they grow: they toil not, they spin not; and yet I say unto you, that Solomon in all his glory was not arrayed like one of these? If then God so clothe the grass, which is today in the field, and tomorrow is cast into the oven: how much more will he clothe you, o ye of little faith?" (Luke 12:24–28 [Authorized (King James) Version]).

Blow Your House Down

SCENE ONE

A spiritualist church. the organ plays "The Church's One Foundation." On the platform (stage) are Mary, who is leading the service, and Harry, who is the medium. Brenda and Maggie, a walking stick by her side, are in the congregation (audience) as is Flo. Harry picks them out by what they're wearing. (And in Flo's case it should, if possible, look as though he is picking on a member of the audience.)

MARY (*stands*) I'd like to extend a warm welcome to everyone here tonight, especially to those who are joining us for the first time.

BRENDA. Maggie?

MAGGIE. (*whispers*) Brenda, shush—

MARY. If you don't have to rush home afterwards there's tea and biscuits as usual, in the back room.

BRENDA. (*whispers*) I think I recognise her from somewhere—

MAGGIE. She does live round here. She's not from outta space. Probably seen her down Nettos.

BRENDA. Her? Wouldn't catch types like her dead in there.

MARY. And now, just before I ask Harry to take the rostrum, I'd like us to take a few minutes to pray, in silence, for those who are unable to be with us this evening for whatever reason. Could we have the lights turned down a fraction, please?

BRENDA. (*suddenly looks as if she's about to leave*) Maggie, you know, I'm really not too sure about this.

MAGGIE. (*squeezes Brenda's hand*) Give it a try Brenda. For me?

BRENDA. Why? What do I want you to get your memory back for? You'll only remember why you weren't talking to me. (*laughs*)

MAGGIE. I'm glad you find it funny.

BRENDA. Do me a favour. Being sat here in this daft shite spiritualist church isn't my idea of a belly laugh.

MAGGIE. Don't swear in here—

BRENDA. The spirits going to get me, are they?

MARY. Dear Lord, keep us in thy angels' care; May we ever feel their presence round about us everywhere. Amen. And now I'd like to welcome back an old friend of ours, Mr Harry Robarts, who's come all the way from Consett to be with us tonight. (*gestures to him*) Harry, would you like to take the rostrum? (*She then sits down.*)

BRENDA. Here we go.

HARRY. (*stands and addresses the congregation*) Thank you Mary. You know my Mother always used to say, before she went over to the other side that is, that I'd be the one to put Consett on the map. Broken her heart to see me come second to a crisp. Somebody accused me the other day of having a chip on my shoulder. I said I said, don't knock it, it's a genuine tortilla is that. I might have been born on the right side of the blanket but what good has it done me? I'd rather have been born on the right side of Meadomsley Road.

BRENDA. (*to Maggie*) I thought he was s'posed to be a medium, not a Phileas Fogg wannabe.

MAGGIE. Bren.

BRENDA. Well, it's boring.

HARRY. But on a brighter note ladies and gentlemen, what a pleasure it is to be back here, in your beautiful church. And Mary here, I don't know how, but she always manages to choose my favourite hymns. Bless her. Now I'm going to take a moment to collect meself and pray that the spirit world will, once again, open itself to me. (*He closes his eyes and pinches the bridge of his nose with his thumb and forefinger, as if in deep concentration.*)

BRENDA. You know who he reminds me of?

MAGGIE. Not now—

BRENDA. That man in the adverts. You know—

MAGGIE. No.

HARRY. (*starts to wander up and down, mutter to persons [spirits] unseen. then nodding towards someone in the congregation/audience*) And, I have someone here for you. That lady there in the blue cardie thing. (*then to the spirit*) No? Not her? Well, who then?

BRENDA. (*to Maggie*) Yes, you do, does the one for the beer with the widget doda in the can.

MAGGIE. Shush.

HARRY. Okay, got yer. Sorry. The lady next to you. (*to Flo*) I've got someone here for you called Bet or Betty. Do you know anyone called Bet or Betty?

BRENDA. (*to Maggie*) Come off it. Who doesn't, that's what I'd like to know?

FLO. Err yes.

HARRY. Can you speak up dear? We need to hear your voice.

FLO. (*louder*) Yes.

HARRY. Thank you. She says you've been worried about something? That be right?

FLO. Yes.

BRENDA. (*to Maggie*) How daft. There's not a person alive not worried about something.

HARRY. Well now, she says you're not to worry. She watching over you and she loves you very much.

FLO. Thank you.

BRENDA. (*to Maggie*) Anyone could have said that. It could apply to anyone. He's just making anything up.

MAGGIE. Brenda, for Christ's sake—

BRENDA. Maggie, remember where you are! Bloody hell.

HARRY. (*who's been pacing up and down in a trance-like state, muttering to the spirits, since talking with the woman in the blue jumper, nods towards Brenda*) Yes, that lady there.

Brenda turns round, thinking he must mean the person behind her.

HARRY. No you, yes that's right, you next to the lady with the stick.

BRENDA. (*rather shocked, surprised and embarrassed*) Me?? (*again looks behind her*)

HARRY. Yes, we're here. Up here, not behind you.

BRENDA. Me?

HARRY. Yes you. Do you know someone called, Carol?

BRENDA. No.

HARRY. (*listening to the spirit, then back to Brenda*) No? Are you sure?

BRENDA. Not a dead one no.

HARRY. No, someone on this side, in this world.

BRENDA. Yeah. (*to Maggie*) Who doesn't? Name's common as muck.

HARRY. Bit louder, please.

BRENDA. Yes, yes. I do.

HARRY. I have someone here from spirit world for you who's very concerned about her.

BRENDA. (*to Maggie*) Oh aye?

HARRY. Do you know a Kath?

BRENDA. (*shocked*) Kath?

HARRY. Yes. Do you know a Kath in spirit world?

BRENDA. (*gulps*) Yes.

HARRY. Bit more volume, my love.

BRENDA. Yes, yes I do.

HARRY. She's here. I'm getting a picture of bottles. Did she work in a bottling plant?

BRENDA. (*half laugh*) No.

HARRY. Oh, wait up. Hang on. She's telling me she lived in the spirit world even when she was in this world. She'd be making a joke about the fact that she liked a drink. Right?

BRENDA. Yes. (*tries to keep the tears back*) Yes she would.

HARRY. Says you've been very unhappy and frightened over the past few months?

BRENDA. Yes.

HARRY. But, she wants you to know that you've no need to be because she loves you and is watching over you.

BRENDA. Than—thank you.

HARRY. (*listening to the spirit*) Oh and Carol? She says to say, she's looking after Carol. No, no. No, she doesn't. What then? She says will you look after Carol? Does that make sense to you?

BRENDA. Yes. Please say that's what I've been trying to do. I was round there this afternoon.

HARRY. Yes, dear. She knows that already. That lady next to you, the one with the stick? You know her?

BRENDA. Yes.

HARRY. Well, Kath's also got a message for you, dear. Can I hear your voice?

MAGGIE. Hello.

HARRY. Good. Thank you. Now it's something like. I'm sorry it's very faint. (*to the spirit, i.e., Kath*) Alright, alright, keep your hair on. I'm doing me best. (*then to Maggie*) She might be faint but she's forceful. She's saying, "You know" . . . about something, if you think back, you'll remember. I don't know if I can follow that, can you?

MAGGIE. I don't—

HARRY. She's saying very clearly now. "But you know." About something that's been puzzling you. Perhaps the both of you. She's telling me to tell you that, you know—

MAGGIE. I've . . . I've been in . . . an accident . . .

BRENDA. She's lost her short term memory—She probably can't remember. See?

HARRY. I'm very sorry to hear that. Come and see me at the end of the service. But, I'm afraid I have to move on. Now, I've got someone here who's very anxious to speak with the man there with the beard. (*pointing to a man in the audience*) If you'll bear with me a moment. (*Harry goes into silent conversation with the spirits.*)

BRENDA. How does he do it?

MAGGIE. It's not a trick.

BRENDA. Okay. I admit it's got me. Not the other stuff but Kath—

MAGGIE. I can't remember anyone called Kath but that's not saying nothing. Was she someone else I stopped talking to?

BRENDA. You never knew her. You might have seen her with me when you weren't talking to me. But I don't think you ever even spoke to her.

MAGGIE. How come she knows me?

BRENDA. Dunno.

MAGGIE. Who is she?

Brenda can hear Jean's voice in her memory.

JEAN. (*voice off*) She's a fucking liability, she is. As you'd say up here, she's nowt but a tanked up, old tart.

SCENE TWO

The Palmerston. Jean and Carol sit at a table. Brenda stands, ready to go over to the bar to help Kath with the drinks.

BRENDA. Won't ever catch me saying owt like that, pet.

CAROL. Jean. Leave off her, will you? She's really kind hearted.

JEAN. Oh, excuse me. It's only a life and death situation we're staring in the gob and, correct me if I'm wrong but piss-heads aren't exactly noted for their quick wits. Kind hearts count for nothing.

CAROL. Shush, she's coming back—

BRENDA. I'll go and give her a hand. (*then*) Oh would you look at that, Bert's only given her a tray.

JEAN. Wonders will never cease—

BRENDA. I'll believe that when you stop laying into Kath.

JEAN. Yeah? And how long before she goes on another bender and you don't see her for a fortnight?—

BRENDA. Then I'll team up with you and Carol, like before. Unless you're saying—

JEAN. No, no. I aint saying anything.

Kath arrives at the table with the tray of drinks. Gin and tonic for Carol. Vodka and lime for Jean. Gin and bitter lemon for Brenda and whisky and ginger wine for herself.

KATH. See that bleeding great alsatian at the bar.

BRENDA. Revolting.

KATH. I just complained to Bert about it. Shouldn't have bothered. He turns round and says "Kath, you and your mates are living testament that no dog's ever been thrown out of this establishment."

Carol laughs.

JEAN. Bastard.

BRENDA. (*to Carol*) What's funny about it?

CAROL. Oh lighten up. It was only a joke.

JEAN. You'd put up with any shit you.

CAROL. Oh would I? Would I?

BRENDA. My Lindsey told me a joke this morning. Didn't half give me a turn. Says Mam, can I tell you a joke? I said yes. She said but you won't be cross if it's about a prostitute. I said, why should I? Sweating mind. She said, cos it's rude. Was I relieved.

KATH. That funny, eh?

BRENDA. Eh?

KATH. That you wet yourself. Said you were relieved.

JEAN. That's funny, Kath.

CAROL. Oh please, just get on with it.

BRENDA. Right. Oh hang on I don't know if I can remember it.

KATH. If it's got a punch line to do with maggots, scabs or her being dead three weeks don't bother. Only Jean finds those funny.

BRENDA. No, no, it hasn't. Shut up. Now stop me if you've heard it. This Panda.

JEAN. That 'un. That's as old as, why did the chicken cross the road, that.

KATH. No need to go spoiling it for the rest of us. Go on Bren.

BRENDA. Eee, let's see. Yes, this Panda is walking down the street when he's sees this woman standing outside a house. The woman says to the Panda, want to come in?

So he thinks "why not?" and goes in. On the table is a take-way pizza. She says fancy a bit of pizza? He says "yeah okay" and eats the pizza. Then she takes him into the bedroom and has sex with him. He says he's had a really nice time and is about to go when she says "Hang on you can't just go, I'm a prostitute."

KATH. Too bloody right and all.

BRENDA. He says "I'm a Panda. How do you expect me to know what a prostitute is." She gets out the dictionary and looks up the word prostitute. She says "See. Prostitute. A woman who has sex in return for money." The Panda gets the dictionary and Looks up the word Panda. "See" he says. "Panda—eats err fresh greens and veg."

No response.

KATH. I don't get it.

CAROL. Me neither.

BRENDA. I'm glad you said that. Cos I didn't actually when she told it to me.

JEAN. You got the punch line wrong you daft, daft . . .

CAROL. Panda fucker.

KATH. Watch yerself.

CAROL. I was only joking.

KATH. Mind, in your case fucking the contents of a panda car would be nearer the truth.

JEAN. The panda eats the pizza, has the prostitute, gets up to go. She stops him, she looks up the word prostitute in the dictionary. The Panda looks up the word Panda in the dictionary and says, wait for it. After three, one two three,— "Panda—eats shoots and leaves."

They all laugh.

BRENDA. (*looking round*) Eee, keep it down a bit, Bert'll throw us out.

JEAN. You're kidding, we're his investment, we are. Better and cheaper than any poxy pension plan.

KATH. Just how d'you make that out?

JEAN. If anything happens to one of us, he's laughing. This will have been the last place we were seen alive.

BRENDA. Shutup.

JEAN. Give it a couple of months and he'll be doing guided walks from here and selling tee shirts.

CAROL. I wonder if we'd then get one of them blue round what-do-you-mercallits thingys on the walls of our houses.

KATH. The only plaque we'll ever get pet, is on our teeth.

CAROL. What did you mean about me and Panda cars? What do you do, when they shove their vice squad card up your nose, like they was American Express?—

KATH. One good thing about being the wrong side of thirty is I don't have to put up with them any more—

JEAN. You're joking, they'd fuck a pig in knickers, they would.

KATH. You what?

BRENDA. Jean?

CAROL. She meant they're all pigs in knickers. They're nice earrings, Bren. New?

BRENDA. Yes.

JEAN. Busy pigs in knickers, Get it? Okay, not so busy pigs—(*to Brenda*) You're not going to work in them I hope.

BRENDA. Don't worry, I've got me clip ons in my bag.

CAROL. (*to Jean*) You're such a worry guts.

KATH. Yeah and a bloody rude one—

JEAN. For Christsakes, why d'you have to take everything so personal, Kath?

KATH. Oh and how are you s'posed to take it when some one calls you a pig in knickers?

JEAN. That's not what I meant.

CAROL. I got bought something today. Shut your eyes, I got to blow it up.

JEAN. Controlled explosion will it be?

CAROL. Shut up and close your eyes.

Kath, Jean, and Brenda close their eyes, Carol takes an inflatable Mr Blobby out of her bag and starts to inflate it.

KATH. Another free blow job, by the sounds of it.

BRENDA. Kath—

KATH. I'll just shut up and get on with my truffle hunting—

JEAN. I wasn't insulting you, I was insulting them.

KATH. Shame they weren't around to hear it—

JEAN. Would you just bloody leave it?

KATH. I'm waiting for a little word—

JEAN. Yer what?

BRENDA. Jean, just say sorry—

JEAN. I'm sorry, sorry, sorry. Okay?

CAROL. (*Mr Blobby is now inflated*) There, you can open your eyes now. (*they do so*) What d'you reckon? Only two pound down the 50p shop—

KATH. Eee, you don't know what to spend your money on next—

CAROL. Can't even get a packet of blobs for that price.

BRENDA. I think I'll get our Sharon one. She's mad about Mr Blobby—

JEAN. Well, seeing as how she's only four, she's got an excuse—

CAROL. (*manages to tap Jean on the shoulder with Mr Blobby's arm—or uses it in some other way to make her jump*) Hey darling, don't shame Blobby unless you want to go the same way as the others.

Carol, Jean, and Kath laugh.

BRENDA. Stop it. Stop it—

KATH. We're only messing around Bren—

JEAN. Where's your sense of humour?

CAROL. Same place as her virginity.

BRENDA. I don't know what you're doing wasting your money on that for. I thought you were saving up so you could go back to London with Jean—

CAROL. We're not going for ages—

KATH. I can't see what's keeping you. Everyone that could buggered off weeks ago.

JEAN. I'm not going back to working the streets down there.

CAROL. No, we're going to be in the money, real money.

BRENDA. Oh yeah?

JEAN. Start working the hotels.

CAROL. And saunas. And for that you got to pass for class.

KATH. Can't see you ever getting down there then.

CAROL. Why do you think I'm so popular with the police? They can tell I'm a cut above.

KATH. Oh aye. According to her majesty here, one cut's much like another to them. They're all s'posed to fuck pigs in—

JEAN. I've said I'm bleeding sorry, what d'you want, a self flagellation session?

KATH. That would be a start—

CAROL. Would you two stop being narky and count yourselves lucky that it's not you that has to do it.

BRENDA. Well, lets just hope all this free business will bring results—

JEAN. Yeah. Have they got any idea who he is?

CAROL. They haven't got a clue. The one I had this afternoon, said they were so stuck that they've brought in a medium.

KATH. (*tops up her drink from a bottle of whisky in her bag*) Whose round is it?

BRENDA. At this rate, we won't even be earning the price of the blobs.

JEAN. I tell you something, having to work in pairs is really slowing our takings down—

CAROL. I've got an idea of how to get round that.

BRENDA. You're mad if you ditch that. That's the only protection we got—

CAROL. Don't forget Mr Blobby—(*she starts to deflate him.*)

JEAN. Yes, forget Mr Blobby. I'm not taking part in any scheme which includes him.

BRENDA. Oh come on, this won't buy the baby new shoes.

CAROL. (*stands*) Right. One two three follow me. And we're off.

Fade down. Fade up to the Chicken man, alone in a locker room, getting ready for work. He takes a brand new boiler suit out of its packet and puts it on. He takes a hammer and a knife out of his locker and puts them into a leather work bag. Maggie comes in.

MAGGIE. Forgot my lunch box. (*gets a Tupperware container from a locker*)

C. MAN. You'd forget your head, you would.

SCENE THREE

Brenda, Kath, Carol, and Jean walk down the street.

CAROL. (*singing*) Hi ho, hi ho, it's off to work we go—

BRENDA. What is she like?

JEAN. Come on dopey, this way—

CAROL. D'you remember the bit where he puts the diamonds in his eyes?

KATH. What are you on about?

CAROL. In "Snow White," right—

JEAN. Shut up and come on or you won't be able to afford mascara never mind diamonds.

KATH. See you tomorrow girls, don't forget, it's your round—

BRENDA. Hang on, what about where he has diamonds in his eyes?

CAROL. Nothing. It was good though wasn't it? See yer.

Jean and Carol walk off. Brenda and Kath walk on. Unseen by Brenda and Kath, the Chicken Man walks past them and off in the same direction as Jean and Carol.

BRENDA. She's such a bairn—

KATH. Except a bairn's got more nouse.

Brenda sees Maggie waiting at the bus stop.

BRENDA. Let's cross over.

KATH. (*seeing Maggie and realising that she's the cause, loudly*) Don't let her make you go out of your way—

BRENDA. Don't show us up Kath—

KATH. Then say hello to her. What's she to you now anyway—?

BRENDA. I know but she was my best friend.

KATH. Why you told her in the first place beats me.

BRENDA. Yeah well. (*as she walks past*) Hello Maggie.

Maggie ignores her and turns her back to both of them.

KATH. (*for Maggie's benefit*) When a human being can't respond to another human being there's only two excuses. One ignorance or two, they're too knackered. So, let's be kind and go for too knackered. Cos by the looks of it she's having to do more than one job these days.

BRENDA. How d'you make that out?

KATH. Well, what's she doing waiting for a bus this time of night, if she's not working? She certainly doesn't strike me as the type to be going out enjoying herself.

BRENDA. She's probably on her way home. She and her old man do shift work.

KATH. I thought he had that lock shop down Battle Hill.

BRENDA. Yeah but someone, can't remember who, told me it went bust—

KATH. It went bust? That's a bit like an ammunition factory not making a profit in a war. What happened?

BRENDA. It got broken into.

They both laugh.

BRENDA. (*seeing Greg in the shadows*) Keep it down. You're scaring off the punters.

KATH. Where?

BRENDA. Him. Over there. We best split up. Which side of the road d'you want?

KATH. Looks to me more like a window-shopping-wanker from where I'm stood. (*Greg approaches them*) Eee no, tell a lie. Looks like one for you Bren. Too young for this old sperm bucket. (*She moves away from Brenda.*)

BRENDA. Looking for business?

GREG. (*seems shy*) I . . . (*but he's looking at Kath, not Brenda*)

BRENDA. It's okay—Oh I see. (*to Kath*) Looks like it's you this young gentleman is interested in.

KATH. Howay, up.

BRENDA. I'll wait here for you.

Kath and Greg walk on.

KATH. I know some place quiet round back of the chicken factory. Alright for you?

GREG. Yeah. . . . err . . . How much?

KATH. Depends. What d'you want?

GREG. Err . . . you know . . . the usual.

KATH. One man's usual is another man's unusual, you know what I mean? (*Pause. Greg doesn't know what to say.*) A straight fuck?

GREG. Yes. That's it. Yes, please.

KATH. Twenty.

GREG. Great.

KATH. Pounds.

GREG. Yeah, yeah.

KATH. Up front.

GREG. Yes, yes of course. I ain't—. How can I put it? The err . . . back passage isn't really my cup of tea.

KATH. I meant—the money. Up front.

GREG. Oh, right. Right. (*He takes out twenty pounds and gives it to her.*)

KATH. Thank you. (*slightly apologetic*) I'm old enough to be your mother.

GREG. I like older women. I can talk to them.

KATH. Oh aye.

GREG. Can I tell you something?

KATH. (*handing him a condom*) You better be thinking about putting this on while you're doing it.

GREG. (*takes the condom*) First wet dream I had, I dreamt I was doing it with my Mother. She was showing me where to put it.

KATH. Oh.

GREG. Not the sort of thing I can tell a girlfriend.

KATH. I don't suppose you can.

GREG. I hope you don't mind me telling you.

KATH. No. Still live at home, do yer?

GREG. Yeah.

KATH. With your Mum?

GREG. No.

KATH. Oh, where's she, then?

GREG. Dead.

SCENE FOUR

Jean and Carol are shagging their clients in such a way that they can mouth to each other over each other's shoulders. Jean is rather embarrassed by this but to Carol it's a laugh.

CAROL. (*mouths*) Alright? (*and gives Jean a thumbs up sign*)

JEAN. (*smiles but looks embarrassed, mouths*) Shut up.

CAROL. (*mouths*) What? (*then*) Hang on. (*then groans twice for the client's benefit*) *Jean's client tries to turn his head.*

CLIENT 1. What the fuck's going on back there?

JEAN. Nothing.

CLIENT 1. Cos whatever it is it's putting me off my stroke.

JEAN. Just a dog.

CAROL. (*tries but fails to stifle a laugh*)

SCENE FIVE

The Chicken Man is in the pub, an almost empty pint in his hand, playing darts with his mates. He retrieves his darts from the board.

C. MAN. No you're alright. I've had enough. I've got to get going.

He drains his glass and leaves. Fade down and fade up to Brenda and Kath outside the chicken factory. A car draws up. Brenda goes over to it and gets in it. Kath ostentatiously writes the number down. She then gets a quarter full, half bottle of whisky out of her coat pocket and takes a large swig from it. She sees or thinks she sees someone in the shadows, (the Chicken Man walks behind her). She turns but she doesn't see anyone.

SCENE SIX

Brenda is waiting on the street. Kath comes back. Before she reaches Brenda she takes a large swig from the bottle and swiftly returns it to her pocket before Brenda turns round.

BRENDA. That was quick.

KATH. Aye, and I managed to get away with a decent price. Mind for an awful minute I thought he might suggest doing it again but luckily he started sneezing. Put him in a bit of a dilemma seeing as he'd only brought one hankie and he's already used it to wipe his cock. Anything doing?

BRENDA. Plenty. But I told them to come back in fifteen minutes. Always slow when there's more than one of us out here but picks up soon enough when you're on your own. (*re. car headlights*) Here we go, get the notebook out.

Kath moves back but the car doesn't stop.

BRENDA. Spoke too soon.

Kath goes back towards Brenda.

BRENDA. Eee, no stay there man or we'll get nowt done.

KATH. Suits me. (*While Brenda has her back to her, she takes another swig of her whisky and puts the bottle back in her pocket.*)

BRENDA. (*turns*) What are you doing?

KATH. Nowt. Just regretting not putting anything into one of them pension plan thingys. What about you?

BRENDA. What d'you mean, what about me? I'm just standing, stood here, trying to earn a living. (*then*) I promised the bairns that I'd take them to choose something at "Toys R Us" on Saturday. At this rate they'll be lucky to get a jamboree bag.

KATH. Best keep your eyes in front of you then. This one looks a dead cert.

BRENDA. (*Goes over to Client 2*) Looking for business. Yeah, don't worry, I know somewhere quiet.

CLIENT 2. You should have said the car park behind the woofters' pub, I'd have known straight off

BRENDA. I didn't know that was a gay pub.

CLIENT 2. Oh aye. You'll be grateful to me for pointing it out to you then?

BRENDA. How d'you make that out?

CLIENT 2. Obvious. Init. You'll get no business done trolling round here. (*laughs*) My boy. You know, my boy, he's only in the first year of infants, right. But he told me this joke. You want to hear it?

BRENDA. Yes.

CLIENT 2. How d'you catch homosexual mice? With a poofy cat. First year of infants. What d'you make of that?

BRENDA. (*not sure what she should make of it but feels she should respond*) Terrible.

CLIENT 2. (*not hearing*) Telling a joke like that not five years old. Bloody genius, I call it. I'm not keen on them, are you?

BRENDA. No, to tell the truth, I never seem to get the punch line right.

CLIENT 2. Na, I was meaning nancy boys. I can't abide them, can you?

BRENDA. Like you say, I don't exactly come across them in my line of business. Talking of which—

CLIENT 2. Shall I tell you why the average straight bloke hates queers? (*pause*) I said, shall I tell you why the average straight bloke hates queers?

BRENDA. Yeah, I heard you.

CLIENT 2. I like a bit of chat, see. Makes it less clinical, don't you think?

BRENDA. Yes.

CLIENT 2. Just a bit of a response. That's what I like. I get edgy if I think I'm being ripped off.

BRENDA. Noone's ripping you off, Mister.

CLIENT 2. Good. Now where was I?

BRENDA. Why straight blokes hate queers.

CLIENT 2. Jealous. That's why. Oh not jealous of what they do. No, they don't want to be puffs. No, but they do want to be able to have a fuck when they want and walk away. No questions asked. No more, no less. That's all. Know what I mean?

BRENDA. Sure. (*hands him a condom*)

CLIENT 2. (*takes the condom but doesn't seem aware of what it is except to wave it about in his hand to emphasise his point*) That is great sex to all blokes. Why? I'll tell you why. It's nature, aint it. If you're bent, great. You go to a club, get sucked off, fuck and be fucked—buggered, you name it. You can have it without so much as buying the other one a drink. See that's where us proper men are at a disadvantage. We've got wives, or girlfriends and we've got to take them out to restaurants, tell them we love them, and then most of the time they don't fucking want to know or we have to fucking pay for it.

BRENDA. Talking of which—

CLIENT 2. How much cheaper is it for a hand job?

BRENDA. Fiver.

CLIENT 2. Fiver? Fucking queers have got it fucking made. No wife or kid to tie them down, they can go out any fucking night of the fucking week and get free fucking no strings a-fucking-ttached fucks for fucking free.

BRENDA. Can I ask you something?

CLIENT 2. Fuck yes. We're having a fucking conversation, aint we?

BRENDA. That's just it. If you want no strings attached stuff. Why do you want to chat?

CLIENT 2. Are you fucking daft?

BRENDA. No—

CLIENT 2. Because if I fucking didn't you might go thinking I had something in common with those fucking queers.

BRENDA. Oh.

CLIENT 2. You don't do you?

BRENDA. No, of course not.

CLIENT 2. Good, cos if any one so much as hinted I was like a poof, I'd fucking kill 'em.

SCENE SEVEN

Jean and Carol's flat. (It has a hat or lamp stand in the corner.) Carol and Jean come in laughing. Jean has two bags of Chinese take away. Carol has inflated Mr Blobby and she holds him in front of her.

CAROL. (*mimicking Jean*) No, Mr Blobby, it's just me and you. Of course nobody's watching us. Now come on don't go limp on me—

JEAN. You are out-bloody-rageous. I'll go and get us some plates. (*She goes into the kitchen. Off.*)

CAROL. We got away with it though and almost doubled the evenings takings—Put the grub in the oven for a couple minutes will ya?

JEAN. I couldn't handle it—

CAROL. What?

JEAN. Doing it, knowing you were there—

CAROL. Don't be daft. Do you never kiss them?

JEAN. (*coming back into the room*) Never. Do you?

CAROL. If I like the look of em.

JEAN. You don't. How could you?

CAROL. (*sings*) You must remember this, a kiss is just a kiss; a shag is just a shag. As time drags by—

JEAN. D'you enjoy it?

CAROL. Sometimes. I used to have one regular and I even looked forward to him—

JEAN. What happened to him?

CAROL. Accident at work. Fingers cut off at the knuckle, completely lost his touch.

JEAN. You're such a wind up.

CAROL. Na, he got married.

JEAN. So?

CAROL. And then he had an affair. He didn't have either the time or the money for me. Why? Don't you ever get anything out of it?

JEAN. Never. I'm always somewhere else. That's the only way I can deal with it.

CAROL. Why d'you do it?

JEAN. I dunno. Used to it. How else would I earn money, now? I don't even have an excuse like you.

CAROL. Oh please. I'm really grateful to my step dad. He taught me to give great head—

JEAN. Carol.

CAROL. And I didn't think you were shockable. (*going into the kitchen*) It's all warmed up. Shall I put it on the plates?

JEAN. Bring it in and we can help ourselves as we want—

CAROL. (*comes back in with the plates and take away and a couple of spoons to put it on the plates with*) Couldn't I just have a fork?

JEAN. No.

CAROL. I can't even see how eating with chopsticks will better myself.

JEAN. Because we're going to do the sort of work where you have to go out to restaurants before you fuck them and you're going to be a bit stuck if yours like Chinese. Now get your chopsticks like so. (*she shows her*)

CAROL. Kath told me a story about chopsticks. Apparently when you go to hell—

JEAN. Watch me. (*takes some more food with her chopsticks*) See. Do what? Where?

CAROL. (*trying to imitate Jean but not having any success*) Shit, it's harder than it looks. Hell. You know, where you go to when you die.

JEAN. Oh right.

CAROL. What did you think I said?

JEAN. Hill.

CAROL. When you go to Hill. That doesn't make sense.

JEAN. I thought it was short for Ferry Hill or somewhere. Here. (*She holds her hand over Carol's to help her pick up the food.*)

CAROL. (*once alone manipulating the chopsticks the food falls off*) Bugger! Don't worry, I'll get the hang of it. (*and although she continues trying throughout the next couple of speeches she doesn't seem to be*). According to Kath's story, hell is filled with people and food. Only the people have to eat it with chopsticks.

JEAN. (*mouthful of food*) Sounds more like heaven to me.

CAROL. Ah but, in hell the chopsticks are three feet long. So no one can manage to get the food into their mouths.

JEAN. Really.

CAROL. There's no need to sound so interested.

JEAN. Good, cos it's a fucking boring story, if ever I heard one.

CAROL. That's the last time I tell you anything. (*dropping more food*) Mind, they don't need to be three feet long far as I can see—

JEAN. (*helping her*) There, that's it. What's it supposed to be like in heaven, then?

CAROL. That's the thing see? It's exactly the same but there they feed the person opposite. See, they feed each other. See, that's the only way to manage to eat with three feet long chopsticks.

JEAN. Oh right. I wonder where Kath heard something like that.

CAROL. Dunno but if you go by that story I reckon she definitely a candidate for heaven. She'd watch out for anyone—

JEAN. If she was sober enough to see—

CAROL. She's okay.

JEAN. She's a loser. Her and Brenda. Knackered as they'd say up here. Fucked as we'd say back home.

CAROL. You miss it so much, I can't understand why you're waiting around. At least down there, there isn't a killer on the loose. (*sees that Jean's looking down so takes the opportunity to use the serving spoon and stuffs her mouth*)

JEAN. I feel safer up here, for the time being. I don't know. You sort of learn to trust your gut, after a while on the street, don't you?

CAROL. (*mouthful*) Ummm.

JEAN. There was some stuff going down with drugs and pimps and you name it, then this kid, I never really knew her, O.D.'d—

CAROL. Yeah? (*Carol takes another spoonful when Jean isn't looking.*)

JEAN. I just felt I had to get out. Had to that day. Funny ain't it. But it felt right. It still does.

CAROL. Oh I thought it was to do with—Sorry. Nothing.

JEAN. The scar on my neck?

CAROL. Yeah.

JEAN. No. After that, I knew I had to get back on the street, the same street as soon as I came out of hospital otherwise I'd have been finished.

CAROL. Doesn't make you twitchy that it might happen again?

JEAN. Oh I got a good remedy for that. (*She brings out a flick knife.*) I could get you one if you want.

CAROL. Christ no. They'd only use it against you. I don't want to be scarred for life—oh shit. Sorry, I didn't mean—

JEAN. It's okay but you have to know how to handle yourself—

CAROL. Ooh, don't worry mate, I know how to hold me own—

JEAN. (*looking at the dent in the food*) Well, judging by what's left of the food, you're getting the hang of chopsticks.

CAROL. Well me manual dexterity's always been one of me biggest assets.

JEAN. And it's going to lead to big money, big cars, big houses—

CAROL. Yeah, we're going to have it all.

SCENE EIGHT

The Chicken Man is plucking a chicken. He puts the feathers in his pocket. Fade down. Fade up to Kath, waiting for Brenda. The bottle is now empty. She flings it away. Brenda comes towards her.

KATH. I was getting worried there pet. You seem to have been gone ages.

BRENDA. Kath me jaws are dropping off.

KATH. This bloody AIDS business. They all want blow jobs.

BRENDA. Oh no, turns out he only wanted a hand shandy but he wanted plenty of chat.

KATH. More of this (*mimes "talking" with her hand*) than this. (*mimes wanking*) Eh? I could go on "What's My Line?" Do you remember that?

BRENDA. Course I do but right now I'm looking forward to some of this. (*lays her head on her hands and mimes being asleep*)

KATH. One last trick. I've been lucky tonight. But I've not quite got me rent money. I'd like enough for a bottle of whisky an all.

BRENDA. Kath.

KATH. Give it a few minutes and then if nothing's doing, I'll call it quits.

BRENDA. Oh alright. (*pause*) Well, don't look like anything's doing.

KATH. Bren—

BRENDA. Just two more minutes. (*pause*) The smell of this place. Mind, it's worse when you work in there. You know, our form teacher at our school when I was in the fifth year, when she wanted to upset us would say—

KATH. Your jaws don't seem too knackered from where I'm standing—

BRENDA. Only passing the time but if you'd—

KATH. Tell the truth, I'd rather be earning my beer money and we're less likely to attract custom if we're stood here, jangling.

BRENDA. Okay. No, fine. Fine. No problem.

KATH. Don't be like that, you daft shite. What did she say? Go on tell us—

BRENDA. As soon as we hear a car or any one coming, don't worry, I'll cross over. Only used to threaten us by squawking "You'll end up working in the chicken factory." Mind, now I'd take that as a compliment. Even she didn't imagine I'd end up giving head outside the gates before the cock crows. Make her day if she could see me now. Malicious old rooster.

KATH. D'you know the only person who ever had any time for me when I was a bairn—

BRENDA. Was your Sunday school teacher—

KATH. Aye well, don't think I haven't heard that about your teacher more than once. But my Sunday school teacher was really—

BRENDA. Kind to you—

KATH. Aye and she didn't judge—

BRENDA. That's a rare thing ain't it?

KATH. What?

BRENDA. To find a Christian what don't judge—

KATH. You win. Come on, I'll do what I always do and buy the whisky outta the rent money.

BRENDA. Huh, and why would I want my job back at the stinking chicken factory? I can earn as much in one night than I took home in a week there. And I have the day free to spend with the bairns.

KATH. I met her, that Sunday school teacher, about a year ago.

BRENDA. What?

KATH. She must have been in her nineties.

BRENDA. How come you never told me?

KATH. Tell the truth, Bren, I never rightly knew if it was real or not. So I kept stumm.

BRENDA. What d'you mean, you don't know. What you on about?

KATH. Sometimes I get so pissed. Oh not on the job. Never on the job. Never when I'm working with you. Any rate, it makes you forget, you know. It blocks stuff out. It gives you a bit of peace.

BRENDA. Where did you meet her?

KATH. I don't know. I can't even remember that much. I wish I could. I don't even know whether I dreamed the whole thing up. All I remember was that I told her the bairns was in care. She—well, she didn't think "it serves you right" I could tell. She was on my side. Not that she should have been, I was a fuck awful mother.

BRENDA. I'm sure you weren't.

KATH. Oh I was.

BRENDA. You've been like a mother to me.

KATH. Bleeding cheek.

BRENDA. I don't mean you're old enough. I mean you've been right good to me.

KATH. Open your eyes. I'm nothing but an impediment to you. Look at me. Glorified Pisshead.

BRENDA. I couldn't have survived out here without yer.

KATH. Go on, get off home with yer.

BRENDA. Where you off then?

KATH. Only to the Palmerston for a take-out then I'm away to me bed.

BRENDA. I'm surprised Bert will answer the door to you this time in the morning.

KATH. He'd sell you booze from his death bed, he would.

BRENDA. Kath—

KATH. What?

BRENDA. Nothing.

KATH. Tell me, go on.

BRENDA. Na, it's soft.

KATH. What? Just say it.

BRENDA. She'd be proud of yer—your Sunday school teacher.

KATH. Just fuck off out of it—

BRENDA. No, not of what you do maybe but for how generous you are—

KATH. You are an arsehole.

BRENDA. Night.

KATH. Morning.

Brenda starts to walk away.

KATH. (*pause then Kath starts singing to herself*) "The Church's one foundation is Jesus Christ her Lord. She is his own creation by water and by word."

Brenda looks round, hears Kath singing and reassured, goes.

KATH. "Midst trials and tribulations, 'midst tumult of the war, she waits the consummation of peace forever more."

The Chicken Man comes up behind her.

C. MAN. (*joining in with the last line*) "Of peace forever more." Lovely hymn, that. One of my favourites.

KATH. Mine too. (*then, as though she knows him*) Oh hello.

C. MAN. If you'll pardon my saying so, you don't strike me as a churchgoer.

KATH. Sunday school.

C. MAN. Was a time when all bairns went.

KATH. Aye. These days it can't compete, can it? Not with joy-riding and ram raiding.

They walk on in silence.

C. MAN. Tickle your cunt with a feather?

KATH. Yer what?

C. MAN. What d'you reckon to this weather?

KATH. (*laughs*) I've not heard that for years. Where did you hear that?

C. MAN. I dunno.

KATH. It's a very old-fashioned way of starting business, if you don't mind my saying.

C. MAN. I don't mind at all. Look, I even brought the feather.

He takes a feather out of his pocket and holds it up. Several others fall to the ground.

SCENE NINE

A month later. Night. Brenda outside the chicken factory.

Carol comes back.

CAROL. Jean not back?

BRENDA. Been back and off again.

CAROL. I don't know how she does it. Lucky cow. Most of her regulars are them premature ejac— whatdoyoumercallit types.

BRENDA. Yeah?

CAROL. She told me that none of her regulars take more than two and a half minutes.

BRENDA. No?

CAROL. You know how she times them? She learns the words of songs that are three minutes long and she reckons if they've not come by the time she finished the words in her head she don't even consider making them a regular.

BRENDA. Really.

CAROL. Bren, are you suffering from the "lights are on but nobody's home," virus?

BRENDA. Yeah.

CAROL. What is it?

BRENDA. It's nothing. I had a dream about Kath last night. That's all. But it's stayed with us, you know how they do?

CAROL. Oh, Bren—

BRENDA. See, I knew you wouldn't want to hear it—

CAROL. She's been gone for a month. Now if she'd had been—if he had got her—they'd have found her body by now. The longest it's taken is three days. You know better than anyone that she's prone to go off on a bender for a couple of weeks—

BRENDA. Yes, but I didn't know she'd been chucked out of her flat. I'd feel better if I knew where she was living.

CAROL. Wherever she is, you can bet your life, she's not worrying over you. (*seeing the headlights of a kerb crawler*) Buck up. Your next punter. (*She steps back into the shadows.*)

BRENDA. (*goes forward to meet the man. It's Client 2*) Oh hello. Usual?

CLIENT 2. Yes, hop in. Shall, we go to the carpark?

BRENDA. I dare say, you'll be wanting a bit of chat on the way.

CLIENT 2. Oh, you've got my number. I like that.

BRENDA. I always remember a face. (*Goes to get in the passenger seat. To do so she has to pick up the copy of the evening paper off the seat. Kath's photo stares up at her from the front page. Her mouth moves but no sound comes out.*)

CLIENT 2. Fucking fondly, I hope, in this case. (*then seeing that Brenda seems to be reading the paper*) See he's got another one. He don't half pick em, don't he? Right old sperm bucket, that'n. Sorry, fuck, didn't mean to be crude.

(*but Brenda has put the paper down and is backing out of the car*) Oh look. Did you know her? Shit, Fuck me backwards. I'm sorry, I didn't think. You don't sort of imagine you lot have friends. I mean not that you all know each other, like. Not. Oh fucking shoot me, shoot me. Don't go. I didn't mean fuck by it—

Brenda stares at him, backing away all the time.

CLIENT 2. (*bit unnerved*) Sod you then. Plenty more where you come from. Two bit whores are ten a fucking penny round here. (*He slams the door and drives away.*)

Carol runs forward to Brenda.

CAROL. What happened? Brenda? Did he hit you? (*looks carefully at Brenda's face and satisfies herself that she's not been hit*) What did he say? Come on let's get off and get you a drink. Shit, me bag. Hang on. (*She goes back a few paces to get her bag.*)

Maggie walks down the street. She is about to walk past Brenda but when she draws level she stops.

MAGGIE. (*brandishing paper in Brenda's face*) I hope you're satisfied. If there weren't women like you, there wouldn't be bloody atrocities like this. We've all had hard times but you don't catch me doing this, do you? Look, look at the evil you've brought on your own doorstep. (*She looks as though she's about to hit Brenda.*)
CAROL. (*taking Maggie's arm*) Leave her alone.
MAGGIE. Don't touch me you cheap little slut.

Maggie goes, dropping the paper.

CAROL. What in hell's name is going on? Who the fuck's she?
BRENDA. I used to work with her. She sort of took care of me.
CAROL. She did?
BRENDA. Yeah only I seem to have this thing with people what do that, mothers, foster mothers, stepmothers and them what's mothered me. They love me, then I do something they don't like and they hate me or the ones who loved me no matter what, leave me—
CAROL. (*goes to put her arm round her*) Brenda. Bren—
BRENDA. (*shakes Carol off, falls to her knees, shouts*) No. No.
CAROL. (*bends down to put her hand on Brenda's shoulder*) Bren? (*then sees the paper*) Oh Bren.
BRENDA. (*screams*) Kath! (*She bangs her head on the pavement.*) Kath!

Carol looks at Brenda and feels completely helpless.

SCENE TEN

The next day. The Palmerston. Brenda, Jean, Carol sit with four glasses and a new half bottle of brandy in front of them.

JEAN. Wouldn't Kath have appreciated Bertie's generosity? (*The others look at her.*) She always reckoned he was tight as a gerbil's arse. (*pause*) It's no good thinking that if we don't talk about her, we're all going to feel better all of a sudden. (*She raises her glass.*) Cheers Kath.
CAROL. Don't get pissed. That's the way he likes them—
JEAN. Don't kid yourself, girl. It ain't *them* any more. I don't know about you two but I've had it. I want out—
CAROL. Calm down.
JEAN. I am calm. All I'm saying is that I don't want to take my chance up here any longer cos whatever else Kath's murder is, it's an omen that our luck just ran out—

CAROL. Yeah that's just it. Up to now we've just taken our chances. We done nothing to make sure it doesn't happen to us—

BRENDA. Carol, please. Kath's not yet buried—

CAROL. And how you planning to get yourself out there? Or was you planning to retire on your pension?

JEAN. What's got into you?

CAROL. Just hear us out, eh? What do we know about him?

BRENDA. Can't you just shut up about him?

CAROL. I know this sounds mad but try and not think about Kath or him as real. Like the only way to do this is to pretend that we was talking about something on the telly or something. Do you know what I mean—?

BRENDA. We know he hates whores—

CAROL. And?

BRENDA. I dunno. I don't reckon he's got a car.

CAROL. How d'you make that out?

BRENDA. I dunno. I just thought it. Because none of them have been found in a car.

JEAN. That don't mean anything. Course he's going to dump them. He's hardly likely to be driving round town with a load of corpses in the back, is he?

BRENDA. S'pose not. It was just a hunch.

CAROL. Let's stick to the facts—

JEAN. He hates us and one by one he's bumping us off—

CAROL. But how?

BRENDA. According to the papers either strangling them or stabbing them or both.

CAROL. Right. So rule number one, never walk in front of the punter.

JEAN. I never do anyway. Do you?

BRENDA. Only if he's a regular—

CAROL. Next we ask them if they'll remove their ties if they're wearing them and put them—

JEAN. Round our necks—

CAROL. Jean, I'm being serious. Somewhere, where they can't then use them as tourney whatdoyoumercallits—you know strangling things—

BRENDA. Oh I can just see them agreeing to that.

CAROL. And why not? Be in their interests as well. They're only customers and we're only providing a service after all. Most of them are okay. All they want is a fuck. It's in their interests to follow a few instructions cos if things carry on like they are soon there won't be any whores left round here.

BRENDA. Would you hark at her, explaining it like she was on "Richard and Judy."

JEAN. I have to admit though she's got a point—

CAROL. Thank you—

JEAN. Not that many wear ties. I'm more worried about belts.

CAROL. Just have to ask them to take them off.

BRENDA. Come on—

CAROL. Well, okay then. Drop their trousers to the ground, so they can't suddenly reach for their belt. And no doing it from behind or blow jobs—

JEAN. You reckon they'll swallow that?

CAROL. Think about it. When there's a bomb scare you don't mind them searching your bag. It's a bit of a nuisance but you'd only really kick up a fuss if you had a bomb in there—

JEAN. Actually, I do mind—

CAROL. You don't know till you try it.

BRENDA. She has got something. Was a time none of them wanted to wear a blob, now, next to their willies, jonnies are their most treasured possessions.

JEAN. I dunno—

BRENDA. Having said that, I don't know as I'd have the nerve, mind.

CAROL. Come on, I'll show you how it's done. Would you just move yourselves. It's not as if you've got anything to lose.

SCENE ELEVEN

Street. Carol waits for a customer. Jean and Brenda are hidden where they can hear what goes on between Carol and the customer.

CAROL. Now you two don't try ruining it on purpose—

JEAN. Believe it or not, I want this to work as much as you.

BRENDA. There's no reason why it shouldn't. You're right, most of them would be horrified if they thought we thought they wanted to kill us.

CAROL. Shush. Here's one.

Client 3 approaches.

CLIENT 3. Looking for business?

CAROL. Sure.

CLIENT 3. How much for a blow job?

CAROL. I don't do them, sorry sir. Straight sex and it's twenty-five.

CLIENT 3. Fair enough. (*He hands over the money.*)

CAROL. (*takes the money*) I'm sorry to have to ask you, but as you know several working girls in this area have been murdered and we're asking all our customers, to comply to a couple of safeguards for our safety.

CLIENT 3. Terrible business ain't it and terrible for business I bet. So, what d'you want me to do?

CAROL. I umm. Well, thank you. Err . . . would you mind showing me what's in your pockets—

CLIENT 3. (*eager for a fuck turns out his pockets*) Nothing to write home about. D'you want me to use me own blob, then?

CAROL. No, here. (*She hands him a condom.*) But, if you wouldn't mind, first giving me your tie. (*pause*) Just until we've finished.

CLIENT 3. Oh I never thought of that. Yeah, yeah, course. (*Takes it off and gives it to her.*)

CAROL. And if you would just drop your trousers—

CLIENT 3. Now we're getting somewhere. (*He undoes his trousers and pulls them down slightly.*)

CAROL. To the floor—?

CLIENT 3. To the floor—(*does so and for a second still looks eager, then*) Hey, this is a fucking set up, ain't it—?

CAROL. No, no.

CLIENT 3. You got me here with my arse in the wind to take the piss—What d'you think my name is, Jack arse, Jack shit. Give me, me money back. (*He grabs her handbag and tries to hit her, his trousers still round his ankles.*) You fucking stupid tart—

CAROL. Please, look. I (*She takes the hand bag from him, gets the money out and gives it back to him.*) You can have the money—

CLIENT 3. (*But he's trying to hop off. He grabs it and takes a swing at her. She jumps out of the way.*) You ugly, piddling trollop. I wouldn't want to fuck you if you paid me. (*He pulls his trousers up and goes.*)

Jean and Brenda come out of their hiding place, laughing despite themselves.

JEAN. Good try—

BRENDA. Yeah, I think you just went a bit far that's all.

CAROL. Oh shut up.

JEAN. (*picks up a tenner*) Here, he dropped it. You certainly earned it.

BRENDA. Yeah. Much less hard work to fuck him and get it over with.

CAROL. Let's go back to the pub then and think of another plan.

BRENDA. Not me. I'm off home to me bairns. I don't know how I'm going to tell them about Kath.

JEAN. I never knew they knew her.

BRENDA. Yeah she was always buying them presents and stuff. Used to call her auntie. Christ, are they going to miss her.

Brenda goes. Jean and Carol start to go home together.

JEAN. Carol—

CAROL. Don't start. I feel stupid enough.

JEAN. I wasn't going to. I was going to tell you that I'm going to London.

CAROL. When?

JEAN. The next train—

CAROL. Don't be daft, you can't just—

JEAN. Daft or not, that's what I'm going to do.

CAROL. What about your stuff?

JEAN. It's in the left luggage—

CAROL. What about me?

JEAN. Come with me—

CAROL. I can't just—

JEAN. Then you can have the flat. I've left some money in a shoe box in the wardrobe. It'll cover my share of the rent for the next couple of months. You can easily get someone else to—

CAROL. What? Come back, just come back to the flat and talk about it—

JEAN. No. If I go back, I'll be persuaded to stay another day and another day. I've got to get out of here now, tonight—

CAROL. Jean—

JEAN. I've said you can come an all—

CAROL. But I've not got no clothes or nothing—

JEAN. Go back to the flat and get them. I'll wait for you by the ticket office—

CAROL. You're joking—

JEAN. The train doesn't go for a couple of hours—

CAROL. A couple of hours? I couldn't even pack me knickers in that time. And what about all me pals up here? Don't go—

JEAN. When he's gone, I'll come back. It won't be forever.

CAROL. You're behaving like something possessed. Come back to the flat. We don't have to go out to work this evening or anything—

JEAN. No. (*She starts to walk off.*)

CAROL. Jean?

JEAN. If you change your mind, you'll know where I am.

CAROL. Fuck off. I'm not packing my stuff and trotting off to the station in a couple of hours—

JEAN. I'll drop you a line when I get there—

CAROL. I bet you haven't even got anywhere to stay. Joke of it is you'll probably die of hypo-whatsit-thermia under bloody whatdoyoumercallits Charing Cross or somewhere—

JEAN. Carol.

CAROL. No, go on then, just fuck off out of it. Just piss off back where you came from. No skin off my nose.

She walks off. Jean watches her and then walks off in the opposite direction. Fade down. Fade up to the Chicken Man. He gets another new boiler suit out and puts it on.

SCENE TWELVE

Three days later. Carol reports Jean missing.

POLICEWOMAN. You can hardly report her missing when you say yourself that she told she was going to London and she'd taken a suitcase with her.

CAROL. Yes but it's been three days now—

POLICEWOMAN. Is she a relative of yours?

CAROL. You know she isn't. You know all about me. I've a file for soliciting as fat as your arse.

POLICEWOMAN. I can do without the crack.

CAROL. You really think so?

POLICEWOMAN. Yeah, yeah. Very funny. What was she to you then, your partner?

CAROL. We worked together, yeah but on the street. We never worked from home so don't go quoting no brothel laws at me.

POLICEWOMAN. I meant . . . Lovers.

CAROL. We was not. Your mind. Jesus! When I split up from my *boyfriend* I didn't have anywhere to stay and she said I could share her place. It's two bed-roomed, so you know what you can do with your filthy suggestions—

POLICEWOMAN. It's not unusual these days—

CAROL. It might be in Eastenders and Brookside but it's not reached Byker Grove yet.

POLICEWOMAN. You'd be surprised. (*laughs*)

CAROL. What's so funny?

POLICEWOMAN. The stuff you must have to do for a living and you find something like that distasteful.

CAROL. Look, can you try and trace her or not?

POLICEWOMAN. From what you've told me, it sounds like she's done what dozens of other tarts have done and simply moved out.

CAROL. It's just I'm sure she'd have rung—

POLICEWOMAN. Did you have an argument before she left—

CAROL. Yeah sort of—

POLICEWOMAN. Well—

CAROL. I know, I know. But she said she'd write.

POLICEWOMAN. You said she's only been gone three days. Nothing you've said even suggests that she's gone missing—

CAROL. You haven't got any way of checking if she got on the train?

POLICEWOMAN. Would she have paid for her ticket with a credit card or a cheque?

CAROL. Na.

POLICEWOMAN. Then I don't see how—

CAROL. She put her case in a left luggage locker. Yes, that's it. She told me she'd put her stuff there, ready. If it's gone then she's—

POLICEWOMAN. But if it's still there—

CAROL. Don't let's think about that—

POLICEWOMAN. No.

CAROL. Can you go and see though?

POLICEWOMAN. Not just like that. I'd need permission and we've not really enough to go on—

CAROL. Please.

POLICEWOMAN. If I put myself out, I'd need a bit of help in return—

CAROL. Oh yeah?

POLICEWOMAN. You know we've not made much head way, if you'll excuse the pun, with this case.

CAROL. Yeah, yeah. When it's only whores what gets murdered no one's bothered—

POLICEWOMAN. Rubbish. It's you lot yourselves. You won't be seen dead cooperating with us. That's what's hampering our enquiries most—

CAROL. You reckon? You better ask your male colleagues how much free sex—

POLICEWOMAN. I meant in terms of information—

CAROL. I just told you about a missing whore and you didn't want to know.

POLICEWOMAN. Yes and I'm saying I'll try and arrange for the left luggage lockers to be searched if you'll give me the car numbers of the punters—

CAROL. You what?

POLICEWOMAN. We know you take them to protect each other—

CAROL. I can't do that—

POLICEWOMAN. Then I'm sorry—

CAROL. But? Hey, no way. You know nowt. I don't betray my own, not for no one, not for nothing.

SCENE THIRTEEN

A week later. Kath's funeral. "The Church's One Foundation" is being sung. Mary carries a wreath with "Katherine" written across it and places it at the grave side and then goes. Carol and Brenda come up to the graveside.

CAROL. This send off must have cost an arm and a leg, Bren. Where'd the money come from?

BRENDA. Search me. Far as I knew she spent all her money on booze. She was kicked out of her bedsit cos she didn't pay the rent.

CAROL. Odd init?

BRENDA. Weird.

CAROL. D'you know what I reckon, it was one of her regulars.

BRENDA. That . . . that killed her?

CAROL. No, that paid for it. (*then*) Although yes! Come to think, you're probably right. Why didn't I think of that? Why would she have gone off with someone when you'd gone home? Either she was desperate which she wasn't, not really, or she knew him and thought he was okay—Bren?

BRENDA. (*not listening*) What I want to know is who was that woman at the back?

They turn round but Mary has gone.

CAROL. Who?

BRENDA. She's gone.

CAROL. I never fucking saw no one else.

BRENDA. Shush, this is consecrated ground.

CAROL. You're so naff, Brenda. (*then at the sky*) Come on God, strike me down I dare yer.

BRENDA. For Christsakes Carol, the vicar will hear you.

CAROL. I'm not frightened of him or God. Come on Father Almighty what are you waiting for? (*She puts two fingers in the air.*)

The Policewoman comes over to them.

POLICEWOMAN. I realise that this is an intrusion.

BRENDA. But you're going to do us for soliciting the vicar. You'll never get it to stick, we don't fuck men in dresses.

CAROL. It's okay, Bren. I know her.

BRENDA. Yeah?

CAROL. (*to the Policewoman*) Was it there? Did you find her bag? No? Well, that's something—

POLICEWOMAN. Another body has been found and we need to eliminate the possibility that it's Jean. Would you be prepared to come with me to the mortuary to double-check?

CAROL. Yes.

BRENDA. I'll come with you.

CAROL. No, no, it's okay.

BRENDA. I don't mind—

CAROL. There's no need. See you later.

She and the Policewoman walk on.

POLICEWOMAN. She could've come—

CAROL. Na. She's not like me, see. She don't trust the police.

SCENE FOURTEEN

Jean and Carol's. Carol comes in carrying Jean's suitcase.

CAROL. (*She opens the case and starts to take things out without really being conscious of what she's doing. She hangs up a dress on the coat / lamp stand or hook.*) They thought I was very hard, Jean. I didn't know what to do. I bent over you. I don't know why. I wanted—. I wanted to kiss your face but don't worry, I never. I realised that I'd never so much as touched your face in real life and it seemed too . . . too intruding now. I pulled back and I said. I don't know why, to cover myself or something but I didn't think. It just came out, I said, "Don't worry mate your ears are still intact and I've got your earrings right here in my hand." Stupid. They thought I was a right callous bitch. Like I was just after your earrings or something. But Jean your face is fine—just beautiful— (*Then she opens the top flap of the case and finds Jean's knife and an envelope addressed to herself. So excited is she about finding the envelope that she puts the knife in her pocket without thinking. There is a knock on the door.*)

CAROL. Jean . . . Jean (*Waving the envelope, she goes to open the door.*)

BRENDA. (*from other side of door*) Carol. It's me. Brenda.

CAROL. Hi—

BRENDA. Carol, I'm so sorry—

CAROL. Look, look, I've got a letter from her.

BRENDA. Who?

CAROL. (*waving it under Brenda's nose*) Jean. Jean. (*opens the envelope but there's nothing inside it*) There's nothing here. Those thieving bastard pigs. They nicked her letter. I can't believe it, they managed to give me her earrings back but—

BRENDA. Carol, take it easy—What letter?

CAROL. The letter that should be in this envelope. See, look, see, it's addressed to me—

BRENDA. Where did that come from?—

CAROL. There. The case. It was in her case.

BRENDA. Pet, she probably addressed it already, before she went, so that as soon as she got there she could write you a note and post it straight away—

CAROL. But it was still in her case.

BRENDA. Yes.

CAROL. Cos she never got there.

BRENDA. No.

CAROL. She never even got on the train—

BRENDA. No. No, she didn't

CAROL. I was alright. You know, alright. At the identification. It was her. I knew. They had her suitcase and I could tell from the doorway but I went all the way over to her. Of course I did. Covered in a sheet, she was. Not her face but the rest of her. She looked so quiet, so serene, you know. At peace. Ha. Ha.

BRENDA. She is, Carol. She is.

CAROL. You think? Brenda, what would you know? Your life is so pathetically door-matty. Someone show you that creepy picture of Jesus being the light of the world? With the door and the lamp, when you was a kid or what? Or was it Kath? And made you believe that things never got that bad while there was a long-haired hippy in a robe to take away the sins of the world. How can you say SHE's AT PEACE?? You know NOTHING!

BRENDA. Did they give you any tablets?

CAROL. I was alright. I'm telling you, I was alright. I didn't need them. In fact the police must've thought I was too alright. That was it. That was why she did it. I swear, they wanted to see some demented reaction out of me. That cow-pig-in-knickers let the sheet slip off. Made out she's caught it on her foot by accident but she couldn't stand my self-control. She wanted to see me blubber. She did not like me being alright. Oh no.

BRENDA. The sheet that was covering, Jean?

CAROL. Yes. I never saw her body before. I know, it's odd what with us being flat mates. I suppose I must have seen her in bra and knickers but I don't really remember. She's not the type that ever even leaves the toilet door open, you know. Anyhow, it was like I was seeing it for the first time. And there it was gouged to bits and sewn together again any old how, great big stitches like some bit of old sacking. (*She remembers snatches of what the Policewoman said.*)

POLICEWOMAN. (*voice over*) Not a pretty sight, eh Carol? In fact, her earrings are the only thing intact. Are you sure you can't help us?

BRENDA. Carol? Carol, have you got any brandy?

Fade up on the Chicken Man burning his last boiler suit in a dustbin.

CAROL. How can he be walking around eating, drinking, breathing, working, signing on, with the memories of what he's done going round and round in his head and still nobody guesses it's him?

BRENDA. In the kitchen cupboard, would it be?

CAROL. Bren, don't bother please. I don't want any. I'm really tired. I just want to go to sleep.

BRENDA. Why don't you come round to ours, just for tonight?

CAROL. I just want to be left alone, please—

BRENDA. You'll be alright on your own?

CAROL. Yes, yes. Please Bren I ain't in the mood—

BRENDA. I'll call back in the morning, when I've got the bairns off to school, shall I?

CAROL. Not early, mind. I feel I could sleep for a week.

BRENDA. You know where I am—

Brenda gets up. She goes over to hug Carol but Carol avoids her by getting up and opening the door.

CAROL. Thanks, Bren.

BRENDA. If you want me—

CAROL. Ta.

Brenda goes. Carol comes back into the room, goes over to the mirror and looks in it. As she pulls at the skin under her eyes, she sees Jean's dress out of the corner of her eye. She turns and sees Jean, wearing an identical dress, standing in front of the hat / lamp stand.

JEAN. The darkness is not frightening, it's what comes before—

CAROL. Jean, Jean . . .

JEAN. I was on my way home, but home isn't London any more. I was going back to the flat and Carol.

CAROL. I'm here. Jean, I'm here.

JEAN. She's right. Staying one more night won't make any difference. Besides tomorrow is a blue saver day.

The Chicken Man comes up to Jean. (Carol, of course, can't see his face.)

JEAN. And it was like a bet with myself. If I don't do this one, I'll never get my nerve back.

CAROL. Don't, don't go with him. I'll go to London. I'll go tonight. I want to go. I really want to—

JEAN. I want somebody's hand to hold. Make this stop. Please make it be over. Carol? Carol?

CAROL. I want you here. I want you here. I look forward to seeing you. I enjoy myself with you, being with you. I feel alive. For the first time, I can remember in my life I've felt properly alive.

CHICKEN MAN. That's what I feel like when I'm doing it. Exhilarated.

CAROL. (*Screams. Eyes closed, she charges at him with the knife. He goes. The knife goes into Mr Blobby. Mr Blobby gets ripped to shreds. She opens her eyes.*) Where are you? Oi bastard, where are you? I can wait. I can wait and wait. I'm going to live until I kill you.

SCENE FIFTEEN

Carol by the gates of the chicken factory. Brenda, having just finished with a client, comes back over to Carol, furious.

BRENDA. What was the number of that car?

CAROL. What?

BRENDA. The car I just got out of. What was its number?

CAROL. (*fishing in her pocket for her notebook*) I've got it here.

BRENDA. Come off it. I didn't even see you write it down, so the punter's not bloody going to is he?

CAROL. I said it's here. (*holding out the book*)

BRENDA. First, we swear that we'll never work on the streets again and now not only are we back out here but you're using me as live fucking bait—

CAROL. What's this then?

BRENDA. Give us that. (*snatches the notebook*) Yeah, you've got the numbers—

CAROL. Thank you.

BRENDA. But the punter's got to see you write it down otherwise it's no use to me. (*taking a better look*) My it's very neat. Days and times. Why have you copied out each page twice?

CAROL. No reason. I was bored.

BRENDA. Bored? Bored? I almost shit meself every time I get in a car. The noise of the engine even seems to be whispering "He's the one. He's the one." And you're back here hoping just that. That I'm alone with him cos you've got his car number.

CAROL. I thought you reckoned he didn't have a car.

BRENDA. I'm not prepared to bet my fucking life on it!

CAROL. Shut up you stupid bitch—

BRENDA. If me being butchered meant he was caught, that's a cheap price to pay in your book. You wouldn't use a dog the way you've used me—

CAROL. Just keep it down, Brenda. You're scaring off the custom—

BRENDA. That's nothing to what they've done to me and it's even less compared with what you've done—

CAROL. Stop being so naffing emotional—

BRENDA. (*fists flying, goes to attack Carol who holds her back*) It's easy for you to say. You don't feel like me. You don't feel filthy, dirty, ashamed of every prick you've had inside you. You don't have two bairns to feed, who'd go hungry without the money you make from eating stinking cock. You don't care what you do. You love it. You stone hearted pervert, you love it.

CAROL. Have you finished?

BRENDA. I'm sorry. . . . I'm sorry. . . . (*she sits down on the pavement*) Oh I wish I was dead.

CAROL. Brenda. Get up. Brenda. (*Pause. Brenda doesn't move.*) Tell you what, let me do them all from now on. I'll give you half the money. You just take down the numbers.

BRENDA. (*looks up*) What? You what?

CAROL. You're right, I love it. I can't be on my own. I want to blot it out. I want to fuck em all. Come on, get up.

BRENDA. (*gets up*) Look, Carol, I'm sorry—

CAROL. Brenda, sorry is no pissing use. Go on, let me do them all—

BRENDA. Carol—

CAROL. Will you stop arguing?

BRENDA. I'm not arguing. Okay, tomorrow evening I'll stand here just taking car numbers and if it works out, night after that I'll bring me knitting.

CAROL. But I don't want them to see you take the numbers.

BRENDA. No. Carol—

CAROL. Yes. Face it Bren, the one thing he's not going to do, is catch me unawares.

SCENE SIXTEEN

The scene is split between the Chicken Man and Carol. He is stir frying chicken and vegetables in a wok.

C. MAN. (*calls*) It's ready.

The phone goes. The sound of it makes him jump. It's answered and it's obviously not for him. Fade down and fade up to Carol, in her flat, reading combat-type magazines. She picks up the knife and holding a large, feather-filled bolster in front of her in an embrace she sticks the knife in the back of it. Then refers to her magazine.

CAROL. (*reading*) "Once the knife is in, it is most effective if manoeuvered from its original position. Pulling it in and out is less effective." (*then*) But even you, you fucking coward are made of stronger stuff than this—

She stabs and stabs the bolster and the feathers fly everywhere.

SCENE SEVENTEEN

Carol, notebook in hand, meets the Policewoman in the park.

POLICEWOMAN. We really do appreciate this Carol. (*She offers Carol a ten-pound note expecting Carol to hand over the notebook in return.*)

CAROL. I don't want your money—

POLICEWOMAN. Well, we have become very public spirited, haven't we?

CAROL. (*holding on to the notebook*) No. I want something else.

POLICEWOMAN. Oh aye?

CAROL. I want to know, how I will recognise him when, if we come face to face—

POLICEWOMAN. If I were able to tell you that, we would have caught him.

CAROL. Come on. I know there's always information the police hold back from the public. You can tell me. I'm not going to tell anyone—

The two women look at each other. Carol holds out the notebook.

POLICEWOMAN. He's got a thing about feathers. A hatred or something. Does gruesome things with them. It's his trademark.

She takes the notebook from Carol.

SCENE EIGHTEEN

Jean and Carol's flat. The lamp / hat stand has a sheet thrown over it. Otherwise there should be a sense that nothing has changed and that nothing has been tidied or cleaned. Carol comes in struggling with a heavy shopping bag. She tips its contents out and unwraps it with pleasure. It holds various cuts of meat, the most prominent of which is a rack of ribs. She closes her eyes, stands the ribs up on her lap, feels where the gaps between the bones are and with her other hand takes her knife from her pocket and sees if she can direct it to the flesh in between. Opening her eyes, she then goes over to the hat stand and removes the sheet to reveal the makings of a faceless man. She has made, if it didn't already have one, a shelf to put the ribs on. She places a joint of meat inside them, secures it, then puts a shirt over them.

CAROL. (*She lifts up her skirt, puts her hands behind and presses her body close to the dummy. Then she moves rhythmically against it. She has her knife in her hand, facing inwards and she stabs the dummy from behind.*) What's the matter, lost your hard on?

(*She laughs, but finds it a struggle to get the knife out. When eventually she does, she rips the shirt off the dummy, hurls the meat to the floor, and bursts into tears. *)

SCENE NINETEEN

Brenda is waiting by the chicken factory gates, checking a long list of car numbers in a (new) notebook. She looks up to see Maggie walking along the street. She stands in front of her.

BRENDA. Going somewhere nice?
MAGGIE. Get out of my way.
BRENDA. To get past me, you're going to have to touch me—to man handle me—
MAGGIE. Are you deranged?
BRENDA. No. I'd rather that, than the way you treat me.

Fade down to Carol who is practising opening and closing the knife.

CAROL. Come on, come and get me. I'm all yours.

Fade up to Brenda and Maggie.

MAGGIE. You're completely twisted you—
BRENDA. So?
MAGGIE. Just get out of my way—(*She tries to push past Brenda. There is a tussle. Eventually she gets past.*)
BRENDA. That makes you worse than a punter. At least when they assault me I get paid.

Fade down to Carol. Knife closed but in her hand.

CAROL. Where the fuck are you?

Fade up to Maggie and Brenda.

MAGGIE. (*turns back*) If that's what you want here—Take it. (*She gives Brenda a five-pound note.*)

BRENDA. That wouldn't even buy your hand up my skirt. (*She takes her cigarette lighter and sets fire to the note.*)

Maggie storms off past Carol who comes back to Brenda very much the worse for wear.

CAROL. What did she want?

BRENDA. I'm not sure but certainly not what she got.

CAROL. (*handing over the money she just earned*) Here. I don't know about you but I'm going to call it a day—

BRENDA. (*adding it to the wad of cash in her hand and dividing it*) I've never earned so much in one week in me life and all I've been doing is stood here taking car numbers. Shame I can't bring me ironing out here. (*She hands Carol her share.*)

CAROL. I don't reckon it can be a local man.

BRENDA. Oh aye.

CAROL. Cos I've fucked the lot of them. If I burped the smell of spunk would knock you over.

BRENDA. Even I know that old joke. Anyhow I thought you'd stopped blow jobs—

CAROL. Na, I relented. Losing too much trade. Let's have the notebook, then—

BRENDA. (*gives it to her*) What happened to the other one?

CAROL. I threw it away.

BRENDA. But we'd only used a couple of pages—

CAROL. For christsakes Bren, it's only a school exercise book. It won't break the bank. Oh look a taxi. Let's take taxis home— (*calls*) Taxi! Taxi!

BRENDA. What a waste—

CAROL. Here—take this. (*She presses a fist full of money in Brenda's hand.*) What do I want all this money for—?

BRENDA. What about you?

CAROL. Look, there's one right behind. Go on. Off you go to them bairns. Taxi. . . . Taxi. . . .

BRENDA. Thanks. See yer.

Brenda goes. Sound of cab driving off.

CAROL. Taxi! (*It slows down but then drives off again.*) Hey, over here. What's the matter? Afraid I'd leak on the seat. Don't worry I'd pay the five pound extra. Piss off then you bastard. I hope your brakes fail.

Greg comes up behind her.

GREG. Are you, umm open for business?

CAROL. Never too late for that in my book, Sir. Have you got any idea where you'd like to go?

GREG. No.

CAROL. Okay—

GREG. Except round the back of the chicken factory. The other one took me round there and I didn't like it.

CAROL. What's wrong with there?

GREG. The feathers really got up my nose.

CAROL. You don't like them?

GREG. I hate them. Terrible what happened to her, weren't it. That old one. She reminded me of my Mum.

CAROL. (*She looks at him. He has got to be the one.*) Have you got a car?

GREG. No.

CAROL. There's the derelict houses on Cumberland Street—

GREG. Yes, I think that would be alright. After you—

CAROL. No, no. You lead the way.

GREG. I'm not sure I know where you mean—

CAROL. Oh. In that case we best go together—

They walk along side by side.

CAROL. What d'you want?

GREG. A umm suck—

CAROL. Sure. Thirty?

GREG. Do I have to wear a blob?

CAROL. No but then it's thirty-five.

GREG. Is it alright if I keep standing?

CAROL. Yes.

GREG. Great. (*He hands her the money. Carol kneels. She undoes his flies. And puts her hand inside his trousers. He starts to breathe erratically. He loosens his tie and takes it off. Carol looks up and sees this. He smiles. She seems about to continue with her work when she realises that he is frantically grappling in his pocket. Again she looks up. He seems to be breathing hard and smiling menacingly.*) Don't stop. No, don't look at me.

  (*He's the one. He has to be. She flicks open the knife but he sees it before she can get it behind his back.*) What you doing? What have I ever done to you? (*She lunges it at the front of him. He struggles with her. She plunges the knife in him.*) What's that for?

CAROL. (*absolutely frenzied*) This is for Jean. This is for Jean. This is for Jean. This is for Kath. This is for Kath. This is for me. This is for Carol. This for Carol, Carol, Carol . . .

Blackout

SCENE TWENTY

Carol and Jean's flat. Carol is in her dressing gown, frantically tearing up the magazines. Jean comes up behind her.

JEAN. What are you doing?

CAROL. Oh, Jean.

JEAN. Take it easy. There—

CAROL. I'm so cold—

JEAN. Come here and tell me—

She sits down and pats the space beside her. Carol goes over to her.

CAROL. I want to be safe.

JEAN. Okay. Okay. (*She indicates that Carol should sit on her lap. Carol does so.*) There. Now, what have you done?

CAROL. I can't remember properly but it was terrible, really, really terrible—

JEAN. Shush . . . There, there . . . it's over.

CAROL. Yes, yes. You can come back now—

JEAN. But sweetheart, he wasn't the one.

CAROL. He was. He was.

JEAN. No.

CAROL. You weren't there. Listen, first that thing about feathers, the chicken feathers—

JEAN. Yes but—

CAROL. And he didn't have a car—

JEAN. I know but—

CAROL. And he asked me to go in front of him—

JEAN. He was being polite—

CAROL. Stop trying to spoil it. (*She gets up from Jean's lap and starts pacing around.*) This is how it was. He wanted a blow job. Kneeling. I knelt in front of him. But then he started puffing and panting. Too early in proceedings. Much too early. Then he only reached up for his tie, didn't he? That was it, that was it—He then reached into his jacket pocket for his knife. It was him. It was him or me. Him or me. My knife was in my hand. I flicked it open and stuck it in him. The rest is blank. I couldn't stop. I couldn't stop. I didn't stop.

JEAN. What did he look like?

CAROL. I don't know. I stopped seeing him. I don't think I ever did see him. His face was my stepfather's. Smiling his dirty smiling. And I just had to stop seeing him.

JEAN. It wasn't him.

CAROL. No, of course it wasn't. It was the Chicken Man.

JEAN. No.

CAROL. He was the one. He was. His fist was clenched in his pocket round his knife.

JEAN. It wasn't a knife.

CAROL. It bloody was. I should know I was there. He had a knife. He was reaching for it. It was me or him.

JEAN. It was his asthma inhaler.

CAROL. Knife.

JEAN. That's what all the panting was about. He was reaching for his—

CAROL. Knife, Knife, Knife—

Knock at the door. Carol freezes. Jean goes.

CAROL. Don't go. Don't leave me.

Louder knocking at the door.

BRENDA. (*voice off*) Carol open the door. I know you're there. I can see your foot through the letter box. Come on, I've got some good news.

CAROL. (*opens the door*) Brenda. Oh Brenda.

BRENDA. Steady—

CAROL. I think something terrible's happened.

BRENDA. Howay up, it looks like someone let a fleet of hamsters loose in here. Have you heard?

CAROL. Oh. (*She looks at the torn paper.*) What? (*She bends down to pick up the paper.*)

BRENDA. Don't worry about that now. Guess what? Guess what? They've got him. They've got him, Carol. They've got him. And it's better than that.

CAROL. Better?

BRENDA. He's dead. Someone got there before the police—

CAROL. How do they know he's the one?

BRENDA. Dunno. They don't say, do they, on the news. They've not caught the bloke who done him in.

CAROL. Bloke?

BRENDA. Oh yes. They don't think it was one of us.

CAROL. No?

BRENDA. Strength of the attack. It was carnage.

CAROL. What?

BRENDA. That was what they said on "Look North."

CAROL. What?

BRENDA. That word. Carnage. I think it means big bloody mess.

CAROL. Oh.

BRENDA. I brought this (*produces a half bottle of gin*) to celebrate.

CAROL. Celebrate?

BRENDA. Yeah. Where d'you keep your glasses?

Brenda goes into the kitchen. Cross fade to the Chicken Man who is reading of his demise in the local paper with growing indignation.

BRENDA. (*clinks Carol's glass*) May he rot in hell.

The Chicken Man starts to lay the paper out over the table. Carol in that moment seems to see him.

BRENDA. Now what was it, you wanted to tell me, what's so terrible now, eh?

CAROL. I. . . . —Sometimes Bren, I don't know what's real or not, do you?

BRENDA. Perhaps you'd better only have a small one then. Tell you what is real. I hope you don't mind me saying but when I was looking in your freezer bit just now, it was choc-a-bloc with meat. What happened, you win the meat raffle?

During the following dialogue the Chicken Man gets a chicken and starts plucking it. He then cuts it open and stuffs the feathers inside.

CAROL. What were you looking in there for?

BRENDA. Ice.

CAROL. What for?

BRENDA. The drink. Are you okay? I don't suppose you fancy sharing it? The stuff in the fridge bit looks as though it might turn.

CAROL. Are you sure, he was the one?

BRENDA. Yes, yes.

CAROL. Take it all.

BRENDA. Oh no, we couldn't eat it all—

CAROL. Please. I can't stand the sight of the stuff.

BRENDA. Don't turn veggie on us.

CAROL. How did they say he died?

BRENDA. Cos we don't want you wasting away. I don't think they did. They didn't find the murder weapon.

CAROL. They didn't?

BRENDA. No. The only thing they found at the scene was, would you credit it, an asthma inhaler.

Cross fade to the Chicken Man who is about to take a Polaroid photo of the chicken.

C. MAN. When you get this photo you'll have to sing a different hymn.

The front door opens and shuts and a woman's voice shouts "I'm back." The Chicken Man panics. He tries to hide the mess but realises that it's useless. He goes to his leather work bag, takes out the hammer, and waits behind the door.

SCENE TWENTY-ONE

Street. Three weeks later. Maggie waits for a cab. Brenda walks past.

MAGGIE. (*calling after her*) Brenda? Brenda?

BRENDA. (*suspicious, turns and walks back*) What?

MAGGIE. Brenda, how lovely to see you. It's me Maggie.

BRENDA. Pick on someone else, can't you?

MAGGIE. Brenda? What is it? Please, don't go.

BRENDA. You've changed your tune. Liked seeing me commit arson, did you? That what turns you on, is it?

MAGGIE. What are you on about?

BRENDA. Oh, just piss off.

MAGGIE. What? What have I done?

BRENDA. What's the matter? Have you lost your mind?

MAGGIE. Sort of.

BRENDA. What?

MAGGIE. Well, me memory.

BRENDA. Your memory? You've lost your memory? Oh very convenient that is. Just woke up and puff gone.

MAGGIE. We were burgled. I came home, disturbed them and got an almighty whack on the back of me head. I can remember some stuff but huge chunks are missing.

BRENDA. Straight up?

MAGGIE. Yes.

BRENDA. What are you doing out here, then?

MAGGIE. Waiting for a cab. I've got to go for me check up.

BRENDA. Where's Bill?

MAGGIE. Oh he's coming with me. It's just that I prefer to wait out here. Since it happened I feel sort of shut up indoors.

BRENDA. Oh.

MAGGIE. I thought you might at least be a bit concerned. Why are you so off with me?

BRENDA. Are you having me on?

MAGGIE. No. What is it?

BRENDA. You can't remember that you're not speaking to me?

MAGGIE. Me? Since when?

BRENDA. Since I lost my job in the chicken factory.

MAGGIE. I don't believe it. We're best mates.

BRENDA. Were.

MAGGIE. What did you do to me?

BRENDA. Not a thing. Nothing.

MAGGIE. Then why did I stop speaking to you?

BRENDA. (*shrugs and starts to walk away*)

MAGGIE. Brenda? Brenda, please. Whatever it was I'm sorry. (*Brenda turns back again.*) Could we be friends?

SCENE TWENTY-TWO

Carol and Jean's flat. It looks absolutely terrible, as does Carol. She hasn't slept for days. Plates and cups are flying round the room and smashing on the floor. Greg, the man Carol killed, is the cause of the mayhem. He roams around the room wearing a Mr Blobby mask. Carol kneels in the middle of the room.

CAROL. (*eyes closed, hands over her ears*) I didn't know you weren't the one. Jean? Jean, please help me.

GREG. I've never done any harm to anyone—.

CAROL. You must believe me. You must believe me.

GREG. I'd never have hurt you—

CAROL. Please go and give me Jean back. I want Jean.

GREG. I can't—

CAROL. Then please forgive me. Please forgive me. Please forgive me. Please forgive me. Please forgive me.

There is a knock at the door. Carol is so absorbed that she doesn't hear it.

BRENDA. (*voice over*) Carol, let me in. (*She tries the door but finds it's not locked and goes in. The man disappears. She sees Carol but doesn't take in the state she's in.*) Eee, you gave me a turn then. I didn't know what I was going to find what with the door being open. Thank God, you're alright. (*then seeing her properly*) Carol, the state of you. What's happened? (*She puts her hand on Carol's shoulder.*)

CAROL. (*jumps*) What the fuck do you want?

BRENDA. You didn't turn up for work last night.

CAROL. (*looks round, checks that there is only Brenda and herself in the room*) What? What time is it? Shit. I completely lost—

BRENDA. What's the matter with you? What's wrong?

CAROL. Wrong? Nothing's wrong. Except for you. Why do you have to keep tormenting me?

BRENDA. Oh well if you're going to pick a row with me? (*She turns to go.*)

CAROL. Bren, have you ever been frightened to go to sleep?

BRENDA. Nightmares?

CAROL. Yeah.

BRENDA. Must be all that meat you've been eating. (*laughs*) Either that or a bad conscience—

CAROL. What do you mean by that?

BRENDA. Nothing—

CAROL. Why were you laughing, then?

BRENDA. Because . . . because. I don't know because it's not us with the bad consciences, is it. What is this, twenty bloody questions?

CAROL. I thought you might be meaning about when I used you—you know as live bait.

BRENDA. No, pet. We sorted that out ages ago. And there was no harm done.

CAROL. If I was you, I'd want to pay me back.

BRENDA. I suppose I'm not like you.

CAROL. No you're daft, stupid-daft, you are. A mug.

BRENDA. Thanks a bunch. (*She turns to go.*)

CAROL. What time is it, then?

BRENDA. Time you pulled yourself together—

CAROL. Bren?

BRENDA. Half past four. In the afternoon.

CAROL. What afternoon?

BRENDA. Pardon?

CAROL. What bleeding day is it?

BRENDA. Sunday. (*She starts to go again.*)

CAROL. Don't go. I don't know what's the matter with me. I'm mad. I'm mad with it all. I'm sorry.

BRENDA. (*taking half a homemade pie out of her bag*) What you need is a decent square meal. I've used up the last of the frozen meat. Minced. Lovely. (*She puts it in the kitchen.*) Would you like me to warm it up?

CAROL. (*gags*) No, no. Bren, come back.

BRENDA. Oh, I'll leave it on the side for you. (*comes back into the room with a large rubbish sack*) Now, let's make a start on this. No, you sit still. (*starting to put old newspapers etc in the sack*) I don't know how you manage to keep getting it in such a state but I do know what it's like, the messier it gets the more depressed you feel. (*picking up bits of broken crockery*) There's a broken cup here. And a broken plate. They're all over—

CAROL. Yes.

BRENDA. It's okay, I know all about it.

CAROL. You do?

BRENDA. It always happens to me when I lose some one.

CAROL. It does?

BRENDA. It'll pass.

CAROL. Will it?

BRENDA. Of course. You can't stay angry forever. The more you loved someone the more angry you feel.

CAROL. Me?

BRENDA. When my foster Mum died, I smashed everything in the house. Not that it did me any good. If she was alive to see how I turned out, she'd wish herself dead again. You know the busies picked me up again last night. Kept asking about the punters. Course we was at cross purposes most of the time cos the names they give us ain't the names they tell the police and their real names are different again. Mind you when we sorted it out, they seemed to know every punter I'd ever been with. How I don't know. Have they—?

CAROL. (*about the room*) Brenda, that looks great.

BRENDA. It's a bit better, isn't it? Do you think you can manage to get the hoover out when I've gone?

CAROL. You're not going are you?

BRENDA. I only popped round to see if you were alright. I've already said I'll—

CAROL. It's just that I—I dunno. I haven't been very good on my own—

BRENDA. Come with us. It's just me and Maggie.

CAROL. Her? That stuck-up cow. The one what doesn't talk to you?

BRENDA. Oh she is now.

CAROL. You made it up?

BRENDA. I saw her outside her house the other day. She's not too grand. Came home and got bashed over the head by a burglar.

CAROL. Should have told her that she brought it on herself. Remember what she said to you when Kath was murdered? You should have said, "Well, Maggie, that's the risk you take when you go into your own house. You're asking to be hit over the head really."

BRENDA. But what's the point of being like that?

CAROL. Bit of satisfaction I suppose. Where you going anyway?

BRENDA. Church.

CAROL. Church? Brenda, have you gone potty?

BRENDA. No, not church, church. The spiritualist church. Why don't you come—?

CAROL. Not fucking likely!

BRENDA. Maggie says that people get a lot of comfort from it—

CAROL. Bollocks. A lot of people go mental from it.

BRENDA. Please?

CAROL. No ta.

BRENDA. It's just that I promised—

CAROL. No, you go.

BRENDA. Maybe I could give her a ring—

CAROL. (*feeling that she now has nothing to fear, after all there is only her and Brenda in the room*) No honestly, Bren. You go. Thanks for coming round. I do feel much better for seeing you.

BRENDA. Sure?

CAROL. Yeah. I've just got to stop feeling sorry for myself.

BRENDA. I don't like to leave you—

CAROL. Honestly, I'll do the hoovering and have a bath.

BRENDA. Tell you what, after the service, I'll get rid of Maggie and meet you in the Palmerston—

CAROL. State of me. I better do something to tidy meself up or I'll break the record and be the first dog to get thrown out of there. (*laughs*) Go on.

BRENDA. You sure?

CAROL. By the time I've had a bath and tarted meself up, it'll be time to meet you.

Brenda goes.

CAROL. (*calls after her*) Bren. Thanks. (*She goes back to looking at her self in the mirror and starts humming "I See Her Face Everywhere I Go," but stops when she sees the back of the man she murdered.*)

GREG. I'm still here.

CAROL. Well, you can just fuck off out of it.

GREG. I can't.

CAROL. What are you wearing that stupid mask for?

GREG. Don't you like it?

CAROL. I want to see your face.

GREG. I haven't got one. You cut it up. I don't have any face left. That's why it took the police so long to find out who I was. My Grandmother identified my belongings and my dentist identified my teeth. My Grandmother didn't report me missing for a week. She certainly didn't put me together with the description of the dead man because I was supposed to be on a training course in Sunderland, not being sucked off in a derelict street. But if it will make you happy to—

CAROL. What would make me happy is to be left alone—

GREG. You don't mean that—You're like me, we don't like being on our own.

CAROL. What do I have to do before you'll let me go?

GREG. You have to go out there and find him, then we can both rest in peace.

CAROL. I can't—
GREG. Then it's just you and me—
He stands in front of her with his back to the audience.
GREG. Come here, come on. Please? (*takes the mask off*) Come and give me a kiss.

Carol looks at him, screams and runs out into the night.

SCENE TWENTY-THREE

The spiritualist church. (Continuation from scene 3) The service is over. Mary and Harry stand by the door, shaking hands, and seeing people out. Brenda and Maggie come over on their way out.

BRENDA. Oh Maggie, I reckon he's gone.
MAGGIE. He said to wait behind. Please hang on, just for a bit, Bren. I know you think it's daft but he might be able to help.
BRENDA. No, no. I did think it was daft but that message from Kath seemed real enough.

Mary comes in.

MARY. Tea and biscuits just through here ladies.
MAGGIE. Actually, I'm waiting to see the speaker Mr Robarts.
BRENDA. He told her to wait behind afterwards.
MAGGIE. He said he might be able to sort us out—help me with my memory like.
MARY. I think he's just nipped to the gents. Why don't you come and have a cup of tea while you're waiting?

Harry comes in.

HARRY. Mary, where did I put my coat?
MAGGIE. Mr Robarts I'm—
MARY. Harry, this lady has been waiting to see you.
HARRY. Ah, you're the one with the bump on the head. (*he puts one hand one her head*) Spirit divine, through your healing channel shine. Look down on our sister and restore her in your chosen image. (*then*) Oh Mary, I'll have to get off or I'll miss the last blooming bus. (*Pause.*) I'll get me own coat, then, shall I? (*He goes off humming "The Church's One Foundation . . ."*)
MARY. It's just in the cloakroom Harry. (*then to Brenda*) Excuse me, but I hope you don't mind me asking, did you know a Kath Robson?
BRENDA. (*Looks round to see if anyone's listening. Then feels ashamed of herself so says rather loudly.*) Yes, what of it?
MARY. Was she a friend of yours?
BRENDA. What's it to you?
MARY. I don't know if she ever mentioned it but my Great Aunt used to be her Sunday school teacher—

BRENDA. Your? Yes, yes she did. Often. In fact she saw her about a year ago.

MARY. I don't think she could have, She went over to the spirit world about a year ago. I don't think she'd seen or heard from Kath since the Sunday school days. She'd always wanted to adopt her you know. She loved kids but in those days, single women adopting children was unheard of—

BRENDA. You know Kath's . . . Kath's . . . err. Dead . . . err gone over . . . in the spirit world . . . herself.

MARY. Yes. My Great Aunt left some money for her. But by the time we traced her. . . . Well, it was enough to pay for a decent funeral.

BRENDA. Oh, that's where I've seen you before—

HARRY. (calls, off) Mary, I'm damned if I can see it.

MARY. Hang on Harry. Excuse me—

BRENDA. That's how he must have known about Kath—from her and I almost believed him. I was well and truly taken in for a moment there.

MAGGIE. Why would she do that?

BRENDA. To con us. And he must have thought as we were friends that you knew Kath as well. Only you never did. So what would she be doing giving you a message? It's all been a big racket from start to finish.

Flo comes up to Brenda and Maggie.

FLO. What are you doing, Maggie, bringing her here?

MAGGIE. Leave it, Flo.

FLO. She's nowt but a common tart—

BRENDA. What d'you suppose Mary Magdalene was?

FLO. How dare you soil this place of worship with your tongue?

MAGGIE. She's no different to you or me.

FLO. You've changed your tune—

MAGGIE. Flo?

FLO. And you've obviously lost more than your memory.

MAGGIE. What's she ever done to you, eh?

BRENDA. Nowt. But I've done plenty to her husband and I've never had any complaints about my tongue or any other part of my body for that matter.

FLO. Maggie, how can you put up with that sort of behaviour? I don't know about you but that's it. I'm off.

She goes.

BRENDA. Been off for a long time, by the looks of you—

MAGGIE. Is that true—about her husband?

BRENDA. I've no idea but the point is, neither has she now. (laughs) I don't know why I'm laughing.

MAGGIE. (Her memory comes back.) Brenda.

BRENDA. Do you want to go home?

MAGGIE. No.

BRENDA. You alright?

MAGGIE. No.

BRENDA. Have you remembered you're not talking to me?

MAGGIE. I've remembered too much.

BRENDA. D'you want me to go?

MAGGIE. No. It's more than that.

BRENDA. What?

MAGGIE. She was right.

BRENDA. Who?

MAGGIE. Your Kath.

BRENDA. About what?

MAGGIE. I do know.

SCENE TWENTY-FOUR

Maggie's flashback. Continuation from scene 20. Maggie comes into her living room.

MAGGIE. (*cheerfully*) What would you know? I forgot the shopping list. Bill?

BILL. (*Stands behind the door and hits her really hard over the head with the poker.*) Fuck you. Fuck you. (*He then goes round the room, pulling out drawers, wiping his prints off things, making it look like a burglary has happened.*)

SCENE TWENTY-FIVE

The spiritualist church. Continuation from scene 23.

BRENDA. Maggie, what is it?

MAGGIE. It's Bill.

BRENDA. What's happened? Is he ill? You telling me you've had a premonition about him?

MAGGIE. What was your message from Kath?

BRENDA. I thought you said your memory had come back.

MAGGIE. To watch out for Carol—

BRENDA. I told you, I have been—

MAGGIE. Where will she be now?

BRENDA. At home I hope, having a bath. I said I'd meet her later down the Palmerston.

MAGGIE. Come on—

BRENDA. Where?

MAGGIE. To find her.

BRENDA. Maggie, leave it. She's right pissed off with me keeping pestering her as it is—

MAGGIE. Can't you see that we've got to find her first?

SCENE TWENTY-SIX

Street. Carol, waits alone by the chicken factory gates. She is drunk and slightly out of control. She has her knife clenched in her fist and manages to cut her finger by accident.

CAROL. Oh shit. (*She sucks her finger and puts the knife back in her pocket. She hears Jean's voice.*)

JEAN. (*voice over*) When he's gone, I'll come back. It won't be forever.

CAROL.) (*She looks round, hoping that Jean is there. She turns back, disappointed and looks up as Bill comes up. Smiles.*) Looking for business, sir?

BILL. Tickle your cunt with a feather?

Pause.

CAROL. You can do what the fuck you want cock as long as you're prepared to pay for it.

THE END

Part Two ■ Dialogue under Pressure

CARINA BARTLEET

Bringing the House Down
Pat Barker, Sarah Daniels, and the Dramatic Dialogue

The adaptation of a novel for the stage can present a number of specific challenges for the dramatist. The economics of modern theatrical production often requires that the number of characters present in a novel be reduced. Equally, there are differences in the manner in which both narrative and plot can be handled in the novel and on the stage. Pat Barker's extensive use of dialogue and the preoccupation with extreme or "dramatic" situations in her work lend themselves to adaptation as drama. At the same time, however, Barker's work presents difficulties for stage adaptation as a consequence of her quintessentially novelistic style, which incorporates an interest in the unconscious. This essay is an examination of the 1995 adaptation of Barker's second novel, *Blow Your House Down* (1984), by the playwright Sarah Daniels for Theatre Live, Newcastle.[1] It considers what dramatization reveals about Barker's work and its relationship with the stage. Barker's novel is set in northern England and depicts a group of prostitutes who fear for their lives because there is a serial killer at large. The killer, it is believed, selects prostitutes as his victims. All of the central female characters are prostitutes with the exception of Maggie, a married woman working at the local chicken factory who features in the final part of the novel as a contrast to the other figures. The story that Barker writes has parallels with the real-life Yorkshire Ripper case.[2] Her story differs, however, because one of her characters, Jean, is driven to commit murder as a response to the murder of her lover, Carol.

For the British playwright Sarah Daniels the novel's four-part structure presented a challenging problem.[3] Her response to the difficulty was to alter the plot significantly, change the ending of the narrative slightly, and refocus the perspectives presented in the story. An interesting figure, Daniels has been described as "arguably the most controversial and the most successful representative of a younger generation of women playwrights to emerge in the 1980s."[4] Her predominantly realist and frequently comic dramaturgy is acknowledged as one that integrates feminist concerns.[5] The author of the succès de scandale *Masterpieces* (1983), and one of the few women to have a play premiered at the Royal National Theatre, Daniels has also written for television, notably contributing to *EastEnders* and *Grange Hill* for the BBC. She shares with Barker an interest in the portrayal of both sex and class. A review of Daniels's adaptation of the *Blow Your House Down* described it as "a very layered piece, involving dreams and delusions within a fantasy . . . [in] a tight spare setting . . . [that] feels very real and authentic."[6] Other critical commentary has typified the play as "black comedy" and given little attention to the changes made in the reworking of the novel for the stage.[7]

Adaptation is, necessarily, an intertextual exercise and this essay is also an exploration of the transposition of Barker's novelistic discourse onto Daniels's dramatic one.[8] The relationship between the novel and the playtext is theorized through the work of Mikhail Bakhtin and, especially, the concept of dialogism. In his book on Bakhtin, Tzvetan Todorov identifies dialogism as the "intertextual dimension" of the utterance.[9] According to Todorov, Bakhtin employs the term "to designate the relation of every utterance to other utterances."[10] Within this framework, the adaptation of *Blow Your House Down* can be theorized as a dialogic one that contains novelistic, feminist, and dramatic conventions and ideologies, which are often in opposition or conflict with each other. The strength of Bakhtin's theories for this essay are that Daniels's adaptation can be read as multiple and divergent in meaning and manner. The application of Bakhtin's concept of dialogism to the drama raises a number of questions, however, because of its celebration of the novelistic genre as the dialogic form above all others. Bakhtin barely mentions drama or theater in his discussion of dialogism, and when he does so it is usually identified, as Helene Keyssar has noted, as monologic.[11] Keyssar has argued persuasively that some dramas may be dialogic, observing that

> the most distinctive quality, call it a genre, of modern drama is its rejection of monologism and the patriarchal authority of drama in performance. This genre of modern drama attempts to create a dramatic discourse that celebrates rather than annihilates or exiles difference.[12]

Keyssar includes feminist dramas among those works that exhibit dialogism.

An alternative argument for the application is located within Bakhtin's model and, specifically, in his wide use of the term "novel." As Max Harris has noted, Bakhtin writes of a novelization of other literary forms.[13] In a frequently quoted passage from "Epic and Novel" Bakhtin comments:

> In an era when the novel reigns supreme, almost all remaining genres are to a greater or lesser extent "novelized": drama (for example, Ibsen, Hauptmann, and the whole of naturalist drama), epic poetry. . . . In general any strict adherence to a genre begins to feel like a stylization taken to the point of parody, despite the artistic intent of the author.[14]

Elsewhere, Bakhtin observes "Contemporary realistic social drama may, of course, be heteroglot and multilanguaged."[15] Drama, especially modern drama, is not an exclusively monological form. In this instance, the "novelization" of form has a specific resonance. Adaptation of a novel for theater or film is frequently termed a dramatization but this belies the interdependence between the original story and its transposed "copy." It is the contention here that just as the story must be dramatized, the drama can be seen as novelized, at least in part, by the interrelationship. Thus utterances, phrases, and descriptions that are remade in the dialogue and stage directions can exhibit their hybrid construction. Together, these two arguments provide a compelling reason for the use of Bakhtin's theories in this instance.

The sections that follow explore three key areas of the adaptation of *Blow Your House Down* paying attention to points where the play converges with and diverges from the novel. The first of these will explore the reworking of novelistic conventions into dramatic ones, the second the representation of sex and sexuality in the novel and on the stage, and the third the manner in which the scenes of murderous violence are remade in the play.

A number of striking changes are made in the stage adaptation. One of the most intriguing is the substitution of Jean for Carol. An important narrative strand in Barker's text concerns these two women characters. Like most of the other major female characters in the novel, Carol and Jean are prostitutes; however, Barker also depicts the two as lovers. Carol disappears without a trace one night and is eventually found murdered. Traumatized by the death of her lover, Jean goes out hunting for the murderer, determined to kill him. This is an important storyline that is retained in the adaptation but with the change that Jean is murdered. Hence, in the play, it is Carol, rather than Jean, who is driven to murder by the death of her friend. The modification makes little difference to the plot but the replacement of Jean with Carol establishes substitution as a means for Daniels's transposition of Barker's text that can be applied more widely. Many of the textual transformations that the novel undergoes in Daniels's playtext can, therefore, be likened to transformation via substitution. Thus, Barker's novelistic discourse is transformed into a dramatic one by substituting one element for another.

An avian motif is interwoven throughout the novel. The prostitutes' stories are placed against a working-class backdrop that includes a chicken factory. The women's trade is juxtaposed with the only other work available to them, the preparation of chickens in the factory. In her adaptation, Daniels reworks the avian motif substantially, transforming it into a theme that leads, ultimately, to the identity of the murderer. Here Daniels turns again to the theme of substitution in her invocation of the murderer. Where Barker's novel presents an act of brutal murder through the eyes of the killer and from Kath's point of view, Daniels, in contrast, opts to embody the murderer as the Chicken Man and, eventually, to identify him as Bill, the husband of Maggie. She shows him in scene 1 in the locker room at the chicken factory with Maggie (who has an important role at the end of both the novel and the play). Later scenes detail his elation after the murders: "That's what I feel like when I'm doing it. Exhilarated."[16] Throughout much of the play it is apparent that the Chicken Man is the killer although his true identity as Bill is not revealed until near the end. A number of clues that lead to his identity are peppered throughout the play. In one instance Carol trades the numbers of the license plates of her clients' cars to the police in return for information and learns that feathers are the killer's motif. Daniels plays with the killer's identity in other ways too, most notably in the portrayal of Carol's anger and distress over the death of her friend. In the dramatic text, Carol is shown murdering the killer of her friend, symbolically. Daniels depicts this through the incorporation of a character, Greg and several inanimate objects that function as symbolic substitutes for the Chicken Man. Carol murders Greg and destroys the inanimate objects in her quest to obliterate the killer.

One of Carol's substitutes for the killer is an inflatable toy, "Mr. Blobby." Alone in her flat, Carol believes that the murderer is in front of her and charges at him with a knife only for him to disappear and the toy to be ripped to shreds instead. Other symbolic substitutes for the killer include a feather bolster, a joint of meat, and Greg, a client who is murdered by Carol when she mistakes him for the murderer. The feather bolster that Carol stabs in scene 16 of the play, sending feathers flying everywhere, provides a link from the chicken factory and its environs to the Chicken Man, and this incident serves as part of a wider play on the identity of the murderer.

The final section of the novel concentrates on Maggie, who is not a prostitute but a worker at the chicken factory; but she, like them, is attacked in the street. Maggie survives her assault but loses her memory as a consequence. This section of the novel introduces an element of optimism by detailing Maggie's slow recuperation. In a radical departure from the novel, Daniels rewrites the section in a way that places the focus on the revelation of the murderer's identity. A flashback scene reveals that Maggie is not the victim of a burglary as had been assumed, but of an attack by her partner Bill when she disturbs him photographing a chicken. Daniels's reworking simplifies a complex area of the novel: although the suspicion that Bill might have attacked Maggie is not resolved in the novel, he is identified explicitly as the serial killer in the play. In so doing, Daniels condenses the storyline but at the expense of ignoring Baker's careful exploration of the relationship between Maggie and Bill and, especially, as Sharon Monteith has argued, the parallels between this and a "real life" victim of the Yorkshire Ripper, whose husband was suspected of her attack initially.[17]

While Daniels's alteration to the story can be read as a distillation of it for stage adaptation the modification also has an implication for a possible feminist reading. Whereas Barker's text may be read as exploring the hypothesis that any man is potentially violent only to challenge it in the ambiguous ending, Daniels's dramatic version is, on initial reading or viewing, more emphatic and appears to postulate that every man is potentially violent. Such a reading is reductive and fails to take account of the symbolic substitution of the murderer for Greg that is one feature of this adaptation. Daniels's expressionistic depiction of the murdered client Greg as an unfortunate "innocent," discussed below, is a rejection of this uncomplicated association of "everyman" with murderous violence. In paring down the storyline, Daniels introduces a playful polysemy between the identity of the Chicken Man, the chicken factory where Maggie works, the feathers that provide the murderer's signature, and the eventual identity of the killer as Bill. The name of the killer, Bill, alludes to his modus operandi, creating a symbolic concatenation between trade and murder in a manner that links Eros and Thanatos explicitly. As the beak of a bird, the bill links the twin identities of the Chicken Man / Bill in an avian theme and encompasses the killer's trademark feathers. This wordplay is echoed in "bird" (a colloquial term for a woman) and in "chicken," sometimes used as a term of endearment but which, as Ardis notes in this volume, can also be a slang term for a prostitute. This theme returns to its origins in Barker's novel because, by extension, it refers to the women who work as prostitutes around the chicken factory also. The avian-themed polysemy that surrounds Bill fans out to incorporate violence and again provides a reference to the women's trade. A third meaning of bill is a medieval weapon that has a hook in place of a blade: thus Bill is also a ripper. Finally, a bill is also a written or printed slip of paper setting out an amount of money owed for services rendered. The polysemic play in this grouping, therefore, alludes to the killer, the act of murder, to the women and their trade. Just as, in the play, Bill sheds one boiler suit after he has killed and replaces it with a clean one, the circuit of substitution offers one meaning only to replace it with others.

The avian motif that Daniels reworks has its origins firmly in the novel. In the play the theme is developed in a manner that challenges and contains Barker's novelistic vision. The relationship between this aspect of the novel and its evolution in the play can be seen as a dialogic one. The motif, which in the novel works to link the women who work as prostitutes with the chicken factory and ultimately with the serial killer himself is contained within the play but extends to include the identity of the murderer. The decisive linking of the crime with a specific personality that is the result of the extension of the avian theme to the killer and his murderous acts is a significant shift in emphasis that simplifies important areas of the story. Thus, although the discourse of the novel may be detected within this re-presentation, it is transformed by the dramatic discourse, which by presenting the murderer onstage must, to a greater or lesser degree, unmask him.

In the novel Barker explores the economic and social reasons why a woman might turn to prostitution in the first place. The novel opens with Brenda settling her children down for the night. As her story is unraveled, it is revealed that she was married young, at sixteen, to a man who subsequently left her with three small children and a clutch of bills to pay. Brenda's first reaction to her predicament is to find employment at the nearby chicken factory. When the job proves untenable as a result of unsatisfactory childcare arrangements, she becomes a prostitute. Barker paints a dryly comic description of Brenda's initiation into her new trade. There is the depiction of Brenda's exploitation by her clients and, later, of how she learns to get, in the words of another character, Kath, "the maximum for the minimum."[18] Barker's portrayal of the prostitutes does not glorify their lives. Apart from being subject to arrest by the police and prosecution, the women also risk beatings, rape, and murder at the hands of clients and ostracism from their community. However, the novel presents the women as a closely knit group, who drink at the same pub and enjoy a lively social life.

Daniels presents a depiction of the prostitutes' lives that is both assured and sympathetic toward them. She emphasizes the daily routine of the women's lives by showing them working. According to the stage directions, numerous scenes are set in the streets where the women work. Details about their everyday lives are interspersed throughout the play. In the second scene, for example, Jean warns Brenda about wearing earrings for pierced ears while she is working (presumably because of the risk of the damage that might occur during an attack). Although neither writer is evasive about the women's trade, the visual portrayal of sex and violence can place an audience in a voyeuristic position. For a playwright such as Daniels, who, in previous work, has successfully avoided the dangers of voyeurism, the effective onstage depiction of prostitution can be seen as one of the most sensitive areas of the adaptation.[19] Daniels's solution is to emphasize the humorous aspects of the story when representing the women and their trade. Thus, even in the early scenes of the play, the business of prostitution is grotesque and, at times, Daniels's approach to the subject can be described, in Bakhtinian terms, as carnivalesque, extending Barker's own humor.[20]

In scene 3 Daniels conflates two of Barker's figures, Brenda's inexperienced, young client and the man with the penchant for violet sweets, into Greg. In a point of congruence with the novel, Greg has a preference for older women. This similarity between the two texts is transformed by the construction of this scene as comic. Greg is made the object of the jokes in the scene and his sexual inexperience is at the root of several of them. In Greg's negotiations with Kath, however, Daniels employs punning, word association and comic misunderstanding:

KATH. Twenty.

GREG. Great.

KATH. Pounds.

GREG. Yeah, yeah.

KATH. Up front.

GREG. Yes, yes of course. I ain't—. How can I put it? The err . . . back passage isn't really my cup of tea.

KATH. I meant—the money. Up front.[21]

Although this is humorous, the comic misunderstanding has wider relevance in the text. Greg believes himself to be negotiating for sex while Kath, her attention firmly on the money, is making a business transaction. The extent of Daniels's ridicule of Greg is not confined to this incident and she transforms him, from an essentially pathetic figure in Barker's text, to a comic character with an Oedipus complex:

GREG. Can I tell you something?

KATH. (handing him a condom) You better be thinking about putting this on while you're doing it.

GREG. (takes the condom) First wet dream I had, I dreamt I was doing it with my Mother. She was showing me where to put it.[22]

Barker, in contrast, displays more sympathy in her portrayal of the young client and treats the encounter between him and Brenda with greater seriousness:

"Fiver. Straight sex with a rubber."

She did her best to sound discouraging. She didn't like doing it with younger men, especially if they were good-looking, and this one was. They made her feel shy.

"I don't like them. Rubbers," he said.

The way he said it she knew at once he'd never had it, with or without. Why not, she thought. Shy? Kinky? There had to be a reason, unless all the girls up his way were blind.[23]

In the novel, the young man elicits Brenda's sympathy. Far from being just another piece of business to be concluded, Brenda thinks about him and his presence as a client troubles her. The young man's Oedipus complex is hinted at in Barker's text, but is subtler, expressed in the accusation that Brenda had referred to him as a son and within his comment, "I like older women."[24]

The women's attitude toward their clients is elaborated on in the play when Jean and Carol are depicted onstage in scene 4 engaging in sexual acts with clients while they continue a conversation with each other, without the men even realizing. This scene is primarily comic but it also makes an important point that, for the women, engaging in sex with their clients is a job. The scene is humorous for a number of reasons. The first of these is that what should be a moment of intimacy between two people turns out not to be: rather, Daniels contrives a scene between four people, two of whom are aware that they are not alone.[25] Second, the two women are obviously "faking it": Carol groans in mock pleasure in the middle of her conversation with Jean. When the antics of the two women arouse the suspicions of one of the clients, Jean informs him that the noise is "just a dog" and Carol cannot contain her laughter. Nevertheless, there are also other serious feminist aspects that underlie the humor of the scene. In comparison with the portrayal of Greg in the previous scene, this one ridicules the clients and distances the women (and the audience) from them. In so doing it disrupts conventions of viewing sex as a voyeuristic spectacle in which the woman is positioned as the other. Daniels's construction of the scene counteracts just such a possibility by placing the women both as the focus of the spectacle and the subjects of it. Her dramaturgy can be seen as an ingenious dialogue between the often confrontational and direct depiction of prostitution in the novel, the conventions of stage realism and feminist discourse.

One major point of difference between the novel and its stage adaptation is the depiction of the relationship between Jean and Carol. In the third section of Barker's text, Carol and Jean's lesbian relationship is recalled through the eyes of the latter character after the death of her lover. Daniels's approach in this instance is to depart from the conventions of theatrical and dramatic realism and to construct an expressionistic depiction of Carol's grief over the death of her friend. While this is a stylistic difference between the texts of Barker and Daniels, it is also a point of convergence: Jean's recollection of her lover in Barker's text is mirrored by the expressionistic post mortem conjuring of the character in Daniels's play. In the second half of the scene, Jean materializes from a lamp / hat stand and the (imagined?) events prior to her murder are played out onstage.

In the dramatic text Carol and Jean's lesbian relationship is never realized. Instead, Daniels depicts two close friends for whom a relationship remains in a forever-thwarted future. In scene 12 Carol is cross-examined by a policewoman when she tries to report Jean missing. Carol's response to the question of whether she and Jean were lovers is an emphatic rejection of the suggestion. Later, however, in scene 14 Carol, overcome with grief and the shock of identifying the dead body of her friend, presents a more ambivalent view of her friendship. Addressing the lamp / hat stand in her flat, talking to it as if it were Jean, Carol tells it: "I don't know why. I wanted— I wanted to kiss your face but don't worry, I never. I realized that I'd never so much as touched your face in real life."[26] Later on in the same scene the depth of Carol's feelings for Jean are revealed in the following speech:

> I want you here. I want you here. I look forward to seeing you. I enjoy myself
> with you, being with you. I feel alive. For the first time I can remember in my life
> I've felt properly alive.[27]

The scene concludes with Carol vowing to kill her friend's murderer.

Barker's graphic depiction of the murder of Kath, one of the prostitutes, has been seen as controversial. For example, Ann Ardis observes in her essay, "Political Attentiveness vs. Political Correctness: Teaching Pat Barker's *Blow Your House Down*," in this volume that Kath's murder is "pornographic, in the sense that Barker shows the murderer's association of sex and violence without reassuring us that we are being offered a critique of his behaviour." She argues that both this murder and the third section of the novel implicate readers through a first-person narrative in which Jean relates her past relationship with Carol and the subsequent events that lead up to her killing a man. It "turns the one-way mirror into a window." The juxtaposition of sex and violence in the novel is disturbing. The text can be troubling and, if one follows Ardis, "Barker's narrative does not fit neatly into feminist arguments about male violence against women." These forms of explicit representation become still more contentious when the story is transposed into a visual medium.

It is unsurprising that, given Daniels's reputation as a feminist dramatist, the playtext is more easily reconciled with feminist views on violence (although the play's depiction of Greg's death and his subsequent reappearance onstage mean that Daniels's dramaturgy cannot be reduced to it necessarily). In her celebrated essay on the theater, "*Aller à la mer*," Hélène Cixous has argued that both violence toward women and their mortality are central to theatrical representation:

> Theatre, which is built according to the dictates of male fantasy, repeats and
> intensifies the horror of the murder scene which is at the origin of all cultural
> productions. It is always necessary for a woman to die in order for the play to
> begin. Only when she has disappeared can the curtain go up; she is relegated to
> repression, to the grave, the asylum, oblivion and silence.[28]

Cixous identifies the theater as a site in which violence against women is represented and the women remain silent. It is perhaps one of the central paradoxes of Daniels's dramaturgy that she adheres to Cixous's principle of violence while simultaneously destabilizing the representational processes that it is founded on and by her refusal to silence or repress the experience of her women characters. Daniels achieves this by introducing nonlinear plotting, reducing the number of in-depth representations of murder from two in Barker's text to one onstage and altering the ending of the story: in the play, Maggie recovers her memory and identifies her attacker as Bill, her own partner.

The play retains Barker's story of three murders but alters the plot. The principal way it does so is through selective nonlinear scene construction. The first scene is a self-consciously metatheatrical one in which the stage and auditorium are remade into a spiritualist church, the audience doubling as the congregation. Seated among the audience, as members of the congregation are two of the characters, Maggie and Brenda. Maggie has persuaded Brenda to accompany her to church because she believes the spiritualist medium may help her to recover her memory. During the service, Brenda is given a message from Kath through the medium. The second scene of the play jumps backward in time and Kath is shown drinking in a pub with the other characters. The action then progresses in a linear fashion until the play catches up with itself in scene 23, where it returns to the church. The rest of the play, with the exception of scene 24, which is presented as flashback, is linear. Thus, Daniels's reordering of events in scenes 1 to 5 acts as a preface to the rest of the drama: Kath's death and Maggie's loss of memory are preordained events. This idea is combined with a striking departure from Barker's novel, the omission of Kath's murder scene. The two alterations are an avoidance of the voyeurism of the novel. The dramatic text, rather than implicating the spectators of the play in the representation of violence à la Barker in this important respect, re-envisions Kath's murder as a site of unseen violence. In so doing it relegates the centrepiece of theatrical representation according to Cixous—violence against women—to the wings.

The omission of Kath's murder from the onstage action contrasts sharply with the representation of Greg's murder. Here, Daniels's re-presentation of Barker's novel is at its most effective. Rather than retain Jean's first-person narrative from the third part of the novel (although there is an obvious theatrical counterpart to it in the form of monologue), she creates a buildup to the murder of Greg by using expressionistic scenes that include dead Jean's appearance to Carol. This works to show Carol's psychological state and parallels the depiction of Jean's mental disintegration and concomitant obsession with destroying the serial killer in the novel.

The stabbing of the man, the climax of part 3 of the novel, is presented at its end in chapter 17, and in a similar place within the drama (scene 19). The description of the act in the novel is brief:

> He didn't twist or turn or anything like that. He just stared at me. Then his mouth opened, it opened very wide, and he was gasping and gurgling and trying to speak and I held onto the knife and I watched his lips and I held onto the knife and finally it came, one single word, with a rush of blood, like a baby splitting open a cunt, one single word: "*Why?*"[29]

The death of the man creates a parallel between Jean and the serial killer during the murder of Kath. Jean's actions mirror his: they both wipe the blood away using items of clothing. Jean even repeats the phrase, "Why don't her eyes close?" after seeing the poster of Kath's face on a billboard, which the killer utters after Kath's murder.

Removing the depiction of Kath's death prevents Daniels from creating parallels between the killings of the serial murderer and Carol's act of revenge. Perhaps more surprising for the readers of the novel, is the manner in which the play works within an implicit asymmetry between the murders, which highlights the differences between the serial killer and Carol. This can be seen in a short extract from the scene in which Carol stabs Greg:

> Great. (*He hands her the money. Carol kneels. She undoes his flies. And puts her hand inside his trousers. He starts to breathe erratically. He loosens his tie and takes it off. Carol looks up and sees this. He smiles. She seems about to continue with her work when she realises that he is frantically grappling in his pocket. Again she looks up. He seems to be breathing hard and smiling menacingly*). Don't stop. No, don't look at me.
>
> (*He's the one. He has to be. She flicks open the knife but he sees it before she can get it behind his back.*) What you doing? What have I ever done to you? (*She lunges it at the front of him. He struggles with her. She plunges the knife in him.*) What's that for?
>
> CAROL. (*absolutely frenzied*) This is for Jean. This is for Jean. This is for Jean. This is for Kath. This is for Kath. This is for me. This is for Carol. This is for Carol, Carol, Carol . . .

> Blackout.[30]

The stage directions in this extract are some of the most detailed of the entire play. While there are many similarities between these and the description of the stabbing in the novel (the act of knifing and the emphasis on the perspective of the woman character), there are also differences. The stage directions embedded in Greg's speech do not dwell on his dying moments. Instead, they are a composite of the viewpoint of (an objective) observer and Carol's subjective perspective. In this dialogic stage direction the clash between the drama and the story's novelistic origin is most apparent. The use of interior monologue displays absorption of novelistic technique into the drama in a manner that is not directly realizable on the stage.

Greg's questions to Carol are relentless. Only the last of Greg's questions in this speech is answered, however. "What's that for?" provokes a frenzied response from Carol. Her speech in this instance is an example of what Bakhtin has described as double-voiced discourse. As in the stage directions, above, Barker's depiction of murder can be detected within this speech. The reason for Carol's act is to exact revenge for the deaths of her friends but the last few sentences in the speech reveal that Carol, like Jean in the novel, stabs a man for her own motives. Daniels has, therefore, remade this scene by incorporating the more troubling aspects of the killing into notions of revenge for all the women's murders.

The play develops issues of ambiguity surrounding the murder further by departing from the open ending of the novel. In the novel—in my view—it is unclear whether Jean succeeds in killing the serial murderer but Daniels makes it clear that Carol has murdered an innocent man. Her conjuring of the dead, Jean and Greg, in the aftermath of the murder is powerful and reiterates the ambiguities and complexities of the earlier scene. Jean is first to appear. Sitting Carol in her lap, Jean tells her that she has killed the wrong man. The dialogue between the two characters, one living and the other dead, is an ingenious device that allows Daniels to stage the doubts raised in the novel over Jean's revenge murder.[31] Here, the dialogization associated with the previous scene is replaced by what can be read as an expressionistic depiction of Carol that externalizes and dramatizes the doubts present in the final pages of the third section of the novel. In the play, Jean raises suspicions that Carol's consciousness cannot. Thus, the knife that Carol believes the man to be reaching for becomes, according to the apparition of Jean, an asthma inhaler. The man that Carol has killed is not the murderer. The theme of doubt is developed in the second half of the scene. The bearer of what seems to be good news, Brenda arrives to inform Carol that the police have found the killer murdered. The apparent certainty of Brenda's assertion evaporates, however as Daniels juxtaposes the image of Carol and Brenda celebrating with one of the Chicken Man slashing a chicken and stuffing it with its own feathers. Later on in the same scene the Chicken Man is interrupted. The technique of the killer, as revealed in his preparation of the chicken by cutting it and stuffing it with feathers, mirrors the *modus operandi* of the murderer in the novel's description of Kath's death.[32] The chicken, therefore, becomes emblematic of all the women who are the victims of the killer.

In scene 22 it is not Jean who is conjured by the traumatized Carol, but Greg, the murdered man. This scene is tripartite in structure and commences with Carol and Greg onstage. He disappears as Brenda arrives to visit Carol and on her departure Carol is left alone with Greg again. Each part differs thematically. The first features Greg, dressed in a facemask of Mr. Blobby, the toy that earlier in the play functions as a symbolic substitute for the killer. Greg roams around onstage, smashing crockery and protesting his innocence while Carol pleads with him for forgiveness. Brenda's appearance on the scene causes Greg's disappearance. Thematically, this section concerns the grief and anger that result from Carol's behavior. Her lack of control, the broken china lying smashed on the floor and her ignorance of what day it is lead Brenda to tidy away the mess commenting, "When my foster Mum died, I smashed everything in the house."[33] Greg reappears only after Brenda's departure to attend the spiritualist church. In the third and final sequence of the scene Carol is more hostile toward Greg. She asks questions that draw attention to the horror of her own actions. Greg is still wearing the mask from the first part of the scene and Carol's questions elicit evidence that he is the man she murdered: "I don't have any face left. That's why it took the police so long to find out who I was. My Grandmother identified my belongings and my dentist identified my teeth."[34]

These two scenes echo the novel in one important respect—they each show the influence of the dead on the living. Just as in the novel, Kath's open eyes haunt both the killer and Jean, Greg and Jean are ghostly presences onstage. In this respect the two scenes can be read as a crucial point of similarity between the novel and the play.

Ironically, in the play the visual motif of Kath's forever-open eyes is transformed by the substitution with speech. Both of these scenes also develop the different emphasis that is placed on the representation of murder in the play. The shift from the clear parallels between the murders and the killers in the novel to the visual repression of Kath's death in the play marks a point of difference between the two. Greg's murder in the play displays a high degree of dialogism. Although his murder has connotations of women acting in self-defense against male violence, the action is shown to be in vain because the killer eludes Carol during the course of the play. Daniels's conclusion to the play, which is as open-ended as Barker's, depicts Bill and Carol as they finally encounter one another. Bill's final line, "Tickle your cunt with a feather?" is a repetition of the one uttered to Kath before she is killed.[35] It provides an alternative ending to the story that returns the dramatic focus to the prostitutes for whom the danger is forever present. This is a strategy that, in placing the perspectives of the community of women prostitutes foremost, presents a view of violence against women that is unrelenting.

When read together, the two texts offer strikingly different perspectives on women and violence through the same story. While Barker's novel implicates its readers by virtue of its textual voyeurism, Daniels gains inspiration from the story but does not incorporate violence against women into the drama. In so doing her rewriting of the story presents a vision of male violence that is both more bleak and less equivocal than Barker's. Nevertheless, the playtext retains the complexity of motives surrounding the depiction of a woman's act of murder. Finally, Daniels's stage adaptation displays not only an intertextual dialogue with Barker's novel but elements of dialogism ensure that Daniels's text may be thought of as "novelized" although it remains a dramatic text. The tension between the formal opportunities of the drama and the novel is detected most clearly in Daniels's expressionistic representations of Greg and Jean onstage. Their deaths provide an ingenious parallel to Barker's use of interior monologue reflective of her preoccupation with the psychological workings of the characters. In addition, the altered ending, which provides a resolution in the unmasking of the serial killer, is left open leaving the audience to wonder what Carol's fate will be after having, at the close of the play, come face to face with the murderer. Despite the differences of vision between Barker's optimistic ending and Daniels's bleaker one, both writers present complex depictions of violence, which draw on feminist discourse and transcend any simple view in which women are always the victims and men the violent aggressors.

NOTES

1. The play was a commission from the theater company. After its première, the play toured theaters in northern England. Many of Daniels's plays are available in the two volumes of her collected works published by Methuen. The adaptation of *Blow Your House Down* is published for the first time in this volume.

2. See, for example, Joan Smith, "There's Only One Yorkshire Ripper," in *Misogynies,* rev. ed. (London: Faber, 1993). Smith details how the police constructed their case around the mistaken hypothesis that the killer in this case targeted women because they were prostitutes.

3. Daniels has commented that "I found the way it's written in four separate sections hard to dramatize unless it was done in monologues and that's why I tried . . . to impose more of a dramatic structure on it." Sarah Daniels, e-mail communication with the author, July 9, 2001.

4. Elaine Aston and Janelle Reinelt, "Editors' Note," in *The Cambridge Companion to Modern British Women Playwrights*, ed. Elaine Aston and Janelle Reinelt, 152 (Cambridge: Cambridge University Press, 2000).

5. See, for example, Lizbeth Goodman, *Contemporary Feminist Theatres: To Each Her Own* (London: Routledge, 1993), 128. Goodman discusses Daniels's plays in terms of the themes that they contain.

6. Robin Thornber, review of *Blow Your House Down* by Sarah Daniels, *Guardian,* reproduced in *Theatre Record* 12–25 (February 1995): 232.

7. Lizbeth Goodman, "Representing Gender / Representing Self: A Reflection on Role Playing in Performance Theory and Practice," in *Drama on Drama: Dimensions of Theatricality on the Contemporary British Stage,* ed. Nicole Boireau, 196–214 (London: Macmillan, 1997). Goodman's analysis of the stage adaptation is largely descriptive. She does note, however, that "translation of [the] book to the stage does not improve the story, so much as communicate it through a different form of language, composed of visual vignettes" (210). Goodman's description has striking parallels with Julia Kristeva's description of intertextuality discussed below.

8. See Julia Kristeva, *Revolution in Poetic Language* (New York: Columbia University Press, 1984), 59–60. Kristeva comments that "the term *inter-textuality* denotes . . . [a] transposition of one (or several) sign-systems into another" (Kristeva's emphasis).

9. Tzvetan Todorov, *Mikhail Bakhtin: The Dialogical Principle* (Manchester: Manchester University Press, 1984), x.

10. Todorov, *Mikhail Bakhtin,* 60.

11. Helene Keyssar, "Drama and the Dialogic Imagination: *The Heidi Chronicles* and *Fefu and Her Friends,*" in *Feminist Theatre and Theory,* ed. Helene Keyssar, 88–126 (London: Macmillan, 1996).

12. Keyssar, "Drama and the Dialogic Imagination," 119.

13. Max Harris, *The Dialogical Theatre: Dramatizations of the Conquest of Mexico and the Conquest of the Other* (New York: St Martin's Press, 1993), 10–14.

14. Mikhail Bakhtin, "Epic and Novel," in *The Dialogic Imagination,* ed. Michael Holquist, 5–6 (Austin: University of Texas Press, 1981).

15. Bakhtin, "Discourse in the Novel," in *The Dialogic Imagination,* 405.

16. Sarah Daniels, *Blow Your House Down,* scene 14 (in this volume).

17. Sharon Monteith, *Pat Barker* (Plymouth: Northcote House, 2002). Monteith notes the parallels between Barker's depiction of Maggie and Olive Smelt, an office cleaner, who was attacked by the Yorkshire Ripper, Peter Sutcliffe. Monteith argues that Smelt rather than Sutcliffe provides Barker with the model for this part of the novel (20–24).

18. Pat Barker, *Blow Your House Down* (London: Virago, 1996), 46. All subsequent references will be included in the text.

19. See, for example, the discussion of *Masterpieces* in Tracy C. Davis "*Extremities* and *Masterpieces*: A Feminist Paradigm of Art and Politics," *Modern Drama* 32 (March 1989). This article has subsequently been reprinted in *Feminist Theatre and Theory,* ed. Helene Keyssar, 137–54 (London: Macmillan, 1996). There are parallels between this text and Daniels's play on the subject of pornography, *Masterpieces*. Both, for example, contain

female characters that are driven to the extreme act of murder by male violence against women. Both plays also make use of nonlinear plotting.

20. See Mikhail Bakhtin, *Rabelais and His World* (Bloomington: Indiana University Press, 1984), 11. It is "the 'turnabout' of a continual shifting from top to bottom" and profane aspects of the carnivalesque that is brought to the fore in Daniels's onstage depiction of sex.

21. Daniels, *Blow Your House Down*, scene 3.

22. Ibid.

23. Barker, *Blow Your House Down*, 42.

24. Ibid., 44.

25. According to one of the performers, Gill Wright, in the original production, this scene was played with "Jean" "downstage right, lit as if she's working a client in the shadows, profile to the audience, enabling her to throw the dialogue across the performance space to 'Carol,' who was upstage left against the flat wall, facing the audience with the male actor facing her, trousers around [his] ankles." She also added that the "lighting enabled the girls' faces and bodies to be seen but they were surrounded by shadow." Gill Wright, e-mail to author, January 14, 2002.

26. Daniels, *Blow Your House Down*, scene 14.

27. Ibid.

28. Hélène Cixous, "Aller à la mer," trans. Barbara Kerslake, *Modern Drama* 27, no. 4 (December 1984): 546.

29. Barker, *Blow Your House Down*, 132.

30. Daniels, *Blow Your House Down*, scene 19.

31. See Barker, *Blow Your House Down*, 134–35.

32. Ibid., 65. Barker writes, "He practically had to stuff her with them [the feathers], like stuffing a chicken, before he could get the effect he wanted: a ridiculous little white frill between her legs."

33. Daniels, *Blow Your House Down*, scene 22.

34. Ibid.

35. Ibid., scene 26. The line is spoken first in scene 8.

JENNY NEWMAN

Souls and Arseholes

The Double Vision of *Liza's England*

Pat Barker chronicles the lives that history ignores, and her best characters, though articulate, often find it hard to make themselves heard. Though her early work has been sometimes passed over by academics as gritty but less inventive than the later, she can be seen from her first novel onward to be locating herself in a postmodernist tradition. Her use of dialogue, parody, and pun, and her commitment to the communal and the choric, constantly remind us that her books are textual inventions; the plots of her novels, instead of completing a pattern, seldom allow us to believe that her characters are consistent, or that their lives have a unifying purpose.

Culminating in the Booker Prize–winning *The Ghost Road* (1995), Barker's trilogy, with its command of psychology, anthropology, and military history, its experimental narrative strategies, and its blend of historic and fictitious characters, first gained her widespread critical respect. Her first four novels, on the other hand, though acclaimed in the press, have been seen, for instance, as belated examples of nineteenth-century naturalism[1] or early twentieth-century British realism,[2] albeit with certain modifications; such as excluding "aspects of working-class life that might appear wholesome and attractive, and concentrating on an examination of poverty and the squalor and degradation that it engenders."[3] Barker's early fiction, it seems, is not to be thought radical simply because it takes for its subject working-class life.

Of all Barker's novels *Liza's England,* formerly known as *The Century's Daughter* (1986),[4] has been most frequently attacked for failing to challenge three of the main tenets of realism: that fictitious characters should be consistent and knowable both to their readers and themselves; that they appear capable of choice; and that their story has a point, a privileged relation to the truth. Linda Anderson criticizes the novel as follows:

> Dignified by her position of centrality, Liza is also installed within a narrative with a positive (historical) destination: the fully integrated and all-knowing self. Thus Liza's memories cannot contradict the relation between past and present as unitary and socially agreed, but instead become absorbed into a larger pattern of continuity. . . . The novel moves *towards* a point of understanding—implying that there is only one way of perceiving and representing the world—which can, by

seeming to complete the pattern, stand outside history, and sublate the very differences of epoch, class and gender which have been the novel's supposed theme.[5]

Barker, it is true, sees objectivity in her novels as a duty, albeit an unrealizable one:

> There is in my work the feeling that the most important thing any human being can do is to be as objective as possible about the past, that this is the only thing on which a secure identity—individual or society—can be based. And linked to this is the feeling that doing it is a virtual impossibility.[6]

It therefore seems surprising that, in preparation for her now abandoned fifth novel, Barker read all Dostoevsky's fiction, and planned to stay in the consciousness of one single guilt-ridden character. She has since rejected that method as too claustrophobic, thus pitting herself against much that is contemporary: "A lot of very good books that are being written at the moment are single-viewpoint fragmented narratives in disturbed minds, and that's okay, but you can only take so much of that."[7]

However, her dismissal of the unreliable narrator does not mean that, as Anderson claims, Barker is searching for the one true way of representing the world. As a historian Barker is aware that total detachment, like the above-mentioned objectivity, is not possible. History, she says, is "a body of knowledge that we agree to regard as important" and she is more interested in "what history has forgotten. In the possibility of an unforgettable life that everyone has forgotten."[8] Thus she tends to investigate absence, or what she calls, paradoxically, absence as presence. "Absence," she claims, "is always more recognizable than presence."[9] In the attention paid to the overlooked and the expunged, each of her novels can be seen as partly an indictment of what we accept as history, and partly a meditation on its making.

By choosing to depict the urban proletariat and their world of grueling and disregarded work, Barker has placed herself in a tradition of working-class novelists. It is a challenging role. As Peter Hitchcock points out, their "knowable community" is "problematic because, in general, they do not form an archive of what the knowable community was: they do not constitute a relic so much as a blueprint."[10] Barker cannot rely on the official version of events, prone as it often is to ignore or minimize the role of the proletariat: an idea evoked in the dream of the dying Liza, who is unable to help trampling on the official-looking files and documents that are blowing in a draught from abandoned filing cabinets. Though profoundly influenced by her early reading,[11] Barker claims that in *Liza's England* she draws on an oral tradition—relying mainly on her own recollections[12]—rather than a literary one (a claim to be disputed later in this essay). She has a gift for dialogue, and has described how she acquired a "headful of voices," and knew her current novel [*Regeneration,* 1991] was going well when they started talking to one another: "Once it starts to work, they are walking up and down and talking almost continuously."[13]

Barker's characters not only talk but quarrel, violently and vociferously. In this battlefield of language, each dominant person or group attempts, as Bakhtin puts it, to monologize the word, to impose upon it an eternal single meaning.[14] "If you write in dialogue, as I do," says Barker, "you have to respect and like people who are very different from you. You have to let them say, vividly and persuasively, things with which you profoundly disagree."[15] In *Liza's England* this struggle over words is first presented as a playful tussle. Closely associated with Liza, her parrot is present on the first and last pages of the novel. Having both lived in a pub and belonged to a sailor, Nelson has learnt different jargons; and it falls to him to puncture the pretensions of Stephen, the young social worker sent initially to evict Liza:

> "You know there's a superstition about parrots? That they don't rot when they die." He [Stephen] tried to remember a poem he'd read that said something to that effect, but failed. "They're supposed to symbolize the soul."
> Nelson produced his perfect imitation of Liza's laugh. "Drop 'em, dearie," he said, and poked his beak through the bars. (220)[16]

Ground down as they are by exploitation and poverty, choice is a myth for most of Barker's characters. Yet their discourse often plays two parts simultaneously. Like Nelson, Liza mimics Stephen; and, as is always the case in this novel, the ironist highlights the official's limitations:

> "Your name's Liza Wright?"
> "Yes," Liza agreed, "née Jarrett."
> It was such a perfect imitation of his own official voice that he might have suspected parody, had he believed her capable of it. (5)

Unlike Liza, whose "outsideness" to language enables her to juggle with different speech forms, the monologic Stephen is impaled on them. His father also mimics his social-workerish primness, but Walter's intention is vicious rather than slyly comic, as when Stephen is trying to explain why he left his last job:

> "Look, I got worried about some of the decisions I was taking. I just . . . started to question what I was doing."
> "*Started to question what I was doing.*" The mimicry was accurate and vicious. "Bloody hell, man, where do you think I'd've been if I'd *started to question what I was doing?* Turning the same bloody crank handle forty, fifty, sixty thousand times a day for thirty bloody years. Where do you think I'd've been if I'd questioned that?" (40)

Where Stephen's family is divided by his newly acquired discourse, Liza's is united when her granddaughter, Kath—the character whose experience Barker claims is closest to her own[17]—goes to grammar school. In the scene where Kath is writing her lines we see the two characters being taught not by pedagogues but each other, with Kath playing the part of a working-class Cordelia, robust and unsubdued in her repeated use of nowt:

> "I got wrong for saying nowt."
> "You must've said summat."
> "No! I said *nowt.*"
> "Oh. Well, you know that's wrong. You know you should say *nothing.*"

"Actually, that's wrong too. It's *nuthing*."
"Is that what they said? Oh, tell 'em to get stuffed!"
Kath looked up and waited.
"Oh, nothing," said Liza. *"Nuthing."*
Kath smiled. *"Nowt."* (238)

These women young and old are joining to mock the arbiters of language. But with received pronunciation imposed in British schools, working-class discourse is clearly under threat. Barker's characters are often at risk of being silenced by the indirect state apparatus, and their speech coagulates with words unsaid. For instance, during Liza's childhood, her mother worked as a cleaner at the Wynyards' mansion. When Louise is humiliated by Mrs. Wynyard, Liza observes the apologetic smile that creeps unbidden across her mother's face:

"Why did you smile?" Liza wanted to ask, but you couldn't ask, either because the words didn't come, or because you knew already, without being told, that there were no answers. (34)

Louise's silence is what Tillie Olsen calls "unnatural," one of those that result from the circumstances of being born "into the wrong class, race, or sex, being denied education, becoming numbed by economic struggle, muffled by censorship, or distracted or impeded by the demands of nurturing."[18] Like many people bullied at work, Louise carries her silence back to her family, where its oppression becomes more intimate, as when she cracks her children over the head with her crutch, or squirts the milk from her breast into the face of her daughter (179). In Walter's case, too, silence is a domestic bequest that damages the psyche of his tentative, sensitive son. Browbeaten in his factory like Louise was at the Wynyards', Walter has in his turn bullied his son for years through his "pact with silence" about Stephen's homosexuality, a pact from which Stephen suffers, and Walter makes it his business to profit. Nearing the end of his life, he confides in Stephen his recently acquired habit of ogling young girls outside the local comprehensive. Running through the conversation, thinks Stephen, is the "one unspoken sentence: *You can't afford to judge me*" (119).

At the end of his life Walter's silence reaches its apotheosis: "The mouth was tight, blackish-looking, as if even in life it had never spoken" (122). Yet silence can also be a weapon of resistance, written on the body when the mouth has been stopped. Stephen, for example, sees the strength of the aged Liza as elemental: like "a rock that wind and sea have worked on since the beginning of time, she needed to apologize for nothing, explain nothing" (6). Though Liza may not be what one critic called "an unstoppable old bore,"[19] she can certainly be loquacious, and Stephen's view may to some readers seem sentimental, dangerously "naturalizing" her silence and making it look inevitable, rather than the product of societal injustice. But he also notices how "two deep lines of force had been cut into the skin between nose and lip" (6); and this for him becomes a new way of "reading" a working-class physiognomy. When he later looks at the face of his dead father, the almost identical phrase recurs: "There were two lines of force scored into the skin between pinched nose and clenched mouth"

(122), and these parallel lines give Stephen a new insight into his unsympathetic parent: "But the strongest impression was of silence, as if he [Walter] were bonded into silence, welded to it, and this final speechlessness revealed a truth about his life that Stephen had never recognized till now" (122).

Many of Barker's characters lose their voices not only figuratively, but literally. Long before starting the novel, she had read the work of Dr. W. H. R. Rivers, the early neurologist and social anthropologist who worked for a period at Craiglockhart War Hospital. In his book *Conflict and Dream* he discusses the mutism—or neurasthenic speechlessness—that afflicted shell-shocked men, a topic to which Barker would return in *Regeneration*. Mutism, as defined by the Freud-influenced Rivers, springs from a conflict between wanting to say something, and knowing that if you do the consequences will be disastrous. As an educated man, Stephen understands that the unbearable pain in his throat after he has failed to confront his father is psychosomatic: "There was a sense of enormous pressure, as if his father's silence had somehow got in and impacted there, a lump he could neither cough up nor swallow" (123).

Most characters in *Liza's England* find the speech act difficult. Voices thicken, Stephen's tongue weighs like lead (126), Brian's Adam's apple quivers painfully (74), Liza's tongue feels big and unused (167). The mouths of the ghostly soldiers who died at the front are "mud-stopped"; their lungs, "gas-blistered, blood-frothed" (61). The civilian Walter's throat is blocked not only by his inability to acknowledge that his son is gay, but in the end by the blood clot "like a lump of black liver" (120) that Stephen hooks out. It is an image reminiscent of a line in the poem "Them & [uz]" in *The School of Eloquence* sequence by Barker's contemporary, Tony Harrison, who, like her, is from the Northeast, is a member of the working class, and is grammar school educated.[20] And, also like her, Harrison links physical and psychological impediments to speech: "my mouth all stuffed with glottals, great / lumps to hawk up and spit out." For both these writers stammerers are a major theme, and stammering, like silence, becomes a class issue.

According to Rivers, however, enlisted men sometimes went mute when shell-shocked, but they never stammered. With officers the reverse was true. This is because, alleged Rivers, as middle-class and educated the officers lead a more complicated mental life.[21] Surprisingly perhaps, *Liza's England* bears out Rivers's class-based thesis. All the working-class characters go mute at points (although none neurasthenically so), and no one is given a stammer.[22] Stammering in poetry and fiction is a cause of textual breaks and ruptures, and is also a way of typographically inscribing the war between speech and silence.[23] Taking as its subject the working-class struggle to be heard, *Liza's England* is pock-marked with stammered consonants.[24] For instance, in the above-mentioned incident at the Wynyards' mansion, Louise is wearing her son's cast-off boots, and a loose sole is flapping as she walks: b-b-b-b-b. Though mother and daughter maintain their pact with silence, the ten-year-old Liza thinks that the torn sole sounds like a blocked tongue (34). This may be a less than satisfactory break with realism, with the child bearing too much of the meaning. Nevertheless, it is also an example of the text speaking the silenced woman, where the woman cannot speak the text.

This image of the sole is echoed in the subplot, when Stephen carries his dead father's possessions from the mortuary, and one of Walter's slippers drops out of the parcel. As Stephen bends to pick it up, he notices the loose sole, and the pun prompts in the reader an eschatological question. Do men have souls, and, if so, do they want to utter after death? Though it first surfaces through word play, this question is the most serious in the novel, and is later resurrected through a linked pun.

Louise and Liza, Liza and Eileen, Walter and Stephen. In peacetime, Barker's characters go to war with each other. The longest-running battle is between Liza and her husband, Frank, and they too fight over speech and silence. The trigger of their quarrels is the seances, or spuggies, that Frank holds for the bereaved of the First World War.

Active service has traditionally been a man's topic, and it took Barker a long time to find a "sufficiently original" way of writing about what she calls "one of the most overdone subjects there's ever been."[25] Her fiction approaches the war by degrees, first by way of Frank's spuggies, then to Craiglockhart War Hospital in *Regeneration,* and on to the London of the blitz in *The Eye in the Door,* only arriving at the front itself in *The Ghost Road.* Michèle Roberts remarked in a review that "masculine concerns and experience really inspire Barker now, offering a new world to explore, bigger and brighter than the conventional feminine sphere."[26] Yet Barker repeatedly emphasizes Frank's feminine traits. As a boy, Liza recalls, he was small and thin, with a head too big for his shoulders, who was always getting left behind by the other boys. This physical slowness probably saved his life when the rest of his battalion was blown up. Like the real-life Julian Dadd, who makes an appearance in *Regeneration,* Frank has returned from the front with a bullet wound in his throat, and is obviously shell-shocked:

> The first week after he came out of hospital, he'd gone into the town centre and seen people treading on dead faces, prosperous men with moustaches and cigars, girls with parasols to protect their skin from the sun, treading on dead faces. They couldn't see the corpses that were sprawled there. (84)

All the young men in the neighborhood had signed up on the same day, and were thus wiped out in the one battalion. Such an event, it appears, is too traumatic to be frozen in linear time. When Frank seemingly contacts them through a seance, he, like Walter, Stephen, Louise, and Liza, recognizes the power of silence:

> At first it was the usual silence of people in a crowded room: coughs, breathing, tummy rumbles, a belch politely smothered, the rasp of wool as women crossed and uncrossed their legs. . . . Then, without warning, the silence deepened, became something that was not merely the absence of speech, but a positive force. Positive, or perhaps negative, she [Liza] couldn't tell. At any rate a source of power, binding them together, drawing them in, and it was easy to believe, in that silence, that the white-faced women were no longer alone, that other figures crowded in the doorway and stood in the shadows at the back of the hall. (60)

But where the other characters make a pact with silence, Frank refuses, claiming that his mission is "to give the dead breath" (87). Predictably, he finds giving utterance stressful: "A snakelike vein appeared on his forehead, wriggling down from hairline to temple, the sort of vein you see only on the foreheads of old men" (61). Like the spirits that allegedly speak through him, Frank too has died then returned to a half-life, "set apart from other men" (87). After lying for three days on the edge of a crater in no-man's-land, he wakes in the final hour before dawn, and puts his fingers to the wound in his neck. They come away dry, as though, like Jesus, he has been drained of blood: "He had the strength to crawl, but lacked the will. Who but a fool would want to come back from the dead, and to such a place as this?" (87).

The spuggies are a narrative trope to which Barker returns in *The Man Who Wasn't There* and *The Eye in the Door*. Like the linked voices of the women of *Union Street*, and those of the prostitutes in *Blow Your House Down*, they give the novel its identity, and suggest that Barker is more committed to the collective and the choric than to the life of the individual. This may also explain her decision to change the title of the novel to *Liza's England*, with its shift in emphasis from the individual to the nation. In an interview given near the start of her career, Barker challenges the value currently placed on the unique, individuated fictional voice:

> You know, it says in books on creative writing that everybody must sound absolutely unique. Well, if you listen very carefully to people, you often find a particular group of people that come together as individuals, speaking in a kind of recognizably individual way. As the group gets going and imposes its rules on all of the people in it, those individuals actually tend to sound more and more alike, so that even if there's disagreement going on, you find that the individuals within the group begin to echo each other's sentence patterns. What you get then is a kind of communal voice. I find that I get very interested in the communal voice as well as in the individual voices of the characters, and also try to listen for that and bring that across.[27]

Once the puniest soldier from the neighborhood, Frank goes on to "speak" a whole platoon. But far from holding all the meanings, he depends for interpretation on the dead men's mothers:

> He began to speak again. Or rather he opened his mouth and voices poured out. One voice after another, and all different . . . and woman after woman leaned forward and strained to hear the voice of her son. (61)

If Barker believes that absence is more recognizable than presence, then nowhere is absence more palpable than in Frank's dissociated voices. Previously under orders as a soldier at the front, he obeys what he "hears" at home without question, thus becoming a secular priest for his congregation of bereaved mothers. Bodiless and ignored by official histories, their sons have become immaterial in two senses; but through Frank's mouth they form an incorporeal archive, intimate and demotic; or else Frank can be seen as one in a long tradition of shamans/showmen such as mesmerists, clairvoyants, hypnotists, spiritualists, and automatic writers. His unquestioning obedience to his voices also bears relation to his young life as a factory hand where his work, like Walter's, reduced him to a mindless cog in a larger whole; or, at the very least, his power denotes a complex series of links to his neighborhood, his schooldays, and his time at the front. By living a working man's life he has undergone an immersion, a special training, in multivoicedness. His tortured speech act is an apt demonstration of how, far from belonging to a single individual, as Bakhtin has argued,

> Language for the individual consciousness lies on the borderline between oneself and the other. The word in language is half someone else's . . . it exists in other people's mouths, in other people's contexts, serving other people's intentions.[28]

The polyvocal chorus of the seance confronts a battery of silences: not only the silence of the grave, but also the silence of authority about the progress of the war, and over the details of the men's deaths. Thus the spuggies' heteroglossia can be seen as a riposte to the official history, in which the casualties are not sons but statistics. Through their gift of release for the grieving mothers, the spuggies become a ghostly Bakhtinian carnival, a Mexican day of the dead brought to the streets of northern England. They are also "the combination of many voices [a corridor of voices] that augments understanding, departure beyond the limits of the understood."[29]

By bringing the numinous to the ranks of the underprivileged, Frank defies chronological time. As a postmodernist writer, Barker too is in conversation with the past, in her case not only oral accounts of the Great War, but its representations in the writing of her modernist predecessors. Like, for example, the "familiar compound ghost / Both intimate and unidentifiable" of T. S. Eliot's lines in "Little Gidding,"[30] each of Barker's revenants is both individual and collective. The ghostly soldiers' voices are different enough to be recognizable, but not as easily distinguished as they had been in life, "because there is a limit to what one damaged set of vocal cords can do" (61). The dead are now in a different sort of "no-man's-land," a predominantly female space in which is reenacted not military aggression but the mother-son bond and the woman's loss. The tissue of kindred voices, each one known, it seems, only to the mother of the speaker, is an alternative tongue, a Kristevan semiotic, where the missing soldier is returned to the womb of the neighborhood unconscious.

But Liza thinks from the start that Frank is a charlatan: "Nothing supernatural in what she'd just heard. He was a parrot, that was all. A parrot" (61–62). Although they marry, she remains mistrustful of her husband's powers, and their aims and idiolects stay distinct. Despite his blows to her body, their fiercest battles are verbal, with the less educated Liza victorious at every turn; she nicknames Frank's followers "the ghouls" and his fellow spiritualist Esme looks like "a vampire's droppings" (148–49). Soon Liza turns to the Labour Party while Frank retreats further into his spiritualism: "It would have been nice to talk to Liza [he thinks], really talk, but how could he talk to a woman who said 'arseholes' every time he mentioned the soul?" (146). When abandoned by his voices, Frank starts to mimic or impersonate himself, unintentionally conforming to Liza's first dismissive estimate of his powers. Remaining within the tradition of popular entertainers, he signals his defeat by temporarily becoming a con man.

Although Liza's Yeatsian pun[31] encapsulates their quarrel, it is impossible to say which side of this dialogue between self and soul the novel validates. Clearly Liza, as heroine, is a descendant of the valiant women of *Union Street* and *Blow Your House Down*. But it is the character of Frank, damaged, hallucinating, and haunted, who points the way forward to Barker's later fiction.

Barker's own grandfather was a medium, and there was etiquette in her family about how one should behave with a ghost. "You would treat it as politely as you would any visitor."[32] Having read Wilfred Owen and Siegfried Sassoon in her teens, she is patently aware that in the grand narrative of the First World War, the ghost is a common trope.[33] In her later war trilogy, they come to inform our way of looking at the living: "Ghosts everywhere. Even the living were only ghosts in the making. You learned to ration your commitment to them."[34] During an interview given on the publication of the tellingly entitled *Another World* (1998), she adds that ghosts are "a perfectly acceptable metaphor for the prevailing influence of the dead, which is not a nonsense, but which is a daily reality we all experience. Because the past is not the past. The dead do not lie down."[35]

What engages her most is the overlap between the medium, the historian, and the novelist.[36] In an interview given a year after the appearance of *Liza's England,* Barker observed, as the camera showed women talking to each other in a street of terraced houses, that they, like novelists, were analyzing character and event.[37] Just as Barker's haunted prose may be read as a metaversion of the spuggies, so Frank, with his dead voices packed inside his throat, may be seen as avatar of the postmodern novelist historian. As language is always at least double when it emanates from the unconscious, he is not in a position to control all its meanings. Signifying loss and return simultaneously, his ghostly characters, like the postmodern subject position, are divided between the past and the present, and thus impossible to grasp. As a novelist needs readers to amplify the work's meanings, so he too depends for interpretation on his listeners, whom he is doomed to disappoint when his ghosts, ineluctably, stop obeying his call.

Frank is more of a prophet than a priest, and his adult, woman-oriented spiritualism is contrasted with the patriarchal Baptist orthodoxy of his youth (152). Unlike the real-life Julian Dadd, he does not recover from his experience of war. Further emasculated by unemployment, he is unable to support his wife and family. The Lawrentian scene where he chops off his four-year-old son's ringlets and forces him out of a dress and into trousers projects Frank's sense of the precariousness of masculinity. When he disappears from view, Barker leaves in his life story silences and gaps for the reader to fill.

As with Stephen and Walter, so with Liza and Frank: the dead person is bound to the living by a pact with silence. Although Frank returns to die in the local hospital, Liza does not reach him in time to hear him speak. His body, like Walter's before it, is laid out like a sermon on the pain of working-class life. But where the venal, embittered Walter could only endorse in death what he had in life, the value of silence, Frank's message is more complex. Like much else in popular culture,[38] his spuggies were a secular version of the Resurrection: people are often thought to have risen from the dead, but not always in the way the Church would contend. Like Jesus, Frank as a young soldier had lain in no-man's-land for three days, then returned to life at dawn. It is spring, and while convalescing in England he searches for a text that will give the ultimate answer to the silence of the grave. After rejecting many pictures of the Resurrection, he finds a reproduction of Piero della Francesca's version in the hospital library: "For there He was: white body, wafer-thin against a blood-red landscape, a flag of triumph in His hand, death in His eyes" (87).

Like a ghost, a resurrected character is two people at once, one living and the other dead, and this picture of Jesus as divided between two worlds is the novel's central intertext. Although, predictably, Frank keeps silent about it, its discovery is the most significant event in his life. When he loses his powers as a medium, however, the painting loses its power to console: "Men go down to the grave and do not rise again. The mouths of the dead are stopped forever. They cannot speak" (153). When Frank's life is over, the text of *Liza's England* bears no hint that his voice lives on. Yet with his ivory skin and cold, translucent flesh, he can be seen as a working-class Jesus of the Deposition, with Liza as one of the grieving women who laid him out:

> She was crying not for herself but for Frank. It seemed the people hurrying past denied him: his life, his death, the terrible stone-breaking struggle of his final years. (167)

Though skeptical about his gift while he lived, while bathing his dead body Liza learns the importance of his fight against silence, finding that she herself now needs "words powerful enough to ignite the silence that was densely packed into her, a voice that, fanned by the bellows of her lungs, would stream out of her mouth like a living torch" (167). Just as Frank's doubt ("the mouths of the dead are stopped forever") seems a denial of the familiar compound ghost of "Little Gidding," so Liza's affirmation after his death is an echo of its most famous lines, two of which now form the poet's own epitaph:

> And what the dead had no speech for, when living,
> They can tell you, being dead: the communication
> Of the dead is tongued with fire beyond the language of the
>   living.[39]

Though eloquent, Liza's language does not allow us to forget the fact that Frank has been bludgeoned to death by an uncaring system. Her own death, when it comes, is equally pointless: she is, effectively, murdered by vandals in the mistaken belief that she has money in the house. In the penultimate chapter of the novel we read the final, phantasmagoric version of her life, inspired by the old metal box which most critics identify as the novel's central symbol.[40] Its lid and sides are painted with the figures of dancing women, and the sequence begins with the dream of Stephen, who is heir to her life story. Once again, the prose echoes *The Four Quartets*, this time "East Coker":[41]

Music, thin and reedy, a pipe, perhaps, and one small drum. Loud enough to beat time, but not to cover the *stamp, stamp, stamp* of feet. They circled the bonfire, hands and arms linked, mud-clogged feet pounding the ground, keeping the rhythm of pipe and drum. The firelight glowed on their arms and faces, they seemed to be made of fire, and yet the mud claimed them. And one day, perhaps, they would crumble into it, dissolve away, like the mud dolls that children make. Meanwhile they danced around the fire, and leapt through it, too, sometimes, so the wind of their passing fanned the flames, and the sparks flew upward. (272)

Although the figures in "East Coker" are long dead, their dance is an emblem of seasonal renewal. Barker, on the other hand, does not commit herself to a resurrection, either cyclical or spiritual. For her, the past lives primarily in her characters: through the attention they pay to history, and the way in which they revisit it. For instance, Stephen's dream is not only a dance of death, but a rite of inheritance in which the mystery figure, for him a combination of Walter and Liza, hands him the metal box that is, we presume, at that moment being ransacked by the vandals. We move to the mind of the dying Liza, who also dreams about dancing, first of a childhood clogdance, and then of the canary girls from the munitions factory doing the cakewalk: "With wages in their pockets to equal their fathers', they danced the new freedoms, the new independence. They danced the new freedoms that made it possible" (274).

Souls and Arseholes. Frank wanted to believe in the Resurrection, and was repelled by his wife's physicality. Liza in her turn found him coldly detached from politics and practicalities. The Great War gave fuel to the "sex war" that Liza wages to the end with her phantasmagoric husband. They are antagonists, it seems, even in death. On finding him in a surrealist dissecting room, she "knew she had to close his eyes, and pressed pennies down onto the lids, pennies as black and heavy as night, but his eyes didn't close. He looked at her and said, '*I gave the dead breath, Liza. But you shut them up in a box*'" (276).

After Liza's death, Stephen recalls Skelton's verse about the parrot symbolizing the soul, with its concluding line, "Make much of parrot, that popajay royál" (282), and wishes that he could tell Liza. The symbolism is sustained in the closing lines of the novel, when Stephen takes Nelson to his flat in the converted mansion where Louise once worked as a cleaner: "In the shrouded cage, Nelson stirred and stretched his wings." Although Liza's house will be demolished, on the surrounding wasteland (a further reference, perhaps, to T. S. Eliot) cottony seeds are drifting across, "like wisps of white hair" (284).

Liza's daughter Eileen takes away the box with its ring of dancing figures, and Stephen becomes heir not to a completed pattern that seems to "sublate the very differences of epoch, class and gender which have been the novel's supposed theme,"[42] but to Liza's parrot, and thus to her doubleness, her love of parody and mimicry, her ability to remake herself through new ways of talking, and to use puns. Part consolatory symbol, part foul-beaked satirist, like much else in the novel the parrot remains ambiguous. Says Mrs. Jubb to the departing Stephen: "You'd best take this pillowcase and put it over him. You won't want him coming out with one of his mouthfuls in the street" (281). But on the last page it is Stephen, not Nelson, who comes out with a mouthful. The recipient is a local lad who is implicated in Liza's death. Besides talking officialese, and being able to quote sixteenth-century poetry, Stephen has learnt how to speak to the teenager in his own language, "Oh, come off it, Brian. You're crapping yourself. Admit it" (284).

In a final image of speechlessness, Liza's house is left empty, with its wallpaper hanging in strips "like silent, lolling tongues" (283). Far from reaching her "positive (historical) destination: the fully integrated and all-knowing self,"[43] Liza's future, like her husband's, stays open to doubt, and her parrot is either a popajay royál, or else a mock-medium who will perpetuate her voice beyond the grave in a demotic and provisional resurrection. Thus she will be remembered for a while by the ageing Mrs. Jubb and the childless Stephen. Frank, now that Liza is dead, will be remembered by no one at all. In the uncertainty of their fates and the randomness of their deaths, both characters demonstrate the aspect of history—or absence of history—that most interests Barker, and which was quoted at the beginning of this essay: "the possibility of an unforgettable life that everyone has forgotten."

NOTES

1. Kathryn Dodd and Philip Dodd, "From the East End to *EastEnders*," in *Come on Down: Popular Media and Culture in Post-War Britain*, ed. Domic Strinati and Stephen Wragg, 116–32 (London: Routledge, 1992).

2. See, for example, Flora Alexander, *Contemporary Women Novelists* (London: Edward Arnold, 1989); Linda Anderson, *Plotting Change: Contemporary Women's Fiction* (London: Edward Arnold, 1990); and Lyn Pykett, "The Century's Daughters: Recent Women's Fiction and History," *Critical Quarterly* 29, no. 3 (Autumn 1987): 71–77.

3. Alexander, *Contemporary Women Novelists*, 47–48.

4. This was retitled *Liza's England*, the title originally chosen by Barker.

5. Anderson, *Plotting Change*, 134.

6. Suzie Mackenzie, "Out of the Past," *Guardian Weekend*, October 24, 1998, 31.

7. Donna Perry, "Pat Barker," in *Backtalk: Women Writers Speak Out* (New Brunswick: Rutgers University Press, 1993), 59.

8. Mackenzie, "Out of the Past," 31.

9. Ibid.

10. Peter Hitchcock, "Radical Writing," in *Feminism, Bakhtin, and the Dialogic*, ed. Dale M. Bauer and S. Jaret McKinstry, 95–121 (Albany: State University of New York Press, 1991).

11. See, for instance, Perry, *Backtalk*, 51; "Pat Barker," *Contemporary Authors*, vol. 122, no. 40. Barker's reading in her teens and twenties included Wilfred Owen, Siegfried Sassoon, W. H. R. Rivers, D. H. Lawrence, and David Storey.

12. Donna Perry, "Going Home Again: An Interview with Pat Barker," *Literary Review* 34, no. 2 (Winter 1991): 237.

13. Francis Spufford, "Exploding Old Myths," *Guardian*, November 9, 1995, 3.

14. Mikhail Bakhtin, "Discourse in the Novel," in *The Dialogic Imagination: Four Essays*, ed. M. Holquist, trans. C. Emerson and M. Holquist (Austin: University of Texas Press), 281.

15. Mackenzie, "Out of the Past," 31. For a discussion of dialogue, see Sharon Monteith, "Pat Barker," in Sharon Monteith, Jenny Newman, and Pat Wheeler, *Contemporary British and Irish Fiction: An Introduction through Interview*, (London: Arnold, 2004), 31–32.

16. All quotations from *The Century's Daughter* are taken from the 1986 Virago edition, and will be included in the text.

17. Perry, *Backtalk*, 46.

18. Olsen is quoted in *Listening to Silences: New Essays in Feminist Criticism*, ed. Elaine Hedges and Shelley Fisher Fishkin, 3 (Oxford: Oxford University Press, 1994).

19. Isabel Scholes, "Old, Not Wise," *Times Literary Supplement*, October 17, 1986, 1168. Quoted in Peter Hitchcock, "Radical Writing," 105.

20. Tony Harrison, *Selected Poems* (London: Penguin Books, 1984), 122.

21. Pat Barker, *Regeneration* (London: Penguin, 1992), 96.

22. However, the working-class, fictitious Billy Prior is allowed a riposte to Rivers's view in *Regeneration*. "Are you serious? You honestly believe that that *gaggle* of noodle-brained half-wits down there has a complex mental life? Oh, *Rivers*" (97).

23. In "Anthem for Doomed Youth," a poem written at Craiglockhart War Hospital for shell-shocked officers, where W. H. R. Rivers worked as an army psychologist, Wilfred Owen also used the metaphor of stuttering. He was helped with the poem by Siegfried Sassoon.

24. This is a preoccupation which has remained with her: "Dodgson found *m* difficult, and *p* in consonant combinations, particularly in the middle of words, but his arch enemy was hard *c*" (*Regeneration*, 154). During the writing of this novel Barker had a "nightmare moment" when she realized that everyone in it had a stammer. She discusses the importance of stammering in her interview with Sheryl Stevenson in this volume.

25. Perry, *Backtalk*, 52.

26. Michèle Roberts, "Male Insensitivity, Female Nagging and Children's Selfishness," *Guardian*, October 18, 1998.

27. *Contemporary Authors*, 41.

28. Mikhail Bakhtin, "Discourse in the Novel," 293–94.

29. Mikhail Bakhtin, "The Problem of the Text in Linguistics, Philology, and the Human Sciences: An Experiment in Philosophical Analysis," in *Speech Genres and Other Late Essays*, trans. V. W. McGee, ed. C. Emerson and M. Holquist, 137 (Austin: University of Texas Press, 1986).

30. T. S. Eliot, "Little Gidding" (1942), line 95, in *Four Quartets* (London: Faber and Faber, 1959).

31. See W. B. Yeats, "Crazy Jane Talks with the Bishop."

32. Mackenzie, "Out of the Past," 33.

33. See, for instance, Wilfred Owen's "Strange Meeting."

34. Barker, *The Ghost Road*, 46.

35. Mackenzie, "Out of the Past," 33.

36. Ibid. For a discussion of the medium in *The Man Who Wasn't There*, see Sharon Monteith's essay in this volume.

37. *Bookmark*, BBC TV, January 1987. Cited in Flora Alexander, *Contemporary Women Novelists*, 48.

38. See, for example, many classic films, such as *Nosferatu: eine Symphonie des Grauens* (1922), directed by F. W. Murnau; *Frankenstein* (1931), directed by James Whale; *The Mummy* (1932), directed by Karl Freund; and *I Walked with a Zombie* (1943), directed by Jacques Tourneur.

39. Eliot, "Little Gidding," lines 49–51.

40. Alexander, *Contemporary Women Novelists*, 50; Anderson, *Plotting Change*, 133; Pykett, "The Century's Daughters," 73.

41. Eliot, "Little Coker":

> On a summer midnight, you can hear the music
> Of the weak pipe and the little drum
> And see them dancing round the bonfire
> Round and round the fire . . .
> Leaping through the flames, or joined in circles,
> Rustically solemn or in rustic laughter
> Lifting heavy feet in clumsy shoes,
> Earth feet, loam feet . . . (lines 25–27, 33–37).

42. Anderson, *Plotting Change*, 133.

43. Ibid.

SHARON MONTEITH

Screening *The Man Who Wasn't There*
The Second World War and 1950s Cinema

> Knowledge and reason only play a limited part in a child's life. Its interest quickly turns away from the real things in the outer world, especially when they are unpleasant, and reverts back to its own childish interests, to its toys, its games and to its fantasies.
>
> Anna Freud, *War and Children*

> The screenplay is a structure that wants to be another structure.
>
> Pier Paolo Pasolini, *Empirismo Eretico*

The *Man Who Wasn't There* takes place in September 1955 over three days in the life of twelve-year-old Colin Harper. Colin lives in a community of women, including his mother, Viv, who in her general dismissiveness refuses to tell him anything at all about his father. Barker fills this absence in the boy's life with Colin's imaginings. He loses himself in reveries usually set in wartime, in the year of his birth, 1943, in which he lives with "one eye open for snipers." Where Viv has fed Colin scenes from war films as spurious memories of his father, he creates the textual weave in which fiction and his quotidian reality become inextricably enmeshed. A mysterious "man in black" enters and crosses over into his "real" life saving Colin from an oncoming car as he daydreams his way across a road. The man recedes into the distance only to reappear at different points over the course of the novel. The "man who wasn't there" is Colin's projection of his absent father combined with his future self, or what Barker describes as "a real emanation of his potential."[1] The boy's expressive psychological state develops into a performance of selfhood that may help engineer a way to unravel his future.

Colin lives in a dream world but he is nothing like Billy Fisher, the archetypal daydreaming hero of Keith Waterhouse's *Billy Liar* (1959), the northern working-class young man with his sights firmly set on London. Billy lives in an imaginary country, Ambrosia, where he is prime minister whereas Colin is a marginal, melancholic figure, despite his self-sufficiency on the streets of the northeastern seaside town where he lives. Colin is an unsettled child, afraid of the dark, and in trouble at school for lateness and inattention. The other world he imagines counters but does not compensate for his unsettled present. In some ways, he is an extension of Kelly Brown in Barker's first novel, *Union Street*, another child who seems more comfortable on the streets than in the family home, and Barker allows that he is indeed a pivotal character type for her: "Colin at various stages of his life turns up quite often. When I was writing *Union Street,* the little boy Richard Scaife was a precursor for Colin. In the first draft he became a viewpoint character who functioned as a sort of identifier, like some of the characters in early plays by Dennis Potter: the character who is working-class but about to soar out of this narrow substratum of life so the middle-class reader can hope he gets to university soon!"[2] But Barker decided the boy's viewpoint would have been out of place in her first novel, as did Angela Carter who read an early draft. Instead, Barker largely forgoes the "escaper" as a type. In *The Man Who Wasn't There* Colin is a "scholarship boy" but also a "son of war," and an artist-in-the-making who is visually dominant and whose fantasy is a process of self-making. Colin is a creative survivor; only later does his character mutate into the more disturbed and disturbing Gareth in *Another World.* Gareth, who creates an alternative wartime world in the computer battle zone of "Streetfighter," seeks adventure, but is dangerously out of touch with himself and reality.

If we follow Sigmund Freud, the process of individuation that any young boy undergoes rests on his identification with the father. The father figure represents abstractions like desire and independence, but the boy's autonomy and agency are also learned from the father and defined as separation from the mother. To be without a father is to be caught in an anxious search for a familial past and some way of asserting one's self as separate and distinctive from others. Colin is locked into revealing a past that he has access to but no experience of: "For Colin, the mystery of his father's identity was bound up with the war, the war he'd been born into but couldn't remember."[3] The imperative to "remember" what is impossible for Colin to remember experientially persists across the novel: in playground games in which schoolboys fight the war over and over each break time; in an evening's play on bomb sites in which the boys are bomber pilots, Dambusters, and screaming victims rolling on the ground; and in the films from which Colin gleans most of his images of war.

But Freud also reminds us that we never invent by accident and that the unconscious mind need not prove reliable in distinguishing wishes from memories. "Memory" in this novel is a simulacrum for a deep-rooted emotional response to loss. According to Viv, Colin's father was "shot down"; she attributes him a hero's death in the manner of Anthony Asquith's *The Way to the Stars* (1945) with its paean to "Johnny in the Clouds," the whole emotional story played to effect by Michael Redgrave, Rosamund John, and Douglass Montgomery. His father could *be* Michael Redgrave, or even Van Johnson in *Miracle in the Rain* (1955)—Colin admits that films become jumbled in his head. Hollywood teaches him that such men are brave and Robert Murphy in *Britain, Cinema and the Second World War* (2000) has noted the concentration of war heroes that dominated melodramatic war films of the 1950s: Richard Todd, Kenneth More, Richard Attenborough, Jack Hawkins, and Dirk Bogarde.[4] Colin seeks out heroism and believes in its images, images the reader may recognize from *They Were Not Divided* (1950), or *Appointment in London* (1953) in which Dirk Bogarde has flown eighty-seven missions and is trying to make ninety;

Odette (1951); and *The Dam Busters* (1955). There is evidence of a marked concentration on heroic masculinity in films of the 1950s and melodrama is a prevalent force in war films of the decade. The kinds of films Colin chooses to watch serve to simplify the melée of feelings that reflect the onset of puberty as well as the emptiness he feels yearning for his missing father. In this way, the novel provides a disquisition on heroism and hero worship and, in a Freudian sense, Colin's cinematic reconstructions "screen" the true origins of his buried anxieties: puberty ("his face didn't look normal. . . . It felt almost as if another face was pushing its way to the surface, somebody else's face and he didn't know whose" [92]) and mortality ("Have you ever thought that every year we live through the day or our own deaths?" [154]).

Barker purposely locates Colin in that ambivalent historical moment just as cinema audiences were beginning to wane with the increasing popularity of television which, for her TV-watching character, Mrs. Hennigan, like most Britons, began with the televising of the queen's coronation in 1953 and the onset of commercial television in 1955. Colin watches films at the local Odeon and the Gaumont that tend to fit the "heroic flyer" subgenre of war films epitomized in the poster he sees advertising an up-and-coming movie: "A man in flying helmet and goggles straddled the scene. Between his legs, blazing planes plunged out of the sky, men in parachutes floated down" (29). Nicholas Pronay believes these kinds of war films made in the 1950s were cathartic in a number of ways for filmgoers: "They allowed the people in the audience to relive vicariously their experiences, the fears, guilt and dilemmas of their own particular war; and to catharsise [*sic*] psychological sores still festering."[5]

While Pronay refers most directly to those who lived through and remember the war, Colin lives vicariously through war as for the first time and in so doing he begins to translate his feelings into a film "treatment"—the stage of the screenwriting process before the ideas are fully formed into a shooting script. Colin's Hollywood war heroes begin as atavistic characters that in the largely unequivocal moral world of the movie play out expected roles. But, as the reels in his head unwind, the film becomes more unsettling. Colin's characters are not always what they seem. They become traitors and torturers and play out the boy's anxieties around loyalty to his mother and his friends as well as his fragile sense of belonging. At one point Colin realizes that a film he is watching at the local cinema bears an uncanny resemblance to the only story about his father that his nagging has elicited from his mother. Although not named, the film Colin watches is probably Ronald Neame's *The Man Who Never Was* (1956), a disturbing feature film "based on a true story" of British Intelligence deceiving the Germans over the invasion of Sicily and set in 1943, like Colin's own adventure. It stars Clifton Webb and features Gloria Grahame as Lucy the "good time girl" who pretends that her boyfriend has been killed in action. If this is the case, Barker is surely punning on the film buff's desire to "find the films" in *The Man Who Wasn't There*, to distinguish them through the very few descriptive "clues" in the novel. Neame's was not one of the biggest box office successes of the 1950s: *Reach for the Sky* and *The Dambusters* clearly earned more and were the subject of much more attention. But, *The Man Who Never Was* contains bluffs and double bluffs; characters and corpses are not what they seem and the whole is grounded in deception and secrecy.[6]

In the novel Barker ensures that masculine identity is a complicated site of inquiry. While Barker refuses to depict Colin as an uncomplicated scholarship boy in the mold of Richard Hoggart's definition, Colin does reflect the more uneasy components of the type. For Hoggart, the scholarship boy is always self-conscious and filled with self-doubt. This is especially true of Colin when one considers his anxious efforts to link two discrete environments he is coming to know—the "men's world" he needs to feel he belongs to and the "women's world" he knows best. Hoggart explains: "With one ear he hears the women discussing their worries and ailments and hopes, and he tells them at intervals about his school and the work and what the master said. He usually receives boundless and uncomprehending sympathy: he knows they do not understand, but still he tells them; he would like to link the two environments."[7] Much of Colin's ambivalent relationship with the "other world" of cinema reflects the exasperated hope of reconciling his own position when it conflicts with the traditional class and gender expectations of the community into which he has been born. It is an exasperation that Barker believes continues into adulthood— and one that has preoccupied Richard Hoggart as exemplified in the title of his collection of essays, *Between Two Worlds* (2001).[8] Colin acts out a story to substantiate his sense of selfhood in Erving Goffman's sense of performing the self in order to manage events. He succeeds in managing his behavior appropriately in what Goffman, deploying the language of the theater, calls the "front" of the stage where the use of "fixed props" and "settings" to aid a solid performance allows for a socially acceptable interaction with others. But backstage, because he feels stigmatized as a fatherless child, Colin's other life charts aberrant "scenes"; it is a space where the dissonant feelings that contradict everyday life can be given free rein.[9] Barker asks what it might mean for a young boy to believe his father a hero but to fear that he may not have been; what it means when he sees through his mother's romanticization of his father and her deception of her son, and what the effects might be when those precious, if spurious, images of heroism are transferred into his own life. When he finally realizes that films can tell lies ("they said it was easy to be brave" [151]), he learns a lesson that Barker tells with searing realism in the trilogy that follows this novel, where soldiers like Burns have "missed [their] chance of being ordinary" because extreme situations and injuries become the norm in a war zone.[10] Masculine myths are crippled by actual war.

However, in *The Man Who Wasn't There* Colin creates a romance adventure in his head that has little sense of the horror of war. He sets it in France in a resistance cell, a place that exists on celluloid or in his imagination so he has little sense of the real pressures on resistance fighters tortured for information. Again, the reader's own cinematic experience may draw on films like Anthony Asquith's *Orders to Kill* (1958) and Jack Lee's *Circle of Deception* (1960), in which young men in the Resistance "fall apart" at the end of their missions. In Colin's extrapolation, Gaston can remain twelve years old; he has simply been parachuted into France because of his "superb command of the French language" (48). The scenes Colin creates fail to transcend his own limited experience: the French citizens queuing at a Gestapo checkpoint include "several schoolboys—wearing the maroon-and-gold blazer of Queen Elizabeth's Grammar School" (17). His only research extraneous to the movies involves finding indecipherable papers in his mother's wardrobe and these prompt a plot centered on espionage and codes only spies can decipher. For Colin, suspense is the key and this he relishes; each vignette is suspended and rerun like a soap opera or dramatic serial, just as a child acts out the plot of a favorite movie over and over. The story Colin imagines, however, is antirealist and unintentionally comic in ways that reflect his age and unworldliness; Barker has him create melodrama and she invents a comic narrative-within-a-narrative in which scenes are sutured together in one of her most experimental novels.

In this way, Barker writes a film screenplay that she decants into the novel but, at the same time, she also creates two distinct personae with the one life lived in parentheses. The two narratives are rendered differently, inscribing two different levels of reality that may be "matched by different levels of credibility—or to put it better, a different suspension of disbelief," as Italo Calvino describes in the essay "Levels of Reality in Literature."[11] Calvino warns readers not to confuse levels of reality within the literary work with levels of truth outside it. Barker presents one story framed by another, so that her protagonist Colin Harper exists liminally in the text. Part of his personality is "split off" or projected and it is this part that exists in cinematic form alongside his more theatrically staged self everyday. For example, the first time that Colin meets his projected future self is on a stage. He has wandered into an abandoned open-air theater that is described as "another world," a place to which his future self returns to stand, on the same stage he stood on as a boy (98). However, his cinematically staged self is a much more meaningful presence throughout the novel because it occupies a social as well as a personal space. Christine Geraghty proposes that in the 1950s cinema became "a residual site which provided escape from the obligations and expectations placed on the citizen/consumer of the modern classless state." Colin, though not subject to the social expectations placed on adults, reflects the cinema's new association with youth in the late 1950s and its facility for making war films that "ratified the fathers' wartime experiences, and helped to explain them to their sons," an inherently masculinist undertaking. Sue Harper and Vincent Porter's research on 1950s cinema audiences and their tastes reveals that from 1953 to 1957 popular war films were about "successful escapades conducted by small groups or individuals" in which heroes "retain their identity in the face of the enemy."[12]

The juxtaposition of images and the short chapters / scenes operate according to the principle of editing we understand from the cinema. Film is a kinetic, dynamic form and Colin's "borrowings" from Hollywood cinema ensure that he produces a classical Hollywood narrative but one told as a sequence of stressful events or scenes. Despite the space between scenes, Colin "directs" his film "in the can." That is to say, he follows the process of continuity editing traditionally favored by Hollywood that minimizes the shift from one scene to the next. But he never moves beyond the

assembly stage to refine his film to a "final cut." Editing is fundamental to the construction and generation of meaning in a film text. Colin edits in order to savor for
himself the pleasurable experience of participating vicariously in a strange and dangerous world. The structuring is episodic; there are cliffhangers, dissolves, and fades
to distinguish the parallel editing of Colin's life in 1955 and Gaston's "life" in 1943.
In each scene Colin's alter ego is anxious, threatened, or frightened, many of the emotions the average cinemagoer craves. At one point he feels vulnerable but almost deli-
ciously exposed, "as if a layer of skin had been stripped from his back" (57). In fact,
Colin's "other" life satisfies his requirements as an avid consumer of cinema. During
the 1950s when this novel is set, F. R. Leavis argued that young people should be protected from what he believed to be the corrupting influence of cinema. This general
feeling about commercialized leisure did not begin to be superseded for educators
until the Newsom Report of 1963, which allowed for the incorporation of mass
media studies into school curricula. For Colin in 1955, cinema is an environmental
factor that helps to define his fears and desires.[13] It sharpens his visual and dramatic
sense as a storyteller but he is not a critical reader of his filmgoing experience.

For a twelve-year-old boy, films are personally meaningful not ideologically
loaded and Colin carefully selects a cast for his very own war story, which he writes,
directs and edits only according to his own limited experience. He is Gaston, an
orphan according to his identity papers; Von Strohm, the archvillain Gestapo officer,
is "in another time and place" his headmaster; and his mother is Vivienne a waitress-
prostitute who dies in her son's story. Colin's immediate empirical world is spliced
with the imaginary. The presentation of birth certificates on admission to school
immediately becomes a dangerous Gestapo check point he has to get through, since
his certificate is the "short" version belying the fact that no father is stated. When
Colin guiltily ignores the bullying a fat boy suffers at his school, his alter ego Gaston
becomes a traitor in his movie who plots to give up the names of others in his resistance cell (79–84). Before dispatching his mother's married boyfriend by telling him
she expects marriage, he "transforms" him into a Kommandant and then decides that
a "spiv" is actually more in keeping. Colin's villains confirm to war stereotypes that
have become more entrenched with time; the contemporary British reader in particular recognizes his caricatures in popular BBC television comedies like *Dad's Army*
and *'Allo, 'Allo*. These popular cultural associations underline the light comedy that
pervades each aspect of the novel. The latter ran successfully on BBC from 1984 to
1992 and Barker was surprised to discover that "the dominance of *'Allo 'Allo*, which
has almost made the serious treatment of the French Resistance impossible, is actually an asset to the book."[14]

Colin generally reverts to his fantasies when confronted with fear or apprehen-
sion. The associations that trigger his performance are often sensory, as when he lies
in his "favourite place," a bomb crater that has not been filled in. As he lies there,
smelling dusty nettles, he becomes aware of "other life here, small animals that darted
and burrowed," and immediately drifts back to his life on celluloid (123). He could
be said to be involved in a mirror exercise of the type Constantin Stanislavski used in

acting workshops to promote naturalistic performance, a model that became very popular in 1950s cinema. The actor "becomes" the character. Stanislavski's emphasis on psychological realism was based on the idea that each aspect of the imaginary world the actor creates onstage—and in his head—must be real.[15] Breaking through the distance between the actor and his role took on progressively Freudian overtones down the twentieth century, an affective response to emotional "memory" as "method acting." But, while Liza in *Liza's England* has a box filled with props to prompt her memories, Colin's fantasy world is so real that it is expressive of his estrangement from the empirical world. It signals his dissatisfaction with what his life entails, and in this influence of Dennis Potter, a writer Barker admires, can be felt. For example, Potter's Casanova (first screened on BBC in 1971) declares: "The only way to dissolve these walls around us is to use the magic of our minds."

A network of images derived from cinematic performance delivers the war safely as story in this novel, where the story is the passage between the real and the imagined (the present and an imagined past). War—its conflicts, effects, and emotional scars—is the ostensible subject of the novel but Colin fails to apprehend it outside the bomb sites where he plays or the stories that proliferate in his postwar environment. In fact, in *Border Crossing* set in the 1990s, boys play a game of war that has hardly altered at all, "setting fire to enemy buildings" and "living off the land."[16] In *The Man Who Wasn't There* it is the cult of compulsory masculinity that is actually explored and found wanting. If the novel is read as a search for role models with whom Colin might identify on the postwar domestic front, it is both comic and filled with pathos, as Pat Wheeler discusses in her essay, "Transgressing Masculinities: *The Man Who Wasn't There*," in this volume. Barker ensures Colin encounters varying examples of masculinity: neighbor Adrian, who fulfils the role of older brother; Viv's married boyfriend, Reg, who refers to Colin as "Sonny Jim" and becomes a Gestapo officer in his "other world"; Roy Rogers at the Gaumont cinema. Closer in age are the older boys he worships from a distance:

> Boys with braying laughs and sudden, falsetto giggles, boys who stood on street corners and watched girls walk past, who punched each other with painful tenderness, who cultivated small moustaches that broke down, when shaved, into crusts of acne thicker than the moustache had ever been, who lit cigarettes behind cupped hands, narrowing their eyes in pretended indifference to the smoke. (28)

Barker captures the fragility of a young boy's ego and his yearning to identify with others in a masculine continuum. Most unsettling for Colin in this context is Bernie Walters, sweetshop owner and transvestite, who in a deep baritone tells Colin to "piss off, sonny" (34). When a teacher impresses on Colin the need for a male influence "to ensure that a boy's development is . . . healthy," he weaves Bernie into his story as Bernard the Englishman. Bernard "never had a father . . . no *male* influence. Nothing *healthy*. Nothing *normal* . . . never even joined the boy scouts" and takes to wearing his sister's knickers (68–71). The words that Barker italicizes here map the contours of the terrain that Colin must occupy in order to begin to find his place. However, Colin never finds himself in safe territory in the story he concocts. His personality is not fixed but fluid and it is possible for him to lose sight of the coordinates of masculine identity that society finds the most comfortable. As theorists of gender from Michel Foucault to Judith Butler have maintained, identity is performance, constituted Butler has argued by the very dramatic "expressions" that are mistakenly taken to be gender's core components.[17] Colin, for example, is subject to the plethora of clichés around homosexual panic, as in his portrayal of Bernard. His tacit understanding of homosexuality underpins the character he imagines in ways that reflect those fictions of empire of the early twentieth century in which homosexuals were constructed as potential traitors who could be led to value sexual favors over patriotism. It also reflects the fact that the 1950s was a difficult decade for homosexuals. While the Wolfenden Report recommendations of 1954 began the decriminalization of homosexuals, the age of consent was not introduced until 1967 and the social and sexual upheaval that so fascinates Barker across the novels was particularly rife with witch hunts in the years immediately following the war.[18] In *Regeneration* W. H. R. Rivers bitingly compares "The Great Adventure," the umbrella term for the stories schoolboys devoured before the First World War, with the reality of a war that "consisted of crouching in a dugout, waiting to be killed."[19] Rivers gives the lie to "adventure"; "manly" activity has become passivity. Colin's imaginary action-packed world remains the stuff of tenacious cliché as fortified by classical Hollywood.

A significant facet of *The Man Who Wasn't There*, also favored by Hollywood in films like *Tender Comrade* (1943) and *Ladies Courageous* (1944) and in Britain with *Millions Like Us* (1943), is the depiction of women relishing the freedom of the home front, like Lucy in *The Man Who Never Was*. They are "out of the cage," to borrow a phrase repeated by so many women interviewed about their war work.[20] Colin's mother and her friend Pauline reminisce about their time in the Auxiliary Territorial Service (ATS), "manning" anti-aircraft guns—though Winston Churchill had forbidden women from actually firing them. Pauline is wistful: "I think the first two years of war were the happiest of my life" (102). Both women regret their loss of status in the workforce at the end of the war. In this novel Barker looks seriously at the role of women in war, a topic she first considered in *Liza's England* and develops in more detail in the trilogy but there is also something of the vaudevillian in Barker's representation of Viv and Pauline. They waitress in a club dressed as fawns, a bizarre take on Hugh Hefner's equally bizarre idea that bunny tails made his girls seem untouchable. Colin is expected to steam Viv's fawn ears each evening before she departs for work. Rather than lament leaving her young son to fend for himself, Viv is more worried that "thirty-six was over the hill, for a fawn" (36). Colin, understanding little of her desires or her loneliness, manages, like Kelly Brown in *Union Street*, to frighten his mother's boyfriends away with his childish precocity. Despite the pathos in the relationship, there is much salt at its edges. It often circles around sex: one young woman, Enid, becomes pregnant by the back end of a pantomime horse and is the talk of the town. Colin is privy to the gossip his mother and grandmother bring into the house about women and "women's problems" and one character, Mr. Stroud, is even described as "a small, balding, sperm-shaped man" (110). Much of Colin's self-doubt relates back to his adolescent fears—about sex and sexuality, courage and manhood—and to his desperate search for meaning in masculinity. When an actor in a film he watches fears his parachute will not open in descent, a nagging doubt invades the boy's clear-cut definitions of heroic fighter pilots. Before the pilot jumps, "the camera moved in close until you were looking at one eye, and in the pupil of that eye a shape formed, the shape of a parachute that didn't open but fluttered endlessly towards the ground." When the jump is successful, the camera zooms in on the pilot's face and Colin sees his terror, "Again and again, he saw the man dangling from his harness, as the plane hurtled towards the ground" (31). Rather than reproducing the propaganda of *The First of the Few* (1942) or the dazzling pyrotechnics of *The Flying Leathernecks* (1951), Barker unsettles Colin's fixed ideas of courage in war. Colin's disquiet is exacerbated by a grotesque sideshow taking place at the local fairground where a man "dies" with a rope around his neck, in a gruesome pastiche of Dr. Crippen who was hanged in 1910. Colin thinks of Derek Bentley and Ruth Ellis (executed in July of 1955) and wonders about the real stories that outdo the imaginary for sheer audacity—or horror. It is fear that "kills" Gaston at the end of Colin's "movie," breaking out of the line the Gestapo has initiated for the checking of documents he flees until he is shot dead. In killing off his own character, Colin leaves Bernard, ironically the most equivocal male in the novel. In the final frames Bernard is reshaped into a classical film role: he is left to "turn up his collar" Bogart-style and walk away as an Allied plane carries off the remaining resistance operatives (158) in a *Casablanca*-style ending. Barker ensures that Colin's images of heroism are embattled, ricocheting back and forth so that he is at once comforted and confounded by the movies.

Colin uses various kinds of performance as strategies for psychological management but the splitting off of a performed self and the uncertainties of material reality are reinforced in other ways in the novel, most specifically Barker's preoccupation with the spiritual medium as a metaphor for the artist who demonstrates the power of fantasy in everyday life. Film director and theorist Michael Roemer's definitions of the artist seem to best fulfill the tenets that Barker explores most distinctively through Colin but as elaborated through the figure of the medium:

> The artist's permeable identity places him on a threshold between being and not being. Like the hero, he is a coincidence of opposites and riven by contradictions. His parentage, like the hero's, is often obscure or in doubt. . . . The modern artist secures his identity by being deeply different.[21]

The medium reflects Barker's fascination with the supernatural and ghosts, ideas she takes up in more detail in *Another World*. Here, Barker domesticates the supernatural in her descriptions of the "spuggies," the seances popular in a grieving postwar Britain. Mrs. Stroud manufactures her "second sight." However, her performance is disturbed when she focuses on Colin and is able to "see" a spirit at his shoulder and to detect in the boy untapped psychic powers, the artistic powers that have driven his imagination throughout the novel. Ironically, it is precisely what is *real* about Mrs. Stroud's role of medium that shocks a comfortable congregation out of the fraudulent routine she manages so successfully for them each session. Faking the real also highlights that which is not quite faked and reminds us that real communication between two worlds is always possible. In *Liza's England* Frank Wright knows when his power as a medium fails and he has to choose whether he will continue in a motivational role for those mourning parents who hang on his every word. In this novel, Mrs. Stroud makes a living by giving her clients and neighbors the very advice they need from "the other side." She is more community counselor than medium. In the early novels Barker's literary exploration of therapy begins in interesting ways. In *Regeneration* Prior both is mute and fakes mutism and in *The Ghost Road* Barker has the spiritual medium in Melanesia show that he knows how to fake divination, "he savvy gannon lang naasa." Where the rational explanation does not fit the facts, Barker posits another version of the real, and it is in *The Man Who Wasn't There* that this key feature of her aesthetic vision really begins to come into play. Mrs. Stroud imagines her spirit guide as a Hollywood-style Native American, complete with bow and arrow, head band and eagle feather, who Colin immediately recognizes as Jeff Chandler in Delmar Davies's *Broken Arrow* (1950), the first example of Hollywood making a hero of a Native American Indian. Colin taps into Mrs. Stroud's thinking almost as surely as she taps into his but while he recognizes her appropriation of a screen images, she senses a boy in crisis. He is clinging to cinema in order to supply the story of how his life began.

Barker often writes against the grain and against expectations but perhaps not more so than in *The Man Who Wasn't There*. One reason, one supposes, that this novel has failed to receive as much critical attention as her other works is that the surreal elements in Colin's cinematic story push the novel further outside the predominantly realistic framework of the earlier fiction. With a nod to Kafka's *Metamorphosis*, Barker has Viv tell her feverish son that when she had a high temperature as a child, "I thought I was a cockroach. I could hear me wings rubbing together and everything" (144). While Gaston fakes an illness, over the days in which the action takes place Colin has become progressively ill until he faints and falls into a fever. When Gaston sees a dead Vivienne propped up on a chair next to her resistance colleagues, he panics and the scene fades out until Colin sees his mother seated in the very same chair in his bedroom talking him through his fever. Surrealism bleeds out of the film in Colin's head and into his quotidian life. The novel twists and turns on what may be "real" and what "fake." Perhaps because of this too, the novel has been subject to some misreadings. Herbert Mitgang in the *New York Times*, believes that father and son "fuse" in Colin's imagination.[22] But this is a surface recognition of only one role that Barker has Colin play. Discrepant or partial readings of the novel may reflect Barker's own writing practice, in that she circles Colin: "I knew at some point that Colin . . . would have to face the man who wasn't there, but I didn't know it was himself. There was a point at which I thought it was a ghost and at one point I thought it was a prowler."[23] The Freudian psychoanalyst Bruno Bettelheim in his discussion of fairy tales argues that the less specific the writer is about the hero, the more readers empathize and endow him with their own meanings.[24] This idea holds true for *The Man Who Wasn't There*. Colin is unable to control the fiction he creates, no matter how carefully he scripts his story, and the reader feels his anxiety, the source of his creativity, as the dominant effect.

The novel has been under-read, as though a child protagonist relegates the fiction to a space outside Barker's best work. This is a pity since *The Man Who Wasn't There* is a central text in coming to understand many of the themes and ideas that circulate in Barker's fiction. A child's yearning for an absent father is a feature that resonates for Kelly Brown in *Union Street* and Danny Miller in *Border Crossing*. The inadequacy of fathers who are present in their children's lives is just as central: even psychologist W. H. R. Rivers is plagued by memories of a cold and distant father for whom his childhood stammer makes of him a case to be observed rather than a son to be supported. Barker's later work is often very visually effective. In this way too it recalls *The Man Who Wasn't There*. When Nick examines the transcript of Geordie talking about the war in *Another World,* for example, he notices the "wordless, hallucinatory filmic quality" of the centenarian's memories "a flare goes up, illuminating bleached sandbags and tangled wire."[25] In the trilogy, especially, Barker succeeds in creating powerful antiwar images of waste and chaos in the trenches and when questioned Barker has allowed that the unfolding of story via the nuancing of repeated imagery could be considered "filmic."[26] Among some of the most visually evocative images are the mystical scenes set in France in *The Ghost Road*. They seem more reminiscent of Alain-Fournier's classic *Le Grand Meaulnes* (1912)—translated into English as "The Lost Domain"—than British writing out of the war.[27] Barker's officers are granted temporary respite in a deserted house in a French village where there are "extraordinary jagged shapes of broken walls in moonlight, silver mountains and chasms, with here and there black pits of craters thronged in weeds."[28] The house the men share is baroque and seems enchanted and they prepare their new environment theatrically, moving furniture from other derelict properties and creating visual set pieces like "still life." Director Gillies MacKinnon's opening panoramic shots when adapting Barker's *Regeneration* for the screen in 1997 remind us that skulls are a key visual motif across the trilogy and in this way something of the symbolic resonance of the novel is captured. Glen Macpherson's cinematography studs the trenches with skulls embedded in the mud. It is a reminder that on the first day of the Battle of the Somme, for example, the British lost some sixty thousand men in full-frontal attacks against the German Second Army and that by the end one and a quarter million men had lost their lives. In the film, the camera pans across the dead and dying in no-man's-land as bombs whistle and light up the killing zone. It cuts to the Edinburgh countryside around Craiglockhart hospital where small animals are strung up in a tree and a naked man sits amid their detritus. Two bleak scenes coalesce to evoke the horror of a war that cannot be confined to the battlefields. The juxtaposition of such images really begins for Barker in *The Man Who Wasn't There,* the novel in which she first experiments with cinematic form and features and fuses one world with another.

Toward the end of his "film," Gaston/Colin has become a traitor, killed Vivienne / his mother, and imagined his father into being, but failed to link them. He conjures up an adult self far removed from his childhood setting. In one of the most moving scenes of the novel Colin watches his adult self return to the home he shares with his mother to attend her funeral, a traitor to his class and to his family. The "man in black"—dressed for a funeral rather than espionage—wears Colin's face but seems to feel very little emotion. Colin rejects this cold, alien figure and in so doing kills off his alter ego Gaston and the idea of his father as the absent key to his latent destiny. No longer believing himself to be solely the extension of an elusive father, but also deeply connected to a less-than-perfect but present mother, he lets the curtain fall on his acting apprenticeship for the last time. In fact, Barker shows that Colin has always been rather more like his mother than he might suppose: as a child Viv escaped to the cinema immediately after her own father's funeral, for example. Out of a fragmented, volatile self, made and remade in performance and fantasy, Colin gains a sense of a more *integral* self. He begins to realize that his personal history is connected to a larger collective history of war—and, by extension, to film history in which war finds one of its most potent representations.

NOTES

1. Sharon Monteith and Pat Wheeler, "Interview with Pat Barker," Durham, February 1999. Parts of this essay derive from earlier work completed in Sharon Monteith, *Pat Barker* (Plymouth: Northcote House, 2002).

2. Examples of the "escaper" type occur in Richard Hoggart's grammar school boy, in the postwar classic exploration of popular and mass culture *The Uses of Literacy* (1957), and in novels by David Storey and poetry by Tony Harrison. See Pat Wheeler's essay, "Transgressing Masculinities: *The Man Who Wasn't There*," in this volume for a full discussion of the concept.

3. Pat Barker, *The Man Who Wasn't There* (New York: Picador, 1988), 32. All subsequent references will be included in the text.

4. Robert Murphy, *Britain, Cinema, and the Second World War* (London: Continuum, 2000), 179.

5. Nicholas Pronay, "The British Post-Bellum Cinema," *Historical Journal of Film, Radio, and Television* 8, no. 1 (1988): 51. For a full discussion see, Robert Murphy, "Fifties British War Films," *Close-Up: Electronic Journal of British Cinema* 1 (Winter 1996) at http://www.shu.ac.uk/services/lc/closeup/fiftiesa.htm; and Andy Medhurst, "1950s War Films," in *National Fictions*, ed. Geoff Hurd (London: BFI, 1984).

6. *The Man Who Never Was* (1956) tells the story of an Intelligence scam whereby the dead body of a British citizen is disguised as a fictitious major with false I.D., a love letter from a false girlfriend, and a letter from Mountbatten describing the intention to attack Greece rather than Sicily. The body is allowed to wash up on the coast of Southern Spain where a German agent can find it. British and German Intelligence pit their wits against each other for the rest of the film.

7. Richard Hoggart, *The Uses of Literacy* (Harmondsworth: Pelican, 1957), 296.

8. Richard Hoggart, *Between Two Worlds* (London: Aurum Press, 2001). See also Hoggart's *An Imagined Life: Life and Times 1959–91* (London: Chatto, 1992). D. J. Enright's

review of the latter is entitled rather ironically in the context of this discussion, "Double Agent in a Class of his Own," *Independent on Sunday*, May 3, 1992, 30.

9. Erving Goffman, "Regions and Region Behaviour," in *The Presentation of Self in Every-day Life* (London: Penguin, 1959), 109–40.

10. Pat Barker, *Regeneration* (London: Penguin, 1991), 184

11. Italo Calvino, "Levels of Reality in Literature" in *The Literature Machine* (London: Picador, 1989), 108.

12. See Christine Geraghty's illuminating overview "Cinema as Social Space: Understand-ing Cinema-Going in Britain, 1947–63," *Framework* 42 (Summer 2000) at http://www.frameworkonline.com; and Sue Harper and Vincent Porter, "Cinema Audience Tastes in 1950s Britain," *Journal of Popular British Cinema* 2 (1999): 77.

13. For a detailed discussion of the ways in which cinema refines definitions of national identity, see Jeffrey Richards, *Films and British National Identity: From Dickens to Dad's Army* (Manchester: Manchester University Press, 1997), esp. chapter 5, "National Identity Post-War."

14. Monteith and Wheeler, "Interview with Pat Barker."

15. See, for example, Constantin Stanislavski's 1926 book *An Actor Prepares* (London: Penguin, 1967), which places the actor at the center of the creative process, as taken up by Lee Strasberg and the Group Theater in their emphasis on psychological realism. By the 1950s, method actors such as Marlon Brando and James Dean epitomized the confusion between actor and role that Barker plays out through Colin.

16. Pat Barker, *Border Crossing* (London: Viking, 2001), 210.

17. Judith Butler, *Gender Trouble: Feminism and the Subversion of Identity* (New York: Routledge, 1990).

18. See Joseph Bristow's "Schoolboys," in *Empire Boys: Adventures in a Man's World* (London: HarperCollins, 1991), esp. 88–89. Although he studies the public school system, Bris-tow points up the kinds of compulsively masculine ideas in fictions of empire that underpin Colin's imaginative world. For a discussion of the 1950s, see Patrick Higgins, *Heterosexual Dictatorship: Male Homosexuality in Post-War Britain* (London: Fourth Estate, 1997). Hig-gins explores, for example, Lord Montagu's trial and imprisonment and Sir John Gielgud's arrest in a public toilet in Chelsea.

19. Pat Barker, *Regeneration*, 107.

20. See, for example, Gail Braydon and Penny Summerfield, *Out of the Cage: Women's Experiences in Two World Wars* (London: Pandora, 1987).

21. Michael Roemer, *Telling Stories: Postmodernism and the Invalidation of Traditional Narrative* (Lanham, Md.: Rowman and Littlefield, 1995), 137–38.

22. Herbert Mitgang, "A Story in the Imagination of a Boy," review of *The Man Who Wasn't There*, *New York Times*, December 8, 1990.

23. Barker in Donna Perry, "Going Home Again: An Interview with Pat Barker," *Literary Review* 34, no. 2 (1991): 239.

24. See Bruno Bettelheim, *The Uses of Enchantment* (New York: Knopf, 1976).

25. Pat Barker, *Another World* (London: Viking, 1998), 241.

26. Pat Barker in Mark Sinker "Temporary Gentlemen," *Sight and Sound* 12 (1998): 24.

27. For a similar aesthetic sense, one might also consider R. H. Mottram's *The Spanish Farm* (1924) but the book has been out of print for a long time. Alain-Fournier was himself killed in action in France in 1914.

28. Pat Barker, *The Ghost Road* (London: Viking, 1995), 179.

PAT WHEELER

Transgressing Masculinities
The Man Who Wasn't There

The *Man Who Wasn't There* is often overlooked in discussions of Pat Barker's fiction despite its charm and complexity but it provides a link across the body of her work. The novel marks a stage in the development of the issues that predetermine her exploration of masculinity and the complexity of the male psyche in the highly acclaimed First World War trilogy. Although reviewers have argued that Pat Barker changed direction with the *Regeneration* trilogy this is clearly not the case, as Sharon Monteith has argued in *Pat Barker* (2002). Neither has she "given up on women" as has also been argued. In *The Man Who Wasn't There* women are the defining influence in the young male protagonist's life and in *Regeneration* and in *The Eye in the Door,* working-class women like the Ropers are powerfully realized. Barker's novels are linked by her critical examination of class and gender. The focus of *The Man Who Wasn't There* falls on the making of masculinity in an all-female working-class family but the acute political sensibility Barker brings to her previous novels is evident here too. Barker's early novels may look more specifically at working-class women but men have a presence in each narrative. In *The Man Who Wasn't There,* her fourth novel, Barker takes her exploration of the working-class male further, addressing the complex diversity of socially constructed masculinity.

Indeed, in each of her novels Barker argues very persuasively that you cannot understand one gender in isolation from the other. In this novel Barker juxtaposes realism and fantasy to explore male identity and sexuality and to show how society sanctions an ideological version of heroic masculinity. *The Man Who Wasn't There* is the story of a twelve-year-old, fatherless boy, Colin Harper, who is brought up by his mother in a small community that is made up almost exclusively of women. He is unable to find out who his father was because his mother will not (or cannot) tell him. Colin turns to films for images of what his father might have been and imagines him to be a war hero, killed in action. This fantasy fuels his own imaginary world of war and espionage where he is a schoolboy hero, Gaston, of the French Resistance. The "action" takes place over three days as Colin searches for a sense of identity after finding his birth certificate with the father's name left blank and ends when Colin comes to accept that he may never know the truth about his birth.

The emphasis in my reading of *The Man Who Wasn't There* is on Barker's use of narrative and genre, reading the novel through a Bakhtinian framework, using the very fundamental Bakhtinian concept of the novel as a dialogic form where words and language come to us already imprinted with the meanings, the intentions, and the accents of previous users. Barker's use (or reuse) of language can be seen as both dialogic and polyphonic. She interweaves and juxtaposes different ways of speaking: interior monologues and double-voiced discourse with carnivalesque irreverence toward authoritarian discourses of class and masculinity. But, as always with Barker, these point the way to a polemical end. In *The Man Who Wasn't There*, Barker juxtaposes the internal world of fantasy with the external world with all its problems and explores male identity through the use of memory and fantasy and ultimately, recognition and redemption. She synthesizes a number of genres, including the bildungsroman and the "working-class novel," drawing upon the supernatural elements of gothic writing—and the western/heroic narratives of Second World War films of the 1950s, as discussed by Sharon Monteith in her essay, "Screening *The Man Who Wasn't There*: The Second World War and 1950s Cinema," in this volume. In the young male protagonist Colin, Barker constructs a multifaceted character, who is instinctively searching for his own sense of self, surrounded as he is by images of masculinity, but growing up in a family of women. The alternative worlds he inhabits are conveyed through the language of the streets, the language of the classroom, and the heroic language of valor. These are not mutually exclusive discourses but reciprocally dependent and together they provide an acute interrogation of the formation of masculinity.

Bakhtin's carnival is associated with the act of "deliberately and emphatically contemporizing" mythical heroes.[1] There are plenty of mythical male heroes in Colin's life, not necessarily the historical figures of myth and legend, but certainly with regard to the mythological heroic manliness exhibited in the films of the 1940s and 1950s and in the war relics that surround the boy. All fathers who fought in the war are mythologized:

> Photographs. On mantlepieces, in friends' houses, dads with more hair than they had now sat astride guns, or smiled against the backdrop of ruined cities. . . . At school too, the endless war between British and Germans was re-fought at every break, and the leaders of the opposing armies were always boys whose fathers had been in the war. Who could produce, when need arose, the ultimate authority: *My dad says.*[2]

Colin has no father so he searches for his own heroes. Barker emphasizes the importance of fantasy in his search for self-knowledge. Reality, in psychoanalytical terms, is frequently associated with "truth" or "knowledge" of the self. Fantasy often occurs when reality becomes unmanageable, or when there appear to be external dangers in the form of an "enemy" to be fought. Colin is constantly "at war" with himself. His quest for identity is played out through a search for evidence as Colin begins to ask challenging questions about what it means to be a man. In *Messages Men Hear: Constructing Masculinities*, Ian Harris argues that, "a boy constructs his gender identity in messages he receives from his environment as to how he ought to be behave." Harris also believes that from the age of twelve, boys begin to ask themselves, "Am I a man amongst men?" He asserts, "their most powerful teacher about masculinity is their father . . . modelling how men behave."[3] Colin looks for confirmation of himself as a "man" in implicit and explicit projections of masculinity: the cinema, on the sports field, in the schoolroom and in vivid reenactments of war.

Colin's search for masculinity can be usefully read through Bakhtin's idea of the "novel of ordeal" or bildungsroman. The novel of ordeal "is constructed as a series of tests of the main heroes, tests of their fidelity, valor, bravery, virtue, nobility, sanctity and so on . . . the struggle and testing of the hero." He states that, this "always begins where a deviation from the normal social and biographical course of life begins, and it ends where life resumes its normal course."[4] From the opening page ("Colin Harper, one eye open for snipers, turned the corner into his own road") to the final page ("Colin, staring straight ahead, waited for the drone of the Lysander to fade. Then he gave a sharp, decisive little nod, and said, 'The End'"), the novel charts Colin's struggle for self-knowledge and "manliness." His ordeal is enacted and imagined in differing scenarios that reflect states of individual emancipation and survival. Using spatial and temporal indicators, Barker appropriates conflicting genres for the landscape of Colin's journey to selfhood. The tension between the "real time" of Colin's world and the fantasy world with its shifts in time and location nuance Colin's ordeal. The time span of the novel is just three days while the fantasy sequences are not always defined in time. Bakhtin's idea of the "chronotope" makes the "other" time visible, the fantasy world becomes part of the making of Colin's masculinity, but remains outside of, or parallel to, the represented events in his "real" life.[5]

The temporal shifts begin at the very moment Colin discovers the blank spaces on his birth certificate:

Name and surname of father: ———
Rank or Profession of father: ———

Colin stared at the lines of black ink, even ran his finger across them, as if willing them to disgorge words.

He thought: *It doesn't matter.* After all, whoever his father had been, *he* was still the same person, it made no difference to *him.* And all the while he thought this, he knew it did matter. (17)

This discovery is immediately followed by the "appearance" of Gaston—Colin's alter ego, the heroic English schoolboy arriving in France to work with the Resistance with his clutch of false identity papers clearly projecting Colin's anxiety about his birth. Barker subverts certain traditional features of the working-class by allowing Colin an interiority and imaginative awareness, facets that are not conspicuous in writing in this genre. Barker is undoubtedly aware of the problems that exist in the reception of the working-class novel and her narrative serves as an essential constituent in the undermining of those views. Michael Montgomery, discussing the limitations of genre, believes that "in the relationships that are artistically expressed in literature, each genre possesses a specific field that determines the parameters of events even though the field does not uniquely specify particular events."[6] Barker works both within and outside the conventions of the working-class novel; consequently the limitations of realism are held in abeyance. She is, to extrapolate on Montgomery's and Bakhtin's ideas, exploring the discursive patterns in which artistic works take shape and are understood. Rather than striving for verisimilitude, she offers a debate on masculinity, constructed out of contradictory opinions, value judgements, and a series of signifying moments in a young man's life.

Bakhtin's chronotope is the place "where casual relationships . . . are always recognizable as a particular type of text."[7] By using the historically narrative form of the working-class novel, then subverting the expectations of that form, Barker exposes some of the contradictions that are inherent in any specification of genre. According to the Bakhtinian scholar Michael Holquist, a chronotope is also "a fundamental tool for broader social and historical analysis." Colin's search for identity is located both within the sociohistorical framework of his childhood and the psychological fragments of memory, history and fantasy. Holquist points up an idea that helps us to appreciate the complexity of a deceptively simple novel by highlighting the Bakhtinian distinction between "the way in which an event unfolds" and "the same event ordered in a mediated telling of it—the chronology might be varied or even reversed so as to achieve a particular effect."[8] Colin reenacts the events of his life by occupying different spaces and times. He translates the idea of himself from his "inner language," the fantasy sequences, into the, "language of outward expressedness . . . into the . . . pictorial fabric of life as a human being amongst other human beings." Bakhtin argues that the search for identity is carried out through others, "giving one expression or another that we deem to be essential or desirable."[9] As hero of his own personal narrative, Colin exhibits both the need to give expression to a heroic form of male identity and the need to create for himself a persona to present to the world. That these identities merge and separate at moments of disorientation and crisis adds to the disruption of the narrative and problematizes concrete notions of masculinity. Colin "sees" himself as a man, dislikes what he sees and in an encounter with his future self, knows that "only one of them would walk away, and . . . at the last moment, that he didn't know which" (153). He does not know which version of a man he will become.

In Colin's search for suitable male role models he encounters many versions of masculinity. The conflict between these is problematized via a set of images typically characterized in studies of masculinity by "silences, crisis, uncertainty and invisibility."[10] Colin's uncertainty is determined by the empty space on his birth certificate where his father's name should be, by his creation of Gaston, who is both hero and traitor, and his engagement with the "man in black" who allows him to see the man he is likely to become. It is also evident in his hero worship of Adrian Hennigan, a surrogate brother to whom he looks for friendship and affection. This is apparent when Adrian takes him on his motorbike: "Colin stood on the gritty pavement watching until Adrian was out of sight. He had his hand raised to wave, but Adrian didn't look back" (27). When playing games with Adrian "for the first time in [his] life, he'd wanted someone else to win" (145). Barker's narrative embodies the desire for male solidarity and homosocial relationships between men. Roger Horrocks argues that men yearn for each other as sources of maleness and masculinity that blur the boundaries between sexuality and gender.[11] The relationships between Colin and Adrian and between Adrian and local badboy and charmer Brian Combey exhibit those desires.

There is a significant body of writing that raises issues such as gender performance and performativity, postmodern sexualities and male impersonation but working-class men are either ignored, or connected to masculinity in its most essential forms. For example, Andrew Tolson believes that, "manual labour is suffused with masculine qualities and given certain sensual overtones for 'the lads.' The toughness and awkwardness of physical work and effort . . . takes on masculine lights and depths and assumes a significance beyond itself."[12] In *The Man Who Wasn't There* the working-class youth, or to be more specific, the "scholarship boy," is brought into the debate.[13] The invisibility of this aspect of working-class maleness is brought into the foreground when Colin fights to remain within the boundaries of his family and his neighborhood, but becomes increasingly alienated from his peers as a bright scholarship boy. In this way, a useful correlation can be made between *The Man Who Wasn't There,* and the work of Richard Hoggart and Tony Harrison.[14] Both have written about the anxieties of displacement and dislocation from one's class and, in particular, about being a scholarship boy.

In *The Uses of Literacy,* Hoggart contends that "the anxious and the uprooted . . . have a sense of loss [that] is increased precisely because they are emotionally uprooted from their class, often under the stimulus of a stronger critical intelligence or imagination, qualities which can lead them into an unusual self-consciousness before their own situation."[15] What is clear in Hoggart's discussion of all aspects of working-class life is that he assumes that family consists of mother, father, and child. Single mothers like Viv are invisible so Hoggart argues that a boy like Colin will find himself estranged from his father and his friends and that he tends to be "closer to the women of the house . . . at the physical centre of the home, where the women's spirit rules." He concludes that this is probably the reason why many working-class male writers give their women characters "so tender and central a place."[16] Colin's relationship with his mother is much more ambiguous and I would certainly question his view that working-class women are automatically treated so reverently by working-class authors.[17] One thing that can be categorically stated about Barker's women is that they *never* behave in ways that conform to these comfortable representations of themselves. Barker is constantly reevaluating and reinventing working-class women in her writing and *The Man Who Wasn't There* is no exception. But, Hoggart's dislocation of the scholarship boy from his friends and his class is pertinent. Barker engages with this idea in the confrontation between Colin and his headmaster at the grammar school where he is a pupil:

> "You've been at this school, how long. . . ?"
> He knew that as well as Colin did. "Just over a year, Sir."
> "Do you like it here? *Eh?*"

"I suppose so, Sir."

"You suppose?"

Colin didn't know what to say. . . . "Have you made any particular friends at school?"

"No, Sir."

"So whom do you play with after school?" Colin shrugged. "Lads I know."

"I see. You mean lads from the Secondary Modern school?"

"Yes, Sir."

"I don't suppose they get very much homework, do they?"

"No, Sir."

"Isn't that a bit difficult? I mean, when they want to go out, and you have to stay in." (67–68)

Colin and Lorimer, the only other boy from his school to pass the eleven-plus examination, are marginalized. Whereas Colin is able to redeem himself in the eyes of his fellow pupils by excelling at football, Lorimer is "very fat with a rather high-pitched voice" and is picked on by the sports teacher while the other boys watch, exchanging "bright, alert, salivating glances" (73). However, Barker does not homogenize: Colin *is* first to be picked for the team, whereas Lorimer is left until last, put in goal and then beaten up in the showers after losing the match. Colin is able to exist in two different worlds in his "real" life as well as his fantasy world. Although the headmaster recognizes his problem, Colin is apparently able to keep his class allegiances.

In a similar vein, Tony Harrison's poem "Me Tarzan" engages with the problems of moving away from your class through education. He examines the plight of boys like Colin; "Outside the whistled gang-call, *Twelfth Street Rag,* / then a Tarzan yodel for the kid who's bored / whose hand's on his liana . . . no, back / to Labienus and his flaming sword. / *Off laikin', then t'fish'oil* an all the boys, *off tartin', off t'flicks,* but on, on, on." Harrison shows the distance between the two worlds of the young boy by juxtaposing regional dialect and more standard English. "Off laikin'" and "off tartin'" are placed in direct opposition to "De Bello Gallico" and "Labienus and his flaming sword." In Harrison's poem the boy has to stay in, "*Ah bloody can't ah've gorra Latin prose.*"[18] In *The Man Who Wasn't There,* Colin has no restraining figure to keep him home and at his studies, he is allowed free rein and wanders the streets late at night. However, the conflict between his two worlds remains at the forefront of Barker's literary exploration. Colin turns the confrontation between himself and his headmaster into a fantasy interrogation scene between Von Strohm, the head of Gestapo and Bernard, a transvestite member of the Resistance. The headmaster tells Colin that "sooner or later you're going to have to make your mind up whether you belong to this school or not." He allows he does not want to be too hard on Colin because he can see that "life must be quite . . . difficult. It's not easy for a boy, growing up without a father" and "It needs a man to . . . ensure that a boy's development is . . . healthy. *Normal*" (68). In the interrogation of the Resistance member Bernard, Barker turns this argument into wonderful satire:

VON STROHM. Why do you dress as a woman?
Silence

> There's no reason to protect them. A joke is not a crime. We Germans are famous for our sense of humour . . .

(Conversationally, as if asking the question for the first time)
VON STROHM. Why do you dress like a woman?
BERNARD. All right! All right!

> It . . . it comes over me. I try not to. I sit there night after night. . . . I've even thrown away the key to the wardrobe, and then it comes over me again, and I go and break the lock. I used to just do it at home . . . but then I got this urge to go and walk the streets.

Cries.

> I've been like it all my life. Ever since I was twelve years old. . . . You see, I never had a father. There was no male influence. Nothing healthy. Nothing normal. I never even joined the boy scouts. (69–70)

These sections work to emphasize the boy's situation within what he sees as a hostile environment. Inasmuch as Tony Harrison's poem reflects the working-class schoolboy caught between two different worlds from an adult perspective, *The Man Who Wasn't There* addresses this issue through the eyes of the boy. Colin does not yet have the "luxury" of distance from his environment, though he has a glimpse of what is to come with the man in black.

Colin's quest for self-knowledge and a place in the world is represented from the perspective of a twelve-year-old boy. In his fantasy world, he remains twelve even when he "becomes" a member of the French Resistance. These function as two separate existences but, at times, the boundaries become indistinct. The characters in each section are mirror images, with Nazi interrogator Von Strohm taking the place of any male figure who is intimidating or dominating Colin. Such characters form the background to Colin's journey and redemptive experience. Colin is a "man in the process of becoming," as "all movements in the novel, all events and escapades depicted in it" are relevant to his journey of discovery. Bakhtin argues that a key aspect of the bildungsroman form is the hero being "forced to become a new, unprecedented type of human being. . . . What is happening here is precisely the emergence of a new man . . . a historical future."[19]

The "man in process of becoming" and the emergence of a new man are brought together in the man in black who figures strongly as Colin is searching for his self-identity. Throughout the novel, Colin's journey into manhood is problematized by the recurring figure of this man. The man in black is the man Colin will become, but also represents the final separation of Colin from his class, that is, in the death of his mother. At the end of the novel the young Colin confronts the spectral figure of the man in black in his mother's empty bedroom:

> His shadow darkened the doorway. . . . He turned towards the window, and Colin opened his mouth to speak, but the eyes passed over him, unseeing. . . . He was wearing a black suit, and a black tie. He looked out of place in the dingy room,

and not merely because it was empty. He could surely never have belonged here. And yet he looked as if he knew it.

He went across to the place where the bed had been, and stood looking down. He said, in a self-conscious, almost experimental tone, "*Mam?*" . . . Colin backed away. He told himself this was a dream, and soon he would wake up, and all the while he knew he wasn't dreaming. This was more terrifying than any nightmare could have been. He was seeing his own ghost . . .

He didn't like this man. He didn't like his eyes. He didn't like the way he'd said "Mam" as if the word was a foreign language.

"You are not me," Colin said. (152)

The man in black looks completely out of place in the shabby, empty bedroom, but he is clearly a constituent of its history. The excessively uncomfortable behavior emphasizes his estrangement. Colin's response to the sentimentalizing of the man's childhood is "*ballocks.*" It is obvious that Colin rejects this version of himself. The self-conscious tone attached to "*mam*" accentuates the feeling of a life left behind and Barker's precise use of the word is central to the debate on class and estrangement. In "Wordlists 11" Tony Harrison uses the same word about "the tongue I used to know / but can't bone up on now, and that's mi mam's."[20] In both instances, the male's distance from mother, home and class is apparent.

Bakhtin's notion of the carnivalesque also describes Colin's exploration of his masculine identity. According to Bakhtin, carnival abolishes hierarchies and laughter becomes a subversive force. Carnival is approved and sanctioned as a means of averting insurrection and unrest. Traditionally natural "order" is restored at the end of a period of carnival. The disruption of Colin's "real" world by his fantasy world is carnivalesque as identities are transformed and transmuted. This is an exploration of authority as well as identity for Colin. Carnival allows other identities to be tried out and discarded and Barker uses this idea to undercut male authority and to release the male body. Calvin Thomas argues that "the traditional relationship between men and their bodies has never been a spoken one; rather it has been marked by a profound if not pronounced anxiety, one that refuses to speak, refuses to see."[21] The homosocial relationships between young boys are equally important to self-identity and Barker evokes this sympathetically:

A gang of teenage boys had gathered on the steps of the Odeon. Boys Colin knew, from the fourth and fifth year, boys with braying laughs and sudden, falsetto giggles, boys who stood on street corners and watched girls walk past, who punched each other with painful tenderness, who cultivated small moustaches that broke down, when shaved, into crusts of acne thicker than the moustaches had ever been, who lit cigarettes behind cupped hands, narrowing their eyes in pretended indifference to the smoke.

Colin worshipped from a safe distance. (28)

Colin needs to identify with male figures such as these young men as his own insecurity is linked to his lack of identification with a father figure. He is also unsure about the female body, trying to convince himself he is excited by ogling a female undressing via a penny slot-machine and "pressing his cock furtively against the edge of the machine, but he wasn't not really" (40). Just a few moments later, he watches his idol Adrian, "noticing how the brown skin became abruptly white just inside the rolled up sleeves of his shirt"; in looking at another young man, Brian Combey, he notices "the oily skin that seemed to have heat trapped inside it, like tar on roads at the end of a hot day" (41). Colin is clearly moved by these glimpses of the male body, rather than the female. Barker shows the ambivalence of male sexuality and problematizes libidinous pleasures. Whereas Colin remains untouched by a supposedly eroticized female body, he unconsciously recognizes the beauty inherent in maleness and the male body. Colin remains alienated from but identified with the female body but at times he tries to positively reject it. When coming across Brian Combey having sex in the bomb-damaged house, he feels "quite vicious" toward the woman, but "doesn't quite know why" (127). The sexuality of the adult Colin is unknown, and references to his "sensitive mouth" are open to interpretation. However, we are left in no doubt that sexuality and masculinity remain unfixed and transmutable.[22]

In Bernie, the cross-dresser, Barker examines other areas of male identity. Robert Stam agrees that "the notion of bisexuality and the practice of transvestism [are] a release from the burden of socially imposed sex roles."[23] Von Strohm accuses Bernard of dressing as a woman because they "carry fewer identity papers—therefore [have] a lower chance of being found out. *And* they're not liable to forced labour." He asserts that "there are a lot of advantages to being a woman, if you can get away with it. It makes life so much easier" (76). But in Colin's day-to-day world Barker ensures that Bernie's life is not easier because of his appropriation of femininity. Colin first sees Bernie as a grotesque figure, "blond hair, piled high, a black dress with lace round the collar." This incident occurs immediately after he is disappointed with the masculinity exhibited in the war film he has seen. He dislikes the film he saw as "he didn't want to be told about men being frightened. He wanted to be told about heroes" (33). Disbelieving that the woman he sees could be a man, Colin is dared to go and speak to Bernie:

> It isn't true, he thought. And the closer he got the more he was sure that it couldn't be true, because she'd got nylons on, high heels, everything. . . . Colin took a deep breath. "Excuse me, Miss. Have you got the time?"
>
> The face that turned towards him was heavily made up. A shiny cupid's bow mouth had been painted over a thin mouth, and the lipstick had leaked into the creases of the upper lip. As Colin stared, the lips opened and a deep, baritone voice said, "Piss off sonny." (33–34)

The juxtaposing of the two incidents is significant since Bernie becomes Bernard, hero/ine of the Resistance in Colin's fantasies. Is Barker representing transvestite men as heroic? Barker certainly represents those male characters who go against conventional gender performance as brave on one level. Mark Simpson states in "Dragging it Up and Down," that the appropriation of glamor and desirability to the masculine body against the cultural grain does not signify the desire to become a woman: "Men wish to keep their penises" but need to "bind the fear and fascination of the feminine to the male body."[24] Transvestism is thus seen as "a respite" from socially engendered hypocrisy and fear of the body. The feminization of the male body is often equated with weakness and vulnerability but Bernie/Bernard appears to be neither weak nor vulnerable.

Interestingly, it is other men's fears of the male body made grotesque through feminization that are subverted by Barker. Bernie is the hero of the fantasy, but he remains a troubling figure for the other men. Pierre, asks him, "Bernard. . . . There's something that's always . . . worried me. All this dressing as a woman—you *do* do it just for France?" (emphasis added). Bernard does not answer, merely smiles. Barker leaves the question unanswered but demonstrates the fear other men may have of transvestites and the feminized male body. Because Bernie appears in the "real" world as a transvestite we are left to surmise that he does it for his own sense of self. Calvin Thomas also argues that "the dark incontinence of male anxiety" is prevalent in much of male discourse and that masculinity is "always an uneasy process of fluidic self-alteration that calls the solid boundaries of masculinity into question."[25] Colin begins to understand that masculinity is not something that can be easily recognized and understood. He begins to see outside of the constructed images of heroism and bravery that are portrayed in the war films of which he is so fond. He recognizes that masculinity takes many forms. Barker is engaged in the remaking of knowledge about masculinity and Colin's refusal of a single male figure as a role model is important in this context.

The "grotesque body" is also a form of celebration of carnival. Via Bakhtin, Calvin Thomas in his examination of the male argues that the relationship to mythological figures in carnival is "deeply critical and at times resembles a cynical expose." By having the transvestite Bernie/Bernard as the mythical hero of the Resistance, Barker is drawing upon traditional ideas of carnival as a world turned upside down. The authority that is exposed is that of compulsory heterosexuality and its concomitant sense of masculinity. There is a strong sense of "life creating and transforming power" within Bernie/Bernard and a "weakening of [the] one sided seriousness . . . and singular meaning and dogmatism" that is attached to hegemonic masculinity.[26] For Thomas, again following Bakhtin, carnival is characterized by

> its bold and unrestrained use of the fantastic and adventure [that] is internally motivated, justified and devoted to a purely ideational and philosophical end: the creation of *extraordinary situations* for the provoking and testing of a philosophical idea, a discourse, a *truth* embodied in the image of a wise man, the seeker of this truth.[27]

In a further subversion of this idea, Colin, the boy, becomes the "wise man" who is the seeker of truth in male identity. The hero has to descend to other worlds and to wander through fantastic landscapes. Whether Colin *descends* to another world is open to debate, but he indubitably travels to a *different* world. Colin's quest takes him to a fantasy world, a magical place where he finds an *idea* of what it is to be a man, not the truth of masculinity. In Bakhtinian fashion the possibilities of another life are revealed to him at the end of his journey. Colin becomes aware of the possibilities that are open to him as a man and he may choose or reject those possibilities as he wishes.

Barker blends the highs and lows of moral dilemmas, using dialects and jargon, and combining prosaic and poetic speech, also in keeping with carnival. In one short section each of these elements can be seen clearly. Colin is rebuked by his class teacher for being late (as usual) and for answering him back: "'I'm afraid I can't let this go on,' he said. 'You'll have to go and see Mr. Sawdon after Assembly.'" He then turns his attention to all the boys clamoring to leave in a disorderly fashion:

> "What do I mean when I say walk?"
> Most of the class looked puzzled.
> "Jenkins?"
> "You mean WALK, Sir." (60)

Colin's daydreaming in assembly immediately afterward demonstrates the key areas of carnival impudence:

> Mr. Sawdon's prayers, like Pond's lipstick went on and on and on. Colin, forced to keep his eyes shut, passed the time trying to imagine what Mr Sedgewick would be like in bed.
> *"Mildred, what do I mean when I say fuck?"*
> *"Oh, Cedric," gasped Mildred, her long scarlet fingernails plucking at the knot of his pyjama cord. "You mean fuck."* (61–62)

The mask of authority that Mr. Sedgewick dons is swiftly removed; the situation is a form of moral and psychological exploration in both fantasy and reality. By implicating his teacher in the sexual act Colin succinctly undermines any sense of command his teacher has and makes him ridiculous. The incorporation of advertising jargon represents the outside world and the power of media language, while the use of "fuck" conforms to prosaic and "vulgar" speech patterns. This extract shows clearly a style that rejects the "stylistic unity" of a single-voiced narrative.

In examining Barker's narrative techniques and the role of masculinity in *The Man Who Wasn't There,* there is clearly another more shadowy area of the text that is important: the significance of Viv/Vivienne in Colin's search for identity. The mother is often presented as the most meaningful influence in a boy's formation. Boys in one-parent families are frequently seen to encounter problems in the determination of themselves as individuals. Viv is a "glorified waitress . . . dressed as [a] fawn." Every night before she goes to work she has to "steam her ears" as "fawns with bedraggled ears got into trouble, and Viv couldn't afford trouble" (11–12). Even the other women comment on this, "'What is it she calls herself?' said Mrs. Hinde. A waitress? . . . not what they called it in our young day" (25). Colin's teacher also tries to belittle his mother when he discovers Colin does not have a school tie. Colin responds that his mother has better things to spend her money on and Mr. Sedgewick is scathing, "like floppy ears and a cottonwool tail, I suppose" (60). Colin understands the relevance of these comments, but cannot really imagine what it could be like to have another sort of family. He tries to imagine "what it would be like to have been adopted. But of course you couldn't imagine it. Instead of Nan and Viv and Pauline and Mrs. Hennigan, there was just a circle of blank faces" (92). Barker emphasizes the importance of the women, to Colin: "He went to his bedroom, and lay on the bed, and listened as he'd listened many times before, to the sound of women's voices, bringing memories out of their shared store" (92). Importantly, while recognizing the impact of the women, Colin realizes that, "this work of remembering, so careful, so detailed, so intricate, left one enormous gap": knowledge of his identity.

In "The Role of the Father," Ian Harris advances a set of statistics regarding the upbringing of sons, by fathers. He states that in the period in which Barker is writing (the 1980s) 23 percent of fathers are physically absent during their sons' upbringing; 29 percent are psychologically absent; 18 percent are austere, unrealistic and uninvolved; 15 percent are dangerous or out of control, while a mere 15 percent are appropriately involved.[28] Patriarchal law is intrinsically linked to a father figure so what happens when there is literally no father? Danae Clark asserts that "the symbolic power of the father increases where the father is dead or killed," and for Colin this is indicated by the blank space on the birth certificate.[29] Clark also argues that along with the absence of the father there is often a wish to be in the father's place. Colin's feelings for his mother remain problematic throughout the novel. The identification with the mother-figure and the sexual awakening of the adolescent Colin become entangled. When Viv brings home her manager from work Colin watches them furtively:

> His right hand slid down her back, and he felt her bottom, then moved on to her thigh and began rucking up her skirt till her stocking tops showed. . . .
>
> Colin retreated to his bedroom, and shut the door. He lay on the bed, hearing their whispers, the rustle and click of clothes going off, and then the clanging and creaking of springs. . . . He imitated the thrusts of Combey's pelvis but this time it wasn't funny. He felt himself swell and stiffen, his breath caught in his throat, and then all at once, the tension was bursting and flowing out of him. When it stopped, and he could be still again, he flicked back through the images and knew that in the end it hadn't been . . . the unknown woman he'd been thinking about.
>
> He began to rub himself dry on the sheet, feeling small, grubby and alone.
> (129)

Colin's identification with the sexual act and his arousal at the thought of his mother having sex culminate in his ejaculation. This provokes another moment of crisis for Colin and his escape is instantaneous. The fantasy sequence that immediately follows results in the death of Vivienne, the Resistance member who has been sleeping with the Nazi Von Strohm. Fantasy and reality are conjoined as Colin enacts and reenacts the Oedipal myth. When the son's need to displace the father in the mother's affections occurs and there is no father to metaphorically kill, Barker transposes the Oedipal urge onto the mother. Viv has to suffer and Vivienne has to die.

Barker presents the death of his mother's mirror image in the fantasy world and the metaphorical "death" of his mother's lover in a wonderful scene where Colin gets rid of Reg and Colin/Gaston, hero of the resistance, betrays his fellow freedom fighters:

> He turned as Colin came in. "Hello, son."
> *Poking my mother does not give you the right to call me "son."* "Lo."
> . . . Colin stared at Mr. Boyce, turning him first into the Kommandant brutal, blue eyes, skin the colour of pork sausages—and then into a spiv with slickly Brylcreemed hair, shielding a cigarette in his cupped hands, jacket pulled out of shape by dozens of black market nylons. *That* was more *his* style. (136)

Colin is determined to eliminate the man he believes will supplant him in his mother's affections. Whenever he says anything rude to him, Mr. Boyce looks at him "with a tolerant and understanding expression. *Brought up without a father,* he seemed to say. *What else can you expect?*" But Colin knows exactly what will get rid of the rival for his mother's affections:

> "You know me mam and me were talking the other day about what I ought to call you."
> "Ye-es?"
> "Well, you know, 'Mr. Boyce' sounds a bit stand-offish, doesn't it? So me mam was saying she thought I ought to call you Uncle Reg."
> "Good idea," said Mr. Boyce, without a great deal of enthusiasm.
> "I said, why don't I call him 'Dad'?"
> Mr. Boyce seemed a little startled, as if, Colin thought, somebody had just rammed an electric cattle prod up his arse.
> "But me mam says, 'No, Colin, it's a bit early for that.' She says, 'I know it means a lot to you, son, but believe me it's better to wait till we're living together.'"
> *"She said that?"* (136–37)

When he drives away he does not look back and as Viv waits in vain for her lover to return, Colin feels guilty at his annihilation of Mr. Boyce and the assuaging of his guilt occurs in his fantasy world. Gaston must be eliminated as he has betrayed the Resistance and Vivienne is now dead as a result of his duplicity. His death is watched by the people he has betrayed: "*Rifle-fire cracks out, civilians scatter and Gaston throws up his arms, caught like a runner breasting the tape, and held there for a moment before he slowly falls*" (155–56).

By setting the novel against a backdrop of the Second World War, Barker is able to use the unreality of war against Colin's unmanageable reality of having no father. The link between war and psychoanalytic theory is well known. Jacqueline Rose in *Why*

War? persuasively argues that war "has something to say about psychoanalysis . . . [and] its own conception of what constitutes truth." Rose also states that the relationship between war, truth, and knowledge is strong and that the language and discourse of war can evoke "the present as a trope."[30] Colin uses the language of war in his own, private battle to gain selfhood and knowledge of himself. To know himself becomes of primary importance as without that knowledge he cannot resolve the dichotomies and mutually exclusive features he perceives within his personality. Inevitably, the enemy to be fought is none other than himself, the man in black. What Colin knows of reality is insufficient to fight that battle; fantasy enables Colin to locate himself in the interior and exterior worlds that comprise his existence. The internal and external war that Colin is fighting come together when Pierre and Pauline look down from the Lysander and watch Bernard walk away into the distance. Bernard survives the war in order that Colin can understand that masculinity and self-knowledge are never finished products. Bernie/Bernard represents the mutability of masculinity and sexuality. In the final words of the novel, "The End," we see that in his own way Colin begins to understand that. Viv's mothering of Colin bears no resemblance to Hoggart's view of a "good" mother. She is however, a "good" mother. Viv's ability to let Colin "look after himself" allows him to finally destroy the man he *could* become. Barker clearly engages with outmoded ideas of women's roles and regimens through Viv and her extended "family."

In conclusion, Barker debates how society forms and influences masculine models and deploys interrogative narrative techniques to explore how environment forms and shapes us. Colin is a reflection of the society around him, in that both are undergoing profound changes. He is a "man in process" and the events that occur throughout the three days of his "real" life, together with the fantasy world he evokes, form a rites of passage and a transition point in his life. It remains unclear at the end of the novel which direction these changes will take, but Barker answers one of the key questions she believes the novel poses:

> What if you had been born into an all-female family as a boy rather than a girl? Would you not be debilitated by the same facets of your life which for a girl were sources of strength? . . . If a boy were raised by these women, to what extent could he take strength from them and to what extent would it be a threat?[31]

The novel debates that question very specifically and in the end, despite the problems that exist as a boy in an all-female world, Colin derives great strength from his extended "family" of women. Barker examines the response Colin receives from a society that only determines him as a child of an unmarried mother. Angela Hague believes that many writers in postwar Britain use a "picaresque" structure for their observations of "a new class of uprooted people."[32] Barker is part of that tradition of reworking and expanding representations of class, but she takes the debate further, stating: "A great many of the writers I had read, like David Storey and D. H. Lawrence, notably deal partly with growing up in a working-class background, but I didn't find that particularly helpful. I felt the experiences of women was so minimised in their work, and to some extent distorted, that to me there was no way into it."[33] She brings her own special intimacy with her subject to bear, giving primary focus to the position of a child growing up in postwar British society, with all the problems a single, working-class mother has. While foregrounding the experiences of Colin in a mock-heroic journey to selfhood, Barker uses language innovatively and forcefully to celebrate working-class experiences. The multiplicity of voices exemplifies the polyphonic nature of her writing. Through Colin's narrative we see constructions of masculinity being formulated and debated. Barker carries this debate even further in the novels that comprise the First World War trilogy.

NOTES

1. Mikhail Bakhtin, *Problems of Dostoevsky's Poetics,* ed. Caryl Emerson (Minneapolis: University of Minnesota Press, 1984), 108.

2. Pat Barker, *The Man Who Wasn't There* (London: Penguin, 1990), 32–33. All subsequent references will be included in the text.

3. Ian M. Harris, *Messages Men Hear: Constructing Masculinities* (London: Taylor & Francis, 1995), 50, 22.

4. Mikhail Bakhtin, "The Bildungsroman and its Significance in the History of Realism (Towards a Historical Typology of the Novel)," in *Speech Genres and Other Late Essays,* ed. Caryl Emerson and Michael Holquist, trans. Vern W. McGee, 11–12, 15–16 (Austin: University of Texas Press, 1986).

5. Bakhtin's chronotope offers a sense of space and time allowing "the relationship of the artistic image to the new geographically and historically concrete, graphically depicted world" (Emerson and Holquist, 25). Peter Hitchcock also discusses Barker in relation to Bakhtin. He argues that in *Liza's England* the use of time and space offers an analysis of the chronotope: "a key interpretive model of the fundamental historicity of the novel," linking it specifically to Liza's box, which he sees as the "chronotopic locus of the story." Hitchcock is interested in "the possibilities of reading memory through a specific set of time/space relations" in a working-class woman's narrative. This foreshadows how the time-space disruption in *The Man Who Wasn't There* serves to reinforce Barker's interrogation of masculinity. See *Dialogics of the Oppressed* (Minneapolis and London: University of Minnesota Press, 1993), 75.

6. Michael Montgomery, *Carnivals and Commonplaces: Bakhtin's Chronotope, Cultural Studies, and Film* (New York: Peter Lang, 1993), 125–26.

7. Michael Holquist, *Dialogism: Bakhtin and His World* (London: Routledge, 1990), 110.

8. Ibid., 113.

9. This idea may be linked to Jung's concept of mask/face. The mask that is shown to others is described as the reality that is not reality, but that which others see as real. When applied to Colin/Gaston in *The Man Who Wasn't There,* the face/mask becomes inseparable at some points while at other points the distinction is clear.

10. See Anthony Rowland, Emma Liggins, and Eriks Uskalis, "Introduction," in *Signs of Masculinity: Men in Literature 1700 to the Present* (Amsterdam and Atlanta, Ga.: Rodopi, 1998), 3.

11. Roger Horrocks, *Male Myths and Icons: Masculinity in Popular Culture* (London: Macmillan, 1995).

12. Andrew Tolson, *The Limits of Masculinity* (London: Tavistock Press, 1977), 25, quoted in Lynne Segal, *Slow Motion: Changing Masculinities, Changing Men* (London: Virago, 1990),

94. This idea can be said to arise, in part, from D. H. Lawrence's glorification of the phallus and George Orwell's fetishistic description of Chesterton miners: "It is impossible to watch the 'fillers' at work without feeling a pang of envy for their toughness . . . as though they were made of iron . . . splendid men . . . nearly all of them." See *The Road to Wigan Pier* (London: Penguin, 1985), 20–30.

13. I am aware that the "scholarship boy" is an obsolete term, but it is one that pertains particularly to Colin. I use the term as a point of reference to locate Colin within a particular period, the 1950s, and also to dislocate him from his background and his class.

14. See Richard Hoggart, *The Uses of Literacy* (London: Penguin, 1958) and Tony Harrison's poetry, in particular *The School of Eloquence, V,* and *The Loiners.* All references to Harrison's poems are from Tony Harrison, *Selected Poems* (London: Penguin, 1984).

15. Richard Hoggart, "The Scholarship Boy," *The Uses of Literacy,* 292.

16. Hoggart, *The Uses of Literacy,* 295.

17. For example, see Kathleen Woodhead, *Jipping Street;* Arthur Morrison, *A Child of the Jago;* Walter Greenwood, *Love on the Dole;* Alan Sillitoe, *Saturday Night and Sunday Morning;* and Stan Barstow, *A Kind of Loving.*

18. Tony Harrison, "Me Tarzan," *Selected Poems* (London: Penguin, 1984), 116.

19. Bakhtin, *Speech Genres,* 24–25.

20. Tony Harrison, "Wordlists," *Selected Poems,* 118

21. Calvin Thomas, *Male Matters: Masculinity, Anxiety, and the Male Body on the Line* (Urbana: University of Illinois Press, 1996), 12.

22. It is interesting to compare Colin with Billy Prior, especially in terms of Colin's ambivalent sexuality and Prior's bisexuality. *The Man Who Wasn't There* provides a clear framework for the discussion of masculinity and male sexuality that is further debated in the First World War trilogy.

23. Robert Stam, *Subversive Pleasures: Bakhtin, Cultural Criticism, and Film* (Baltimore: Johns Hopkins University Press, 1989), 93.

24. Mark Simpson, "Dragging it Up and Down," in *Male Impersonators* (London: Cassell, 1994), 132

25. Calvin Thomas, *Male Matters,* 16.

26. Ibid., 108.

27. Ibid., 114.

28. Ian Harris, "The Role of the Father," in *Messages Men Hear,* 25.

29. Danae Clark, "Father Figure," in *Boys: Masculinities in Contemporary Culture,* ed. Paul Smith, 23 (Boulder and Oxford: Westview Press, 1996).

30. See Jacqueline Rose, *Why War?* (Oxford: Blackwell, 1993), 25.

31. Donna Perry, *Backtalk: Women Writers Speak Out* (New Brunswick: Rutgers University Press, 1993), 43–61.

32. Angela Hague discusses the narrative style of authors including John Braine, Alan Sillitoe, David Storey, Kingsley Amis, John Wain, and Muriel Spark. See "Picaresque Structure and the Angry Young Novel," *Twentieth Century Literature* 32, no. 2 (Summer 1986): 209–20.

33. Interview with Pat Barker, *Contemporary Authors,* vol. 122, no. 40 (Detroit: Gale, 1986), 40–43. Barker returns to the same idea in Monteith's "Pat Barker," in Sharon Monteith, Jenny Newman, and Pat Wheeler, *Contemporary British Fiction: An Introduction through Interview,* (London: Arnold, 2004), 18–35.

Part Three ■ Men at War

RONALD PAUL

In Pastoral Fields

The *Regeneration* Trilogy and Classic First World War Fiction

In *Heroes' Twilight* (1965), his major study of the literature of the Great War, Bernard Bergonzi paraphrases J. B. Priestley's remark that "the Great War is now as far removed from us in time as the Napoleonic campaigns were from Tolstoy when he began *War and Peace*," adding that "the subject would make a splendid challenge for an ambitious young novelist."[1] Since this was written a similar gap in time has occurred between the publication of the cluster of First World War novels that Bergonzi's critical work covers and the appearance of Pat Barker's *Regeneration* trilogy (1991–95). However, in her own, award-winning literary treatment of the First World War, Barker consciously sought to project a radical shift in ideological perspective, describing the trilogy in an interview she gave for the *Guardian* soon after the Booker Prize ceremony as representing "very much a female view of war."[2] Indeed, apart from Rebecca West's *The Return of the Soldier* (1918) and Virginia Woolf's *Mrs. Dalloway* (1925), which both deal with the traumatic domestic effects of shell shock, all of the contemporary, classic novels of the Great War were written by men whose literary response to war was conditioned by their own personal experience of fighting in the frontline trenches.

On completing *The Ghost Road*, Pat Barker received overwhelming critical acclaim for her trilogy as a work that extended the artistic boundaries of the war novel; the implicit suggestion being that her three novels could be more than equally measured against the great classics of the genre. Although there is no reference to any of these Great War novels in the lists of sources provided in her trilogy, they remain an obvious starting point for any critical appraisal of Barker's work, not least when one considers her own stated literary intention to "humanise the experience of men by thinking of it in terms of what women do."[3] The present essay seeks to explore this particular critical comparison in order to ascertain more exactly what key characteristics the classic war novels might have in common and in what ways Barker's trilogy subsumes or subverts them. To do this, the following selection of some of the most important novels of the period has been made in order to situate Barker's work within a context of internationally recognized First World War narratives written by men: Henri Barbusse's *Under Fire* (1916), John Dos Passos's *Three Soldiers* (1921), Erich Maria Remarque's *All Quiet on the Western Front* (1928), Ernest Hemingway's *A Farewell to Arms* (1929), and Frederic Manning's *The Middle Parts of Fortune* (1930).

Perhaps the greatest antiwar novel from this same period is Jaroslav Hasek's *The Good Soldier Svejk* (1921). However, because of the almost surrealist and certainly satirical mode in which it is written, Hasek's work stands out as a wonderful yet absurdist, literary anomaly within this particular genre. It seems, therefore, rather inappropriate to include it in a critical discussion of the basically naturalistic, semi-documentary approach that Barker shares with the other war novelists mentioned above. A further aesthetic restriction is made in relation to the thinly disguised auto-biographies that were written by several English and American writers who were themselves based as soldiers in France, such as e. e. cummings's *The Enormous Room* (1922), Edmund Blunden's *Undertones of War* (1928), Robert Graves's *Goodbye to All That* (1929), Richard Aldington's *Death of a Hero* (1929), and Siegfried Sassoon's *The Complete Memoirs of George Sherston* (1937).

One particularly fruitful way of addressing some of the fundamental aesthetic dif-ferences between Barker's trilogy and the above selection of classic war novels writ-ten by men is through the concept of the pastoral. Perhaps this may seem a somewhat surprising critical choice at first when one considers the violent aspect of both the setting and the individual experience portrayed by all of these First World War novelists. Indeed, as Paul Fussell points out, the "opposite of experiencing moments of war is proposing moments of pastoral. Since war takes place outdoors and always within nature, its symbolic status is that of the ultimate anti-pastoral."[4] However, when seen as stories primarily written about ordinary working men, albeit in uni-form, there is in fact a precedent for such a critical move. The analytical point of departure here is, of course, William Empson's seminal study, *Some Versions of the Pastoral* from 1935, which sought to reveal how this traditional literary mode could still exert a powerful metaphorical influence on, among other things, the working-class novel. Moreover, by beginning his survey of the pastoral with a chapter on "Pro-letarian Literature," Empson was not seeking to pay only lip service to the vogue of critical appreciation that working-class writing provoked among many intellectuals in the 1930s.

On the contrary he uses a discussion of the more socially oriented versions of the pastoral as a means to pick out some of the fundamental political and aesthetic con-tradictions of so-called proletarian writing itself. Thus by extending the meaning of the pastoral to cover more than mere Arcadian subject matter, Empson indicates how questions of class and ideology, even in works of "good proletarian art," are very often rendered in terms of what he calls "Covert Pastoral."[5] For example, in his focus on the latent political ideas of an early Romantic poem like Thomas Gray's *Elegy Written in a Country Church-Yard* (1751), Empson links the pastoral convention to the way in which peasants and workers are often viewed stereotypically as being either passive victims of fate or wise fools who see further than their more educated masters. Such pastoral tropes Empson found often reproduced uncritically also in the working-class novel, a genre that in the proletarian literary climate of the 1930s tended to transform the worker into something of a "mythical cult-figure." In reality, however, such an aestheticized view of the lower orders only represented a new play on what

Empson describes as the "essential trick of the old pastoral, which was felt to imply a beautiful relation between rich and poor," a narrative strategy that involved making

> simple people express strong feelings (felt as the most universal subject, some-thing fundamentally true about everybody) in learned and fashionable language (so that you wrote about the best subject in the best way). From seeing the two sorts of people combined like this you thought better of both; the best parts of both were used.[6]

Thus, because of the similarly stereotyped perception of the working class found in the novels of the Great War, Empson's critical discussion of the proletarian pastoral appears to have more than a rhetorical bearing on these classic narratives of war. Indeed, a closer examination of the pastoral images of working-class soldiers, as well as of the perceptions of the central male—and often middle-class—protagonist, will not just reveal some of the implicit ideological paradoxes of these First World War novels. Within this context of class and ideology the radical female vision of Barker's trilogy can be viewed as a conscious subversion of the pastoral conventions of such fictionalized encounters between high (officers) and low (soldiers). Moreover, the pastoral subtext that underpins much of the narrative fiction of the First World War has, I would argue, not only a negative influence on the psychological credibility of individual characters, but also affects the whole impact of the antiwar message of the novels themselves. Finally, as a further contrast, the comparison here will also attempt to reveal how Barker's critical awareness of the pastoral tradition allows her to expose such metaphysical images of men at war and bring out the essentially patri-archal and class nature of the military conflict itself.

Another fundamental way in which Barker's trilogy differs from most other Great War narratives is in the absence of any pastoral link between the horrors of the trenches and the idealized images of life at home or behind the lines. At the heart of this lack of illusion is Barker's understanding of the class nature of society, the con-tradictions of which the war only tends to sharpen. In *The Eye in the Door* for exam-ple, Barker projects a view of the home front in Britain as being a place torn by sexual and political tensions, a country at war with itself, a society both repressed and re-pressive. This profound sense of all-pervading social division is given explicit expres-sion through the consciousness of Billy Prior, the central working-class character in the trilogy, who sees little difference between the exploitation of ordinary soldiers in the trenches and the oppression of their lives at home. Thus, the image of Britain, socially and economically divided along class lines, is in complete contrast to the patriotic concept of a nation at one with itself, epitomised by the romantic idea of a rural English retreat far from the rigors of war. In the trilogy, Barker explodes the myth of a classless, pastoral England that was nostalgically evoked and celebrated in prewar Georgian poetry:

> One of the ways in which he felt different from his brother officers, one of the many, was that *their* England was a pastoral place: fields, streams, wooded valleys,

medieval churches surrounded by ancient elms. They couldn't grasp that for him, and for the vast majority of the men, the Front, with its mechanization, its reduction of the individual to a cog in a machine, its blasted landscape, was not a contrast with the life they'd known at home, in Birmingham or Manchester or Glasgow or the Welsh pit villages, but a nightmarish culmination. "Equality not at home in either," Mac had said. He was right.[7]

In comparison, the First World War novels of Hemingway, Dos Passos, Remarque, and West all contain a fundamentally idealized pastoral element that recurs by no means randomly throughout the text. It is in fact used as a central narrative device to underscore the unnatural conditions of life in the war zone. In her analysis of form and ideology in First World War fiction, Evelyn Cobley suggests that these often quite lyrical episodes merely represent a "stilistic luxury" reserved for "nostalgic passages about life before the war or for pastoral moments during which the destruction of war is suspended."[8] However, this narrative antithesis also has a clear ideological edge —the trauma of the trenches is made to appear even more devastating by the inability of the protagonist to ever again feel at ease in the prelapsarian surroundings of home. In Remarque's novel for instance, the stark realism of the portrayal of active service at the front is suddenly displaced by the bucolic sentimentalization of the narrator's description of the peasant village to which he returns on leave, yet toward which he feels a growing sense of alienation:

> It is pleasant to sit quietly somewhere, in the beer garden for example, under the chestnuts by the skittle-alley. The leaves fall down on the table and on the ground, only a few, the first. A glass of beer stands in front of me, I've learned to drink in the army. The glass if half empty, but there are a few good swigs ahead of me, and besides I can always order a second and a third if I wish to. There are no bugles and no bombardments, the children of the house play in the skittle-alley, and the dog rests his head against my knee. The sky is blue, between the leaves of the chestnut rises the green spire of St. Margaret's Church. This is good, I like it. But I cannot get on with the people.[9]

In the narratives of both Hemingway and Dos Passos these pastoral interludes are extended even further, turning the escape into the country—to the mountains of Switzerland or down the river Seine—into a metaphor of the whole personal rejection of war on the part of their main protagonists. Indeed, the war zone itself is quickly relegated to that of a violent but distant backdrop to the more important emotional and aesthetic issues that are raised in the text—in Hemingway, concerning the nature of love and in Dos Passos, the duty of the artist to himself. At this juncture, however, the pastoral element becomes rather more ideologically equivocal. This ambivalence lies, as Terry Gifford points out, at the very heart of the literary convention itself: "Pastoral's celebration of retreat is its strength and its inherent weakness. When retreat is an end in itself, pastoral is merely escapist."[10] In Dos Passos's *Three Soldiers,* the intellectually escapist concerns of Andrews, the artist, are thus set against the romantic peasant nostalgia of Chrisfield, the stoical farm hand, who is more "dully" oblivious to his fate as a soldier. The psychological representation of Chrisfield as the worthy but simple-minded trooper is moreover framed by Dos Passos in terms of almost classic pastoral:

> Then he thought of the spring in the hills of southern Indiana and the mockingbird singing in the moonlight among the flowering locust trees behind the house. He could almost smell the heavy sweetness of the locust blooms, as he used to smell them sitting on the steps after supper, tired from a day's heavy plowing, while the clatter of his mother's housework came from the kitchen. He didn't wish to be back there, but it was pleasant to think of it now and then, and how the yellow farmhouse looked and the red barn where his father never had been able to find time to paint the door, and the tumble-down cowshed where the shingles were always coming off. He wondered dully what it would be like out there at the front. It couldn't be green and pleasant, the way the country was here. Fellows always said it was hell out there. Well, he didn't give a damn. He went to sleep.[11]

As part of the overtly political purpose in writing his antiwar novel, *Under Fire,* Barbusse endows the pastoral elements of his own narrative with an even more pronounced ideological meaning, such as when he portrays a group of French soldiers—poor peasant poilus—on leave in Paris wandering round goggle-eyed at the pleasures of the big city. Here the traditional pastoral binary of nature and culture is reversed in order to underscore the novel's central moral message about the corruption of urban profiteers behind the lines and the sacrifice of ordinary soldiers at the front:

> They have stayed behind in the heart of their own firesides; they have only to stoop to caress their children. We see them beaming in the first starlights of the street, all these rich folk who are becoming richer, all these tranquil people whose tranquillity increases every day, people who are full, you feel, and in spite of all, of an unconfessable prayer. They all go slowly, by grace of the fine evening, and settle themselves in perfected homes, or in cafés where they are waited upon. . . . They make haste into the shadows of security where the others go, where the dawn of lighted rooms awaits them; they hurry towards the night of rest and caresses.
>
> And as we pass quite close to a ground-floor window which is half open, we see the breeze gently inflate the lace curtain and lend it the light and delicious form of a chemise—and the advancing throng drives us back, poor foreigners that we are![12]

Comparing this uncritical reproduction of pastoral tropes in the classic novels of the Great War with, for example, the third volume of Pat Barker's trilogy—*The Ghost Road*—a further narrative break with the tradition can clearly be perceived.

When intertwining scenes from the front line with Rivers's recollections of life in Melanesia, it would certainly have been tempting for Barker to slip into a pastoral transition from images of the slow collapse of Western civilisation on the battlefields of Europe to a contrastingly idyllic representation of noble savages in their South Seas paradise. However, Barker takes care to avoid this Arcadian trap by turning the thematic focus of Rivers's flashbacks onto the patriarchal power structure of these communities themselves, torn between the decline of their own primitive head-hunting culture and the imposition of an encroaching imperialism that is set upon its own brutally exploitive mission. Thus, not only does the fact that the First World War was fought over a redistribution of such colonies implicitly underpin Barker's narrative of Melanesia. The whole attempt by Rivers to come to terms with his own ideological role at Craiglockhart is shown to involve a feverish retrieval of repressed thoughts and emotions concerning the savage behavior of the British in the South Seas:

> Look, you know what the penalties are. If they go on a raid there's no way the British Commissioner isn't going to hear about it. And then you've got a gunboat off the coast, villages on fire, trees cut down, crops destroyed, pigs killed. Screaming women and children driven into the bush. You *know* what happens.[13]

Similarly, in *Regeneration,* the hospital at Craiglockhart, despite its peacefully rural surroundings, is from the outset never depicted as a pastoral haven for the soldiers. On the contrary, the "sheer gloomy, cavernous bulk of the place"[14] provides Barker with an almost Gothic-like setting in which to explore the ideological tensions of Rivers's experimental treatment of his patients and the blood-filled nightmares of death and destruction that haunt them. It is in this context particularly revealing to compare Barker's work with the other two classic First World War novels to deal directly with the same sort of traumatic experience of shell shock—Rebecca West's *The Return of the Soldier* and Virginia Woolf's *Mrs. Dalloway.*

Not only does West rely heavily on the convention of the pastoral in terms of setting—both the rustic glories of Baldry Court and the nostalgic recollections of Monkey Island Inn are painted as delightful, peacetime idylls. The marital conflict resulting from Chris's frontline amnesia is also resolved with predictable pastoral simplicity when Margaret, the wise, working-class matron, defeats the efforts of a Freudian doctor by curing Chris's shell shock herself with a homespun psychological remedy that returns him to the bosom of his upper-class wife. In her discussion of the literary representations of both male and female hysteria, *The Female Malady* (1985), Elaine Showalter praises West's literary handling of the subject, stating that women "understood the lesson of shell shock better than their male contemporaries: that powerlessness could lead to pathology."[15] In particular, Showalter points to "West's understanding of the unconscious motives and symbolic meanings of shell shock" as being both "moving and complex."[16] However, perhaps in her zeal to reassert the literary credentials of neglected female writers, Showalter ignores the fact that West's pioneering attempt to confront the domestic impact of the traumas of war remains marred by a melodramatic adoption of pastoral plot convention and a socially stereotyped portrayal of working-class character.

In her study, *The Great War and Women's Consciousness* (1990), Claire Tylee claims instead that both *The Return of the Soldier* and *Mrs. Dalloway* are not really war books at all, reflecting neither the conditions of fighting at the front, nor the state of British society at home. In contrast Tylee sees these two "women's best-sellers" as attempts to shift the focus onto gender issues raised in the wake of the war:

> Their novels take for granted a common fund of images of the war-zone and of home-front reactions to it. I think these novels have continued to be of interest precisely because of their reliance on generally accepted ideas about the Great War, the use they make of these ideas in their analysis of women's gender identity, especially as it is defined in relation to men.[17]

In Woolf's case, this "common fund of images" includes the use of a classic pastoral binary contrasting the lower-class character of Septimus Warren Smith and that of Clarissa Dalloway, an upper-class society lady. Indeed, Woolf admitted in her own introduction to the novel that Septimus "is intended to be [Clarissa's] double."[18] The prime function of Septimus's condition of shell shock is therefore to act as a pastoral foil, paralleling the novel's real concern, which is with Mrs. Dalloway herself. As Claire Tylee states, Septimus is "the scapegoat for his society's denial of humanity,"[19] whose tragic personal fate provides only the backcloth for Woolf's more fundamental exploration of another trauma—the spiritual death of Clarissa Dalloway, her seemingly perfect party hostess.

It is clear from the above discussion that the reemergence of the pastoral in the ostensibly realistic classics of First World War fiction remains somewhat problematic. However, it is not only the overall narrative thrust of these antiwar novels that is undermined by their authors' reliance on conventional binary contrasts. A further complication involves the portraits of the main protagonists themselves, whose protest against their murderous exposure to trench warfare is more often than not determined by purely aesthetic considerations of personal nonconformity and worth. At the same time, the sensitive, psychological depiction of their individual revolt is often juxtaposed with more brutalized collective images of ordinary soldiers, a narrative contrast that again tends to reproduce the pastoral stereotype of high and low sensibilities.

Thus, when both Henry in *A Farewell to Arms* and Andrews in *Three Soldiers* become deserters, the implication is that their actions represent not a rejection of war itself, rather of the impositions of army discipline that interfere with the fulfillment of their own private—emotional and spiritual—pursuits. The personal and not political nature of Henry's act is strikingly revealed in his unhesitant shooting of an Italian sergeant who tries to run away himself during the retreat from the front. Moreover, in *Three Soldiers,* as Evelyn Cobley points out, Andrews's "liberatory aspirations are not intimately connected with the war."[20] In actual fact, the whole purpose of novel's wartime setting seems merely to provide Dos Passos with an excuse to portray the more existential problems of individual, aesthetic creation, rather than explore the essential nature of the conflict itself. Similarly, Bourne, the intellectually dissident hero of Frederic Manning's *The Middle Parts of Fortune,* is also shown to express a remarkably insensitive reaction to the repeated desertion of one of the other ordinary soldiers at the front:

He would be better dead, and then a man's riddling conscience would ask no more questions about him: one felt even a little impatient at the thought of a court-martial and a firing-party, senseless parades clothed in the forms of law. To keep him like this, exhibiting him to the battalion, was not a warning or a deterrent to other men: it merely vexed them. He should have been killed cursorily: but as they evidently did not intend to kill him, he should have been sent away. He was no longer a man to them: he was a ghost who unfortunately hadn't died.[21]

Perhaps even more noteworthy in these classic male narratives, when one considers their literary reputation as outstanding examples of antiwar protest novels, are the individual attitudes to the war itself on the part of their main characters. Again, these appear often much more ambivalent than one might expect. Bourne, for instance, admires the pastoral stoicism of the French peasantry, whom he thinks view war as "one of the blind forces of nature"; something as metaphysically indeterminable as the occasional ruin of their crops:

Their attitude, in all its simplicity, was sane. There is nothing in war which is not in human nature; but the violence and passions of men become, in the aggregate, an impersonal and incalculable force, a blind and irrational movement of the collective will, which one cannot control, which one cannot understand, which one can only endure as these peasants.[22]

In other novels, such passive resignation is sometimes translated into feelings of almost active moral support, at least with respect to the war effort in general, rather than one's own personal contribution to it. Henry, in *A Farewell to Arms,* argues, for example, with those ordinary Italian soldiers in the ambulance corps who are instinctively against the war for reasons of personal and class allegiances. With the usual male bravado of the classic Hemingway hero, Henry defends the fighting in terms of the private honor of the men:

"I believe we should get the war over," I said. "It would not finish it if one side stopped fighting. It would only be worse if we stopped fighting."
"It could not be worse," Passini said respectfully. "There is nothing worse than war."
"Defeat is worse."
"I do not believe it," Passini said still respectfully. "What is defeat? You go home."
"They come after you. They take your home. They take your sisters."[23]

This aesthetic blurring of the private and the public is also one of the prime, ideological focal points of Pat Barker's trilogy, where the complex psychology of the individual response to war is set clearly within a framework of warring social forces. At the same time Barker never compromises the critical realism of her narrative by a recycling of pastoral tropes in an attempt to add a seemingly mythic quality to the text.

On the contrary, by moving from the individual, pacifist protest of Siegfried Sassoon against the mismanagement of the war to the more militant antiwar campaign of working-class socialists like Mac and Beatie, the whole thrust of Barker's trilogy is toward a comprehensive rejection of war as being the result of a patriarchal, class-based society, against which it is necessary to struggle. "Looking straight at the world is part of your duty as a writer," is how she herself defines this function of her work.[24] Moreover, even the central question of shell shock itself is socially contextualized in terms of the murderous monotony of life in the trenches. Apart from this radical gender twist she gives to the psychological breakdown of men domesticated and totally disempowered in their dugouts, even the different symptoms of their neurosis are shown to be determined by the class background of the victims, as in the case of Billy Prior's inability to speak:

> Mutism seems to spring from a conflict between *wanting* to say something, and knowing that if you *do* say it the consequences will be disastrous. So you resolve it by making it physically impossible for yourself to speak. And for the private soldier the consequences of speaking his mind are always going to be far worse than they would be for an officer. What you tend to get in officers is stammering. And it's not just mutism. All the physical symptoms: paralysis, blindness, deafness. They're all common in private soldiers and rare in officers. It's almost as if for the . . . labouring classes illness *has* to be physical. They can't take their condition seriously unless there's a physical symptom.[25]

Barker has admitted that she "loves" Billy Prior who, as a character, was "constructed to get up Rivers's nose."[26] However, his function is not only to play the Devil's Advocate whose comments and questions are meant to engender doubts in Rivers himself about his treatment of the patients. Billy's own emergence as the key character in the trilogy also brings together the issues of gender, class, and collective violence that form the connecting themes of Barker's three novels and that are refracted through the rebellious consciousness and behavior of this working-class underdog, homosexual, and shell-shocked soldier. Moreover, it is this conflation of the personal and the political that makes Barker's portrait of First World War Britain such a powerful, ideological statement. Thus, Billy's voluntary return to the front lines at the end of the trilogy is not meant to represent a confirmation of the personal success of River's particularly brand of Freudian therapy, but the ultimate condemnation of the whole patriarchal edifice on which it rests. Despite the relative humaneness of his treatment, in the final analysis it remains a fundamental support to a war effort that keeps on sending young men to their deaths. Barker's trilogy concludes, therefore, with a rejection of war that is neither aesthetic nor metaphysical, but stems from a realization of the very tangible and often devastating, ideological impact that patriarchal structures have on the lives of ordinary people.

Like Barker's trilogy, most of the classic narratives of the First World War also share a reliance on the revulsion produced in the reader's mind toward the horrors of trench warfare that are graphically depicted in the text. Indeed, they all tend to include a climactic set-piece in which an actual battle is described naturalistically in all its confusion and terror. In the novels of Manning, Remarque, and Barker herself the moral force of this final scene is also linked to the death of the main protagonist.

As part of his didactic purpose, Barbusse, for example, uses the aftermath of the battle at the end of *Under Fire,* when the surviving soldiers are literally stuck in a sea of mud in no-man's-land, to orchestrate a Greek chorus of antiwar protest and lamentation. However, the image of the ordinary soldiers foundering helplessly in mud-filled craters, is not only one of both physical and mental entrapment. The men themselves are also rendered metaphorically in terms of wild animals, herded together for slaughter:

> They snarled and growled like wild beasts on that sort of ice-floe contended for by the elements, in their dismal disguise of ragged mud. So huge was the protest thus rousing them in revolt that it choked them.
>
> "We're made to live, not to be done in like this!"
>
> "Men are made to be husbands, fathers—*men,* what the devil!—not beasts that hunt each other and cut each other's throats and make themselves stink like all that."
>
> "And yet, everywhere—everywhere—there are beasts, savage beasts or smashed beasts. Look, look!"[27]

Similar dramatic tropes of men portrayed as beasts are to be found throughout the classic narratives of the Great War. Their recurrence, however, involves more than just a question of unreflected, figurative catchphrases. Once again, it can be traced to a basic pastoral perception of ordinary people as always being on the receiving end of fate, as an anonymous and often brutalized mass, against which the lives of heroic and certainly more emotionally complex characters may be set. In classic First World War fiction, the stereotyped pastoral images of simple shepherds are, however, taken a metaphorical step further with the peasants themselves being turned into sheep. Such animal imagery abounds in all the Great War novels and reflects the perennial literary trap into which middle-class writers often fall of portraying working-class or peasant characters as either worthy victims or comic dupes. Even Barbusse—whose novel was regarded by Lenin himself as representing a new type of revolutionary fictional reaction to war, which was, he said, "depicted with extraordinary power, talent and truthfulness"[28]—makes a clear, aesthetic distinction between the elevated mind of his narrator and the obscurer mentality of his fellow soldiers:

> I look at them all, plunged in the abyss of passive oblivion, some of them seeming still to be absorbed in their pitiful anxieties, their childish instincts, and their slave-like ignorance.[29]

Although mostly written by authors who came from the middle-class, the narratives of the Great War nevertheless all seem to share a certain ambition to capture the experience of the ordinary working-class soldiers at the front. In fact, Barbusse himself wrote explicitly that "the ex-soldier bearing the scars of war is nothing other than the bloody symbol of the entire working class."[30] However, the semiautobiographical narrative technique of focusing primarily on a protagonist, usually a member of the middle class, creates an inevitable psychological distance between the observer and the social world from which he feels personally estranged. Moreover, at this very juncture the pastoral convention begins to jar and the whole gamut of animal imagery loses its Arcadian appeal. Empson's "mythical cult-figure" of the worker in proletarian novels becomes transformed in classic Great War fiction into an alien creature, at once less romantic and clearly more threatening. Thus, the soldiers are perceived as animals not only by Barbusse; they appear as "wild beasts" in Remarque's novel,[31] while Manning describes them as "nocturnal beasts of prey, hunting each other in packs."[32] Similarly, Dos Passos's favorite antiwar trope is the collective brutalization of the troops which also turns the three main protagonists into dumb animals, an image that is constantly repeated in the text. On joining up, Andrews feels he is being carried away "as in a stampede of wild cattle";[33] Fuselli experiences a similar sense of "being as helpless as a sheep in a flock";[34] while Chrisfield "felt powerless as an ox under the yoke."[35] Even in Hemingway, whose novel centers almost exclusively on the emotional life of an individual suffocated by war, the metaphor he uses to symbolize the death of ordinary soldiers is once more that of the slaughterhouse—their "sacrifices were like the stockyards at Chicago if nothing was done with the meat except to bury it."[36]

Although Barker herself refers early on in her trilogy to soldiers being "pack animals," the context is that of an angry retort by Billy Prior directed against the fundamental class distinctions between officers and men at the front: "What you wear, what you eat. Where you sleep. What you carry. The men are pack animals."[37] Thus, as throughout her trilogy, Barker complicates the image of working-class soldiers being marginalized and then mangled as mere cannon-fodder by focusing on the essential class nature of their predicament. Through the conflicting range of Billy's reactions to the war Barker not only succeeds in giving working-class soldiers a representative voice, but also avoids the pastoral trope of portraying them as a mass of potentially dead animal meat. It is significant also to note that Barker repeats the pack horse metaphor at the end of *Regeneration* in order to explode the whole concept of control and manipulation that underpins the perception of ordinary soldiers as being dumb, brutalized victims. The harrowing scene of Callan's oral electrocution that culminates the first volume of the trilogy (*Regeneration*) evokes this expressed animal connotation, when Rivers reflects upon his own and Dr. Yealland's role in the forced rehabilitation of the soldiers in their care:

> *A horse's bit.* Not an electrode, not a teaspoon. A bit. An instrument of control. Obviously he and Yealland were both in the business of controlling people. Each of them fitted young men back into the role of warrior, a role they had—however unconsciously—rejected.[38]

The whole question of the authorial choice of figurative language is therefore not just a purely linguistic one. On the contrary, the uncritical recoining of pastoral conventions in classic Great War fiction creates in fact a damaging deflection of their aesthetic preoccupations away from the realistic and toward a more stereotypical depiction of the experience of war. It also seriously undermines the ideological—

antiwar—message of the novels themselves, as transmitted through the thoughts and experiences of the protagonists. It is this final critical point that I wish to explore in more detail in the latter part of the essay.

In *The Outsider* (1956), his post-postwar study of existentialism in modern literature, Colin Wilson singles out Hemingway's portrait of Frederick Henry in *A Farewell to Arms* as a "skilful evocation of the sense of meaningless, of confusion, of the soldier in a strange country."[39] Barbusse's work is also mentioned as portraying the classic figure of the outsider. The alienation of twentieth-century man is, of course, one of the great themes of modernist literature of which Hemingway's war novel in particular is a prominent, early example. There is, however, a critical point that can be made in connection with Wilson's existential characterization, which applies to all the classic Great War narratives and that reflects a fundamental aesthetic contradiction in their depiction of war. The sense of psychological estrangement experienced at the front appears curiously ambiguous when such individual feelings of alienation are directed against the mass of fellow soldiers rather than the war effort itself. The fact that the actual fighting is, as has been noted, relegated to a dramatic backcloth, against which the emotional turmoil of the main protagonist is set, is also something which fits uneasily with the otherwise epic scope of the novels themselves. Even when this is politically motivated, as in the case of Barbusse's literary narrator who seeks expressly to retell the story of the common soldier, his encounter with the other poilus in the trenches has all the pastoral elements of paternal condescension:

> Barque notices that I am writing . . .
>
> "Tell me, you writing chap, you'll be writing later about soldiers, you'll be speaking of us, eh?"
>
> "Why yes, sonny, I shall talk about you, and about the boys, and about our life." . . .
>
> "Tell me, then . . . if you make the common soldiers talk in your book, are you going to make them talk like they *do* talk, or shall you put it all straight—into pretty talk? It's about the big words that we use." . . . "I shall put the big words in their place, dadda, for they're the truth."[40]

In the case of Manning's *The Middle Parts of Fortune,* a novel that Hemingway himself considered "the finest and noblest book of men in war that I have ever read" and that he said he reread every year in order to remember "how things really were so that I will never lie to myself nor to anyone else about them,"[41] the narrative is perhaps more than any other Great War novel defined by this pastoral ethos. Despite his bold reproduction of the obscenities of authentic working-class speech, Manning's portrayal of the relationship between Bourne and the rest of the men in the battalion remains ideologically enmeshed in the pastoral tropes of patronizing aloofness:

> They were mere automatons, whose only conscious life was still in England. He felt curiously isolated even from them. He was not of their county, he was not even of their country, or their religion, and he was only partially of their race. When they spoke of their remote villages and hamlets, or sleepy market-towns

in which nothing happened except the church clock chiming the hour, he felt like an alien among them; and in the vague kind of home-sickness which troubled him he did not seek company, but solitude.[42]

Furthermore, the pastoral stereotyping of these narratives seems to have produced another critical blindness that impinges once again upon the apparently comprehensive, epic realism of their portrayal of war. Despite the fact that, according to Elaine Showalter, by 1916 shell shock "accounted for as much as 40 per cent of the casualties in the fighting zones,"[43] its existence is hardly acknowledged in these early war novels written by men. Such a remarkable case of collective literary amnesia suggests that perhaps the writers themselves shared a sense of masculinist denial of the trauma at the time. Indeed, the few cursory references in their novels to individual cases tend to support this supposition. Dos Passos for instance mentions only one shell-shocked trooper whose constant screaming causes the victim to be strangled by the orderlies because he "got their goat."[44] In Remarque's novel, a similarly brutal male response is also clearly condoned when a hysterical young recruit is beaten up by the older men:

Though he raves and his eyes roll, it can't be helped, we have to give him a hiding to bring him to his senses. We do it quickly and mercilessly, and at last he sits down quietly.[45]

This obliviousness to patriarchal attitudes on the part of the male chroniclers of war is in stark contrast to the way in which Barker genders the trauma of shell shock by portraying men who feel emasculated and threatened by such traditionally female expressions of hysteria. At the same time, her narrative strategy of moving the focus away from the trenches and onto the victims at home not only questions the mythically heroic connotations of the battlefield. The view that underpins such a narrative shift is that shell shock represents, in fact, one of the most sane and healthy reactions to the madness of war. This same madness Barker sees spreading throughout the whole power structure of society, the claustrophobic and conspiratorial neuroses of which she hauntingly evokes in *The Eye in the Door*. Moreover, in the final volume of her trilogy (*The Ghost Road*), the switch between Melanesia and the mud-filled trenches of Western Europe provides the narrative basis for a profound exposure of the patriarchal cult of violence that is promoted by both the headhunters of the South Seas and the Chiefs of Staff in London. Her conclusion, as she herself has admitted, is as disconcerting as it is unequivocal: "Violence is the negative core of masculinity."[46] This fundamental awareness of the ideological nexus between patriarchy and the organized mass murder of young working-class men in the trenches forms the core of Barker's literary indictment of war.

In this comparison between Pat Barker's *Regeneration* trilogy and a selection of classic First World War fiction I have sought to reveal some of the characteristic pastoral limitations of these earlier narratives, as well as the literary accomplishment of Barker's work in revitalizing the genre of the antiwar novel. Through her deep insight into both working-class life and the ideological workings of patriarchal society she has, I believe, succeeded in bridging the aesthetic gap between literature and the politics of gender and class by portraying the experience of men at war in a radically innovatory way. In critical retrospect, her prize-winning *Regeneration* trilogy not only represents a crowning artistic achievement, but will, without doubt, stand out as one of the finest works of antiwar fiction the twentieth century has produced.

NOTES

1. Bernard Bergonzi, *Heroes' Twilight: A Study of the Literature of the Great War* (London: Constable, 1965), 219.
2. Quoted in Francis Spufford, "Exploding the Myths: An Interview with Booker Prize–Winner Pat Barker," *Guardian Supplement,* November 9, 1995, 3.
3. Ibid.
4. Paul Fussell, *The Great War and Modern Memory* (Oxford: Oxford University Press, 1977), 231.
5. William Empson, *Some Versions of the Pastoral* (Harmondsworth: Penguin Books, 1996), 13.
6. Ibid., 17.
7. Pat Barker, *The Eye in the Door* (1993), rpt. in *The Regeneration Trilogy* (London: Viking, 1996), 307.
8. Evelyn Cobley, *Representing War: Form and Ideology in First World War Narratives* (Toronto: University of Toronto Press, 1996), 96.
9. Erich Maria Remarque, *All Quiet on the Western Front,* trans. A. W. Wheen (St. Albans: Mayflower Books, 1976), 110.
10. Terry Gifford, *Pastoral* (London: Routledge, 1999), 47
11. John Dos Passos, *Three Soldiers* (New York: Modern Library, 1932), 136.
12. Henri Barbusse, *Under Fire,* trans. W. Fitzwater Wray (London: Dent, 1975), 300–301.
13. Pat Barker, *The Ghost Road* (1995), rpt. in *The Regeneration Trilogy,* 537.
14. Pat Barker, *Regeneration* (1991), rpt. in *The Regeneration Trilogy,* 10.
15. Elaine Showalter, *The Female Malady: Women, Madness, and English Culture, 1830–1980* (London: Virago Press, 1996), 190.
16. Ibid., 191.
17. Claire Tylee, *The Great War and Women's Consciousness* (Iowa City: Iowa University Press, 1990), 141.
18. Virginia Woolf, quoted in David Bradshaw, introduction to *Mrs. Dalloway* (Oxford: Oxford University Press, 2000), xxi.
19. Tylee, *The Great War,* 164.
20. Cobley, *Representing War,* 160.
21. Frederic Manning, *The Middle Parts of Fortune* (Harmondsworth: Penguin, 1990), 122–23.
22. Ibid., 108–9.
23. Ernest Hemingway, *A Farewell to Arms* (London: Grafton, 1987), 40.
24. Quoted in Spufford, "Exploding the Myths," 3.
25. Barker, *Regeneration* (1991), rpt. in *The Regeneration Trilogy,* 87–88.
26. Quoted in Spufford, "Exploding the Myths," 3.
27. Barbusse, *Under Fire,* 329.
28. V. I. Lenin, *On Literature and Art* (Moscow: Progress Publishers, 1970), 132.
29. Barbusse, *Under Fire,* 185.

30. Henri Barbusse, "Writing and War," in *New Masses: An Anthology of the Rebel Thirties*, ed. Joseph North, 212 (New York: International Publishers, 1972).

31. Remarque, *All Quiet on the Western Front*, 78.

32. Manning, *The Middle Parts of Fortune*, 40.

33. Dos Passos, *Three Soldiers*, 23.

34. Ibid., 72.

35. Ibid., 166.

36. Hemingway, *A Farewell to Arms*, 133.

37. Barker, *Regeneration* (1991), rpt. in *The Regeneration Trilogy*, 61.

38. Ibid., 209.

39. Colin Wilson, *The Outsider* (London: Victor Gollancz, 1956), 34.

40. Barbusse, *Under Fire*, 167–68.

41. Quoted in Paul Fussell, Introduction to Frederic Manning, *The Middle Parts of Fortune* (Harmondsworth: Penguin Books, 1990), xvi.

42. Manning, *The Middle Parts of Fortune*, 54.

43. Showalter, *The Female Malady*, 168.

44. Dos Passos, *Three Soldiers*, 92.

45. Remarque, *All Quiet on the Western Front*, 76.

46. Quoted in Spufford, "Exploding the Myths," 3.

KARIN E. WESTMAN

Generation Not Regeneration

Screening out Class, Gender, and Cultural Change in the Film of *Regeneration*

A dapting a novel for the screen often requires selecting one or two of the narrative threads of the novel to stand for the whole. Faced with the difficult task of bringing Pat Barker's intricately woven *Regeneration* (1991) to the big screen, director Gillies MacKinnon and screenwriter Allan Scott chose to focus on the relationship between the older Dr. W. H. R. Rivers and three young patients at Craiglockhart War Hospital: Siegfried Sassoon, Wilfred Owen, and the fictional Billy Prior. Though the result is a very fine film that speaks to the psychological damage of war, *Regeneration* (1997, 113 minutes) is not the cinematic embodiment of Barker's *Regeneration*.[1] MacKinnon and Scott streamline Barker's narrative to emphasize the conflict between the old and the young. As a result, the themes of class and gender that shape the narrative of *Regeneration*—the very themes that mark the continuity of the novel with Barker's earlier fiction—are muted on the screen. Barker's novel shows men and women seeking regeneration from debilitating psychological pressures brought into relief by the war; in the hands of MacKinnon and Scott, the novel becomes a film about the conflict between two generations of men, a conflict enacted through war. The film resolves this conflict by ending with the end of the war and by granting wisdom to the old through the sacrifices and experiences of the young. Its streamlined narrative, though, leaves both generations powerless to explain fully *why* the conflict persists in their culture. Bereft of Barker's commentary on class, gender, and the shaping power of the imagination, the characters of the film as well as its audience are left without the means to alter the future of their culture—a much more certain, and yet less hopeful, conclusion to the characters' predicaments than the novel provides.[2]

Generational conflict is certainly one of Barker's themes in *Regeneration,* just as it appears in other novels, for example in the tension between Tom Seymour, a child psychologist, and the now-grown child murderer Danny Miller of *Border Crossing* (2001). Yet Barker has always been as interested in beneficial similarities between generations as much as divisive differences. Her first novel, *Union Street* (1982), traces the debilitating consequences of inherited pain and suffering, but at the end of the novel we also watch the dying Alice encounter the youthful Kelly as "the withered

hand and the strong young hand met and joined."[3] The growing friendship between
the elderly Liza Jarrett and the young social worker Stephen in *Liza's England* (1986)
is an extended example of generational conflict resolving into emotional, if not
social, change. In *Regeneration,* the benefits of cross-generational connection take on
additional thematic and symbolic weight, so that Barker's historical novel may represent and interrogate the culture that has created the possibility for war and for its
continuation. Barker has challenged the designation "historical novel" for *Regeneration;* the term too frequently suggests that a novel has no connection to the present,
she tells interviewer Wera Reusch. However, Barker also believes that "the historical
novel can be a backdoor into the present."[4] To connect past and present, older and
younger generations, seems very much the goal behind Barker's decision to write
about the First World War. Encouraging her readers to see the past as part of the present, Barker seeks both to represent and to initiate cross-generational exchange.

In the novel *Regeneration,* cross-generational connections develop from Rivers's
unspoken reflections on his own life and on his patients' experiences, as well as from
Rivers's contributions to conversations with Sassoon, Prior, and other patients. These
comparisons appear quite explicitly within the narrative's free indirect discourse: "In
some ways the experience of these young men paralleled the experience of the very
old," Rivers thinks, after visiting his men's club with Sassoon.[5] Other comparisons
emerge from the development of Rivers's thoughts, as when he pauses to analyze the
link between a vivid dream from which he has awoken (a disturbing memory of his
experiments on nerve regeneration with his friend and colleague, Henry Head) and
the method of treatment he employs at Craiglockhart. His mind turns to the gender
roles he and his patients are expected to assume, and Rivers realizes the degree to
which he is implicated in the process of treatment:

> In leading his patients to understand that breakdown was nothing to be ashamed
> of, . . . he was setting himself against the whole tenor of their upbringing. They'd
> been trained to identify emotional repression as the essence of manliness. . . . And
> yet he himself has been a product of the same system, even perhaps a rather
> extreme product. . . . In advising his young patients to abandon the attempt at
> repression and to let themselves *feel* the pity and terror their war experience
> inevitably evoked, he was excavating the ground he stood on. (48)

Rivers's comments to his patients similarly acknowledge their common ground.
Rivers can admit, with biting humor, to Prior's ability to make him feel more like a
patient than a doctor: "Is that the end of my appointment for today, Mr. Prior?" (97),
and he can reassure Sassoon about his hallucinations by sharing his own hallucinatory experience on the Solomon Islands, when he heard the paddling of the dead
across the bay (188). In both cases, Rivers readily allows his authority over his
patients to be complemented by his empathy for them. Indeed, he even acknowledges
to himself during a session with Prior that "he would have tackled [the traumas of
warfare] in exactly the same way" (79). Rivers also recognizes how the authority and
comfort he offers to his patients casts him as a "mother," just as his patients enact a

maternal role for their soldiers in the field (106–8). As readers, then, we learn that Rivers considers himself a patient as much as a doctor, a son and a mother as much as a father.

Cross-generational connections appear through the representation of social class in the novel as well. Rivers's friendship with Sassoon and his relationship with Prior reveal how class privilege is a recurring pattern of cultural experience across generations, not representative of one moment in history. The strong friendship Rivers develops with Sassoon builds a bridge across the thirty-odd years between their ages, and that bridge is built upon their shared cultural capital. Rivers's form of address to Sassoon indicates class difference: Second-Lieutenant Sassoon soon becomes "Siegfried" while Second-Lieutenant Prior remains "Mr. Prior" or "Prior" for the duration of his stay in Rivers's care. The world to which Sassoon belongs—a world of hunting, university, and powerful friends—is familiar to Rivers even if, as the son of a clergyman, he did not participate directly in its riches. Having quickly established so comfortable a relationship with his patient that they are able to discuss Sassoon's homosexuality, Rivers offers to suggest Sassoon for membership at his club, so Sassoon can have "an alternative base" beyond the walls of Craiglockhart (70). Sassoon's ready assent and his familiarity with the world of the club speak to his willingness to partake of this privilege. Prior and Rivers's other patients, by contrast, do not receive such accommodation; it never crosses Rivers's mind to extend to them the same opportunity. Although otherwise attuned to the ideological obligations and tensions within his culture, Rivers remains relatively blind to his own role in its class system. When Rivers hears Prior's Northern accent, he judges it in conjunction with his combative demeanor; he cannot but peg Prior as a "little, spitting, sharp-boned alleycat" (49). Prior's determination to open Rivers's eyes to class difference reveals Rivers to be a man who resides on the borders of upper-class affiliation as much as a man firmly entrenched in the world of "the club": the khaki of Rivers's shirt is "borderline," according to Prior, while Prior admits his own is "nowhere near" what it should be for an upper-class officer (66). Although Rivers drifts toward Prior's social position, he only ever grudgingly accepts a cross-generational connection with Prior; instead, Rivers fosters his connection to Sassoon.

The film *Regeneration,* in contrast to the novel, repeatedly elides the cross-generational connections briefly outlined above in order to emphasize its selected theme of generational conflict. As a result, the film locates the persistence of war in an older generation's belated awareness of its failings, rather than in systemic tensions within the culture as a whole. Elision of the cross-generational connections of the novel—and consequently its complexity of themes and its social commentary—occurs in four ways. The film maintains a single, omniscient point of view based primarily on visual cues in place of Barker's shifting third-person narrative and free indirect style; the film transposes and reassigns characters' speeches; the film alters the plot of the novel's narrative and its ending; and, finally, the film erases an important narrative thread central to a novel about memory, creation, and regeneration: the power of the imagination.

A DIFFERENT KIND OF REALISM

From its opening scenes that pan across a gruesome battlefield writhing with inde-terminate life and shift to observe the liquid brilliance of the Scottish woods, the film *Regeneration* emphasizes a visual experience of Barker's novel. By offering the novel's narrative from the omniscient camera eye,[6] the film removes the shifting perspectives that Barker's free indirect style creates and undermines our emotional alignment with individual characters, particularly Rivers. Of course, restriction to a single view-point is often necessary when transposing a realistic novel for the screen; the audi-ence would expect a degree of realism in the cinematic form and a consistent point of view is required to convey this realism. Yet for the novel Barker employs psycho-logical realism; this type of realism tends to place greater emphasis on the develop-ment of characters' thoughts and on their emotional responses to their world rather than emphasizing the visual details of the world they inhabit. Barker also keeps her third-person narrator in constant motion, moving between characters' minds and experiences, even venturing at moments into first person. In the nine pages of chap-ter 1, for instance, the point of view shifts from Rivers to Sassoon, and then back to Rivers. As readers, we are constantly in motion between characters and aligned with any one character's point of view, most often Rivers. As a result, we therefore stay connected to *one* of the character's experiences at each moment of the narrative. The decision to film *Regeneration* from an omniscient point of view, therefore, prevents the degree of movement *between* generations which the narrative of the novel allows. Without this degree of movement, the audience loses the narrative impetus to see connections between characters and their emotional experiences.

Barker's chosen narrative form is also relatively uninterested in setting: while read-ing the novel, our focus remains on the characters' emotions and not on the room they are in or the landscape outside their window. The film, by contrast, revels in its recreation of hospital and grounds. One of the few details the reader learns about Craiglockhart, for instance, is the absence of locks on patients' doors. That single detail conveys a wealth of emotional experience about those who live within its wards. To recreate the world of Craiglockhart for a realistic film, however, demands an influx of visual detail: plush carpets, dark gleaming woods, doors, blankets, and so on. Such visual cues do attune the viewer to the class privilege of Craiglockhart's facility as well as the year of the action of the novel (1917), but the consequences also include a greater emphasis on the patients' immediate surroundings rather than their emotional experiences.

Adding to this shift in emphasis, the film persistently relocates scenes between patients from the nondescript interiors they occupy in the novel to the lush grounds of Craiglockhart, exposing them to a natural world (idyllic or destructive) which buffers or buffets their relationships. Why relocate conversations between Rivers and Prior or between Rivers and Sassoon to a stone terrace or path outside the hospital, instead of presenting those doctor/patient meetings as they occur in the novel, within Rivers's office or the patient's room? The shift from a private to a public space increases the formality of the conversations, particularly in the case of Sassoon, who remains "Sassoon" and does not become "Siegfried" as he does in the novel. This change of setting also alters our relationship to the characters, who appear as smaller figures against the bulk of Craiglockhart's façade or upon the horizon of the landscape. At such moments in the film, then, we experience the characters from distant vantage points as figures in the natural scene, in contrast to our experience during the narrative of the novel, where we only know about the weather or trees when those natural features become important to an individual's experience of the world. Add to these changes the willingness of the film to offer visual representations of the war itself right from the opening (an observation addressed in greater detail below) and to juxtapose images of war with scenic vistas of Scotland, and we have arrived at a very different experience of Barker's characters: a vision that asks us to remember the historical moment of 1917 and the characters' place in a larger canvas of action, rather than to observe the similarities between their emotional experiences in the present of the film's narrative.

SPEECH ACTS

Just as MacKinnon creates a single omniscient point of view in place of Barker's multiple perspectives, reversing our proximity to the characters' emotional experiences, the film's translation of Barker's prose to the screen discourages cross-generational connections between characters and even reassigns characters' speeches to heighten tensions between the old and the young. When Rivers's private thoughts are not translated to the screen and when his public responses to his patients are altered, generational difference and antagonism dominate the film. The omission of Rivers's private reservations about taking Sassoon's case exemplifies these changes. Near the beginning of the film, when Rivers and Sassoon meet for the first time, the camera privileges the development of Sassoon's character over Rivers's character: the camera allows us to observe what Barker calls Sassoon's "small, private victory over fear" as Sassoon enters Craiglockhart (9). However, we are not privy to the struggle that has been simmering within Rivers or to Rivers's own "small, private victory" in deciding to take Sassoon's case, since doing so will require him to wrestle with his own beliefs about the war (8–9). In omitting some expression of Rivers's reservations, the film denies its viewers the initial complexity of Rivers's character: he is a medical officer who proceeds with his duty, rather than a doctor who wonders if he can fulfill his duty as an officer. This pattern of omission and revision, established at the start of the film, persists throughout, with the result that much of the insight we gain into Rivers's character through third-person narrative in the novel is not translated into dialogue or action in the script of the film.

Even more surprising for the reader of Barker's novel might be the film's alignment of *both* Prior and Sassoon against Rivers, as revision comes close on the heels of omission in the development of Rivers's character. In the screenplay it is Rivers, not Sassoon's friend Robert Graves, who questions Sassoon's pledge to his country. Instead of the young Graves telling Sassoon that the uniform is a "contract" of "honour" that must be upheld once accepted (23, 198), the film has Rivers voice these views to Sassoon. In the world of Barker's novel, such a statement would be quite uncharacteristic for Rivers, a man not only at odds within himself about the war but openly sympathetic with Sassoon's position when he is speaking to Sassoon. In the film, this statement clearly places Rivers and Sassoon on opposing sides and aligns Sassoon and Prior, both against Rivers. This alignment in turn diminishes the shaping power of class within the characters' cultural experiences because it removes the friendship between Sassoon and Rivers as well as the grudging respect with which Prior and Rivers view each other by the novel's end. It also solidifies the audience's view of Rivers as part of the establishment, not the avant-garde. Thus, a scene that represents in the novel a schism *within* a younger generation becomes emblematic of the rupture *between* the generations. Our sympathy for Rivers's character alters between book and film accordingly: in the film, we are more likely to feel sympathy for the position represented by the younger Sassoon and Prior, not the older Rivers.

Even when many of the scenes between Rivers and his patients in the film do echo the novel's dialogue, the film's script has Rivers withhold more from his patient and, by extension, from the audience. While in the novel Rivers and Prior read each other's handwriting, for instance, in the film only Prior shares his handwriting with Rivers— a small difference, except that Rivers's act of writing levels the playing field of power between Prior the patient and Rivers the doctor in that scene, forcing Rivers to communicate as Prior requests and to reveal his own handwriting as generally impossible to read (42). The way the film translates the dialogue of the scene further emphasizes an unequal power relationship, transforming Dr. Rivers into Dr. Lewis Yealland, a London doctor whose success in curing patients of mutism relies upon the opposite principle to Rivers's treatment. "The last thing these patients need is a sympathetic audience," Yealland informs Rivers, and soon fulfills this injunction when he tells a patient: "*You must speak, but I shall not listen to anything you say*" (228, 231). When Rivers observes Yealland's method, he hears Yealland command his patient to recover: "You must talk before you leave me," adding, "You will leave me when you are cured, remember, and not before" (229, 231). The film requires Rivers to address Prior in similar tones and phrases: "Officers don't suffer from mutism, Mr. Prior," Rivers announces, "You won't leave here before you have your memory back. And you will recover your speech." These commands are hardly representative of the dialogue in the novel, in which Rivers responds to Prior's inability to remember by saying: "No, not at the moment, perhaps, but the memory will start to come back" (42). Qualification ("perhaps") becomes assertion ("you will") in this transformation, establishing Rivers to be firm, rather than reflective, about his authority as doctor.

As readers, we are likely to dismiss Rivers's concerns at the end of the novel that he may be like Yealland, since we have observed his measured demeanor with his patients. The audience for the film, however, might hesitate before dismissing the comparison; they have observed many scenes between Prior and Rivers that are similarly altered to emphasize the differences between the older doctor and his young patient. When Rivers learns from Prior that his previous doctor suggested hypnosis, Rivers's response changes from, in the novel, "How did you feel about that?" (51) to

"When I feel you want to get better, hypnosis may be appropriate" in the film. Prior's forced submission appears in the staging of scenes, too. On-screen, we watch Rivers standing and pacing in front of Prior as the hypnosis conversation occurs in the film, while the novel indicates that Rivers and his patients are typically seated for their sessions, one across from the other. Assuming an unquestionable authority over his patient, the Rivers in the film insists upon Prior's subservient position within the doctor/patient relationship; as a result, Prior becomes the beleaguered young man thwarted by the forces of patriarchy and class. The persistent omission of Prior's tendentious humor in his responses to Rivers's questions—"It's hardly a reason to stay out of the trenches, is it? 'Not tonight, Wilhelm. I've got a headache'?" (50)—and his love/hate relationship with the upper classes creates an uncomplicated Prior to match the uncomplicated Rivers, as Barker herself has remarked.[7] Prior appears earnestly and appropriately antagonistic rather than shrewdly complicated, as he rightly chafes under so strong a hand as Rivers's.

Because the hints in the novel that Rivers sympathizes with his patients must be absent from a script that asks Rivers to echo Yealland, Rivers's character must undergo a sudden epiphany as we reach the conclusion of the film. On-screen, Jonathan Pryce, who plays Rivers, lets his face register true surprise as Prior announces to Rivers that he had been "rather assuming" they were on opposite sides rather than the same side. This exchange, relocated to near the end of the film rather than appearing early on as it does in the novel (80), suggests that Rivers arrives belatedly at an understanding of his patients' experiences *as* patients. Only as his patients are leaving Craiglockhart does he begin to realize how his actions may be other than sympathetic and how he might openly question the accepted view of war. The film must arrive at this rapid realization because it has completely omitted Rivers's experiences in part 3 of Barker's novel. The cinemagoing audience does not return with Rivers to his childhood church or to his memories of struggling against his father's faith, politics, and enforced speech therapy. The film consequently sidesteps the shaping power of patriarchy within Rivers's own life and his angry struggles against its authority. Whereas the novel provides ample opportunities for readers to observe Rivers analyzing his own troubled relationship to authority, we arrive at the end of the film without such context. Rivers asserts unity with the younger generation in the film when he tells Sassoon, "Perhaps it's the protest of the old that will bring things to an end." This speech does echo an unspoken thought that readers encounter near the end of the novel: "Perhaps the rebellion of the old might count for rather more than the rebellion of the young" (249). What sounds in the film like the start of a new belief, however, is for the reader of Barker's novel a confirmation of Rivers's very first response to Sassoon's file.

PLOTTING CONFLICT

In tracing the numerous alterations that the film makes to the plot of Barker's novel, one irony particularly stands out: the film *Regeneration* embodies what several reviewers desired the novel to be, in place of what it is. Historian Samuel Hynes, for example, questioned Barker's decision to end the novel with Sassoon being discharged to duty and not with the end of the war: "Why there, when the rest of the historical story is so dramatic and moving?" Hynes asks, "Why not follow Sassoon to the front, where he fought again until he was wounded by one of his own men and was evacuated to England?" Hynes believes that there is a "narrative cost in stopping where she does, short of the story's natural closure."[8] Scott and MacKinnon must have felt a similar unnaturalness to the conclusion of the novel, as they fulfill Hynes's request: not only do they begin the film with scenes from the battlefield, but they choose to end the film with the end of the war. However, this revision to the plot of the novel, in conjunction with the elision of the novel's other plot lines involving female characters, prevents the film from performing the novel's critique of British culture. Barker's novel becomes what many reviewers believed it to be: a break from her earlier fiction about class and gender rather than a continuation of her sustained interest in those cultural identities.[9]

By selecting only the theme of generational conflict for development, the film trims complexities of character that add dimension and depth to the world Barker's characters inhabit. We first lose Barker's sustained presentation of gender and class roles during wartime. None of Rivers's insights into the conflict between the socialized masculinity of his patients and their forced passivity during trench warfare remain in the film (107–8). In denying us the knowledge that Rivers has been an anthropologist and ethnographer, the film forfeits Rivers's active attempts to tease apart the larger cultural patterns of the social fabric that, in the novel, Rivers observes, queries, and, in his own limited way, attempts to change. Antagonism between the older and the younger generations does appear in the conversations between Rivers and Prior that the novel contains, yet the narrative of the novel, unlike the film, asks the reader to see how Prior's antagonism emerges from his frustration at Britain's class system, its faith in institutional authority, and his conflicted feelings about his own father and mother, rather than from generational difference per se. In the film, the force of Prior's antagonism against Rivers is *only* based on class and without a clearly defined motive, because Prior's portrait lacks the complexity of his parents' visit and his many conversations with Rivers. We never learn in the film, as we do in the novel, how much Prior both hates and loves that world of privilege and power. Just as the film's audience is not encouraged to see Rivers as another angry son, as another Billy Prior, the audience cannot see Prior as Barker's "temporary gentleman" who still gets a bit of a rush when reciting Tennyson's "Charge of the Light Brigade" (66) even as he mocks the "strangled" accents of public school (66, 52).

As well as removing Rivers's cultural insights and Prior's complex relationship to social class, the film also omits the comparatively brief yet pointed dialogues between working-class women. Consequently, the film sidesteps the role of women within the culture it presents, thereby obviating discussion of how prescribed gender roles and compulsory heterosexuality underpin the older generation's cultural authority and precipitate the very neuroses Rivers's patients experience in war. Absent is the novel's evidence of women's roles during war, how they have "expanded" (90) in some ways (better salaries) but remained confined to the biological (the duty to bear healthy children for the Empire, according to Major Huntley). To lose the working-class women who are part of Sarah's life at the munitions factory is indeed a double blow; as in the revisions that the film makes to Prior's character, we lose the intersection of gender and class. Madge, Betty, and Lizzie are mere background in one pub scene, while Madge makes a brief appearance during a trip to the hospital; muted on the screen, these women cannot offer their plainspoken observations about prewar spousal abuse or wartime liberties. Even the memorable line from Lizzie—"Do you know what happened on August 4th 1914? . . . I'll tell you what happened. *Peace* broke out" (110)—disappears. So, too, do the women's persistent concerns about prewar feminine appearance and behavior, for all their talk about sexual promiscuity and wartime freedoms. In many ways, the film's transformation of Sarah into an active partner contradicts her counterpart in Barker's novel. Whereas on screen Sarah places Prior's hand on her breast and later approaches him in the pub before he addresses her, on the page she struggles to balance her desires against her fear of appearing too available, too soon (93).

The complex view of sexuality that the novel offers suffers in the translation to the screen as well. The rescripting for the film of Sarah and Prior's heterosexual love-making, spliced at the end of the film with Owen's unrequited homosexual love for Sassoon, creates a composite scene that simplifies the novel's commentary on male-female relationships and dehistoricizes the novel's presentation of homosexuality. Without the complexities of Sarah and Prior's relationship before us on the screen, their meeting in Sarah's room becomes a way for Prior to escape from the war and not a window into his confusion about who or what women should be—a confusion that suggests the possibility for productive change. In the novel, Sarah is a complex character: she can be one of the working class whom Prior feels comfortable with but whom he has left behind, she can be an ignorant civilian, she can be a female inhabiting a feminine space apart from worldly pain, and, just maybe, she can also be a person who connects all three facets at the same time. In the film, she is only two: a woman who can never understand the war because of her ignorance and a woman who allows her man to escape the war because of her ignorance. The image of Prior resting his head upon her naked body near the end of the film presents Sarah as a retreat, a place of temporary relief; sleeping upon her upright figure, his head upon her breast, he returns to the security of the female maternal. The scene is also stripped of the dialogue and free indirect narrative that accompanies the presentation of their lovemaking in the novel: there, Prior and Sarah voice their love for one another, and Prior silently acknowledges his equal desires to have Sarah know him fully and for her to remain a haven for him (216). In the film, heterosexual love becomes the only satisfactory way to escape the trauma of war, especially when the scene of Prior and Sarah in bed is spliced with Owen's solitary figure, holding Sassoon's picture and not his body. Indeed, the film assiduously erases homosexuality from its dialogue or action until the end. There, Owen's lingering stare at Sassoon's portrait risks implying that homosexual desire is impossible and silenced while heterosexual desire is possible and productive. Granted, in 1917, homosexual desire *was* silenced, but in Barker's novel Rivers and Sassoon discuss the social and political reasons behind this erasure; the film, by contrast, offers only a veiled reference to

Sassoon's "private life" as jeopardizing his attempt to protest the war. Not only, then, does the film emphasize a conflict between generations, favoring the young against the old, it also grants its *heterosexual* youth the physical pleasures and psychological comforts of love and denies its homosexual youth such possibilities.

Finally, in plotting conflict, the additions that the film makes to the plot of the novel are as telling as its omissions and revisions. Determined to emphasize the youth of the patients and the age of the medical officers who treat them, the film inserts two new scenes to depict the patients as boys rather than men. When the film introduces a character named Timmons to inspect the methods at Craiglockhart, he encounters a group of patients making toy boats and other arts and crafts. Another scene shortly follows this one, in which we, with Timmons, observe the nurses escorting the patients, boats in hand, to the creek by the hospital. The patients are seen splashing in the water, as they set their boats to sail. Aside from injecting humor into a medical treatment that remains serious in the novel, the decision to play up the youth of the patients runs counter to Barker's repeated efforts to show continuity between the old and the young—even to find the two side by side within the same individual, as Rivers reflects when he observes Burns:

> Rivers thought how misleading it was to say that the war had "matured" these young men. It wasn't true of his patients, and it certainly wasn't true of Burns, in whom a prematurely aged man and a fossilized schoolboy seemed to exist side by side. (169)

While one can see how Scott and MacKinnon interpreted a passage like this one to suggest the dominance of the patients' youth, the translation of this idea to the screen loses the other part of Barker's description and Rivers's insight: that the young officers have aged. Rivers's comment about Burns is therefore an echo of his earlier reflection about Sassoon: "In some ways the experience of these young men paralleled the experience of the very old" (118). Both of these interpolated scenes deny the insistence of the novel, voiced through Rivers, that two generations coexist within the same person.

What, then, is the combined result of these omissions, revisions, and additions to the novel's plot? In the film we experience a narrative that separates one selected theme—generational conflict—from the cultural nexus that fosters it. The conflict enacted on-screen between Rivers and his young patients, writ large in the conflict of war, is not in any way linked to other relationships within British society; therefore, the conflict apparently cannot be altered by society. This pessimistic and fatalistic response is secured with the addition of the war's end as the film's concluding scenes and with its omission of the force that motivates that art of the poets themselves: the imagination.

A FAILURE OF IMAGINATION: SHUTTING THE DOOR ON HISTORY

Barker's novel, like Sassoon's "Declaration," encourages everyone to have "sufficient imagination to realize" (3) that an official or traditional view of war is not the only one and that cultural patterns are open to change. However, the film of *Regeneration* does not end, as the novel does, with Sassoon's, Prior's, and Owen's discharge to duty but with the end of the war. This alternate ending implies that the conclusion of the film's cultural narrative is already written, closed off from the present. The streamlined approach and revised ending of the film also deny its audience the opportunity to experience Barker's discussion of the imagination and to see the imagination at work across the generations. We are left instead with a familiar cultural parable about fathers, sons, and the inevitability of war, in place of Barker's cautious optimism for the future of the characters in the novel and their culture.

In the film, the imagination is aligned with the youth of Sassoon and Owen, their growing friendship, the poetry they produce, and the green world of Craiglockhart's grounds—a sharp contrast to the novel's insistence that the recuperative powers of the imagination are of a piece with war and everyday life and are often responsible for its horrors. To this end, the film's dialogue revises an important exchange between Owen and Sassoon near the beginning of their friendship that squarely sets poetry within war. In the novel, Sassoon admonishes Owen for having an art that cannot "face the facts" of war and encourages him to incorporate war into his art (84–85), while in the film, Sassoon nods and accepts Owen's claim that poetry cannot challenge war because war carries the force of history behind it. This revision alters the thematic development of Barker's narrative in two ways: first, it suggests art is powerless against the course of present history; and second, it places Owen the unpublished and aspiring poet in the position of instructing the published poet, Sassoon. Indeed, the scene furthers the film's tendency to privilege Owen *over* Sassoon and other character's points of view, even giving him the position of the camera's eye in three scenes of the film. At the opening of the film, we observe the naked Burns in his primal scene through Owen's eyes; we observe the Scottish landscape first through Owen's eyes; and, at the end of the film, we hear Owen's voice and words as they have been transcribed by Sassoon in his letter to Rivers. These three alternative camera perspectives seem out of place, given the use of the camera in the rest of the film, but consistent with the scripting of Owen's character. Is the film a representation of Owen's view of the war? Is Owen the hero of the film? That the film concludes with Rivers reading Owen's poem suggests Owen may be. Owen, the poet who dies in war, becomes the fallen hero of the film's narrative and its voice for the imagination—a voice that is, as one might expect for this film, a young voice challenging the older generation. The novel's narrative, by contrast, emphasizes the voice and vision of Sassoon, the poet who lives through the war to share his experience with a future generation.

By consolidating the imagination into the poets, even into one poet who questions the power of the imagination to shape experience, the narrative of the film flattens what in the novel is a layered discussion of the shaping power of the imagination. That only Owen and Sassoon exercise their imaginations in the film creates a cordon sanitaire around such generative acts, preventing us from hearing the other characters' reflections on the power of the imagination. Prior ponders how his imagination can transform the reality of no-man's-land into a "vast unimaginable space" (214), a fearful place. Rivers's other patient, Burns, who hardly speaks during the film, becomes quite eloquent on its force. He shares with Rivers his realization of how the biblical phrase "The imagination of man's heart is evil from his youth" all too aptly identifies how horrific acts of human violence are possible: "Somebody had to *imagine* that death," he says of Christ's death by suffocation on the cross (183). Barker's decision not to have her narrative "tell" us about the war but have the patients show Rivers and the reader the effects of its horrors engages the reader's imagination. As in Greek drama, just because violence happens offstage does not mean that the legacy of that violence will be any less horrific; indeed, it may be more so, because of the imagination. If someone can imagine such horrors and enact them, however, then these events are of human making and therefore, to some extent, within human control. A society that has "sufficient imagination" to envision another reality, Barker's logic runs, can alter its way of being. The film, by contrast, provides the images of war for the audience at the beginning and end of the film—telling, not showing—and closes off the imaginative enterprise from all but the poets, who communicate belatedly through their poems.

In the film, then, not everyone has equal access to the imagination, and art becomes a Romantic storehouse of past experiences to be passed belatedly to another: the conclusions that Rivers arrives at on his own in the novel, as he reflects on his experiences with his patients, must be *told to him* by letter at the end of the film, when Sassoon encloses a copy of Wilfred Owen's "The Parable of the Old Man and the Young." The film's selection of this poem by Owen, in place of the several poems by Sassoon that appear in the novel, is telling: the film undoes Barker's rewriting of "the expected World War One elegy,"[10] forestalling the novel's assertion that the old fathers will not always and without consideration sacrifice the sons. The film of *Regeneration* thus tells an accepted and acceptable tale of youth suffering under the heavy hand of an older generation tied to honor and custom, a older generation of men unable to recognize or to act against the signs of its own ideological infirmities. The film's inclusion of children, as a revamped Campbell drills young boys like recruits, emphasizes this destructive repetition across generations. The process of old commanding young begins once more: as each generation matures, it will again show how extreme youth too often falls to the power of the old.

If Barker's historical novel offers a "backdoor into the present" by encouraging us to consider those social and imaginative forces which shape our cultural experiences, the film shuts the door on that history and those potential insights. It strives to fulfill a "modern" view of history; it seeks to contain the war within the past, rather than granting the novel's assertion that the past is part of the present and the future and that it returns in a "postmodern" form.[11] The timing of the film's release in 1997 seems auspicious, given Niall Ferguson's concerns about the public rituals of Remembrance Day: for Ferguson, there is a tendency for such displays to replicate the "high diction" that war poets like Sassoon countered in the art.[12] By representing the First World War as a past cut off from present understanding, the film becomes just such a monument to the sacrifice of the dead at the hands of old men, rather than a living critique of a society that has fractures within as well as between generations. In the film, understanding comes only from the imagination of doomed youth, rather than the novel's imaginative and regenerative dialogue between generations.

NOTES

1. *Regeneration,* directed by Gillies MacKinnon, screenplay by Allan Scott, (Fine Line, 1997).

2. For one of the few, if not the only, critical analyses of MacKinnon's film, see Sharon Monteith, *Pat Barker* (Plymouth: Northcote House, 2002), 76–78.

3. Pat Barker, *Union Street* (London: Virago, 1982), 265.

4. Wera Reusch, "A Backdoor into the Present: An Interview with Pat Barker," 2000, trans. Heather Batchelor, LOLA Press, January 16, 2001 http: //www.lolapress.org/reue.htm.

5. Pat Barker, *Regeneration* (New York: Penguin, 1992), 118. All subsequent references will be included in the text.

6. There are three exceptions to this general rule: near the opening of the film, the camera, somewhat shakily, follows Owen through the woods; at another point, the camera appears to take Owen's point of view, looking down a dark canal tunnel to the light and trees at the other end. This second image recurs during the film, most notably as we approach Owen's body at the end of the film.

7. Barker remarked upon this devolution of her characters' complexity at a book festival in August 2001. In the words of David Robinson, writing for the *Scotsman,* Barker questioned the ability of a film "to show what that psychologist made of his memory." He says, "And even though she enjoyed the film version of her novel *Regeneration,* she couldn't help but notice its tendency to over-simplify. Siegfried Sassoon was, she pointed out, an immensely more complicated character than was ever portrayed" by the film. See David Robinson, "No Easy Answers," *Scotsman,* August 21, 2001, 6.

8. Samuel Hynes, "Among Damaged Men." *New York Times Book Review,* March 29, 1992, 1.

9. For Justine Picardie of the *Independent, Regeneration* "comes as a surprise"; Philip Hensher, writing for the *Guardian,* sees Barker as "a rare example of an author who has drastically, and successfully changed course." Candice Rodd makes use of this same rhetorical gesture—"you could almost be forgiven for thinking there are two Pat Barkers"—but her review then argues for important thematic connections between Barker's previous fiction and her turn toward the First World War. See Picardie, "The Poet Who Came Out of His Shell Shock," *Independent,* June 25, 1991, 19; Hensher, "Getting Better All the Time," *Guardian,* November 26, 1993, S4; and Rodd, "A Stomach for War," *Independent,* 12 September 12, 1993, 28. For a full discussion of the reviewers' responses, see Monteith, *Pat Barker,* 2–10, 108–10, and Karen E. Westman, *Pat Barker's "Regeneration": A Reader's Guide* (New York: Continuum, 2001), 61–64.

10. Catherine Lanone, "Scattering the Seed of Abraham: The Motif of Sacrifice in Pat Barker's *Regeneration* and *The Ghost Road,*" *Literature and Theology* 13, no. 3 (1999): 259.

11. See Anne Whitehead's essay "Open to Suggestion: Hypnosis and History in the *Regeneration* Trilogy," in this volume. Whitehead applies Peter Nicholl's paradigm of "modern" history and "postmodern" history to explore how Barker acknowledges, but ultimately rejects, a view of the past "which depends upon a notion of authorship" and control of personal history.

12. Niall Ferguson, "Do Today's Public Rituals Hinder Our Understanding of War?" *Independent,* November 11, 1998, 4.

SHERYL STEVENSON

With the Listener in Mind

Talking about the *Regeneration* Trilogy with Pat Barker

STEVENSON: What led you to write *Regeneration*?

BARKER: A long-standing interest in the First World War. My grandfather, who was my grandmother's second husband but was the man who brought me up, fought in that war, and my stepfather who was older than my mother by sixteen years also fought in that war. He was in the trenches as a boy of fifteen. So for me, in a sense, that was *the* war in terms of the conversations I had on a day-to-day basis. My father, of course, was involved in the Second World War, and my uncle, but these were not such salient people in my life, in my childhood. So the experience of the older war was paradoxically closer to me, in that sense. My grandfather had a bayonet wound that was something I noticed particularly as a small child, and he didn't talk about the war. So in a sense the bayonet wound was speaking for him. Silence and wounds were therefore linked together in that particular way. And my stepfather was certainly also marked by that war: he had a paralytic stammer, and my grandfather was very deaf. So the idea of war, wounds, impeded communication, and silence, of course— silence about the war, because the war was not a subject of revelation—all became entwined in my mind with masculinity.

STEVENSON: When did you decide that this work would be part of a trilogy?

BARKER: At the end of *Regeneration*, when I realized that I'd sent Sassoon back to the war—or rather, since he's a historical character, Sassoon sent himself back to the war—with his opposition to it actually intensified. He went back *more* against the war than he had been when he made his protest originally. And there is no way of writing the final chapter of *Regeneration* to make it a genuine "ending," because any soldier prepared to do that is going to run the risk of further breakdown or further protest. Rivers also has all the guilt—perhaps he wouldn't have said it was guilt, but he has the moral responsibility for having encouraged Sassoon to go back. He will have to face the consequences of that, just as he has to face the consequences of sending all these patients who are well enough back into the trenches. Because of this, of course, it cannot be the ending. I wrote and rewrote the final chapter of *Regeneration*, trying to give the sense of completion, and in fact I couldn't make it complete because the story ends with the end of the war.

STEVENSON: So did you decide then that you would write two more novels?

BARKER: Two more, yes. It was originally one, and then it became three. But it was never two. The ending of *The Eye in the Door* is even more indeterminate, because you have Prior going back to the war with all his hang-ups and difficulties. And, by implication of course, Owen going back.

STEVENSON: What were some of the difficulties that challenged or fascinated you, particularly in writing about Rivers?

BARKER: Rivers took good care that people didn't know much about him, personally. He was a great burner. He burned letters and left instructions to his executors to burn letters. He was an intensely private, intensely discreet man. And that is useful for a novelist, because you don't want to know too much. You want that blank screen; you want to be able to project. Really, I knew too much about Sassoon and Owen. Owen in particular is difficult, because Owen comes with his own preexisting myth. And you don't want a preexisting myth in a novel.

The difficult thing about Rivers was not his sex—that's what people generally imply, that it must be hard to write about a man. One difficult thing was his stammer and the stammer of everybody else in the hospital, which is very hard when you're writing dialogue, to indicate that without producing something that would have been impossible to read. And yet you have to indicate that communication is being impaired. I was particularly interested in the stammer because of my stepfather's stammer. I think my stepfather would have been a lot less violent if he hadn't stammered. If he'd been able to articulate his anger it wouldn't have exploded in the way it did—not against me, but against other members of the family.

The other difficult thing about Rivers was the lack of visual memory—that, except in dreams or when he was suffering a feverish illness, he had no memory at all, no visual memory. If you're very strongly visual yourself, as I think most of us are, it's very difficult to see how Rivers thought about anything. It's very difficult to see how he got from A to B, but, you know, he did. He didn't wander around the world saying "I'm lost." He seemed to know where he was, but he didn't have any kind of mental map. I find that extraordinary. I find it extraordinary that someone like that could learn anatomy well enough to pass his medical exams in record time. I still don't understand how he did that.

STEVENSON: Do you see the *Regeneration* trilogy as exploring how Rivers tries to understand the causes of his stammer and lack of visual memory—how they relate to his childhood?

BARKER: Yes. In the Rivers-Head experiment, they cut a nerve in Head's arm. Rivers, in much the same spirit, experimented on himself; he used himself as his raw material. He became convinced that there was a reason why he could remember the ground floor of his childhood home, but not the upper floor. When he says this to my fictional character Billy Prior, Prior reacts very much as I think a modern therapist would and assumes there was either violent abuse or sexual abuse. And Rivers is quite shocked, because he doesn't believe his parents were like that, forgetting of course that it doesn't have to be his parents—that he was brought up by servants. But he thinks about it differently. Rivers is an Edwardian in the way he thinks about this, in spite of being influenced by Freud, and Prior is much closer to the modern framework that we have. Also, having been himself abused as child, Prior is drawing on his own experience here. He doesn't believe Rivers's very timid explanations and says, in effect, "What was so impossible to look at that you blinded yourself in order not to see it?" Rivers never recovered that memory, and because he never recovered it in real life (or he never records that he did), he doesn't really recover it in the books either, since I always try to stick to historical facts. What I did tentatively suggest was that the thought of his grandfather, the original Rivers who got his leg shot off on *The Victory*, combined with his father's profound conviction concerning the importance of inculcating Christian manliness in boys, would produce an excessive amount of pressure in a small boy to be prematurely tough and stoical and brave. The stammer was probably a reaction to that.

Rivers himself was from a generation of stammerers. There are two kinds of stammers: one, a reaction to shock, was almost universal among officers of the First World War, and the other was the lifelong stammer, where there's a troubled background of some kind. So Rivers was—oddly enough, since he was a psychiatrist—always rejecting the psychological explanation.

I see Katharine Rivers as being parallel with Rivers himself because he has a stammer and she, having been a very free and lively little girl, becomes in adult life increasingly confined. The daughter of the vicarage, she becomes a spinster, she does good works, stays home with her parents, takes care of her father after her mother dies, and then is finally confined to her bed, for no obvious reason. Her whole life is a process of increasing confinement. And I see her as being a double for the woman on the island who's confined into a tiny space.

Although women in the trilogy characteristically play rather small roles, I would say that each of the roles that the women play is absolutely vital, and that actually if you wanted a key to the whole work, you could do a lot worse than just to go through from woman to woman. Essentially what women are doing and talking about is—as much as Rivers was—the underlying moral question of the entire work.

For example, I was attracted to Katharine Rivers because it was discovered by Rivers's biographer, Dick Slobodin, that she had written this very little memoir of Lewis Carroll. And I'm quite certain that Lewis Carroll was attached to Katharine Rivers in the way she said he was—probably in other ways as well. I was influenced in writing about it by Dennis Potter's wonderful screenplay called *Dreamchild*, in which the adult Alice Liddell recalls her childhood with Lewis Carroll. There is a particular incident when they're punting on the river. Just as Katharine Rivers and Lewis Carroll went boating together on their river, so of course did Lewis Carroll and the much more famous Alice. And in Potter's *Dreamchild*, Alice throws water into Lewis Carroll's face. She's supposed to be a nice little girl, so her mother is absolutely horrified by this. Yet Lewis Carroll says, "No. Don't say anything to her. She's right." Of course, what he recognizes and admits is that in his glance at this small girl, there is an adult sexual demand. Although she can't name it or articulate it, she is aware of it being there, and she throws water in his face to protect herself from it.

I think it's reasonable to assume that Katharine Rivers was subjected to something like this. Not abuse—there's never been any evidence of abuse by Lewis Carroll. But it doesn't have to be physical; there can be an emotional pressure and emotional demands that call something out of the child that the child is not ready to give. You see this explored in the work of D. H. Lawrence, with Paul and his mother in *Sons and Lovers* and also in *The Rainbow,* even more explicitly perhaps, in the father-daughter combination. Once again, there is no abuse but the demand on the child. And it links to what happens to Kelly Brown at the beginning of *Union Street,* although it's much more brutal there. It is a continuum of the same kind of seductive and quasi-parental relationship.

STEVENSON: Another point of connection is that one of the wards where Rivers works has drawings from *Alice in Wonderland* on the wall.

BARKER: Yes. The hospital had been a children's hospital, but I doubt very much that the ward would have been enlivened by any kind of painting. So I did make that up. What was in my mind was that Alice gets into all kinds of fixes and, especially at the beginning of *Alice in Wonderland,* she solves them by manipulating her body in some way: she gets tall, she gets short, she goes back again, she gets stuck halfway. What a lot of the men, the real hysterics, were doing was to use that manipulation of their bodies as a way of solving *their* problem, which was the intolerable nature of the war. I was quite fascinated by the idea that a man had projected onto a little girl, in this fairy story, such a profound understanding of the way in which humans solve conflicts by manipulating their own bodies. So I applied those insights to adult men who were doing what men were never supposed to do, which is to speak through their bodies.

STEVENSON: In the trilogy, you present mute soldiers who "speak" their protest through their wound, their symptoms, but you show other kinds of silence as well, like Rivers's silences with his patients and also the presence of the unsaid in a conversation, often suggesting what can't be spoken. So I wondered about your views on this issue of silence.

BARKER: Sharon Monteith has said, "At the heart of your work there is a conversation between men that they need to have, and they're not having. So that all these dialogue-laden books of the trilogy are revolving around an essential silence." I think that is probably the silence of my stepfather, who stammered so that he could hardly get to the end of a sentence, and was violent. My grandfather certainly wasn't violent, but he also could not take part in conversations very easily.

So, in part, it is that. But you're quite right. There's also a suppressed narrative, as well, in my books. There's this feeling that a narrative is always a selection. And the selection is always done with the listener in mind. Even if you're talking to yourself, you divide yourself—you have a concept of yourself as a listener, and you are framing what the listener wants to hear. So that narratives are shaped to the point where they are only a very imperfect approximation of the truth of what really happened. I think that's particularly true of the narratives elicited during therapy.

So it isn't a simple matter. You know, silence—bad. Speech—good. Not by any means. In *Regeneration,* when Callan starts to speak, he is in fact silenced, because he's only permitted to say what Yealland is prepared to allow him to say. Another representative character—who's very different but also follows after Callan—is Geordie in *Another World,* who comes back with a stammer and doesn't want to talk about the war, even if he could, because nothing is being said in his culture about this war that relates to his actual memories of it. In a sense, through every decade of his life, what Geordie is allowed to say about the war is different. When he gets to be quite an old man, seventy or even eighty, he's suddenly allowed to talk about the horror. What people in the 1960s, 1970s, and 1980s wanted to hear about was the horror of the trenches, whereas in the 1920s they wanted to be told about patriotism and self-sacrifice or glory. So he can talk about the horrors, and he feels liberated. But Helen, the woman who interviews him, quite rightly points out that there are still things he can't say. He can't talk about the fact that the class divisions were still there, at the front, and they were still there after the war. There was an awful lot that Geordie can't say and doesn't say. And, at the end, neither speech nor silence is helpful. He's delivered back to his memories, because his brain, as it decays, loses all the ways of coping with that raw experience of terror and pain that it had acquired over the years. So he's simply back there. And this actually happened to my husband's father, who became an American citizen in the 1930s. At the end of his life, he was living in his little apartment in New York City with his American wife, and he was fighting in the trenches. He attacked his wife, because he thought she was the German soldier who killed his brother. That is how wars last, whether it's the Falklands or the Gulf War or the Vietnam War; what tends to happen is that however well the veterans have coped, at the end of their lives there tends to be this enormous resurgence of buried war memories. This is the final insult of war.

STEVENSON: Violence, in war or other forms, is an issue that connects many of your novels. Are there writers or viewpoints on this subject that have been important to you? Or are you primarily evolving your own conception?

BARKER: I think I am mainly evolving my own conception. My uncle who fought in the Second World War came back to find that he had a certain two-year-old son, who wasn't exactly thrilled to find he suddenly had a daddy, because he'd got used to having the women all to himself. My uncle had been fighting the Japanese, and his nerves were very bad indeed. He was a very peaceful man, a very good man, but he found this little toddler almost impossible to deal with. I remember particular incidents where the child would do something wrong—when he was four or five years old, and I was the same age—and I was startled by the rage, quite out of proportion. Then I'd hear my mother and my grandmother talking about it afterward. So the domestic scene and the war in the background, with explanations applied by the women, were linked for me at a very early age. There was my stepfather too. He was certainly abusive—oddly enough, not to me but to his son from his first marriage, who was, by any standards, an abused child and grew up to be violent himself, as is the way of such things. Now, whether my stepfather's abusiveness was based on his experience in the trenches, I don't know. He may just have been a bastard anyway. There's no point in being sentimental about this—you can't blame everything on the war. But there was that link in my mind, between public violence and private violence, and I've been interested ever since in exploring what they have in common. There's legitimate public violence, domestic violence, and of course criminal violence outside the home—those three types—and I've been interested in the network that grows up between them.

Obviously, as a part of the lifelong working through of personal experience, you inevitably read and are attracted to what other people have done on the subject. I read the ethnobiologists, who explore the root causes not just of violence but also of altruism. One book I read on that subject was Matt Ridley's *The Origins of Human Virtue*, which is actually a rather hopeful book. He argues, very persuasively, that we have in-built, altruistic feelings for those who share our genes, and by extension for those who share our culture and ideas. But he also argues, equally persuasively, that we have in-built mechanisms for rejecting those who are different in all those respects, and in particular for demonizing and for hyping up conflict between our own group and other groups, as a way of reinforcing the altruistic ties within our own group. This is what the women in the cake factory do in *Union Street*. With the pressure of the assembly line, they initially turn on the one black woman there, because she is racially and culturally different from them. But when she proves to be a formidable opponent, they turn on the weakest member of their own group.

I was very much aware, when I was writing that scene, that because these were working-class women, this might be dismissed as trivial. But I saw I was writing about forces within individuals and within groups that are the same forces that in Nazi Germany, for example, wrecked an entire culture. The mechanisms are exactly the same. So that scene was a microcosm of the larger macrocosm—that demonization or discrimination interests me a lot.

STEVENSON: There is a similar scene in *Another World* and *Border Crossing*, in which a young child becomes the target of harmful, potentially deadly actions by an older child or children. I wondered what those scenes suggest about children and issues of violence among children.

BARKER: In *Border Crossing*, the incident involves the psychologist, Tom Seymour, not Danny, the young man who killed an old woman when he was ten. I wanted to say, really this is not something that happens on the other side of the desk or the other side of town. This is something that can happen to us, either to us as children or to our children. What happens with Tom is that he is rescued by an adult who intervenes, just as the killers of James Bulger, Thompson and Venables, were *not* rescued, though thirty-two people saw them with that child. Nobody intervened.

I was reminded too of Catherine Cookson, the novelist, who when she was ten years old tried to drown another child. And, in exactly the same way as Tom Seymour, she is rescued by a man jumping off a tram and stopping her. I was also wanting to say, okay, some children push it all the way, and then you have a tragic outcome, but the minor forms of bullying are very, very common. You see them in any playground, just as you can see disturbed children from difficult backgrounds in any playground. The people who knew Mary Bell when she was a child or who knew Thompson and Venables when they were children probably feel a great sense of responsibility and guilt for not intervening. And yet those children who would become killers were not necessarily very different. I'm not saying they were normal, but they were not necessarily very different from other violent, disturbed kids who don't commit murder.

It's an aspect of the professional detachment issue—that you can only maintain absolute professional detachment easily if you think that what's happening on the other side of the desk is not something to do with you; it's something that happens to *them*. What I admire in Rivers and in Tom Seymour is that willingness to look inside, to admit their own vulnerability, their own guilt. I think Rivers actually manages to maintain his balance, whereas Tom Seymour, though I equally admire his willingness to do it, tilts into complicity with Danny.

STEVENSON: Many writers depict disturbed or damaged people, but you have concentrated, to an unusual degree, on psychologists and the patient-therapist relationship. Why are you, as a writer, attracted to the therapist or to the therapeutic relationship?

BARKER: I'm fascinated by the balance between detachment and involvement that the therapist has to have, between compassion and analytical judgment, which is what I revere in Rivers: the combination of mental toughness with compassion. It seems the best that any human being can be is that combination. So when it works, it's great. I'm fascinated too by the times it doesn't work: when the detachment fossilizes and hardens into indifference, which it very readily can and in many cases does. This same capacity for detachment—for going home, switching off, and saying, "That's over. Now I'm going to live my life"—is one of the characteristics of a good doctor, because if they don't do that, they're no use to anybody. It's also the characteristic of a concentration camp guard. You throw Jewish children onto the truck, and you go home and give your kids a hug. And so this same human quality, this capacity for compartmentalization, can be at the service of supreme good or supreme evil. It's the double face of medicine. It's also the double face of human beings; to a certain extent, we all do it. It's no accident that when people think about medicine or they think about science, they typically think about them with overinflated hopes and overinflated fears, and the figures that come to mind are doubles: Dr. Jekyll and Mr. Hyde, Frankenstein and his monster.

Also, as far as psychologists are concerned, I'm interested in the dialogue and the extent to which people have to listen, as well as the selective nature of the narrative, in response to the listener. As Rivers says, there is no way you can not influence a patient to supply what you want, because even the dilation of the pupils of your eyes reveals interest, and Prior looks to see whether Rivers's pupils are dilated.

So it's not actually one person listening and another person speaking. It's a collaboration most of the time, but it may be quite dangerous.

STEVENSON: There's much the therapist and the novelist have in common, because a writer of dialogue, like you, has to be keenly aware of all that people *aren't* saying or the ways that people go about avoiding saying certain things. Your dialogue is often very pregnant, very weighty, with the unsaid.

BARKER: Yes. The totally unspoken thing is, for example, when Lauren in *Border Crossing* says, "It's always raining *here*"—meaning, "I'm going to leave you. I've decided."

One thing that impressed me the first time I was filmed as a very new writer—a very strange experience—was the bit at the end, after I'd been talking nonstop for about three days. The last thing that happened was that they recorded silence; they recorded the ambient sound in the room, which they need to paste over parts like cars going past. And it occurred to me that that was a very good example of the way dialogue should be written: that if there are two people in the room, you should be able to hear the sound of the room when neither of them is speaking. And everything that anybody actually says comes out of that silence and goes back into that silence. You don't have a clear sense of that in social conversation or even in intimate conversation. But in therapy you have a very powerful sense of the silence. You also hear it in telephone conversations, simply because there is a kind of listening there, which is the sound of silence.

STEVENSON: You were speaking of a level of compassionate involvement and detachment, and a level of conversation, of mutual influence, that may be dangerous for professionals like the therapist. But can't this also be true of the writer? You deal with subjects that have a painful component, perhaps associated with your own past, but they are, in any case, difficult subjects. Is the psychologist a figure you relate to as a writer?

BARKER: Yes, I think so. Sometimes people will say to you, "That must have been a very painful scene for you to write." And I always say, "Yes, it was. But it wasn't a painful scene to rewrite and rewrite and rewrite," because at that point you are using your craft. In fact, the novelist's defense against the power or the pain of what he or she might be writing about is, in the end, the same as the therapist's defense. I think also one of *my* defenses, of course, is to use male-viewpoint characters. They're my asbestos gloves.

STEVENSON: How so? How does that work for you?

BARKER: Two ways. You can't ever identify with a man in quite the same way as you identify with a woman. And actually that works in my favor, because I don't want to identify with my characters in that particular way. And the other thing is that I don't want to be identified with them either. I don't want people to read the work as disguised autobiography. You're an academic working in literature, so it has to be said that the dominant way in which literature is read today is as disguised autobiography. Autobiography is the dominant form; fiction is subservient. And you are left in no doubt about this when you are interviewed, not by academics but by journalists. "Who was that character *really?*" "What made you write that?" "Oh, so it's really about *that.*" It's a very strange way of reading fiction. It collapses the life into the fiction. I'm in favor of a certain degree of detachment, as we've already covered. I don't want to be that autobiographical writer. I couldn't be, anyway. There's too much dynamite there.

STEVENSON: Along with therapy, another profession you write about is that of the anthropologist, as you present Rivers through his memories of work he did in that field. So in *The Ghost Road* you draw upon his experience extensively, and in that way you give the trilogy an ending that has a global, cross-cultural, anthropological perspective.

BARKER: You know, I was aware—though I can't say I initially planned this, because I didn't plan it as a trilogy—but I was aware of *Regeneration* as very claustrophobic. Craiglockhart is a very dark building, with very narrow corridors once you get off the ground floor (they've added skylights that were not there at the time). So *Regeneration* is very claustrophobic, very tight, and the only escape is into nightmare and memory. And then you have Billy Prior, essentially, in *The Eye in the Door* in a much larger world, in the city, but he's also in this slightly claustrophobic world of homosexuals, at a time when being homosexual was almost like being a member of a secret society. And then, in that novel, you have spies, who are inevitably members of a secret society, whatever their sexuality. So, you have another, yet different, kind of rather paranoid, labyrinthine complexity and darkness. I wanted to open it up in the third volume, to go right away from the war, and to get Rivers out of his chair, totally, as he'd been getting more and more out over the trilogy. But I wanted to see him in a dramatically different role. He was an anthropologist before the war, before he was a person who treated these young men—*that* interested me.

Another factor shaped *The Ghost Road*. The death of Wilfred Owen was one of the great tragedies of war—you know, a week before Armistice Day, and he was a personal voice of the compassion and the anger and the pity of war. With his death, Billy Prior's death, and the death of Hallet on the ward—as well as the inarticulate protest coming from the throats of the other desperately wounded men—it could have turned naturally into a very simple antiwar message. So I wanted to counterpoint that by looking at a society that actually succeeded in abolishing war. Or, rather, the British colonial power had abolished it for them. And it had brought their society to a halt, because a man couldn't get married until he had taken heads, a woman couldn't give up mourning until somebody brought a head back in honor of the dead husband. They couldn't make a canoe without a head, and so on. They were warriors through and through. And once you destroyed their capacity to wage war, you destroyed one of the mainsprings of their culture. So I didn't want to settle just for the irony of all these young men dying in a war to end all war with the next war only twenty years away. I wanted to ask a more difficult question, which is, to what extent are we intrinsically violent toward other groups? To what extent is it a part of our biology?

STEVENSON: In *The Ghost Road* you also create parallels between Rivers and the healer Njiru, which make them a good example of the way you often use doubling. I wondered if you would say something about how you view this aspect of your work, or why it's important in literary texts you refer to, such as *Jekyll and Hyde*.

BARKER: I think I was saying that it's very prevalent in literature about human knowledge. *The Strange Case of Dr. Jekyll and Mr. Hyde* and *Frankenstein* are both essentially, it seems to me, parables about science and medicine. You notice very much when geneticists talk about the new genetics that enormous hopes are placed on their work, but they're also quite demonized. Auschwitz is never very far away when people talk about genetic experiments on embryos. You know, in this country at this moment it's illegal to do them beyond fourteen days, and in America it's totally unregulated. So there is that: the excessive hope and the excessive fear.

In the trilogy, I think the very stark doubling comes from the theories of Rivers and Head about the nervous system, the epicritic and the protopathic, which of course they also applied to their society: to the upper and lower classes, to men and women, to "civilized" white people and "uncivilized" brown people on the other side of the world. It was a very useful theory. What's interesting about Rivers, of course, is that instead of being wholeheartedly an advocate of the epicritic and the hierarchical structure of his society, he came more and more to value the protopathic as the parts of the personality that were chiefly involved in creativity, and he included in that scientific creativity. He was very impressed by the fact that the germ of the scientific idea, like the germ of the idea in the arts, seems to come from the unconscious, to be given, to come not from the higher parts of the brain but from the lower, instinctive parts of the human personality. That's an interesting conflict in Rivers's mind, but it's a theory of a deeply divided man. Also, Wilfred Owen was reading *Jekyll and Hyde* in Scarborough immediately after he left Craiglockhart, and I suspect, though I don't know, that it may have been suggested reading from Sassoon, because anything that Sassoon recommended, Owen would go off and read immediately.

I suppose the other source of the double, in the trilogy at least, is the fugue state. Rivers talks about having met one of his patients in the fugue state, which was very undramatic. It was just that he met this guy on Prince's Street, and this guy was so cheerful and happy and well and enthusiastic and optimistic about the future. Rivers went on his way, patting himself on the back, thinking, "Oh, I'm really doing a good job with *that* one." Then Rivers met him in the hospital that evening, referred to the meeting, and realized that the patient had no recollection of it at all. So he had actually met a patient in a fugue state. But generally in literature of course these things are made more dramatic, as sometimes they are in real life. The extreme divided state Prior experiences in *The Eye in the Door* is actually based on a Vietnam War veteran, who, in the other state, the alternative personality, had very striking anesthesia over a very large part of his body, so he had actually turned his skin into armor. And that state went back into his childhood. He was black, and he'd been attacked in his neighborhood by a gang of white youths, all of whom were much bigger than he was, and there was no way he was going to win or survive without a beating. This other personality came and took over and took the pain. Ever since then, but particularly in Vietnam, when he was frightened or in danger or faced with physical pain, he would go into this other state, which was extremely violent.

Looking at *Border Crossing* and *Another World* in terms of the trilogy, what seems to be going on through the work is the theme of violence—the deep roots of violence and the links between criminal violence, domestic violence, and public violence. But I see the rootedness of compassion as well. There's no doubt that, in a very limited way, the altruism is there, equally rooted.

Part Four ■ The Talking Cure

DENNIS BROWN

The *Regeneration* Trilogy

Total War, Masculinities, Anthropology, and the Talking Cure

Pat Barker's recent fictional trilogy—*Regeneration* (1991), *The Eye in the Door* (1993), and *The Ghost Road* (1995)[1]—is concerned with men and war, with men without women (with few exceptions), and with varieties of heroism. It is also, centrally, about the art of healing (as the first title indicates), in a historical context of nation fighting nation, bloc versus bloc, life against death. It mainly concentrates on three characters—the "real life" W. H. R. Rivers and Siegfried Sassoon, and the invented Billy Prior. Sassoon, Prior, and, among others, Wilfred Owen are initially shown as patients at Craiglockhart War Hospital for Officers (reorganized to cope with the newly denominated, and still controversial, phenomenon of "shell shock").[2] Rivers—medical doctor, anthropologist, nerve specialist, explorer, and psychiatrist— is made the central representative of a humane therapy (as opposed to the barbarity of electric shock treatment). A postmodern hero, he appears, as in H.D.'s description of Sigmund Freud, the "blameless physician"[3]—parental in nurturing, a saintly,[4] disciplined, and notably patient individual.[5] He is the lynchpin of the three novels (the first opens with him reading Sassoon's famous "A Soldier's Declaration," the last closes with a "visitation" from his Melanesian informant, on the "edge of sleep"), and his centrality is implicitly shown in Barker's strong endorsement for the republication of Richard Slobodin's *W. H. R. Rivers* (1997).[6] From the standpoint of the new millennium, as we look back at the last century's amazements and mayhem, where the Great War can appear as index of a radical (and scarcely healed) wounding of hubristic modernity, Rivers becomes an important figuration of the age of sociopsychological symptomatology. He is made exemplary as a steady listener, methodical carer (down to details of room-sharing), and a canny interpreter—as much by "tacit knowledge"[7] as by orthodox diagnosis. In this context of total war, however, his gift of healing could be, in effect, ironically paradoxical:

> But yesterday afternoon my reasoning Rivers ran solemnly in,
> With peace in the pools of his spectacled eyes and a wisely omnipotent grin;
> And I fished in that steady grey stream and decided that I
> After all am no longer the Worm that refuses to die.
> But a gallant and glorious soldier;
> Bolder and bolder; as he gets older. . . .[8]

Barker's narrative technique creates a close fit between historical chronology and the ability of literary realism to deliver persuasive mimesis. The foreground of the trilogy encapsulates the last fifteen months of the war—from Sassoon's protest of July 1917 to Owen's (and Billy Prior's) death in November 1918—one week before the Armistice. The period represents the hinge of the culmination of events—swinging first in favor of the Central Powers, then in favor of the Allies. It was also the time scale in which Sassoon and Owen wrote the poems we remember them by, in which Sassoon returned to the front and became hospitalized again with a head wound, and in which Prior could be used first as a home front spy and then, once again, as cannon fodder. The novels inexorably trace a trajectory to disaster, on the brink of a historical ending. However, Barker's method is not seamless naturalistic progression: there is much deft cutting between different viewpoints and disparate locations. And where, say, Virginia Woolf prioritized psychological time yet acknowledged chronology, Barker establishes chronology by constructing present "moments of being" shot through with memories, "fabulations," and personal associations. Nor are these pure "creations" in the classical realist mode. For the trilogy constitutes a tour-de-force of well-researched intertextuality—from Rivers's own many published works (*The Todas* and *Conflict and Dream,* for instance), Sassoon's *Memoirs* and *War Poems,* Owen's poetry, Slobodin's account of Rivers, lines from *The Waste Land,* Eric J. Leed's book on the Great War or Elaine Showalter's on hysteria, and so forth.[9] In this respect, the trilogy reads less like Georg Lukacs's version of historical realism than Linda Hutcheon's view of the postmodern novel as "historiographic metafiction":

> Its theoretical self-awareness of history and fiction as human constructs (historio*graphic meta*fiction) is made the grounds for its rethinking and reworking of the forms and contents of the past.[10]

or more specifically:

> How do we know the past today? Through its discourses, through its texts—that is, through the traces of its historical events: the archival materials, the documents, the narratives of witnesses . . . and historians. On one level, then, postmodern fiction merely makes overt the processes of narrative representation—of the real or the fictive and of their interrelations.[11]

The sheer range of W. H. R. Rivers's expertise and interests makes him an ideal figure to embody a transition from Victorian self-confidence to modernist doubt (he died the same year *The Waste Land* was published), and from the totalizing grand narratives of modernity to the "petit récits" of postmodernism. Barker does not make much of Rivers's upbringing as an Anglican vicar's son, but it probably explains much about his introversion, selflessness, and eventual commitment to socialist politics[12] on the one hand, and, on the other, his passionate pursuit of truth. More importantly, the development from a religious to a scientific environment helped make him an important sociohistorical representative. For as Robert Young has noted, in the first half of the nineteenth century new "scientific findings and theories" were culturally assimilated as "bearing on the demonstration and attributes of God as drawn from the book of nature."[13] However, "the common intellectual context came to pieces in the 1870s and 1880s and this fragmentation was reflected in the development of specialist societies and periodicals."[14]

There was a spectacular growth of "hard" knowledge: the "seventeenth-century concept of uniform natural activity" was expanded "by the 1860s" to take in "chemistry, physics, biology, psychology, medicine and the emerging sciences of society."[15] At the same time, there was a growth of oppositionality between science and theology that neither Boyle nor Newton would have understood: "In the period from 1800 to 1880 . . . the role of theology seems to change from that of providing the context for the debate to that of acting as the point of view in a conflict."[16]

These dates correspond closely to Rivers's background and intellectual development. His uncle James Hunt's Anthropological Society was accepted (as against the Ethnological Society of London) by the British Association for the Advancement of Science in 1866;[17] in 1870 Rivers's father revised Hunt's speech therapy textbook *Stammering and Stuttering*[18] (of obvious relevance to the trilogy), and in 1882 Rivers entered St. Bartholomew's Hospital, and he later received his Bachelor of Medicine in 1886 as its youngest graduate at that date.[19] Rivers was a Kent contemporary of H. G. Wells (later a friend) and for both men—as for their whole generation of intellectuals—the advent of Darwinism and the growth of agnosticism had much to do with a growing rift between Christianity and science. As "Social Darwinism," the mood well transcended the spheres of biology and zoology to inform the very ideology that Barker seeks to address. In 1983, with world wars very much on his mind, the astronomer and mathematician Sir Fred Hoyle wrote:

> Frankly, I am haunted by a conviction that the nihilistic philosophy which so-called educated opinion chose to adopt following the publication of *The Origin of Species* committed mankind to a course of automatic self-destruction.[20]

Whatever Rivers's mature beliefs, there is a Christlike quality in Barker's characterization of him that avoids the implications of such "nihilistic philosophy." Yet the Great War, as represented, might seem to embody them. Another "real life" character in the trilogy deplored the loss of "the Minds" and "bodies, the product of aeons of Natural Selection," yet also remarked in a personal letter: "It is true the guns will effect a little useful weeding"[21]—not a sentiment usually associated with the sanctified Wilfred Owen of contemporary England's classrooms.

In his brilliant and provocative book *The Sexual Fix*,[22] Stephen Heath makes an important point about the psychoanalytic revolution: that, whereas Charcot looked, Freud listened. This encapsulates the essence of the "talking cure," and for all Michel Foucault's theoretical reputation, there is surely little more reason to see its origins in the Catholic Holy Confession[23] than, say, those of the *Oprah Winfrey* show. Freud's genius was in setting up a new psychotherapeutic practice (one now used worldwide in psychoanalysis and "counseling" alike), and Rivers's perspicacity was in recognizing its importance and adapting it to the needs of his Craiglockhart patients, without any doctrinaire adherence to Freud's questionable system of ideas. Barker's trilogy well captures the therapeutic techniques involved:

Sassoon shook his head. "Nothing much. Hunting, cricket. Writing poems. Not very good poems."

"Didn't you find it all . . . rather unsatisfying?"

"Yes, but I couldn't seem to see a way out. It was like being three different people. . . ."

"And the third?"

"I'm sorry?"

"You said three."

"Did I? I meant two."

Ah. "And then the war. You joined up on the first day? . . ."

"I think the army's probably the only place I've ever really belonged."

"And now you've cut yourself off from it."

"Yes, because—"

"I'm not interested in the reasons at the moment. I'm more interested in the result. The effect on you."

"Isolation, I suppose. I can't talk to anybody. . . ."

Rivers watched him staring round the room. "You can't bear to be safe, can you? . . ."

"If you maintain your protest, you can expect to spend the remainder of the war in a state of Complete Personal Safety."

Sassoon shifted in his seat. "I'm not responsible for other people's decisions."

"You don't think you might find being safe while other people *die* rather difficult?"

A flash of anger. "Nobody else in this *stinking* country seems to find it difficult. I expect I'll learn to live with it. Like everybody else."

(*Regeneration*, 35–36)

It was another Great War veteran, Wilfred Bion of the Tavistock Institute, who entitled an influential book *Attention and Interpretation*.[24] The key terms sum up Rivers's method—and they are close to the best practice of literary criticism too. In two pages, Barker encapsulates the way Rivers's caring guidance will lead to Sassoon's so-far-unacknowledged decision to return to the front. Later Sassoon would write: "My definite approach to mental maturity began with contact with the mind of Rivers."[25] Rivers also helped him to affirm: "I haven't broken down; I've only broken out."[26] Barker's whole trilogy is a tribute to the "talking cure" as a form of healing for what is now termed "post-traumatic stress disorder"—as well as a form of counseling for someone simply angry and confused.

Central to the whole process is ultimate trust between therapist and client, and the successful negotiation of the interactive polarities of transference and countertransference. Recent British psychoanalysis has highlighted the therapist's countertransference, in particular. In *The Political Psyche* (1993), Andrew Samuels writes:

People who have never been analysts or therapists are often surprised to find that clinical practice is a red-hot emotional activity . . . the analyst's state of mind often shows signs of altered levels of consciousness and the presence of intense fantasy and aroused emotion. . . . Nowadays there are numerous analysts who see their subjectivity, carried by the countertransference, as a central feature of the clinical encounter. . . . The idea is that the analyst's unconscious somehow "understands" that of the patient in an empathetic, feeling manner.[27]

In a 1995 article, Robert M. Young asserts that "countertransference is everywhere these days"[28] and gives a comprehensive bibliography to substantiate the claim. All this, frankly, is a very far cry from the neo-Lacanian cult of psychoanalytic criticism that assumes the "objective" validity of the theory and then goes hunting among cultural productions for traces of the symbolic "phallus" or the "mirror stage." Young has commented generally on "that other form of madness called orthodoxy." Whether aware of such current emphases or not, Barker is adept at showing how Rivers's sociopsychological intuition allows countertransference relevant play in the interpretative process. This is most dramatically expressed when he breaks the rules, and reverses the roles, under Billy Prior's needling:

> Rivers thought, *all right*. He stood up and indicated that they should exchange seats.
> Rivers saw him look round the study, taking in his changed perspective. . . .
> "I'm going to show you how boring this job is. When I was five. . . ."
> Prior shifted his position, leaned forward, rested his chin on his clasped hands, and said, in meltingly empathic tones. "Yes? Go on." (*The Eye*, 136)

Later in the trilogy, after talking to Prior, Rivers remembers a Melanesian rite (where an illegitimate youth is killed by the man who has brought him up as father) and the Abraham and Isaac "sacrifice" window in his father's church at Maidstone: "He wished this particular memory had chosen another moment to surface" (*The Ghost Road*, 104). However, the memory is a countertransferential association directly relevant to the situation—Rivers is a father figure to Billy as he is to Sassoon, and his job is to make them fit to return to the murderous front. In the outcome, Sassoon, despite almost succumbing to the death instinct, survives to remain haunted by the Great War for the rest of his life; Prior is killed, but in a peculiar variation on the sacrificial exchange, has saved Hallet, thereby "sending" him back to Rivers, who tends him as he dies in the hospital. And where quite might countertransference end?— Rivers, stung into political action by meeting such men, dies untimely in 1922 at the age of fifty-eight, his dying gesture being to sign approval for a young student's diploma.[29]

At the center of the trilogy is a world given over to "Thanatos"—a state of total war. The enormity of that reality has taxed historians as much as novelists, for certain battle experiences are beyond the range of any normal imagination. Here, for instance, is Lyn Macdonald on the ending of the first day of the Battle of the Somme:

> As they neared the wood, behind the sickening gas-soaked mist, in the forefront of the noise that raged at them from every horizon, the small party of the West

Yorkshires became aware of another sound. It was like nothing they had ever heard before. Later—and for the rest of his life—Lieutenant Hornshaw was to remember it as a sound that chilled the blood; a nerve-scraping noise like "enormous wet fingers screeching across an enormous pane of glass." It was coming from the wounded, lying out in No Man's Land. Some screaming, some muttering, some weeping with fear, some calling for help, shouting in delirium, groaning with pain, the sounds of their distress had synthesised into one unearthly wail.[30]

One alternative to the straight realist method of trying to convey the incommunicable was the modernist "impressionism" of the veteran Ford Madox Ford:

It was slow, slow, slow . . . like a slowed down movie. The earth manoeuvred for an infinite time. He remained suspended in space . . .
    The earth sucked slowly and composedly at his feet. It assimilated his calves, his thighs. It imprisoned him above the waist. His arms being free, he resembled a man in a life-buoy.[31]

Over some pages, Ford's technique can build up a powerful "progression d'effet"— yet all narrative methods must ultimately fall short of the reality. When evoking frontline action, Barker is terse, vivid, and simple: "He saw Owen die, his body lifted off the ground by bullets, describing a slow arc in the air as it fell" (*The Ghost Road*, 273). However, most of the trilogy wisely alludes to the front by evoking characters' memories—in the manner of the "oral historian." For her main subject is the home front—the hospital experience of those already traumatized by battle, the gulf between combatants and civilians, and the mounting public hysteria as the Allies appear to be losing the war.

The last theme becomes rooted in the preposterous Pemberton Billing affair, with its nonsense about "the 47,000," the "Cult of the Clitoris" and the demonization of homosexuality (under the guise of patriotism). Fresh evidence continues to come to light on that particular scandal.[32] However, Barker is able to use what was already known to symbolize the state of affairs alluded to in D. H. Lawrence's *Kangaroo*.

From 1916 to 1919 a wave of criminal lust rose and possessed England, there was a reign of terror, under a set of indecent bullies like Bottomley of *John Bull* and other bottom-dog members of the House of Commons.

and

. . . the city, in some way, perished from being a heart of the world, and became a vortex of broken passions, lusts, hopes, fears, and horrors.[33]

The second and third novels of the trilogy, especially, cast a shrewd light on this scenario. As Charles Manning comments: "I used to find a certain kind of Englishness engaging. I don't any more" (*The Eye*, 175). In Ford's *Parade's End*, the corruption of the home front is more melodramatically seen as "the last of England."

The hysteria about homosexuality helps focus a Great War issue that Barker, unusually for a woman novelist, engages head-on: a crisis in ideas about masculinity.

The topic of "masculinities" has become of considerable recent interest.[34] However, to my knowledge,[35] male war experience has not featured largely in gender studies—despite its having been an actual or potential reality for Western men in most of the last century. To "be a man" has at the bottom line a notion of courage *in extremis*—one that total war tests to the full. Billy Prior and his old mate Mac talk about it in suitably down-to-earth terms:

> Mac smiled. "Must be quite nice, really. A foot on each side of the fence. Long as you don't mind what it's doing to your balls."
> "They're all right, Mac. Worry about your own."
> "Oh, I *see*. I wondered when that was coming. *Men* fight, is that it?"
> "No. I can see it takes courage to be a pacifist. At least, I suppose it does. . . ."
> Mac nodded. "Well, since you're being honest. I think a load of fucking rubbish's talked about how much courage it takes to be a pacifist. . . ." (*The Eye*, 111)

Physical courage is clearly important to both men's sense of masculinity. The same is true of Sassoon, and it can make him dismissive of men he sees as less than manly—evidenced when Rivers orders him back to Craiglockhart:

> A silence during which Sassoon struggled visibly with himself.
> "Why can't you?" Rivers prompted gently.
> "Because it would mean I'm one of them."
> Rivers felt a flare of anger, but brought it quickly under control. "One of whom?"
> Siegfried was silent. At last he said, "You know what I mean."
> "Yes, I'm afraid I do. One of the degenerates, the loonies, the lead-swingers, the cowards. . . ." (*The Eye*, 269)

Manifestly, sexual inclination has virtually no relevance to the imagined ideal of masculinity—Sassoon is homosexual and lethal at the front; but nor is it clear how this might differ from feminine courage and sense of duty of a similar kind. The fear of "Otherness" becomes gendered in a way none of the characters really escapes from. Yet it is, at the least, contained: Klaus Theweleit's lurid study *Male Fantasies* shows how brutalizing imaginary masculinity may become when honor is felt to be tainted by betrayal and defeat.[36]

Notoriously, the Great War was largely static and defensive. As the memoirs and novels about it testify, that helped make it a war of compensatory male intercommunication—of shared jokes and rumors, of communal myths (the "Angel of Mons"), of ironic marching songs, of sweetheart talk and moaning and argumentation and mutual bucking-up. David Jones's modernist epic *In Parenthesis* (1937) is, among other things, a carnivalesque celebration of verbal coping, of the intermingled accents, vocabularies, idioms, and registers of the Volunteer Army. The Great War was also a particularly "literary" affair.[37] As Billy Prior notes in his (to me, rather unconvincing) diary discourse: "It's like this every evening. And not just the letters either. Diaries. Poems. At least two would-be poets in this hut alone" (*The Ghost Road*, 115). Barker's early focus on Sassoon, Graves, and Owen shows her interest in the composition of war poetry, yet her larger theme lies less in communication than breakdown in the ability to communicate. Rivers, for all his wisdom, remains something of a stammerer. Prior, when he first enters the novel, is unable to speak at all:

> Prior reached for the notepad and pencil he kept beside his bed and scrawled in block capitals, "I DON'T REMEMBER."
> "Nothing at all?"
> Prior hesitated, then wrote, "NO." (*Regeneration*, 41)

At the "spuggies" Billy and Sarah walk out on an exhibition of glossalalia:

> Not words. A gurgling rush of sound like the overflow of a drainpipe, and yet with inflections, pauses, emphases, everything that speech contains except meaning. People turned towards him, watching the sounds jerk out of him, as he stood with thrown-back head and glazed eyes. (*The Ghost Road*, 78)

Arguably, the whole phenomenon of hysteria (the name has stuck)—speech loss, inability to walk, phantasies of castration, to name a few manifestations—constitutes a dysfunction of communication of one kind or another. In this respect, Rivers (connoisseur of anthropology-through-translation) is a modern embodiment of Hermes —god of boundaries and interpretation ("hermeneutics"), the messenger of the gods. And as I have argued elsewhere,[38] Hermes is an apt figure to preside over the phenomenon of postmodernity.[39]

However, Barker is very much a novelist, and novelists are typically in awe of poetry—if only because it is historically prior to prose, is closer to the sacred, and negotiates the profound boundary between orality and literacy (which Rivers knew all about in his pragmatic way)—theorized by Walter J. Ong.[40] For poetry is the oddly privileged, if mainly marginalized, articulation of what in *The Ghost Road* is called "*talk blong tomate*: the language of ghosts" (208); as T. S. Eliot wrote, "the communication / Of the dead is tongued with fire beyond the language of the living."[41] Just so, do Owen, Sassoon, and Graves still speak to us. And in poetry exactness of "voicing" is paramount, even when the result is in cold print. That requires constant rewriting, as Sassoon insists to the younger Owen:

> "How long do you spend on it? Not that one, I mean generally?"
> "Fifteen minutes." He saw Sassoon's expression change. "That's *every day*."
> "Good God, man, that's no use. You've got to sweat your guts out. Look, it's like drill. You don't wait till you *feel* like doing it." (*Regeneration*, 124–25)

Later, Owen shows Sassoon the draft of a poem now famous:

> What minute-bells for these who die so fast?
> Only the monstrous / solemn anger of our guns. (141)

They work together on this to achieve the final result:

> What passing-bells for those who die as cattle?
> —Only the monstrous anger of the guns.

> Only the stuttering rifles' rapid rattle
> Can patter out their hasty orisons. . . . [42]

The poem, overall, evokes the "pity" of the Great War as Owen intended: yet in the context of the trilogy's interweaving of Melanesian and modern experience, it also typifies the post-Darwinian desolation of a rationalizing generation who have denied any validity to "passing-bells" and "orisons." That generation, despite its rendezvous with death, is cut off from the "'high speech' of ritual, myth and prayer" (*The Ghost Road*, 164). In contrast to the work of David Jones, for instance, the poetry of Owen and Sassoon leaves an odd emptiness, once the "trench realism" has made its point. Yet an exception might be made for the few poems where the uncanny invades the metonymic norm, willy-nilly. Such a poem seems to have invaded Barker's prose, too, at one point:

> [Rivers] picked up the lamp, pushed aside the heavy dark red curtains and opened the window. A big dizzy moth flew in . . . and began bumping against the ceiling. He leant out of the window, smelling roses he couldn't see. The wind had fallen completely now, giving way to a breathless hush. Faintly, over dark hedges and starlit fields, came the soft thud-thud of the guns. . . . Siegfried must have heard it in June when he was at home convalescing from his wound. (*Regeneration*, 156)

Indeed, Sassoon had, for this constructed scene almost certainly refers to the poet's "Repression of War Experience"[43] (dated July 1917—the title being that of a lecture given by Rivers in that year, and reprinted in *Instinct and the Unconscious*). The lonely room, the moth, the roses, the sullen weather, and the noise of the guns are virtually identical (and I believe the poem was influential for two central modernist texts— *The Waste Land* and *Mrs. Dalloway*).[44] However, the uncanny is also there in ways Njiru himself might well have sensed: "There must be crowds of ghosts among the trees,—. . . ."

The Melanesian material, re-"presented" as it is, seems to me essential to the trilogy, and especially to *The Ghost Road*. There have been, after all, many other Great War narratives, and the lives of Sassoon, Owen, and even Rivers of Craiglockhart are scarcely unknown. What the Melanesian "petits récits" effect is a postmodernization of Barker's "Little England" realism. This not only makes the trilogy show affinities with the fictions of such as Salman Rushdie or Ben Okri, where the "historiographic" vision is informed by the idioms and tropes of hitherto marginalized groups, but also places the novels within the ethos of a postmodern social anthropology where communities, kinship systems, rituals, and the like are valued on their own terms rather than "translated" into a post-Enlightenment metanarrative. George Marcus writes, for instance:

> By the mid-1980s, these cross-cutting interests in culture as lived local experience and the understanding of the latter in global perspective have come specifically to be about how collective and individual identities are negotiated in the various places that anthropologists have traditionally, and now not so traditionally, conducted fieldwork.[45]

Similarly, Charles Lemert has commented on the work of Marcus and Michael Fischer[46] in which Captain James Cook's death is described from the Hawaiian mythic point of view. "The narrative focus," Lemert remarks, "is not so much on the early nineteenth-century Hawaiians as it is *from their perspective*."[47] He concludes by affirming "the ironic centrality of differences in a decentred world." Such irony is evident in the trilogy, where both similarities and differences arise from "cross-cutting" between a colonially blighted Melanesian culture and the culture of a European modernity in the process of tearing itself apart.

In the Melanesian sections Barker represents Rivers's encounters *as such*—i.e., the lived reality, out of which classical anthropology was made: narrative fragments not rationalized metanarrative. "Reasoning Rivers" does, of course, speculate on what he sees—but then so does Njiru, by very different lights. Anthropology is here fictionalized as interactive negotiation, and Rivers is shown as aware of "the ironic centrality of differences." After the Melanesians subject him to his own questionnaire on sharing, and dissolve in laughter over the "life of a bachelor don in a Cambridge college":

> He looked up, at the blue, empty sky, and realized that their view of *his* society was neither more nor less valid than his of theirs. No bearded elderly white man looked down on them, endorsing one set of values and condemning the other. And with that realization, the whole frame of social and moral rules that keeps individuals imprisoned—and sane—collapsed, and for a moment he was in the same position as these drifting, dispossessed people. A condition of absolute free-fall. (*The Ghost Road*, 119–20)

Whether such a perception informs the matter of Rivers's published work (or the Cambridge "notes") remains open to discussion—if so, it might further explain the decline in his reputation during the rise of "traditional anthropology" that Slobodin makes evident. However, the perception is certainly consonant with Barker's portrayal of Rivers's countertransferential relationship with his army and flying corps sufferers—pragmatic, interpersonal, relativistic, hermeneutic. And, possibly, this might illuminate the contrast between a doctor specializing in prewar, middle-class Viennese neuroses and a doctor devoted to the mores and sufferings of the Solomon Islands or Eddystone. Yet where Freud and Rivers become united is in confronting the phenomenon which the former would (perhaps paradoxically) call the "death instinct":

> Ave lives in Ysabel. His mouth is long and filled with the blood of the men he devours. . . . The broken rainbow belongs to him, and presages both epidemic disease and war. Ave is the destroyer of peoples. (*The Ghost Road*, 268)

The passage is relevant both to D. H. Lawrence's dark vision (after *The Rainbow*) and to Robert Oppenheimer's—"I am become death, the destroyer of worlds." Njiru trains Rivers in the relevant exorcism with "scholarly exactitude and intellectual impatience." But fully aware of Western ways, he comments: "Now you will put it in your book." "I never have," Rivers reflects. This remains a pity, for Rivers was well placed to provide an alternative to Freud's magisterial *Civilization and its Discontents*, where the old magician of Eros belatedly conjures up his latest trick. Yet Freud himself would have appreciated how the Melanesian term for "death instinct" becomes transcribed as the European Latin word for "Hi there!"—Ave.

The Ghost Road, in particular within the trilogy, does fictional justice to the twentieth-century tension between psychology and social anthropology, which both Rivers and Freud in their different ways, tried to negotiate through, and which has remained for commentators such as Herbert Marcuse, Eric Fromm, R. D. Laing, or Norman O. Brown to try to pull together in the early postmodern period. Rivers (the pragmatist) consented to become the first president of the "medical section" of the British Psychological Society[48] and signed up as Labour Party candidate for the University of London constituency in the year of his death;[49] Freud (the theorist) sought continuously in his later writings (*Totem and Taboo*, for instance) to bridge the personal-political divide. The attempt has been reactivated in recent years—as much in conferences and groupings as in authored treatises.[50] Books such as *Crises of the Self . . . Psychoanalysis and Politics*, edited by Barry Richards,[51] Michael Rustin's *The Good Society and the Inner World*,[52] or Andrew Samuels's *The Political Psyche* suggest that, in Britain at least, the liminal areas between selfhood and society tend to be explored out of ongoing discussion rather than individualistic theorizing. Indeed, Patrick de Maré's *Koinonia* makes just this point: "Cultures . . . concern groups and involve impact, action, and moulding, cultivating, and growing, a matter not of facts and causality but of meaning."[53] That is, surely, what the trilogy in part implies:

> The ghosts were not an attempt at evasion, Rivers thought, either by Siegfried or by the islanders. Rather, the questions became more insistent, more powerful, for being projected into the mouths of the dead. (*The Ghost Road*, 212)

In fact, the realities with which the trilogy is concerned exceed the resources of psychology and social anthropology, as academically understood. They verge on the uncanny. In his book on the Great War, *Death's Men*, Denis Winters reports the following:

> Modern analysts of death and bereavement have made us aware of the long-term effects. One sample found that 12 per cent of widows died within a year; another reported that for a year 14 per cent still saw the ghost of the deceased, 39 per cent sometimes still felt the presence.[54]

In the Great War, when most deaths were of younger men, the incidence of bereavement "visitations" was undoubtedly higher. Ada Lumb may not have believed in the séances she went to, but their very existence points to a communal longing for some higher meaning to the devastation of the war. Just as the Melanesians are deprived of their spiritual mourning rites through the imposition of colonial morality, so have British soldiers and civilians alike had spiritual rites of burial undermined by scientistic agnosticism. One of Sassoon's perceptions that recurs in the trilogy comes from his poem "Survivors": "their cowed / Subjection to the ghosts of friends who died."[55]

The whole poem is bitterly ironic (including the title), playing off propagandistic phrases ("longing to go out again" or "proud / of glorious war"), yet it can offer no compensatory exorcism or ritual of remembrance. The poem is signed "Craiglock-hart, October 1917." Later Sassoon would somewhat disown such sentiments: "Why can't they realise that the war poems were improvised by an impulsive, intolerant, immature young creature, under extreme stress of experience?"[56] Yet that is scarcely the point: "maturity" might merely have blunted the point of the truth he had to tell. For the technological advances of Great War weaponry entailed a "burnt offering" of millions of individuals—and the skepticism of Sassoon's Garsington circle left no satisfactory way to make sense of this. David Jones, by contrast, while he also suffered from war neurosis (he called it "Rosie"), nevertheless found a reciprocity between lit-erary modernism and religious tradition that could make, at the least, poetic sense. Sassoon's war poems reflect a butchered generation; Jones's In Parenthesis, and the later The Anathemata (1952), evoke continuity—for all time.

A recurrent phrase in H.D.'s fictional Great War memoir Bid Me to Live[57] is "the war will never be over." Not only Pat Barker's trilogy, but cumulative First World War paperbacks (or indeed "History Channel" footage) make this factual in the postmod-ern emporium of signs. This is even more the case if the Second World War (and even the Holocaust) is seen as a "psychic" extension of the Great War. The "repressed" returns—and returns and returns. Granted this, the "Rivers question" might be posed as: What is it that heals? . . . Overall, as represented in the novels, Rivers's remission rate is impressive, although the follow-up statistics seem no more evident than for Dr. Yealland. However, Rivers certainly had at least partial success—even among the most ravaged patients—and this owed less to scientific method or know-how than (in Eliot's phrase) to "observance, discipline, thought and action." Again counter-transference is at the heart of the matter—that of the "good-enough" man dedicated to his charges. There is, for example, no scientific technique that could automatically translate "Shotvarfet" as "It's not worth it" (The Ghost Road, 274): Rivers's under-standing arises from empathetic interpretation. Whatever the advances of medical technology, the basis of good medical practice remains the Hippocratic Oath—a bond of human trust between carer and patient devised on an island (Cos) little more "advanced" than Njiru's. And Rivers notices how Njiru's own effectiveness as healer depends on his total and devoted attention to the full person[58] involved:

> Once again that curious hypnotic effect, a sense of being totally focused on,
> totally cared for. Njiru was a good doctor, however many octopi he located in the
> colon. . . . Njiru sat back, smiling, having terminated the physical contact as tact-
> fully as he'd initiated it. (The Ghost Road, 52)

In this Rivers is way ahead of the materialistic orthodoxy of his time, anticipating "holistic" techniques and the "greening of medicine."[59]

The trilogy ends with a portentous "appearance" of Njiru:

> O Sumbi! O Gesese! O Palapoko! O Gorepoko! O you Ngengere at the root of the sky.
> Go down, depart ye. And there, suddenly, not separate from the war, not in any

way ghostly, not in *fashion blong tomate*, but himself in every particular, advancing down the ward of the Empire Hospital, attended by his shadowy retinue, as Rivers had so often seen him on the coastal path on Eddystone, came Njiru. (*The Ghost Road*, 276)

Barker is on mythically poetic ground here—shades of Eliot's "familiar compound ghost," Seamus Heaney's "meeting" with James Joyce in "Station Island," the evocation of the skinhead-double in Tony Harrison's *v*, or Derek Walcott's summoning of Greek Homer in *Omeros*. And the exorcism of mourning, here, applies to all the characters the book has made real—Prior, Owen, and Hallet especially—and to all the Great War dead, and for a cultural mindset that died on the battlefields of France ("never such innocence"), and finally for Rivers, the good doctor, whose early death was surely hastened by the burdens of healing-through-feeling. *The Ghost Road* well deserved the Booker Prize, and Barker's whole trilogy is a worthy testament to "death's men"—and to W. H. R. Rivers in particular:[60] "*There is an end of men, an end of chiefs, an end of chieftain's wives, an end of chief's children. . . . Go down and depart, oh, oh, oh.*" Another notable farewell, written during the next world war, by a survivor of that generation (whose most famous poem laments no-man's-land as an abjection of "waste"), foreshadows the ending of Barker's novel sequence:

> He left me, with a kind of valediction,
> And faded on the blowing of the horn.[61]

NOTES

1. Pat Barker, *Regeneration* (Harmondsworth: Penguin, 1922); *The Eye in the Door* (Harmondsworth: Penguin, 1994); and *The Ghost Road* (London: Viking, 1995) are the editions referred to throughout.

2. See Dennis Brown, *The Modernist Self in Twentieth-Century English Literature: A Study in Self-Fragmentation* (London: Macmillan, 1989), 43–45.

3. H.D.'s epigraph to "Writing on the Wall"; see her *Tribute to Freud: Writing on the Wall* (Manchester: Carcanet, 1985).

4. Beyond simple admiration, I have in mind the thrust of Edith Wyschogrod's book *Saints and Postmodernism: Revisioning Moral Philosophy* (Chicago and London: University of Chicago Press, 1990).

5. Rivers's disciplined attention, and the resultant "countertransferential" change in him, reminds us of the Latin root—to bear or suffer.

6. See the quotation on the paperback front cover of Richard Slobodin, *W. H. R. Rivers: Pioneer Anthropologist, Psychiatrist of The Ghost Road* (Stroud: Sutton Publishing, 1997).

7. See Michael Polanyi, *Personal Knowledge: Towards a Post-Critical Philosophy* (New York: Harper Torchbooks, 1964). For an extrapolation of the implications see Patrick Grant, *Six Modern Authors and Problems of Belief* (London: Macmillan, 1979), 121–52.

8. Siegfried Sassoon, "Letter to Robert Graves," dated July 24, 1918, in *The War Poems*, arranged and introduced by Rupert Hart-Davis (London: Faber and Faber, 1983), 130–33. Barker alludes to the conditions leading to the writing of the poem in *The Eye in the Door*, 220. It is probably the wildest poem published under Sassoon's name (originally in Robert Graves's *Good-Bye to All That* [1929], then withdrawn). It ends: "Does this break your heart? What do I care?—Sassons."

9. Barker acknowledges many of her sources in "Author's Notes" at the end of the novels.

10. Linda Hutcheon, *A Poetics of Postmodernism: History, Theory, Fiction* (London: Routledge, 1988), 5.

11. Ibid., 36.

12. He was a Labour Party candidate for election to Parliament at the time of his death in 1922. See Slobodin, *W. H. R. Rivers*, 2.

13. Robert M. Young, "Natural Theology, Victorian Periodicals and the Common Context," in *Darwin to Einstein: Historical Studies on Science and Belief*, ed. Colin Chant and John Fauvel, 70 (London: Longman, 1980). For an overall view, see J. A. V. Chapple, *Science and Literature in the Nineteenth Century* (London: Macmillan, 1986).

14. Young, "Natural Theology," 70.

15. Frank Miller Turner, "Rainfall, Plagues, and the Prince of Wales: A Chapter . . . of a Common Context," in *Darwin to Einstein: Historical Studies on Science and Belief*, ed. Colin Chant and John Fauvel, 58.

16. Young, "Natural Theology," 76.

17. Slobodin, *W. H. R. Rivers*, 5.

18. Ibid.

19. Ibid., 9.

20. Fred Hoyle, *The Intelligent Universe* (London: Michael Joseph, 1983), 9.

21. From a letter by Wilfred Owen to his mother, in Jon Stallworthy, *Wilfred Owen* (Oxford: Oxford University Press and Chatto and Windus, 1974), 109.

22. Stephen Heath, *The Sexual Fix* (London: Macmillan, 1982).

23. See Michel Foucault, *The History of Sexuality*, vol. 1 (London: Penguin, 1970).

24. W. R. Bion, *Attention and Interpretation* (Tavistock: Maresfield Reprints, 1984).

25. Siegfried Sassoon, *The Complete Memoirs of George Sherston* (London: Faber and Faber, 1972), 534.

26. Ibid., 523.

27. Andrew Samuels, *The Political Psyche* (London: Routledge, 1993), 24–26.

28. Robert M. Young, "The Vicissitudes of Transference and Countertransference: the Work of Harold Searles," *Free Associations: Psychoanalysis, Groups, Politics, Culture* 5, no. 2 (November 1995): esp. 170–72.

29. Slobodin, *W. H. R. Rivers*, 83n34.

30. Lyn Macdonald, *Somme* (London: Macmillan, 1987), 65.

31. Ford Madox Ford, from *A Man Could Stand Up*, in *Parade's End* (Harmondsworth: Penguin, 1988), 637.

32. See Philip Hoare, *Wilde's Last Stand: Decadence, Conspiracy, and the First World War* (London: Duckworth, 1997). Peter Parker's review in the *Observer* June 29, 1997, alludes to Michael Kettle's *Salome's Last Veil* (1977), which, he says, shows: "The generals had discovered that the Government was planning secret peace negotiations and were determined to stop them: all the talk of women with clitorises so enlarged they might need an elephant to satisfy them was an elaborate smokescreen" (17).

33. D. H. Lawrence, *Kangaroo* (Harmondsworth: Penguin, 1980), 235, 240.

34. The reading matter is vast and rapidly growing. See, for instance, Antony Easthope, *What a Man's Gotta Do: The Masculine Myth in Popular Culture* (London: Paladin, 1986); Jeff Hearn and D. Morgan, ed., *Men: Masculinities and Social Theory* (London: Hyman and Unwin, 1990); Lynne Segal, *Slow Motion Changing Masculinities Changing Men* (London: Virago, 1994); Harry Brod and Michael Kaufman, ed., *Theorizing Masculinities* (London:

Sage, 1994); R. W. Connell, *Masculinities* (Cambridge: Polity, 1995); and Martin Mac An Ghaill, ed., *Understanding Masculinities* (Buckingham: Open University Press, 1996).

35. See, for instance, Dennis Brown, "Male Gendering and Education into War Mentality," *New Era in Education* 75, no. 1 (April 1994): 12–17.

36. Klaus Theweleit, *Male Fantasies*, vol. 2. *Male Bodies: Psychoanalysing the White Terror*, trans. Erica Carter, Chris Turner, and Stephen Conway (Minneapolis: University of Minnesota Press, 1989).

37. A point well made by Paul Fussell in *The Great War and Modern Memory* (Oxford: Oxford University Press, 1975).

38. See "W. H. Auden's 'Hermes,'" in Dennis Brown, *The Poetry of Postmodernity* (London: Macmillan, 1994), 15–29.

39. For a salient book on this see Zygmunt Bauman, *Postmodernity and Its Discontents* (Cambridge: Polity, 1997).

40. See especially Walter J. Ong, *Orality and Literacy: The Technologizing of the Word* (London: Methuen, 1982).

41. T. S. Eliot, *Four Quartets* (London: Faber & Faber, 1958), 51.

42. Wilfred Owen, "Anthem for Doomed Youth," in *The Collected Poems*, ed. C. Day Lewis, 44 (London: Chatto and Windus, 1968).

43. Sassoon, *The War Poems*, 84–85.

44. See Brown, *The Modernist Self*, 57.

45. George Marcus, "Past, Present, and Emergent Identities: Requirements for Ethnographies of Late Twentieth-Century Modernity Worldwide," in *Modernity and Identity*, ed. Scott Lash and Jonathan Friedman, 311 (Oxford: Blackwell, 1992).

46. George Marcus and Michael M. J. Fischer, *Anthropology as Cultural Critique* (Chicago: Chicago University Press, 1986).

47. Charles Lemert, "General Social Theory, Irony, Postmodernism," in *Postmodernism and Social Theory*, ed. Steven Siedman and David G. Wagner, 26 (Oxford: Blackwell, 1992).

48. Ernest Jones, *The Life and Work of Sigmund Freud*, ed. Lionel Trilling and Steven Marcus (Harmondsworth: Penguin, 1961), 487.

49. Slobodin, *W. H. R. Rivers*, 79.

50. For example, the "Free Associations" and East London University "Psychoanalysis and the Public Sphere" conferences or the group "Psychoanalysts for the Prevention of Nuclear War."

51. Barry Richards, ed., *Crises of the Self: Further Essays on Psychoanalysis and Politics* (London: Free Association Books, 1990).

52. Michael Rustin, *The Good Society and the Inner World: Psychoanalysis, Politics, and Culture* (London: Verso, 1991).

53. Patrick de Maré, Robin Piper, Sheila Thompson, *Koinonia: From Hate, through Dialogue, to Culture in the Large Group* (London: Karnac Books, 1991), 137.

54. Denis Winter, *Death's Men: Soldiers of the Great War* (London: Penguin, 1985), 257.

55. Sassoon, *The War Poems*, 97.

56. This was in 1965, and quoted in John Silkin, *Out of Battle: The Poetry of the Great War* (Oxford: Oxford University Press, 1972), 165–66.

57. H.D., *Bid Me to Live* (London: Virago, 1984).

58. For a worthwhile "unpacking" of what is involved, see Patrick Grant's trilogy, all published in London by Macmillan: *Literature and Personal Values* (1992), *Spiritual Discourse and the Meaning of Persons* (1994), and *Personalism and the Politics of Culture* (1996).

59. See, for instance, Patrick Pietroni, *Holistic Living: A Guide to Self-Care* (London: J. M. Dent, 1986) and *The Greening of Medicine* (London: Victor Gollancz, 1990).

60. In the chapter, "Ruined Boys: W. H. Auden in the 1930s," Stan Smith cites Rivers's work and indicates how the sense of "Death Instinct" permeated Auden's early poetry. See Gary Day and Brian Docherty, ed., *British Poetry 1900–1950: Aspects of Tradition* (Basingstoke: Macmillan, 1995), 109–30.

61. Eliot, *Four Quartets*, 55.

ANNE WHITEHEAD

Open to Suggestion

Hypnosis and History in the *Regeneration* Trilogy

> "We could try hypnosis now, if you liked."
>
> "Now?"
>
> "Yes, why not? It's the time we're least likely to be interrupted."
>
> Prior's eyes flickered round the room. He licked his lips. "It's odd, isn't it? When you said most people were frightened, I didn't believe you."
>
> "What frightens them," Rivers said carefully, "is the belief that they're putting themselves completely in the therapist's power. That he can make them do anything, even things they'd normally consider ridiculous or even immoral. But that isn't true, you remain your*self* throughout."
>
> Pat Barker, *Regeneration*

In 1915, Dr. Charles S. Myers, a physician serving at casualty clearing stations behind the front line in France, wrote an article in which he observed the lack of correlation between the symptoms exhibited by the soldiers he treated and the explosion of nearby shells, which was (supposedly) their cause. Although the shells burst with considerable noise, the hearing of his patients was almost entirely unaffected; while the memory and the senses of sight, smell, and taste were invariably at the heart of the symptoms that were displayed. This discrepancy led Myers to conclude his 1915 article, "A Contribution to the Study of Shell Shock": "The close relation of these cases to those of 'hysteria' appears fairly certain."[1] Once the correlation between the symptomatology of warfare and the condition of hysteria had been recognized by some physicians, modes of treatment were revised in order to reflect the new diagnosis. In particular, the use of hypnosis entered the scene of therapy for the war neuroses, although the technique had been more or less abandoned since the turn of the century.[2]

The revival of the practice of hypnosis was attended by considerable debate. Not least among the concerns for practitioners was an anxiety about *how* the method of hypnosis achieved its cathartic effect. Writing in 1921, Myers argued in his paper "The Revival of Emotional Memories" that a sudden emotional shock effected a change in the personality of the soldier, so that he was "no longer 'himself.'"[3] With the return of the "normal" personality after the shock had subsided, the affective and cognitive experiences undergone by the "traumatized" self were repressed and were no longer available to the conscious awareness of the patient. For Myers the hypnotic cure thus involved the recovery in consciousness of the disturbing event and the consequent revival of the affective and cognitive experience with which it was associated. By recovering his memory of the traumatic event, the patient was able to integrate in his consciousness the traumatized self with the normal personality and so overcome his fractured state. The emphasis for Myers was thus on the dissociated memory; hypnosis effected a cure in the patient by reinstating the event and allowing the patient to have access to a new knowledge of, or relation to, himself. In 1916 Myers noted that, after the use of hypnosis, the patient reacted to the recovered memory with such delight that it frequently marked a "distinct change in . . . attitude"; in many cases, this transformation was so noticeable that it "appear[ed] like an alteration of personality."[4]

Myers argued further that the *timing* of the hypnotic treatment was crucial. When the soldier was first admitted he was frequently still in a state of shock; Myers terms this condition as one of "stupor." In cases of "severe stupor" the normal personality of the patient is unavailable; he reacts as if he is still involved in the disturbing event that has precipitated his neurosis. Myers observes that the next stage in recovery is an alternation of states: the patient realizes that he is in hospital but he still reacts involuntarily to the conditions of shelling. At this stage the patient also alternates between an intensely animated mode of miming the traumatic event and an ability to narrate to the physician an account of what has occurred. In other words the patient is caught between a present involvement in the event and the recognition that it properly belongs as a part of his past. In 1916, Myers provided a moving record of one of his patients who was locked into this confused mental state:

> One subject, for example, whispered to me, "Did you see that one? . . . It went up on top." "What now?" I asked. "They keep going over," he replied. Unable to catch a remark, I asked, "What did you say?" "I was talking to my mate" was the reply. To my question "What were you saying?" he answered "Get rifles." This patient could be made to realise he was in hospital, but explained his inconsistent behaviour by the remark, "Can't help it. I see 'em and I hear 'em (the shells)."[5]

Myers warns against attempting hypnotic procedures at this stage; in another case he pressed a soldier into dialogue with him who was still in a "stuporose condition" of acting out: in confusion, the patient assumed an attitude of hostility and threatened to shoot an imaginary rifle.

Myers argues that the hypnotic method should be introduced at the point at which the patient emerges from his state of confusion and disorientation. In the hypnotic catharsis, the memory is revived, as far as possible, as part of the patient's past, which he is able to narrate as a story to the physician. The tendency to reenter the experience in an emotional reliving is strong, but Myers argues that it should be discouraged. Myers's therapeutic procedure thus combines a dual approach: in "The Revival of Emotional Memories and Its Therapeutic Value," he discourages an emotional response to the traumatic event, which involves the patient in reliving the trauma, and he thereby encourages the patient to narrate the past event as a part of his own history: "I therefore made a practice of using such persuasions as—'Now when I put my hand on your forehead, you will be back in the trenches again, but you will *not be unduly afraid,* you will be able to live through it all again *calmly* and to tell me all that happened to you.'"[6] The problem that arises for Myers is that the compulsion to repeat the event in an emotional reliving is often overwhelming for the patient. In 1916, Myers noted that all too often the reactions of the patient under hypnosis revealed characteristic signs of "excitement": "His pulse and respiration increased in frequency, he sweated profusely, and not infrequently showed clear evidence of living again through the scenes which were coming vividly to his mind."[7]

The articles that were written by Myers form part of a significant debate as to the ways in which hypnosis was able to effect a cure in the case of the war neuroses. The other key participant in this debate was Dr. William Brown, who had also treated soldiers at the front line in France and at military hospitals in England. Brown believed that the hypnotic cure depended for its efficacy upon precisely the emotional reentry into the traumatic event, which was for Myers a condition to be guarded against. Brown argued that at the time of the traumatic event, the soldier was too preoccupied with his duty and with the conditions of survival to experience an emotional reaction; the affective content of the memory was therefore repressed and became unavailable to him. Under hypnosis the soldier could be made to experience vividly those emotions that he was *unable to experience at the time of the event.* For Brown the acting out of the event in the hypnotic catharsis thus represents less a *reliving* of the past than a delayed or belated experiencing of its affective power. The efficacy of the cure depended on the extent to which Brown succeeded in reviving and releasing the emotion that was associated with the event.

In Brown's account the procedures by which he operates as a hypnotist differ markedly from those of Myers. Writing in 1918, he encouraged the patient to reenter the traumatic event and to experience all the emotion with which it was associated:

> I now tell him [the patient] that the moment I put my hand upon his forehead he will seem to be back again in the trenches, in the firing line, in the fighting, as the case may be, and will live again through the experiences that he had when the shock occurred. . . . I then place my hand on his forehead. He immediately begins to twist and turn on the couch and shouts out in a terror-stricken voice. He talks as he talked at the time when the shock occurred to him. He really does live again through the experiences of that awful time. Sometimes he speaks as if in dialogue, punctuated with intervals of silence corresponding to the remarks of his interlocutor, like a person speaking at the telephone. At other times he indulges in imprecations and soliloquy. . . . *In every case he speaks and acts as if he were again under the influence of the terrifying emotion.*[8]

What appears to be debated in this exploration of the workings of hypnosis between Myers and Brown is the very notion of history itself. The papers with which they present us struggle to formulate a distinction between two different modes of conception of the historical process; what Peter Nicholls has termed (in his essay on Toni Morrison's *Beloved*) the distinction between "modern" and "postmodern" history.[9]

Myers strives to rescue from the ruins of the war a *modern* approach to the past, which depends upon a notion of authorship. The patient repossesses his own history, is enabled to inhabit his past, and this in turn provides a consolidation of his identity. The past becomes a possession; the ability to narrate the event acts as proof of its ownership. However, Myers's project is disrupted by the soldiers' compulsive reliving of the traumatic event. In contrast to his modernist desire to inhabit the past, here the past returns invasively to inhabit his patients, beyond their will or control.

This compulsive reliving represents the incursion of *postmodern* history, which is no longer a chronological sequence of events but an anachronistic collision of temporalities. Originating in a traumatic moment of shock without affect, the postmodern history represents a past that has not been experienced at the time at which it occurred. The event is dislocated from historical process; the affect with which it is associated surges back uncontrollably into the present moment, causing a painful and vivid belated experiencing of the trauma. The patient has been transformed from the subject to the object of possession; the detective story, or the mastery of the past through a process of interpretation, has become a ghost story, in which the specters of the past persistently haunt the present.

IN DREAMS BEGIN RESPONSIBILITIES . . .

Both Myers and Brown shared the common bond of being colleagues of the psychiatrist W. H. R. Rivers. Formerly most famous for his treatment of the First World War poet Siegfried Sassoon at Craiglockhart Military Hospital near Edinburgh, Rivers is currently enjoying renewed fame in his role as the protagonist of Pat Barker's fictional-historical trilogy, *Regeneration.* From the turn of the century Myers was a student of Rivers at Cambridge and assisted him in his early experiments; Myers accompanied Rivers on an anthropological expedition to the Torres Straits; and Myers corresponded with Rivers regularly during the war. In these letters Myers compared his treatment of the breakdown of soldiers at the front with Rivers's experience of the war neuroses in Britain, first at Craiglockhart, the hospital for officers and subsequently in his work for the Royal Flying Corps at Hampstead, London. William Brown served with Rivers in 1915 at Maghull Military Hospital, which specialized in the treatment of the regular soldier.[10] However, despite the close correspondence of these men, Rivers's treatment of the war neuroses differed considerably from that of either Myers or Brown; most notably, he was not convinced of the efficacy of the hypnotic method in the treatment of such cases.

For Rivers, the war neurosis was not the result of a single traumatic event but of a gradual erosion of the psychological defenses over an extended period of time. His primary interest, however, lay in the frequent development of neurotic symptomatology *after* the soldier had been removed from the distressing scenes that had (supposedly) occasioned his illness. Rivers argued that the pathology of war originated not in a specific disturbing event, but in the subsequent efforts on the part of the soldier to banish from his mind unpleasant thoughts of war. Far from removing the shocking experiences, this project paradoxically prolonged their affective power. Rivers thus relocates the cause of the neurotic symptom, so that it no longer originates in an overwhelming traumatic event that is located in the past, but reflects a present conflict between the soldier's desire to banish his recent experiences from his mind and their insistent return.

Within Rivers's framework of belief, the use of the hypnotic method clearly became redundant. In his practice of psychiatry during the First World War, Rivers avoided the use of hypnosis as far as was possible. He distrusted the technique for two well-defined reasons. Firstly, Rivers aimed to encourage his patients toward a state of independence and self-reliance; he felt that the practice of hypnosis fostered a relationship in which the patient came to depend upon the physician. Rivers only considered the use of hypnosis for those cases in which the patient's deliberate repression of his war experiences had succeeded in making his memories unavailable for recall. He argued significantly that this only happened in those cases who already displayed a tendency toward dissociation. Hypnosis therefore became a dangerous technique of intervention in these cases because it entailed the danger, for Rivers, of reinforcing this innate tendency to dissociate. In the worst instance, it could result in a splitting of the personality.[11]

In place of hypnosis, the dream becomes for Rivers the scene for the revival of the past. In his 1923 volume *Conflict and Dream*, Rivers provides the most comprehensive elaboration of his ideas on the phenomenon of the dream. His focus is again on the notion of psychological conflict in the present; borrowing a phrase from Freud, Rivers argues that the "dream-work" (or the function of the dream), represents a transformation of the source of the individual's conflict into a symbolic form, which is lacking in affect, and consequently allows the dreamer to sleep restfully. In the case of the nightmares that are so characteristic of the war neuroses, the conflict that the patient experiences is between the desire to avoid thoughts of the experience of war and the tendency of these thoughts to recur in memory. In this instance, the conflict fails to be resolved, due to the patient's unhelpful method of treating the situation. He attempts by day to repress the memory of his wartime experiences; consequently they return by night untransformed and flooded with painful affect. Rivers points out that as soon as a patient ceases to pursue a policy of avoidance, the "dream-work" can begin; the memories undergo a process of transformation into more symbolic or abstract forms and there is a lessening of affect.

Again, in relation to the dream, Rivers's emphasis on the notion of present conflict entails a resistance to the affective power of the past. Referring to the work of Freud on dreams, Rivers criticizes in *Conflict and Dream* the notion that "an incident of a dream necessarily leads one to experience."[12] However Rivers's own description of the battle nightmare inexorably "leads . . . to experience," for it involves the patient in a painful reentry into the traumatic event. Rivers's description in 1923 of the nightmares of his patients hauntingly returns us to the compulsive behavior of the soldiers under hypnosis:

> The nightmare of war-neurosis generally occurred at first as a faithful reproduction of some scene of warfare, usually some experience of a particularly horrible kind or some dangerous event, such as a crash from an aeroplane. A characteristic

feature of this variety of dream is that it is accompanied by an affect of a peculiarly intense kind. . . . The dream ends suddenly by the patient waking in a state of acute terror directly continuous with the terror of the dream and with all the physical accompaniments of extreme fear, such as profuse sweating, shaking, and violent beating of the heart. Often the dream recurs in exactly the same form night after night.[13]

Rivers describes faithfully here the invasive return of the past. The patient is possessed by a belated experiencing of the traumatic event, which is beyond his will or power to control. The past painfully and compulsively inhabits the present; time loses its chronological sequence.

If Rivers fails to recognize the significance of the phenomenon that he describes so acutely, it falls to Freud to elucidate clearly the importance of the battle nightmare. In 1920, Freud published his essay "Beyond the Pleasure Principle," which represented the revision of his thinking that occurred after the war. In particular, he was concerned to revise his concept of the function of dreams as it was represented in *The Interpretation of Dreams* (1900). There Freud had argued that every dream was based on the principle of wish-fulfillment. Clearly this did not accord with the nature of the battle nightmare; otherwise the soldiers would dream of health and of being cured. Freud argues instead that the nightmare of the war neurosis evidences a compulsion to repeat. This process is of an order distinct from that of memory. Memory figures in Freud's text as a form of narrative; like a detective, the physician prior to the war could follow the clues of the "unconscious material" that was presented by the patient and, like a good sleuth, reveal to the patient the reconstructed story of his past, "at the right moment." The process was thus primarily one of "interpreting." Now, however, the notion of a loss of memory does not appear to Freud to be adequate to the experiences of the soldiers:

The patient cannot remember the whole of what is repressed in him, and what he cannot remember may be precisely the essential part of it. Thus he acquires no sense of conviction of the correctness of the construction that has been communicated to him. He is obliged to *repeat* the repressed material as a contemporary experience instead of, as the physician would prefer to see, *remembering* it as something belonging to the past.[14]

In this passage, the affective power of the past clearly threatens to engulf all awareness of the present moment; for Freud, at least, the aftermath of the traumatic event represents a formidable force.

GHOSTLY IMAGININGS

Pat Barker's 1991 novel, *Regeneration*, represents her fictional-historical account of Rivers's treatment of the war poet Siegfried Sassoon. The novel centers on the intense psychological conflict that Sassoon experienced during the war. Sassoon was Rivers's patient at Craiglockhart Hospital because of his protest against the war, which stemmed from his conviction that the war was being needlessly prolonged, at the expense of the regular soldier, when terms for peace could have been successfully secured.[15] However, this conviction conflicted for him with his sense of duty as an officer; in staying away from the front, as a form of antiwar protest, he was abandoning the men for whose welfare he felt himself to be responsible. In Barker's novel, the crucial moment of Sassoon's decision to return to the front is figured in the form of a dream. This immediately departs from Sassoon's account in his autobiographical memoir, *Sherston's Progress* (1936). In Sassoon's description, his moment of decision to abandon his protest and return to the front occurs when Rivers is away from Craiglockhart on leave. Sassoon is visited by a mysterious figure, a Dr. Macamble, who represents the interests of the pacifists. He exhorts Sassoon to abscond from Craiglockhart to London, in order that he might be certified medically normal and responsible for his actions; by this means, Sassoon's war protest would be legitimized. Sassoon's reaction to this encouragement is represented by the thought: "Good Lord, he's trying to persuade me to do the dirty on Rivers!"[16] The episode forces Sassoon to recognize that his allegiance now lies entirely with Rivers and that he must therefore return to the fighting; once he has arrived at this realization, delay seems fruitless and Sassoon informs Rivers of his new resolution on the evening of his return from leave.

Prior to his description of the visit of Macamble, Sassoon provides a brief account of "an odd experience,"[17] in which he is visited in his room at Craiglockhart by the specter of a young soldier named Ormand, who had been killed in action six months previously. Sassoon initially mistakes the figure for a fellow patient walking in his sleep; unable to see the face of the apparition, he identifies Ormand only by his distinctive pale, buff-colored coat, which he habitually wore in the line. The figure appears briefly only to vanish; Sassoon finds the episode curious but it is not associated with any particular effect.

In *Regeneration*, Barker elides the two visitations that were contained in Sassoon's account; the ghostly apparition of "Orme" also marks for her the moment of Sassoon's decision to return to the front. Her treatment of the dream thus conforms to Rivers's theoretical principles, laid out in his study *Conflict and Dream*. Previously in the novel, Sassoon's visitations by the dead had taken the form of the wounded; covered in gore and slime, they had been figures of horror and were associated with painful affect. The figure of Orme differs in character from these former apparitions. He appears as he had done in life, not in death; and his visitation is consequently not particularly disturbing for Sassoon: "This had been so restrained. Dignified."[18] For Rivers the explanation for this would lie in the resolution of conflict, which the dream comes to represent for Sassoon in Barker's text: the arrival at a point of decision to return to the front allows the "dream-work" to begin, so that the horrifying specters of the wounded are transformed into the figure of the living Orme, and there is no discernible affect for Sassoon.

Barker's treatment of the visitation of Orme thus appears to collude with Rivers's account of the nature and function of the dream as a site for the "working-through" of present conflict. The affective power of the past seems to be absent from the scene. However, this reading of Barker's text omits a vital intertextual layer from her writing of this passage. Barker's textual source for the visitation of Orme is not confined to Sassoon's account of his appearance in *Sherston's Progress;* the description also alludes to the appearance of Cathy's ghost to Lockwood in the opening pages of Emily Brontë's *Wuthering Heights.* Barker signals to the reader the text of *Wuthering Heights* in her description of Sassoon's auditory hallucination of the sound of tapping on the window. Sassoon hears this insistent sound first in Wilfred Owen's room, where the two poets are engaged in revising a draft of Owen's poem, "An Anthem for Doomed Youth." They are preoccupied with the task of *remembering* and articulating the past; discussion between them centers on the precise sound made by a shell passing overhead. It is at this point that Sassoon first hears the noise of tapping, which serves as a prelude to the appearance of Orme, just as the insistent tapping of the fir branch at the window in *Wuthering Heights* heralds the visitation of Cathy:

> At one point Sassoon looked up and said, "What's that noise?"
> "The wind." Owen was trying to find the precise word for the sound of shells,
> and the wind was a distraction he'd been trying to ignore.
> "No, *that.*"
> Owen listened. "I can't hear anything."
> "That tapping."
> Owen listened again. "No." (126–27)

The desire of the poets to possess the past, to capture it in a precise description, is here undermined by the power of the past to return as a form of possession or haunting.

This slippage between "modern" and "postmodern" history is evidenced again in Barker's description of the autumnal weather. The source for her description appears in Sassoon's *Sherston's Progress,* in the following passage:

> Autumn was asserting itself, and a gale got up that night. I lay awake listening to
> its melancholy surgings and rumblings as it buffeted the big building. The longer
> I lay awake the more I was reminded of the troops in the line. There they were,
> stoically enduring their roofless discomfort while I was safe and warm. The storm
> sounded like a vast lament and the rain was coming down in torrents.[19]

In Sassoon's description, the sound of the wind outside leads him by a process of logical reflection to remember the "roofless discomfort" of the trenches and to contrast his present condition with those for whom he ought to be responsible. Their pitiable condition lends to the noise of the wind the quality of a "vast lament." In Barker's description, by contrast, the violence of the storm outside besieges the hospital and itself becomes a force of war. The patients within are involuntarily returned to their wartime experiences; those who are already haunted by the past now take on the appearance of being possessed:

> The wind went on rising all evening. By the time Sassoon left Owen's room, it
> was wailing round the building, moaning down chimneys, snapping branches off
> trees with a crack like rifle fire. All over the decayed hydro, badly fitting windows

rattled and thumped, and Sassoon, passing several of his "fellow breakdowns" in the corridor, thought they looked even more "mental" than usual. (127)

Similarly, the evocation of Brontë's *Wuthering Heights* serves to underline the theme of the haunting power of the past. In Brontë's description, Lockwood is caught uncertainly between nightmare and haunting: the circumstances of his dream collude in the creation of this transitional state. By allusion to Brontë's passage, Barker anchors the apparition of Orme more securely in the realm of the supernatural than Brontë anchors the ghost of Cathy. Where the apparition of Cathy appears only after Lockwood has already suffered one disturbing nightmare, the figure of Orme explicitly appears alone: "And it hadn't followed on from a nightmare either. He thought back, wanting to be sure, because he knew this was the first question Rivers would ask. No, no nightmare. Only that tapping at the window before he went to sleep" (128). Similarly, the rattle of the dry fir cones on Lockwood's lattice derives from the fir branch that is situated immediately outside the window; Brontë deliberately confuses dream and reality. In Barker's text, however, the tapping against the window does not appear to have a readily discernible cause: "There were no trees close enough to touch the glass. He supposed there might be rats, but then whoever heard of rats tapping?" (127). The construction of the dream passage thus operates to subvert Rivers's theories at the same time as it appears to uphold them: by allusion, Barker's description suggests that the power of the dream lies not only in its ability to resolve present conflict but in its haunting return of past experience.

THE RECOVERED PAST

Given what we know of Rivers's resistance to the use of hypnotic catharsis, it is indeed notable that one of the central scenes in *Regeneration* stages Rivers's hypnosis of one of his most resistant patients, Billy Prior. Prior's deliberate repression of his wartime experiences has been so extreme that he has succeeded in rendering them unavailable for recall; hence, he has reached the condition at which Rivers is prepared to consider the use of the hypnotic method. Barker signals clearly in the text Rivers's reluctance to resort to hypnosis in this case: the idea initially comes from Prior, and Rivers insists on trying out other techniques first, including writing to Prior's C.O. for any information about the circumstances surrounding Prior's breakdown. Barker follows here Rivers's description of his treatment of a young officer in "The Repression of War Experience"; in this case, Rivers describes his own hesitancy to use hypnosis and his willingness to explore alternative avenues:

> The gusts of depression to which this patient was subject were of the kind which I was then inclined to ascribe to the hidden working of some forgotten yet active experience, and it seemed natural at first to think of some incident during the time which elapsed between the shell explosion which deprived him of consciousness and the moment when he came to himself walking back from the trenches. I considered whether this was not a case in which the lost memory might be recovered by means of hypnotism, but in the presence of the definite

tendency to dissociation I did not like to employ this means of diagnosis, and less drastic methods of recovering any forgotten incident were without avail.

It occurred to me that the soldier who was accompanying the patient on his walk from the trenches might be able to supply a clue to some lost memory.[20]

In this treatment, Rivers discovered, while waiting for a reply to his inquiry, that his patient was repressing anxieties about his fitness to return to service in France. He was suffering a conflict between his apprehensions regarding his future medical condition and his fears that such thoughts be interpreted by others as cowardice. For Rivers, therapeutic intervention thus lay in persuading the patient to face his worries and hence to banish their powerful affect. Familiarly, Rivers treated his patient for a present psychological conflict, and not for a "forgotten yet active experience" that lay in his recent wartime past.

In *Regeneration*, Barker explores the alternative scenario to that which is provided by Rivers; before the reply to Rivers's inquiry comes back from Prior's C.O., Rivers determines on the use of hypnosis in order to prevent Prior from entering into a state of depression. In contrast to the historical Rivers, Barker's fictional protagonist is motivated by the desire to recover a "forgotten yet active experience," which underlies his patient's neurosis. The resulting passage is one of the most memorable in the novel. On admittance to Craiglockhart, Prior was suffering from the symptom of mutism; although he subsequently recovered the power of speech, he remained unable to remember the circumstances surrounding the formation of his symptom. In order to recover the meaning of his mutism, hypnosis is attempted. The result is remarkable: the memory that Prior recovers provides an unexpected but entirely fitting explanation for the nature of his symptom. On night watch, Prior found two of his men, Sawdon and Towers, crouched in a fire bay making tea. Minutes later, a shell hit the fire bay directly; turning back, Prior found no recognizable sign of the fire, the kettle, or Sawdon and Towers. Together with Logan, he performed his duty of clearing the remains and spreading lime over the area. Barker continues the account of his recovered memory:

> They'd almost finished when Prior shifted his position on the duckboards, glanced down, and found himself staring into an eye. Delicately, like somebody selecting a particularly choice morsel from a plate, he put his thumb and forefinger down through the duckboards. His fingers touched the smooth surface and slid before they managed to get a hold. He got it out, transferred it to the palm of his hand, and held it out towards Logan. He could see his hand was shaking, but the shaking didn't seem to be anything to do with him. "What am I supposed to do with this gob-stopper?" (93–94)

The horror of the event renders it literally unspeakable for Prior; escorted back to the casualty clearing station, he loses the ability to coordinate the movements of his jaw which are required for speech. He is unable to "swallow" or incorporate the traumatic event; it literally acts for him as a "gob-stopper."

The history that Barker offers us at this stage in the text represents the modernist desire to possess the past. Rivers acts to reconstruct the forgotten event in Prior's past, which Prior is then able to reclaim and integrate into his identity. The episode is remarkable in the novel because it marks the transition from a series of ghost stories, in which Rivers's patients are haunted by their pasts and by the recent dead, to a detective story, in which Rivers uncovers a version of Prior's past, just "at the right moment" to rescue him from despair. The memory that Rivers recovers is remarkable for the neatness with which it explains Prior's symptomatology; Prior's last words before losing his powers of speech refer to the "gob-stopper" that he holds in his hand. Having brought Prior out of his hypnotic state, Rivers sits back and waits complacently for Prior to integrate the experience into his consciousness: "Rivers watched the play of emotions on Prior's face as he fitted the recovered memory into his past" (95). Prior's actions at this point in the novel mirror exactly those of the reader. Like Prior, the reader is engaged in a process of connection between past and present; and he or she derives pleasure from the sense of mastering the past through interpretation.

However, this feeling of pleasure in reading, which derives from the sense of possessing a connection between the different elements of the text, is immediately denied to the reader in Barker's novel. The reader, like Rivers, is brought up short by the reaction of Prior to the memory that has been recovered:

He [Rivers] was unprepared for what happened next.

"*Is that all?*" Prior said.

He seemed to be beside himself with rage.

"I don't know about *all*," Rivers said. "I'd've thought that was a traumatic experience by any standards."

Prior almost spat at him. "It was *nothing.*" (95)

At this point in the novel, we are confronted with the seductive power of narrative. Narrative relies on smooth progression and sequentiality; the recovery of Prior's memory satisfies the desire of the reader for an uninterrupted narrative with no unexplained gaps or inconsistencies. However, Prior's reaction disrupts the certainties that seem to be apparent in the text. The narrative of the recovered memory does not appear to him to be as satisfactory as the story with which he himself filled in the temporal hiatus in his memory. In Prior's version of his past he himself was responsible for the death of his men; by losing his way in the confusing geography of the trenches, he opened fire upon his own men. The recovered version of his past appears to Prior inadequate in comparison with his own narrative. Barker's text raises the question of the historical status of the traumatic event: Prior's narrative appears to him to be more immediate, more real than the memory of the past which he recovers. A problem thus arises in relation to modernist history: based on notions of narrative and authorship, the past can become the site for a number of competing fictions. In this situation, the most compelling narrative account can become a substitute for the event itself.

THE PROJECT OF REGENERATION

Throughout the novel *Regeneration,* Barker is negotiating issues of historicity. The act of writing a narrative is always implicitly a mode of repetition, a retracing of ground already covered. In Barker's case this project is explicit: her novel promises that it will "regenerate" the past or return us to the event. This is precisely the seduction of narrative; it appears to be able to recapture the events that it describes, but it always and necessarily disappoints this promise. The paradoxical nature of narrative is exemplified in Barker's description of Prior's recovered memory. This marks the only point in the novel at which the past is possessed as a form of knowledge; for all the other patients, and to some extent for Rivers himself, the past possesses or haunts them in compulsive rhythms and routines. Yet this is also the only episode in the novel that is entirely fictional.[21] Barker's novel is meticulously researched; even those patients who are awarded the most minor roles in the text are based on accounts and case histories written by Rivers in his books and papers. The only exception to this is Prior; at the point at which the past appears most tangible in the novel, where Barker seems to have succeeded in her project of "regeneration," the text paradoxically does not return us to a past event. It is the only episode in the novel where Barker entirely departs from history; it seems that in this instance, the compelling narrative account has been subsumed and substituted for the past event.

What conclusions regarding history can be drawn from a reading of Barker's text? It is clear that the traumatic event problematizes our notion of what history is and how we relate to the past. In the therapeutic context, the traumatic event is either relived or remembered: in either case, it is lost to the individual. If it is relived, this process occurs without any conscious awareness on the part of the patient: there is no sense of the past as past or as a part of the individual's history. If the event is remembered, it is remembered as past but its recall necessarily takes a narrative form. In narrative, the event is altered and new perspectives are taken on it; in short, it is transformed. Barker's novel radically questions the very possibility of the "regeneration" of the past.

Barker's primary interest appears to be in the power of fictional narrative to reshape the historical event. Prior's recovered memory acts as one of the most "memorable" scenes in *Regeneration;* the question arises as to the extent to which this "fictional" episode will redefine the ways in which the historical phenomenon of World War I is remembered both on an individual and a cultural level. This problem is particularly worthy of consideration in the wake of the release of the film *Regeneration* (1997), which derives a great deal of its power from the intensity of the scenes played out between Jonathan Pryce (Rivers) and Jonny Lee Miller (Prior). In 1993, the film of *Schindler's List* reached and affected a very large audience; one result was that tourists visited the scenes of past suffering but wept over the events portrayed in the film. The narrative power of the film shaped an ambivalent collective response to the events of the Holocaust; on the one hand, it remodeled and transformed the past to conform to the language and genre of filmic narrative; on the other hand, it provided an accessible means of approach to an often unthinkable event. It is unclear as yet what impact Barker's novel (and its film version) will have on the ways in which the First World War is remembered. Yet already the power of Barker's narrative has reshaped the reading of the past. Miranda Seymour, in writing her 1995 biography of Robert Graves, *Robert Graves: Life on the Edge,* based her portrayal of the character of Rivers on Barker's fictional account.[22] Barker's construct of Rivers proved more compelling for Seymour than the historical figure and led her to revise her view of the importance of the impact of Rivers on the development of Graves as a poet; the power of the fictional narrative to transform and reconfigure the past is clearly in evidence here.

It is not only in approaching the experiences of others, however, that narrative transforms our approach to the past. The act of remembering one's own experiences is inherently the act of telling the story of the past. In Barker's account of the haunting of Sassoon, the return of his own past is filtered through the literary experiences of Lockwood in *Wuthering Heights.* The First World War has become known as the "literary" war: Paul Fussell has argued convincingly that at all social levels the troops attempted to understand the incomprehensible suffering in which they were immersed by filtering their experiences through the literary tradition.[23] Following Fussell's account of the formation of "modern memory" in the wake of the war, it appears natural that Sassoon should be haunted not only by the recent dead but also by the ghost of the English literary heritage, which no longer seemed applicable to the experiences of modern warfare. Barker's construction of this passage, so that Sassoon's experiences are filtered through and defined in opposition to a literary precedent, mirrors the methods of writing of the First World War poets. By its very nature, the act of remembering or "regenerating" the past involves the production of a narrative: the composition of this narrative account inevitably incorporates the influence of other powerful and affective narratives, which may not necessarily be derived from a literary source. The power of the narrative lies in its ability to render the past accessible to the individual, but in so doing it transforms the event and opens it to the influence of other narrative accounts.

In conclusion, then, Barker's novel interrogates the possibilities of "regeneration." Her writing of the scene in which Owen and Sassoon rework the draft of "An Anthem for Doomed Youth" appears as an analogy of her own methods of writing the past. The two poets are engaged in remembering the scenes of warfare and locating the "precise word" for the sound of a shell passing overhead. They seek to "regenerate" the past by concentration and conscious recall. In his haunting by Orme, Sassoon learns that this is only one process of "regeneration": the past also returns compulsively of its own accord. In writing *Regeneration,* Barker was involved in an intensive programme of reading and research; like her fictional Owen and Sassoon, she sought to "regenerate" the past by a concentrated effort of will. As in the case of Sassoon, the past returned compulsively of its own accord. Barker's researches for the novel coincided with the Gulf War; the television reportage portrayed soldiers in training attacking from a trench with fixed bayonets. The media coverage was continually focused on the threat of gas attacks. The traumatic past compulsively returned to haunt the present in an unanticipated collision of temporalities. Barker's text leaves us finally in an uneasy "no-man's-land" between past and present; although the past cannot be "regenerated" or brought again into existence, its specters compulsively haunt the present and do not readily submit to the processes of narrative transformation.

NOTES

1. Charles S. Myers, "A Contribution to the Study of Shell Shock," *Lancet*, February 13, 1915, 320. The term "shell shock" was in fact a misnomer for the severe and debilitating effects suffered by the soldiers. Although it was initially thought that the explosion of the shells caused the range of symptoms which was displayed, "shell shock" was subsequently found to be a form of hysteria. It was recognized by some, but not all, medical practitioners to be a psychological condition caused by the traumatic circumstances of warfare, in particular the protracted periods of immobility and lack of agency. For an interesting discussion of the medical views and treatments of shell shock during the First World War see Eric Leed, *No Man's Land: Combat and Identity in World War I* (Cambridge: Cambridge University Press, 1979.) For an interesting consideration of the gender implications of shell shock as hysteria, see also Elaine Showalter, *The Female Malady: Women, Madness, and English Culture* (London: Virago, 1987), 167–94.

2. The practice of hypnosis had largely fallen into disuse following a double blow in the 1890s. In 1892 the legal practice of hypnosis in France was restricted to the medical profession and the Catholic Church banned it altogether—a ban that remained in place until 1955. In 1896 Freud rejected hypnosis as a medical tool in his founding of psychoanalysis, claiming that it was subject to the taint of suggestion. In France Pierre Janet, whose work has recently been championed by the Recovered Memory Movement, continued to practice hypnosis, but his work was largely eclipsed by the growing popularity of psychoanalysis. For a more detailed discussion of the debates surrounding the revival of hypnosis in the First World War see Ruth Leys, "Traumatic Cures: Shell-Shock, Janet, and the Question of Memory," *Critical Inquiry* 20 (1994): 623–62.

3. Charles S. Myers, "The Revival of Emotional Memories and Its Therapeutic Value (II)," *British Journal of Medical Psychology* 1 (1921): 22.

4. Charles S. Myers, "A Contribution to the Study of Shell Shock," *Lancet*, January 8, 1916, 68.

5. Ibid., 67–68. In this quotation Myers interprets for us the meaning of his patient's "I see 'em and I hear 'em," as referring to the exploding shells. However the patient's remark could equally refer to his friends, implying that he was able to see and hear them in the present. Myers forecloses this interpretation, which involves a more disturbing and literal form of haunting than his own version.

6. Myers, "The Revival of Emotional Memories," 20.

7. Myers, "A Contribution," 68.

8. William Brown, "The Treatment of Cases of Shell Shock in an Advanced Neurological Centre," *Lancet*, August 17, 1918, 198.

9. Peter Nicholls, "The Belated Postmodern: History, Phantoms, and Toni Morrison," in *Psychoanalytic Criticism: A Reader*, ed. Sue Vice, 51–52 (Cambridge: Polity, 1996).

10. For the only biographical study written on Rivers see Richard Slobodin, *W. H. R. Rivers* (Stroud: Sutton, 1997). In his monograph, Slobodin emphasizes Rivers's career as a pioneering anthropologist over his psychiatric work during the war.

11. It is worth noting that Billy Prior, the fictional character whom Rivers hypnotizes in *Regeneration,* does subsequently suffer from a split-personality disorder in *The Eye in the Door,* the second volume of the *Regeneration* trilogy. Barker's presentation of the character of Prior, who is a bisexual, working-class officer, implies that he has an innately divided character; following hypnosis this results in pathological consequences. However Barker's primary interest does not lie in an examination of the hazards of hypnosis, as perceived by Rivers, but in a broader exploration of the split nature of the war experience, in terms of gender and class positions.

12. W. H. R. Rivers, *Conflict and Dream* (London: Kegan Paul, 1923), 61.

13. Ibid., 66.

14. Sigmund Freud, "Beyond the Pleasure Principle," in *On Metapsychology: The Theory of Psychoanalysis,* ed. Angela Richards, 288 (Harmondsworth: Penguin, 1991).

15. The historical Sassoon thus lay outside the range of patients who were treated by Myers and Brown. He was not suffering from a psychological disorder but was admitted to Craiglockhart on a false diagnosis in an attempt to discredit his protest against the war. Barker's treatment of the fictional Sassoon in *Regeneration* suggests that he is on the verge of a psychological breakdown and thus to some extent validates Rivers's treatment of him. Sassoon's daredevil behavior in the trenches, earning him the name of "Mad Jack," and his nightmares and hallucinations are treated by Barker as evidence of his impending "shell shock."

16. Siegfried Sassoon, *Sherston's Progress* (London: Faber, 1936), 42.

17. Ibid., 32.

18. Pat Barker, *The Regeneration Trilogy* (Harmondsworth: Penguin, 1996), 128. All subsequent references will be included in the text.

19. Sassoon, *Sherston's Progress,* 31.

20. W. H. R. Rivers, "The Repression of War Experience," *Lancet,* February 2. 1918, 75.

21. Hilary Hinds of Lancaster University has pointed out to me that Prior's memory bears a strong resemblance to a passage from Edmund Blunden's *Undertones of War* (Harmondsworth: Penguin, 1940). The relevant passage reads as follows: "Not far away from that shafthead, a young and cheerful lance-corporal of ours was making some tea as I passed one warm afternoon. Wishing him a good tea, I went along three firebays; one shell dropped without warning behind me; I saw its smoke faint out and thought all was as lucky as it should be. Soon a cry from that place recalled me; the shell had burst all wrong. Its butting impression was black and stinking in the parados where three minutes ago the lance-corporal's mess-tin was bubbling over a little flame. For him, how could the gobbets of blackening flesh, the earth-wall sotted with blood, with flesh, the eye under the duckboard, the pulpy bone be the only answer? At this moment, while we looked with dreadful fixity at so isolated a horror, the lance-corporal's brother came round the traverse. He was sent to company headquarters in a kind of catalepsy. The bay had to be put right, and red-faced Sergeant Simmons, having helped himself and me to a share of rum, biting hard on his pipe, shovelled into the sandbag I held, not without self-protecting profanity, and an air of 'it's a lie; we're a lie'" (51). Barker's rewriting of the passage emphasizes the failure of strategies of self-protection and distancing in the face of such horror. Barker's choice of Blunden as a literary source underlines several of the points made in this essay. Blunden's writing of *Undertones of War* highlighted the role of memory: it was his second attempt at a war memoir, because his first account was written too close to the events. In his "Preliminary," Blunden also draws attention to the nature of narrative as repetition, with the reiterated phrase, "I must over the

ground again" (vii). For the reader, Prior's memories not only fill in his own experiences, but are also filtered through Blunden's literary account of the war, highlighting the nature of memory (and narrative) as a rehearsing of already familiar tropes.

22. The information here and in the concluding paragraph is derived from an interview between Pat Barker and Miranda Seymour, held in St. Nicholas Parish Church, Durham, England, on June 12, 1997. The theme of the interview was the relationship between biography and fiction; the event was organized as part of the 1997 Durham Literary Festival.

23. Paul Fussell, *The Great War and Modern Memory* (Oxford: Oxford University Press, 1975), 61–169.

The Uncanny Case of Dr. Rivers and Mr. Prior
Dynamics of Transference in *The Eye in the Door*

Consider a consummately metafictional moment: two characters, a psychoanalytic therapist and his soldier-patient, discuss the latter's episodes of amnesia,
"fugue states" that leave the soldier anxiously gazing at his hands, expecting that they
will be transformed—suddenly hairy and unfamiliar, uncanny. "You've read Jekyll
and Hyde?" he asks. The doctor opposes his patient's identification with Hyde, claiming that the fugue state is rarely "the darker side of the personality." Still, he goes on
to think about his own "deeply divided" nature in terms of Jekyll's words, quoted as
"almost" his own: "It was . . . in my own person, that I learned to recognize the thorough and primitive duality of man."[1] Appearing in the central chapter of Pat Barker's
The Eye in the Door (and thus at the center of the *Regeneration* trilogy), this scene
provokes our awareness of reading characters who are engaged in analysis, both psychoanalytic and literary. They are simultaneously "reading" themselves as they interpret a fictional text, Robert Louis Stevenson's *The Strange Case of Dr. Jekyll and Mr.
Hyde.* That dual mirrors (such as two texts or two consciousnesses) can produce a
sense of multiple selves is hinted by the first chapter of *The Eye in the Door,* when the
soldier Billy Prior gazes into a mirror that faces another, showing "a long corridor of
Priors."[2] Barker's mirrors or mirror-like surfaces that harbor and connect multiple
selves reflect specific moments in Stevenson's novella, in which both Jekyll and Utterson see themselves, yet imagine "Hyde," in the same mirror.[3] Thus, through shared
motifs, explicit quotations, and near-quotes from *Jekyll and Hyde,* Barker's novel
presents the case history of Rivers and Prior—the story of a psychoanalytic treatment
—as a parallel to Stevenson's "strange case." Just as Barker's doctor, based on the historical W. H. R. Rivers, sees "Jekyll and Hyde" as having "passed into the language"
(143), so too Stevenson's novella has "passed into" *The Eye in the Door,* appropriated
and subtly reworked by the characters and their author. Moreover, since Dr. Rivers
works not only with "Mister Prior" but also with Charles Manning and Siegfried Sassoon, contrasts between these therapeutic encounters further define the dialogic,
transferential process of reading selves, both in texts and in psychoanalysis.

Seeing *The Eye in the Door* as a reworking of *Jekyll and Hyde* can be useful in ways
discussed by Brian Rose in *"Jekyll and Hyde" Adapted: Dramatizations of Cultural
Anxiety.* Though he concentrates on films, Rose can generate awareness that Barker's
novel is part of an immense, diverse cultural context of Jekyll and Hyde adaptations,

including musical and even restaurant versions. Such strikingly frequent, ongoing revisions (starting with the first theatrical production, staged less than a year and a half after the publication of the novella) suggest that *Jekyll and Hyde* is a "tracer text," a means to map "shifts in attitudes" by comparing its adaptations.[4] Thus our own period's understanding of working-class consciousness can be seen in the recasting of Stevenson's "apelike" Hyde in Barker's Billy Prior and Valerie Martin's Mary Reilly, the protagonist of Martin's 1990 retelling of *Jekyll and Hyde*.[5] In addition, as a historical novel, *The Eye in the Door* suggests how Stevenson's story may have been interpreted and appropriated during the First World War (Barker is aware, for example, that Wilfred Owen read *Jekyll and Hyde* in 1918, perhaps at Sassoon's suggestion).[6] Barker's adaptation, like Martin's *Mary Reilly*, also brings out undeveloped, perhaps even repressed, aspects of the original text. Hence, such reworkings convey that *Jekyll and Hyde* offers "knowledge never possessed or . . . knowledge that is partially useful but requires redesignation or updating to achieve maximum resonance and value."[7]

In particular, *The Eye in the Door* develops valuable insights about the psychoanalytic process that Robert Louis Stevenson anticipates without, of course, fully defining. The portraits of analyst and patient that Barker presents are both psychologically astute and culturally representative, encapsulating concerns prevalent before and during 1918, while also defining, for our own time, relationships that promote healing and growth. In *The Eye in the Door*, Rivers describes, without intending to, qualities that make his and Prior's psychoanalytic encounters extraordinarily dialogic, and thus effective, when he notes Prior's "very marked tendency to probe. To insist on a two-way relationship" (70). Dialogic partnership between analyst and patient is a striking feature of the historical Rivers's experimental therapy. Similarly, Freud redefined the involvement and exchanges in the psychoanalytic relationship, especially as he came to emphasize the "transference" that occurs when "hidden and forgotten . . . impulses" from the past are attached to present situations and people.[8] The rejection of hypnosis, which enhanced the patient's passivity, in favor of dialogical therapy is thus a keynote for both Dr. Rivers and Dr. Freud at the time around the First World War. Stevenson's Dr. Jekyll also undertakes an experimental two-way method of exploring selves, but, as he regretfully observes, his research is "incomplete," in part because of its dependence on external controls—the drugs that work much like hypnosis, by bringing out and then submerging the repressed self that Hydes within.[9] Depicting a disastrously inadequate working-through of deep-seated conflicts, Stevenson's novella offers an instructive contrast with Barker's, Rivers's, and Freud's texts.

ACTING OUT THE HIDDEN SELF

Prior's deeply embedded conflicts begin to emerge in an opening paragraph of imagined violence, encapsulating the acting out of unconscious impulses that psychoanalysis contrasts with remembering, as alternative "ways of bringing the past into the present."[10] Prior walks with a pretty girl by "formal beds" of flowers in Hyde Park. The erotically resonant beginning of spring is evoked by "early tulips . . . in tight-lipped rows," but rather than admiring the flowers with Myra—whose name might convey such appreciation or the wonder she soon feels—he perceives troops in a position that exposes them to gunfire: "Billy Prior spent several moments setting up an enfilade, then, releasing his companion's arm, seized an imaginary machine-gun and blasted the heads off the whole bloody lot of them" (3). Of course this action may seem merely a joke, which is Myra's reading of Prior's playful claim about time spent "in a loony bin" (3). But, as Freud realized, jokes are like dreams, able to convey unconscious feelings, and the fact that Prior later repeats the same pretended gunfire as he imagines "striking munition workers" invites analysis of this "childish gesture" (110–11). Though the enfilade of "tight-lipped" tulips might suggest a reenactment of Prior's extensive trench experience, the echoed sounds of "lips" and "lipped" suggest a much closer target for his violent impulses, a possibility that becomes clearer when he rejects "tight-lipped" Myra and is aware of being "made physically sick by the sight and sound and smell of civilians," including "whiffs of perfume that assaulted his nostrils whenever a woman walked past" (7). Moreover, Myra's vacillations about having sex, even after she and Prior are aroused, elicit a remark that implies his repressed violence: "Myra, you're the sort of girl who ends up in a ditch with her stockings round her neck." [11] The intense hostility Prior expresses toward noncombatants, and particularly women, fits the First World War's paradoxical pattern of "the enemy to the rear," described by Paul Fussell and seen by Sandra Gilbert and Susan Gubar as a more persistent "battle of the sexes." [12] Prior's rejection of the female is accompanied by conscious preference for soldiers and their "stench" (7), followed by his illicit sexual liaison with another officer, Charles Manning. The impression that Prior is unconsciously acting out deep impulses based in his past increases as this sexual encounter unfolds in a setting whose symbolic imagery and sense of forbidden sexuality vividly recall *Jekyll and Hyde*.

In Stevenson's first chapter, "Story of a Door," two men stand outside a tellingly divided, decayed residence and share in the knowledge that it has become a place of forbidden access, that "Hyde" has a key to enter. Barker brilliantly adapts this symbolism as she depicts Prior and Manning's entry into the latter's house, which has become—due to bombing that has demolished residences nearby—a place of secret, nocturnal, homosexual assignations. Imagery of the surrounding neighborhood, with its "huge gap" and white dust marking the absences war creates, is compounded by Manning's struggle with his front door, whose damaged lock seems to require forced entry, along with an "ominous" crack over the living room door, and the photograph of his wife and sons, funereally covered by a sheet, just as the furniture too is "shrouded" (9–10). With his female-centered family relegated to the country for safety, and he himself living at his club while using his house to pursue his dangerous "other" side, Manning updates Stevenson's tale of "the double life," which Elaine Showalter describes as "a fable of fin-de-siécle homosexual panic"—a panic that multiplied as the 1914–18 war dragged on and homosexuals were blamed. [13]

Within Manning's ominously divided, somewhat uncanny house (a home that has become unhomelike, unfamiliar), Barker describes a sexual encounter shadowed by Prior's potential sadism, which he expresses inwardly, yet controls, perhaps in part through a joke, when he thinks of the "raging homicidal mania" Manning inspires

(13–14, 15). Revealing Prior's moments of sheer hatred toward the genteel, class-conscious Manning, Barker elaborates the symbolism of Jekyll's divided house/laboratory and his mirror, as she brings out the class conflict that is one of the roots of Prior's violent impulses (as can also be seen in Hyde and Jekyll). Thus after "transform[ing] himself into" a Hyde-like "working-class boy," coolly and contemptuously playing to Manning's need, Prior is mockingly aware of being taken "to the *servants'* quarters" (11, 12). Yet in the housemaids' small space his mood suddenly shifts as he glimpses their mirror, and holds one of their uniforms to his face, "inhaling the smell of sweat," a response that strongly contrasts with his previous reaction to women's perfume: "This impulse had nothing to do with sex, though it came from a layer of personality every bit as deep" (11–12). Feelings of class consciousness and hostility continue through the sexual encounter, after which Prior moves the maids' mirror to face him, exactly as Jekyll moves his mirror in order to see "Hyde." However, Barker presents Prior's gaze as probing not only his class roots, but also his identification with his mother, who was once a housemaid: "Prior reached out and turned the looking-glass towards him. Into this glass they had looked, half past five every morning" (14).[14] As Prior later sees, the conflict in himself is one he continues to play out from both sides, identifying with and disliking both figures, his proudly working-class, violently abusive, manly father and his delicate, upwardly striving mother, a division that reflects Hyde and Jekyll: "*He* and *she*—elemental forces, almost devoid of personal characteristics—clawed each other in every cell of his body, and would do so until he died" (90). This passage powerfully articulates the nature of "acting out" as an unwilled repetition of the past, for which the psychoanalytic, therapeutic relationship is both a venue and an antidote.

REPETITIONS AS STORIES, DREAMS AS DOORS

Reenacting the past can be seen as unconscious storytelling. As Jean Laplanche and J.-B. Pontalis observe, through the "compulsion to repeat" a person "deliberately places himself in distressing situations, thereby repeating an old experience, but he does not recall this prototype; on the contrary, he has the strong impression that the situation is fully determined by the circumstances of the moment."[15] Such an unconscious compulsion could explain how Billy Prior gets himself into the stressful position of serving as an Intelligence officer assigned to spy on working-class pacifists whom he has known since childhood, including imprisoned pacifist Beattie Roper and the highly sought resistance leader Patrick MacDowell ("Mac"). Prior's current relationships with these war resisters, as well as with the Resistance infiltrator and government agent Lionel Spragge, uncannily reenact his childhood conflicts. When he was a young child, Beattie, who calls him "son," became his surrogate mother when his mother's supposed tuberculosis required separation (40, 208, 56). In the spring of 1918, Prior feels forced to stand by and watch while Beattie suffers in prison, just as his childhood memories focus on nights when he sat at the top of the stairs, hyperaware of the violence his mother often faced. Though Beattie is in danger (like his mother, due to ill health), and he takes risks to incriminate Spragge (the witness against her) and thus to win her release, still Prior finds himself torn, quite literally divided, as he experiences dissociated fugue states that he connects with Spragge. Prior's irrationally intense, physical hatred for this man resembles reactions to Hyde, and these feelings seem to spring from the older man's similarity to Prior's father, as well as a feared likeness to Prior himself, as is shown in the uncanny moment when Prior is afraid he will find his own face when Spragge turns toward him (185).[16] During this confrontation, Prior experiences a fugue, threatens to "brain" Spragge with his cane, and, when he comes back to himself, remembers a time in childhood, when he was "walking with his father's hand" and his father made him a silent accomplice in the philandering that betrays Prior's mother (190, 187–88). Since Prior does not see a link between this memory and the incident with Spragge, this passage offers a perfect example of the "textual unconscious," while also echoing Jekyll's recollection of his childhood, when, as he says, "I had walked with my father's hand," a memory that occurs immediately after Hyde has used his cane to brutally kill Sir Danvers Carew, an elderly father figure.[17] Thus both Jekyll's and Prior's responses suggest an unrecognized parricidal impulse in their violence toward Carew/Spragge. Moreover, since Mac was also Beattie's adopted son (113), and is large, overtly masculine, and against the war (traits shared with Prior's father, making Mac the son Harry Prior would have wanted), the rivalry of Billy and Mac, and Billy's betrayal of his "brother," can seem compulsively repetitive. Prior, the correctly dressed boy on the rise, has always been spared the beating that Mac received and continues to endure at the novel's close, for not putting on the demanded uniform (109, 263).

Describing such repetitions of past conflicts, Laplanche and Pontalis draw upon Freud's words to suggest that "the repressed seeks 'to return' in the present, whether in the form of dreams, symptoms or acting-out" arguing that: "a thing which has not been understood inevitably reappears; like an unlaid ghost, it cannot rest until the mystery has been solved and the spell broken."[18] *The Eye in the Door* vividly depicts psychoanalysis as a laying of such ghosts through the process of reading and solving a mystery. A hallmark of this psychoanalytic process is the analyst and patient's partnership in dream analysis. This process is described by the historical Rivers in *Conflict and Dream* and vividly rendered by Barker as Rivers and Prior focus on the latter's nightmare concerning the eye in the door.[19] After Prior recounts his dream, Rivers seeks to elicit his understanding of it through "guarded inquiries" and minimal use of "leading questions."[20] Rivers's silences also not only allow Prior's associations to emerge, but also compel him to overcome the inevitable resistance that is evidence of deep feelings coming out through barriers of repression. In this way, Prior and Rivers gradually determine that Prior's first, intensely emotional association—with the detached eyeball of a soldier in his platoon, depicted in *Regeneration* —unexpectedly screens a more immediately threatening association, the current conflict that the dream seems to express. Prior questions Rivers's view of dreams as "attempts to resolve conflict," since he feels he is on the pacifists' side against the prison-state's "constant surveillance," represented by the eye that relentlessly stares at the pacifist-prisoner from his or her cell door (74–75).[21] Given Prior's resistance, mounted through an interpretation that protectively blinds the dreamer, Rivers finally has to ask him to identify "who was the spy" in the situation with Beattie and the deeply disturbing eye (75). The therapist thus elicits an interpretation that is clearly a mutual construction, though Prior states it: that "eye" is the pun of the unconscious for "I." In Prior's view, this outrageously bad pun does indeed convey his conflict: "I hate what I [as "eye"] do" (74–75). Moreover, the oval mirror on the back of Prior's bedroom door (53) reinforces the identification of the eye in the door with Prior, so that his nightmare image of stabbing the eye possibly conveys a desire to stop his own seeing, the prying suggested by his name (53, 58).

Ambivalence about seeing, even the impulse to blind oneself, is a response to threatening experiences exhibited by both Prior and Rivers—the one through periodic memory gaps, the other through an even more striking suppression of visual memory since he was five. Noting that William Rivers studied vision, carrying his research from physiology to anthropological field work, Anna Grimshaw holds that *The Eye in the Door* "establishes a fundamental opposition . . . between seeing as insight and seeing as surveillance."[22] The symbolism of the novel hinges on the fact that the eye in the prison cell (and in Prior's bedroom door) "looks inward," which to Grimshaw represents William Rivers's stance of "look[ing] into the self as a prelude to engaging with the world." Though most of the displaced or singular eyes in Barker's trilogy evoke feelings of dread, I believe that Grimshaw is right concerning the duality of the symbol. For inward vision is both fearful and necessary, painful and yet desired, as *Jekyll and Hyde* suggests through the compulsion of several characters (Jekyll, Utterson, Lanyon) to see Hyde. Indeed, an image William Veeder notes in the printer's copy of Stevenson's novella seems to anticipate Barker's focal symbol, when Utterson's desire to see within Jekyll's house/identity motivates him to looks at the shops near the laboratory, "all the time still with one eye over his shoulder, spying at the door."[23] If the door represents, as Rivers implies, the way into "the innermost part of one's identity" (155), is not such looking necessary? Moreover, is not the dream, when analyzed, an eye of the door into the psyche?

THE MIRROR OF TRANSFERENCE

For Freud, another way to access the unconscious—a way he compares to dreams—is the transference that occurs in the psychoanalytic relationship. Freud's revised, positive assessment of this process, strongly presented in two essays, "The Dynamics of Transference" (1912) and "Remembering, Repeating and Working-Through" (1914), is based on the perception that memory is not enough. He holds that people repeat and act out the past more fully and revealingly than they remember it, and that the "compulsion to repeat" is expressed not only with the analyst "but also in every other activity and relationship."[24] Though Freud did not see therapeutic value in the reverse process, the analyst's countertransference, Barker powerfully demonstrates the opening of doors past resistance that may occur when two people engage in a two-way transferential relationship.[25]

The moment in which Rivers and Prior "exchange seats" both symbolizes this transference and marks a deeper engagement of Rivers with his own buried impulses and problems (136). Structurally, this scene occurs at the midpoint of Barker's trilogy, in the central chapter (eleventh out of twenty-one) in the second book of the trilogy. Before this pivotal point, Prior has certainly possessed the power to disturb Rivers. For example, being described as an insufficiently forthcoming "strip of empathic wallpaper" has stuck in Rivers's mind, and he has found Prior's "jeering flirtatiousness" to be "surprisingly difficult to handle" (70). Yet in chapter 11 of *The Eye in the Door* Prior interprets Rivers's unconscious eye-covering gesture in a way so "disconcerting" that Rivers lets slip the fact that he has "no visual memory" (135–36). This revelation elicits Prior's imitation of the cliché therapist's line ("Have you always been like this?"), followed by their changing places, and Prior's unforgettably camp parody of Rivers's manner, forcing the doctor to tell of his buried self while looking into a mirror (136–37). Their discussion of what happened to Rivers at age five seems to go far beyond Rivers's conscious intentions, not only profoundly shocking him (due to Prior's assertion that the traumatic event was rape), but also eventually leading to Rivers's admission, after repeated denials and stammering, of the enormity of the event, shown by his acting out its impact. As Prior says, "Whatever it was, you *blinded* yourself so you wouldn't have to go on seeing it. . . . You put your mind's eye *out*" (136–39). Rivers opposes Prior's insistence that loss of memory necessarily indicates the repression of an objectively horrific event: "You must be wary of filling the gaps in your memory with . . . with monsters" (139). This projection of fear, says Rivers, is comparable to "the guide for medieval map-makers," "*Where unknown, there place monsters*" (139). But his rationalizations, hesitations, and stammering all strongly convey the resistance that marks the emergence of something very deep and thus reveals Rivers's transference. Moreover, the obvious inadequacy of "the Rivers guide to map-making" ("*Where unknown, there place dressing-gowns*") is not merely shown by Prior's mockery (though Barker does give Prior all the scene's best lines). After Rivers tries to deny the mind's "monsters," that word keeps returning to his mind and then seems to take form as he dreams of a monster.[26] It thus appears that his exchange with Prior truly "touches a nerve" (135).

Rivers's pivotal action of facing his mirror and changing places with his patient recalls Carroll's Alice going through the looking-glass: from this point, Rivers seems to reflect Prior's journey.[27] Mirroring Prior's attack on his nightmare eye/I and his expressed loathing for himself in his job, Rivers repeatedly conveys distrust for doctors and psychologists. He thus worries about the medical researcher's disengagement from feeling, jokes that he "hate[s] psychologists," and mocks the psychologist in the Pemberton Billing trial, who refers to homosexuals and lesbians as "monsters" (146–48). Like Prior, too, Rivers confronts his conflicts about himself indirectly, through a terrifying nightmare. In his dream, a cadaver rises up, like Frankenstein's creature, from the "dissecting table" where his friend Henry Head prepares to operate on the "shaven head" (163). This monster seeks Rivers in his bed, coming through doors that "flap open with a noise like the beating of wings."[28] Rivers interprets his

Frankenstein-like dream as expressing his fear of the doctor's "suspension of empathy," potentially "the root of all monstrosity," since "the torturer . . . practises the same suspension" (164). Yet this interpretation, like Prior's of his own nightmare, serves as a screen that shields Rivers from a more immediate, disturbing fear, conveyed in his depression and anxiety just before the dream, apparently aroused by the Pemberton Billing trial and talk "about monsters and hereditary degeneracy" (160–61). Since the trial stirred public fears of homosexuality, the current news causes Rivers to think, in a worried and fond manner, about Siegfried Sassoon, the homosexual whom Barker suggests Rivers loves (161). Hence, it is possible for Barker's reader to decide, in contrast to Rivers's conscious understanding, that his nightmare deals with conflicts stemming from his sexuality as well as his work (164). Knowing of Head's reputation as the doctor who "can cure sodomites" (71), Rivers has dreamed of a naked man whom he tries to stop Head from operating on. The man's "genitals are shriveled," yet his rising from the table of dissection (or analysis) is represented in sexual images of "bone," "mouth," and "a hand [that] grasps Head's hand at the wrist" (163). Moreover, echoes of "hand" and "Head"/ "head" suggest the inseparability of doctor and "monster." In other words, the figure that "thrusts its anatomical drawing of a face *into* his" (163; my emphasis) seems to represent Rivers himself, specifically his sexuality. Since Rivers also, like Head, is assigned to "cure sodomites," his nightmare encapsulates the conflict between his professional role and his sexual self, though Rivers's dream analysis only recognizes a more general conflict. Thus Rivers, along with Prior, exemplifies resistances that form barriers to recognizing one's selves— ways of putting out the eye in the door.

Yet the doors that burst open in Rivers's dream, like "the door to the innermost part of one's identity" that is "smashed open" in his earlier thoughts (155), can suggest the possibility of getting through barriers of repression. Barker's motif of doors that are forcibly opened reworks Stevenson's novella, which foregrounds the story of a problematic door that is finally broken down when others enter Jekyll's inner compartment, where his secret identity lies. Building on this imagery, *The Eye in the Door* presents the revelation of Prior's dissociated self to Rivers as a breakthrough, an impression Barker creates by making Prior's late-night entry in chapter 19, though announced by the maid, seem unexpected and rushed, as perceived by his doctor:

> [Rivers] felt very unfit to cope with this, whatever it was, but he buttoned his tunic and looked vaguely around for his boots. Prior seemed to be climbing the stairs very quickly, an easy, light tread quite unlike his usual step. His asthma had been very bad on his last visit. He had paused several times on the final flight of stairs and even then had entered the room almost too breathless to speak. The maid must have misheard the name, that or—
>
> Prior came into the room, pausing just inside the door to look around. (238)

Coming to "Dr. Rivers," as he calls him (238), announced by the "odd light footstep" that constitutes Utterson's first perception of Hyde (*Jekyll and Hyde*, 40), Prior's alternate self claims never to feel pain or fear. His taunting dialogue then culminates in a demonstration of power, the unmoved burning of his hand and transformation back into his familiar self, that seems intended to amaze the good doctor, like the showy Hyde-to-Jekyll transformation that fatally shocks Stevenson's Dr. Lanyon (*Jekyll and Hyde*, 74–75). Similarities of Prior's other self to Jekyll's Hyde include that the alter rejects Prior's father, is stronger than Prior in a crisis, yet is also peculiarly undeveloped and childish, because he was "was born two years ago. In a shell-hole in France."[29] Despite the odd, uncanny aspects of this encounter, Rivers sees that "to feel no pain and no fear" in overwhelming circumstances "was not impossible, or even abnormal" (245). Prior differs from others only in the separation of his "warrior double" from his ordinary consciousness, intensifying the other self's frightening aspect (245). Freud sheds light on this duality, with words that recall Jekyll and Hyde, in his explanation of war neuroses: "The conflict is between the soldier's old peaceful ego and his new warlike one, and it becomes acute as soon as the peace-ego realizes what danger it runs of losing its life to the rashness of its newly formed, parasitic double."[30]

Numerous echoes of *Jekyll and Hyde* in Rivers's meeting with Prior's double emphasize differences that mark this coming together of selves, in the doctor's presence, as a crucial step toward healing. Even though the "newly formed" self replicates many features of Stevenson's Hyde, this side of Prior also brings out crucial knowledge—that Prior has coped in childhood and the trenches through a type of self-hypnosis that produces dissociation. This knowledge leads to a mutual, dialogic construction of the way he can work through his problem. As Prior proposes that he could perhaps use self-suggestion to get himself to remember, rather than coping through dissociation and amnesia, he wonders whether merely remembering is sufficient "to heal the split" (249). Rivers responds with an image and a quoted statement from the scene in which Jekyll first sees himself in the mirror as Hyde and thinks, "This, too, was myself" (*Jekyll and Hyde*, 79). As Rivers puts it, "I think there has to be a moment of . . . recognition. Acceptance. There has to be a moment when you look in the mirror and say, yes, this too is myself" (249).

It is clear that the "recognition" Rivers describes matters equally to him, and it also applies to the present relationship between himself and Prior. This "moment" exemplifies transference at its best. Rivers models the needed acceptance when he asks Prior to stay with him, calls him "Billy" for the first time (as he would a social equal and friend), as well as affectionately reprimanding the ever-exasperating, rule-breaking "*Mister* Prior." Dr. Rivers marks this transition to greater closeness with a symbolic gesture, giving Mister Prior a key to the house and planning to inform the servants to admit him, just as Dr. Jekyll acts when he most fully accepts "Mr. Hyde" (250; cf. *Jekyll and Hyde*, 80). The mutual transference between Rivers and Prior, who mirror each other's self-blinding and need for self-acceptance, is clinched, perhaps, in Barker's reworking of the symbolic imagery of hands and handwriting from *Jekyll and Hyde*. Where the hand of Hyde is repeatedly contrasted with that of Jekyll, thus serving as a sign of their difference, their handwriting (which Jekyll twice calls "my own hand") is the same, as Prior's writing is the same in his dissociated state.[31] Barker repeats this deconstruction of apparent difference when Prior shows that, unlike anyone else, he can easily read Rivers's handwriting, which is so illegible to others that it functions as a way to hide the self. As Prior observes (with his offhand, sharpest insight), it is "the graphic equivalent of a stammer"—a written embodiment of what Rivers "couldn't say" and "didn't intend to write" (257). Because Prior gets through the resistance put up by Rivers's repression, he becomes the doctor's assistant, his Hyde, though a better word might be "amanuensis," as he becomes literally Rivers's hand by typing for him, thus helping his work move forward.

INCOMPLETE WORK: READING AND WORKING-THROUGH AS OPEN-ENDED PROCESS

Just as Jekyll's "discoveries" remain limited and unfinished (*Jekyll and Hyde*, 77), Rivers does not complete the investigation of his repressed problems from childhood, the "gap" or "darkness at the top of his own stairs" that he begins to face with Prior (252). Hence Prior, as his name implies, precedes his doctor in the psychoanalytic process that Rivers will take further as he remembers his past in *The Ghost Road*. The differences in their progress emerge in two sets of paired scenes that conclude *The Eye in the Door*. At the end of chapter 20, when Rivers meets with Sassoon in the hospital, he squashes the vulnerable soldier's dream of living near the homosexual Edward Carpenter and gets him instead to put on his uniform, which he has been resisting (259–61). Rivers thus merely repeats his past role at Craiglockhart, with little expectation of progress, as Barker suggests through his final words in the scene: "We needn't go far" (261). In sharp contrast, when Prior meets with Mac in his prison cell (261–66), Mac's war resistance, also represented by the rejected uniform, is never an issue. Instead, the scene focuses on Prior's need: he must talk with Mac to work against his own resistance, to reach an acceptance of his profound act of betrayal, which he faces without any evasion: "Though he still had no memory of doing it, he had betrayed Mac" (266).

Reinforcing the novel's focus on duality, Barker's ending also consists of paired scenes in chapter 21. Rivers and Sassoon walk by the Serpentine in the first of these scenes, so that the novel seems to circle back to its first page. Moreover, the harm in merely repeating past roles and conflicts is conveyed in their planned return to Craiglockhart, with Sassoon's depressed sense of going "back to the beginning. Only worse" (270). As Rivers also feels trapped, his last words in *The Eye in the Door* lack either comfort or insight: "Let's go back." The scene showing Prior's return to Manning's house, also a setting from chapter 1, is contrastingly filled with repetitions that bring out differences, suggesting changes in Prior, while Manning's progress seems more ambiguous. With the bomb site nearby "tidied up," the absence of dust-sheets that had shrouded the furniture, the repaired crack, and the presence of his beloved family, Manning seems to be "mending." However, he also notes that "the wallpaper might be holding the plaster up" where the crack had been, which suggests that Rivers, the "empathic wallpaper," might be similarly supporting, and covering up, the divided family man and "sodomite" (271). In contrast, Prior genuinely seems, as he claims, much better, in part through his affectionate acceptance of "Charles," in spite of the latter's again assuming that Prior might want help getting a job. But perhaps

Prior's progress emerges even more clearly in his somewhat amused, playfully non-confessional owning up to what he did during his memory gaps, as well as the outright laughter with which he lightly mocks Manning's famous friends.

Prior's last gesture, "laughing," is incomplete, as are his plans to return to the front, Manning's "mending," and Sassoon's repeated rejection of "admitting" he is mentally ill (269–70). At the end of *The Eye in the Door*, the incompleteness and uncertainty of these "cases," along with persistent gaps in the understanding of these soldiers and their doctor, exemplify how Barker's novel both depicts and teaches the psychoanalytic process of reading selves and texts. Her use of multiple limited viewpoints—both in third person narration reflecting different characters' perspectives and in incorporated, quoted texts—enhances the analyst-reader's role. Anticipating Barker's method, Robert Louis Stevenson's fragmented narrative shows Utterson inheriting the texts that may enable him to interpret Jekyll's selves. Yet Utterson disappears at the end of "The Last Night," so that readers are simply given the final chapters of the novella, Lanyon's narrative and Jekyll's statement, as two documents in a case. Achieving a similar effect, Barker's narrative presents viewpoints of characters who are discontinuous, split, characterized by gaps in their memory and conscious understanding. Her novel's explicit focus on psychoanalysis—not as a theory but as a lived experience of relationships, dialogues, dream interpretation, and hard "*work*" (275)—provides frequent reminders of the need to read psychoanalytically. *The Eye in the Door* shows that this reading process starts from the understanding that unconscious feelings and selves emerge in impeded, indirect forms of communication: dreams, slips of the tongue, hesitations, jokes, symbols, stammers, handwriting, symptoms, acting out, forgetting, silence, and even memories or interpretations that try to screen out threatening knowledge. Subtly incorporating an archetypal text of the hidden self, Pat Barker demonstrates that such conflicted modes of communication require critical readers and a dialogue between interpretations, analogous to the psychoanalytic encounter. What Barker reinforces in our reading of selves is awareness that the most productive relationships involve transference, bringing the past into the present so it can be recognized and worked through. What she strengthens in our reading of texts is the awareness that texts are like selves, often most fully known through what they cannot say and never intended to write.

NOTES

1. Pat Barker, *The Eye in the Door* (London: Viking, 1993), 134, 142. All subsequent references will be included in the text.

2. Such multiplied reflections in two mirrors are like the mise-en-abyme that occurs when a text incorporates, as a subtext, a story that shares elements with the story of the text as a whole. I will suggest that *The Eye in the Door* incorporates images and scenes that evoke *Jekyll and Hyde* as a subtext that mirrors Barker's novel.

3. For examples from *The Eye in the Door*, see the following passages: when Manning perceives threatening Captain Spencer in a mirror, when Prior gazes "sightlessly at his reflection" but thinks of Spragge, and when Rivers looks at his reflected image and sees "behind

it, Siegfried and the rumpled bed" (80, 176, 233).

4. Brian A. Rose, *"Jekyll and Hyde" Adapted: Dramatizations of Cultural Anxiety* (Westport, Conn.: Greenwood Press, 1996), 1–2.

5. Numerous illuminating similarities, beyond the scope of this study, link Mary Reilly and Billy Prior, as traumatized children and working-class heroes; perhaps the most fascinating is their replacement of a brutal father with a benign doctor-surrogate, with differing results.

6. See my interview with the author in this volume where Barker expressed her interest in the fact that Owen read *Jekyll and Hyde* at Scarborough in late 1917. See also Dominic Hibberd, *Wilfred Owen: The Last Year, 1917–1918* (London: Constable, 1992), 71.

7. Rose, *"Jekyll and Hyde" Adapted*, xi; see also R. McClure Smith, "The Strange Case of Valerie Martin and *Mary Reilly,*" *Narrative* 1 (1993): 245–64, esp. 245.

8. Sigmund Freud, "The Dynamics of Transference" (1912), *The Standard Edition of the Complete Psychological Works of Sigmund Freud,* ed. and trans. James Strachey (London: Hogarth, 1958), 12: 97–108 (here cited from 108).

9. Robert Louis Stevenson, *The Strange Case of Dr. Jekyll and Mr. Hyde* (1886), ed. Martin A. Danahay (Peterborough: Broadview Press, 1999), 77. All subsequent references will be included in the text.

10. J. Laplanche and J.-B. Pontalis, *The Language of Psycho-Analysis,* trans. Donald Nicholson-Smith (New York: Norton, 1973), 4.

11. Barker, *The Eye in the Door,* 5. Prior's comment anticipates his later fear, connecting his unknown actions during periods of amnesia with Jack the Ripper's horrific crimes (132). See Danahay for evidence that Stevenson's contemporaries linked Hyde and the Ripper, whose brutal 1888 murders led to the closing of the first London stage production of *Jekyll and Hyde,* when newspaper accounts revealed that the actor who played Hyde was a suspect (17). Dr. Jekyll may also have been controversial since doctors were among those suspected, due to the murderer's surgical precision (Martin A. Danahay, introduction and notes, *The Strange Case of Dr. Jekyll and Mr. Hyde* (Peterborough: Broadview Press, 1999), 194–96.

12. Paul Fussell, *The Great War and Modern Memory* (Oxford: Oxford University Press, 1975), 82–90; Sandra M. Gilbert and Susan Gubar, *No Man's Land: The Place of the Woman Writer in the Twentieth Century* (New Haven: Yale University Press, 1988), 3, 62

13. Elaine Showalter, *Sexual Anarchy: Gender and Culture at the Fin de Siécle* (New York: Viking Penguin, 1990), 106–7. Exploring the focus on homosexuality at the time of *Jekyll and Hyde,* Showalter highlights intensified scientific studies as well as legislation that criminalized homosexual behavior, both being forms of scrutiny that might contribute to the need for duplicity and the images of spying and being spied on that are prevalent in Stevenson's text. *The Eye in the Door* similarly examines First World War conditions that led to increased use of discipline and punishment targeting homosexuals, such as the discipline Rivers is supposed to provide, as a therapist enlisted to "cure sodomites" (16). The way in which Manning exemplifies "homosexual panic" especially emerges in the second chapter of the novel, which eerily echoes Elizabeth Bowen's "The Demon Lover" when a letter Manning takes as an accusation arrives mysteriously at his house, with an uncanny sense of strangeness and dread.

14. For evidence that dissociation (or multiple personality) was linked, in the late nineteenth century, to identification with the mother, see Leys 633. Prior's identification with his mother is shown particularly in their scene together (89, 91). Leys points out that First World War psychological theories blamed the mother "as the source of her son's 'feminine'

hysteria and lack of virile courage in actual battle"; moreover, "the war neuroses came to be conceptualized . . . on the model of the child's earliest reaction to the threatened loss or disappearance of the maternal figure." Ruth Leys, "Traumatic Cures: Shell Shock, Janet, and the Question of Memory," *Critical Inquiry* 20 (1994): 623–62, esp. 633.

15. Laplanche and Pontalis, *The Language of Psycho-Analysis*, 45.

16. For some of the evidence suggesting that Prior's hatred for Spragge (described on 130) springs from the sense of likeness and connection that makes Spragge his double, see passages where the shadowy figure follows or is followed by Prior, where he echoes Prior's words (196), and where he appears in Prior's flat (whose L-shaped bedroom resembles the captain's cabin in "The Secret Sharer"). The latter scene recalls not only Conrad's nocturnal confrontations between doubles, but also Utterson's fantasy that Hyde comes into Jekyll's bedroom at the time of sleep, exerting control over him (*The Eye in the Door*, 196, 53; *Jekyll and Hyde*, 39).

17. For several ways of regarding the "textual unconscious," see Smith, "The Strange Case," 251–52. I use this term to highlight how Barker's fiction is characterized by discourse that often suggests what is not stated by the narrator or recognized by the characters. For Jekyll's description of "maul[ing]" Carew's body, followed by the memory of his father, see *Jekyll and Hyde*, 85.

18. Laplanche and Pontalis, *The Language of Psycho-Analysis*, 48–49.

19. For Rivers's views on dream analysis, a crucial basis for the mode of psychoanalytic understanding presented in the many dream scenes of Barker's trilogy, see W. H. R. Rivers *Conflict and Dream* (New York: Harcourt, 1923), chapter 4, where Rivers stresses means of reducing the therapist's intrusive influence and thus "mak[ing] the analysis a matter in which the patient and I are partners" (59).

20. Rivers, *Conflict and Dream*, 59.

21. Barker's motif of disturbing, singular eyes persists from Towers's detached eye in *Regeneration* through the last pages of the trilogy, as Rivers closes Hallet's single eye. This motif suggests not only a trend toward pervasive government surveillance, but also the threat to individual vision posed by modern institutions and warfare.

22. Anna Grimshaw, "The Eye in the Door: Anthropology, Film, and the Exploration of Interior Space," in *Rethinking Visual Anthropology*, ed. Marcus Banks and Howard Morphy, 36–52 (here cited from 39) (New Haven: Yale University Press, 1997).

23. Quoted in William Veeder "Children of the Night: Stevenson and Patriarchy," in *"Dr. Jekyll and Mr. Hyde" after One Hundred Years*, ed. William Veeder and Gordon Hirsch, 107–60 (here cited from 135) (Chicago: University of Chicago Press, 1988).

24. Sigmund Freud, "Remembering, Repeating and Working-Through" in *The Standard Edition of the Complete Psychological Works of Sigmund Freud*, ed. and trans. James Strachey (London: Hogarth, 1958), 12: 145–56 (here cited from 151).

25. Barker's representation of the therapist-patient relationship is consistent with William Rivers's psychoanalytic writings, since he frequently discusses his own dreams, conflicts, and even symptoms of neurosis, while he also describes the impact of Sassoon (as "Patient B"), conveying an awareness of inevitable countertransference (this awareness permeates *Conflict and Dream*). For an able summary of views of the countertransference, see Laplanche and Pontalis, *The Language of Psycho-Analysis*, 92–93. Roy Schafer offers an especially satisfying exploration of the psychoanalytic relationship that includes "the analyst's also being subject to analysis," both through self-scrutiny and through the patient's becoming a "coanalyst" ("Narration in the Psychoanalytic Dialogue," *Critical Inquiry* 7 (1980): 29–53, esp. 37–38.

Murray M. Schwartz also emphasizes the "dialogic aspect" of this relationship; see "Critic, Define Thyself," in *Psychoanalysis and the Question of the Text*, ed. Geoffrey H. Hartman (Baltimore: Johns Hopkins University Press, 1978), 1–17 (here cited from 8).

26. For repetitions of the word "monsters" after Rivers disputes the medieval guideline, see *The Eye in the Door*, 143, 144, 148, 160; see also "monstrosity" on 164, and Rivers's nightmare of the cadaver that is brought to life (163).

27. The narrative structure of Barker's trilogy strengthens the mirroring of Rivers and Prior, since Rivers's perspective is the dominant viewpoint in *Regeneration*, as is Prior's in *The Eye in the Door*, and *The Ghost Road* presents their perspectives in alternating order, chapter by chapter as well as within the final chapter.

28. This passage, characterized by images from *Frankenstein* and *Jekyll and Hyde*, also contains verbal echoes and images from Rivers's final dream in *Regeneration*, as both dreams include an "elongated" corridor and the "flapping" open of doors, "like the wings of an ominous bird." The earlier nightmare was triggered by Rivers's passively watching another doctor subject a soldier-patient to disciplinary electric shocks, a "treatment" hard to distinguish from torture; the nightmare in *Regeneration* thus dealt with Rivers's guilt concerning his work as a therapist.

29. See *Jekyll and Hyde* (90, 87, 79) for Hyde's similar traits. Note also that the alternate self explicitly refuses to discuss Prior as "I," just as Prior earlier states, "How can I say 'I'" to describe someone he cannot remember or recognize, and just as Jekyll says, when discussing Hyde, "He, I say—I cannot say, I" (*The Eye in the Door*, 239, 191; *Jekyll and Hyde*, 88).

30. Freud, "Introduction to *Psycho-Analysis and the War Neuroses*" (1919), *The Standard Edition of the Complete Psychological Works of Sigmund Freud*, ed. and trans. James Strachey (London: Hogarth, 1955), 17: 205–10 (here cited from 209).

31. *Jekyll and Hyde*, 82, 87, 90. Barker develops the symbolic motif of hands by incorporating Stevenson's words, without identifying the source; when Rivers watches Head at work, noting his hand, he quotes Jekyll's description of his own hand: "professional in shape and size; . . . large, firm, white and comely" (*The Eye in the Door*, 147; *Jekyll and Hyde*, 82).

Part Five ■ Regenerating the Wasteland

MARGARETTA JOLLY

Toward a Masculine Maternal
Pat Barker's Bodily Fictions

Pat Barker has stated that she wishes to pose moral dilemmas without offering any solutions, and yet it has proved hard to accept that this is what she does. Part of the reason lies in her strong didactic impulse. Her enthusiastic (sometimes bald) lecturing lures us away from the implications of the mire in which England is shown to be wallowing. Self-destructiveness, she suggests, is endemic, perhaps inescapable, and this renders ambiguous her political protest. Her use of psychoanalytic theory heightens this tension. Is humanity doomed to war with its own unreason or potentially curable? A similar argument could be made for her mining of anthropology, in which the splendid diversity of human culture is measured against a depressing recurrence of women's oppression, male violence, and social hierarchy.

If these theoretical debates constitute the anatomy of Barker's work, they are muscled with prose that revels in the body. An extraordinary sense of the corporeal animates her writing from the appearance of a used and stinking sanitary towel in the opening scene of *Union Street* to the description of penises as decaying cabbage stalks and breasts as lard-white footballs in *Another World.*[1] This dark sensuality focalizes tensions between an England that is condemned or an England that can be saved. In this essay I will argue that the body functions in all of her work as the visible face of psychological and social unreason. Her characters' often grotesque physical symptoms and extreme desires (hemorrhages, phlegmatic coughs, scars, sadism), like those of the hysterics and neurotics who visited early psychoanalysts, are displacements, that is, social and psychological forces that have been internalized and accepted.

At the same time, the body is a figure of hope. This is in part because of its very ability to "speak" the socially illegitimate but also is in part because the body exceeds or ignores the social altogether, in the material processes of birth, growth, and death. Articulated through the life cycle and reproduction, Barker constructs the body as the shape of an alternative narrative to a death-filled social history. In the context of contemporary discourses of bodily flexibility and manipulation, Barker suggests that the body is less knowable than we would like to believe, even as she displays it in its most intimate aspects. This is frightening but also encouraging.

I will therefore consider the body's representation in two parts. Firstly, I will argue that it signifies Barker's skepticism about social ideals of enlightenment and political liberation. Secondly, and in contrast, I will show how physical life is also posed as a liminal source of hope for change, as the mouth of the socially repressed, and as the foundation for a metaphysics of birth rather than death. In this latter sense, I propose that Marianne Hirsch's theory of "maternal" narrative form provides a fruitful context for understanding Barker's interest in the body's alternative "reason." However, Barker modifies Hirsch's conception of "maternal form" by expanding maternity to encompass male as well as female nurturing, and by considering its relationship to England's class struggle. This controversially situates men at the point of greatest pessimism, and yet also grants them the greatest potential for a general redemption.

This leads me to ask how the symbolic role of physical life relates to another strikingly consistent element of Barker's fiction: the spiritual and ghostly. From the mystical symbolism of birds, trees, "magical" consciousness, and hallucinations to spirit mediums and ghosts both New Guinean and English, it becomes apparent that the disembodied is not so far from the embodied. Both are symptoms of social displacement, of memory returning to haunt history, and both retain a quasi-religious alterity. Yet however inspiring we may find the completeness of Barker's cosmology of body, mind, and spirit, it raises troubling questions about the status and function of working-class fiction in England today. If the body and spirit rather than the mind become the places of hope, a narrative of progress based on material change and rational agency would appear to have disintegrated. Can we recover the notion of "maternal form" or perspective as an alternative basis for political agency and collective transcendence? Or are we being asked to accept mere physical survival as the best that history can offer?

Probably the most unpleasant aspect of Barker's unflinching depiction of working-class life is her characters' own submission to and even complicity in their degradation. Oppression is physically internalized. A concise example is the story of Joanne Wilson in Barker's first novel *Union Street*. In this story the characters perceive their bodies and not their social circumstances as traitors: Joanne is trapped in pregnancy, Ken in sexual desire, Joss in the apparently undesirable body of a man of restricted growth. All three possess better judgment about their predicament; Joanne in particular harbors no illusions about maternity, nor Ken's weak commitment to her. But none of them appear able to assume agency or control. This is graphically indicated in physical submission, most literally in Joanne's pregnancy and sexual submission to Ken, but also, paradoxically, in Ken's sexual brutality and emotional detachment. In this context, Joss's physical difference is resonant. Forced outside of the conventional sexual and gender contract, he gains a possible perspective on masculinity and is strikingly caring compared to the other men in the book—an anticipation of what I will term Barker's later exploration of a "masculine maternal." However, as he "look[ed] down at his legs as if for once in his life he needed to be reminded of their length," his disability acts as symbolic castration, and he submits quickly to defeat in winning Joanne's interest (*Union Street*, 105).

Such self-division is implicitly defined in Freudian terms, in which the body testifies to a continual negotiation between ego and id, reason and desire. Barker's application of psychoanalysis to working-class contexts is challenging even today, both to those who continue to believe that only the middle classes are capable of fine feeling, and to those who would have the oppressed as the repository of common sense. In scenarios like the above, we are shown how the unconscious can harbor self-destructive as well as aggressive desires that do as much as external circumstance to trap their miserable possessors. Indeed, it is the combination of internal and external entrapment that makes (Northern) working-class life, as she presents it, so bleak. In *Blow Your House Down*, the "switching off" described as necessary to do sex work paradoxically both severs the mind from the body and submerges it there, tellingly figured in the description of Brenda's acclimatization to the job as "a skin [that] had formed over her mind."[2] Even the lesbian Jean, the strongest of the prostitutes, is given a scar across her neck that seems emblematic not only of the dangerous conditions within which prostitutes are forced to work, but of an emotionally repressive fracturing of mind from body. If the women's unconscious traps them in masochism, as in *Union Street*, the masculine unconscious, represented through the Ripper, contains essentially sadistic needs and desires. Jean, who makes it her mission to kill the Ripper, has an epiphany when she realizes that the key to finding him is in working out not only that he "*need[s]* to kill," but that he will be attracted by a pregnant woman (*Blow Your House Down*, 102; 97). His motive—although chilling—is implicitly presented as a kind of womb envy.

Perhaps the most eloquent, certainly the most explicit, of Barker's physical figuring of the unconscious occurs in the *Regeneration* trilogy, in which shell-shocked First World War soldiers are displayed as suffering from all manner of bizarre psychosomatic illnesses.[3] Here, however, they are less a sign of the sadistic desires of conventional masculinity, than of fear, horror, and self-revulsion engendered by the war. Their bodies protest not only against war but the terms on which their masculinity has been constructed. This signifies a shift in Barker's work toward a hopeful understanding of the fracture between conscious and unconscious in the context of the breakdown of an Enlightenment model of progress, often located historically as partly an effect of the First World War itself. I will return to this more positive exploration of the body shortly. For the moment, I wish to concentrate on the way that the portrayal of physical trauma and mental violence in the trilogy continues Barker's testing of reason, or rather what is designated as reason in such an oppressive historical period.

In the trilogy, war—and its connection to masculinity—is posited as in part an element of the unconscious, both social and individual, that must be confronted. Through the ambivalent desires of the soldiers, doctors, headhunters, and even the pacifists we encounter, we are asked to confront the appeal as well as necessity of violence. Barker personifies this most acutely through the almost-Mephistophelean character of Billy Prior, who is distinguished from the others not only by his social in-between-ness, but by the extent of his self-knowledge. In the first two books, Prior's own physical symptoms are presented as beyond his control: muteness, stammering, dramatic fugue states in which he is prone to violence, most tellingly "nocturnal emissions" during his nightmares of being at the front. But to his therapist Rivers he acts as the analysand from hell, as adept at analysis as his therapist. This is often enormously comic, yet ultimately reflects the sober fact that Prior does not share Rivers's faith in the possibility of cure in a society that he has personally experienced as cruel and unjust in a way that the upper-class Rivers has not. His inner debate over how to act justly in the war is a darker one than Rivers's for all Rivers's moral self-examination over his own contradictory position. Prior's response to the amorality of the war is therefore positioned as the more logical one: the eventual, if qualified, acceptance of his sadistic "id"—Blake Morrison views him as disturbingly guilt-free.[4] In *The Ghost Road,* Prior returns to the front, open-eyed to the pointlessness of the war, ready to kill and be killed. A memorable example of Barker's technique of embodying this sensitive cynicism is Prior's copulation with a French boy by a river, in which his principle excitement is the knowledge that the boy had recently also sold himself to Germans. Prior makes the unconscious conscious, aware of the relation between desire and aggression, and how it brings enemies and allies on to the same side.

Through Prior's realism and Rivers's curing his patients only in order to send them back to war, Barker suggests that even in the subversive infancy of psychoanalysis, it was institutionalized for ends that made a mockery of its therapeutic promise. If psychoanalysis appears to be cruelly limited to diagnosing its own impotence, anthropological theory enters the trilogy as another language through which modernist claims to enlightenment are severely tested.[5] The elaborate parallel between Europe and Polynesia's head-hunting society in *The Ghost Road* suggests the ubiquity of masculinity as destructive violence, femininity as destructive, complicit passivity, and most of all, of war. Furthermore, just as psychoanalysis is shown to have been historically implicated in repression, anthropology is implicated in the suppression of the cultural difference that is its object. As part of the colonizing of Polynesia, the locals are ironically suppressed through banning the practice of headhunting, which is crucial to their identity. The psychoanalytic and the anthropological come together in the suggestion that the headhunters are Europe's own repressed and indeed the headhunters' explicit ritualization of blood sacrifice may be shown as more "civilized" and "conscious" than the hypocritical slaughter of the First World War. Barker asks us how far sadistic and masochistic patterns are deep parts of English cultural institutions in ways that we have yet to admit. Blake Morrison suggests the resistance to this idea that we can expect: "Whatever the waste of human life, isn't war fundamental to the human spirit? It's a dark and distinctly un-nineties thought with which to end this complex trilogy."[6]

Ann Ardis measures the extent of Barker's pessimism, and throws light on the sense in which the body is implicated in her exploration of social irrationality. In her discussion of teaching *Blow Your House Down,* Ardis shows that underneath its powerful explorations of both class and male domination lies a still more threatening assertion that *all* humans have the capacity to dominate and kill.[7] She draws this conclusion through her reading of the scene in which the anonymous killer rapes and murders a woman, in which the reader is forced to adopt his narrative viewpoint. Ardis explains the full horror of the murder in Hortense Spillers's terms of the distinction between "the body" and "the flesh," such that this murder involves an objectification that actually combusts the hatred of women that provoked it. It would seem that though the unconscious is shown continually shaped by the social, Barker asserts another level at which it gives way to an even more primitive relationship of dominance and submission, in which the psychological disappears into the physical.

Ardis speculates on her students' discomfort at Barker's techniques of implication, their own wish to "freeze" an opposition between oppressed and oppressor, in which they are invariably on the side of the victim. We might extend her observation to that of critics and other readers who have not confronted Barker's attack on conventional political narrative, nor how close she comes to asserting a biological narrative of exploitation. Barker has stated:

> In my books, the characters themselves are not political. People want to read a message of hope for the people in Britain in my books, *but it isn't there in political terms.* When Liza [in *Liza's England*] has to go out scratching for coal, she has to fall out of political activity.[8] (emphasis added)

In my view, her fiction goes further than showing how political consciousness depends upon having time and money, to suggest that it must incorporate psychological and even *biological* change. The Labour Party that worked for Liza is now not enough, for we must engage with the destructive socializing of the sadomasochistic desires of the "flesh." Barker's interest in psychoanalytic therapy, staged in the trilogy and *Border Crossing,* is one response to this. But as we shall see in the next section, physical stoicism and birth, even "without any idea of the alternatives," forms the basis of her most consistent response to human violence.

Barker does provide some traces of hope in the moral dilemmas posed by her fiction. Although her bodily figuring of the unconscious delineates the limits of a politics that fails to take into account people's inner contradictions, this lays out a more sophisticated political vision. I would argue that a tentative optimism is anchored precisely in the split between body and mind, as the body is perceived as partially independent from a corrupt social order. Moreover, this exceeds the psychoanalytic model of body as unconscious protest. It is as a materialist biology, one that exists as much outside as inside of history, that Barker constructs the body as source of political hope.

My point of departure for this thesis is the work of Marianne Hirsch, whose feminist reworking of psychoanalytically based narratology provides terms for such bodily plotting. In *The Mother/Daughter Plot: Narrative, Psychoanalysis, Feminism,* Hirsch designates the bearing and regeneration of life as a formal concern that has been neglected as part of a symbolic rejection of mothers and mothering throughout the Western literary tradition. By contrast, the gradual cultural enfranchisement of women over the last two hundred years has produced the grounds upon which maternity can be associated with creativity, without simply returning to the mindless immanence of reproduction. Citing such writers as Toni Morrison, Alice Walker,

Luce Irigaray, and Julia Kristeva, Hirsch defines maternal narrative through birth and futurity, rather than through a desire bound up with mortality as it has been theorized by narratologists. Maternity is not simply the introduction of mothering as a new subject for writing, but the basis of a new "radically prospective" aesthetic, or "form." "Birth rather than death would have to motivate the dynamics of plot," she says, grandly:

> Death would have to cease being associated with healing and birth would have to cease being associated with fear and destruction. Beginnings and endings would have to stand in a more complex relationship to each other.[9]

Hirsch is tentative in defining these "maternal" plots more concretely, but suggests that iterative, circular, and open-ended structures might more successfully mimic the more relational life story of mothers (and daughters looking to maternal rather than paternal identification) than narratives of linear development, closure, and singulative construction. Rather than viewing the maternal as only outside or at the end of time, as in the mythical and psychoanalytic paradigms of our inheritance, "spiral" structured plots of departure and return may bring the mother into narrated history, while recognizing the liminal cultural position that she inhabits. Significantly for our purposes, this involves a new exploration of the corporeal dynamic of writing, as it is reoriented away from a sexual—and usually heterosexual—metonymy of desire to one of the sensations, pains and pleasures in bearing new life.

Hirsch is highly conscious of the apparent essentialism of her assertion that narrative form can be characterized by gender and parental position, arguing that her intent is to "make space for differences [between men and women and] among women from the perspective not of *biology* but of *experience*."[10] Maternal representation, in fact, must be characterized less by an absolute symbolic, such as those proffered by French theorists Hélène Cixous and Luce Irigaray, in an idealized "pre-oedipal" language, than a shuttling between the assertion and denial of gender position in different narrative contexts. But Hirsch works from the controversial belief that gender is deeply defined through the bodily differences between male and female, nonreproductive and reproductive, paternal and maternal. While theorizing about the way gender inhabits the body has become a topic of much more focused interest since *The Mother/Daughter Plot*'s first publication in 1984, Hirsch's relative conservatism on the matter is most useful for a reading of Barker's work. Barker's bodies, as we shall see, are marked by their ability or not to reproduce. At the same time, Barker's biological materialism is in many ways more challenging than Hirsch's body of "experience." Her dramatization of the essentials of birth, physical survival, and death as preoccupations of the poor suggests the class and national interests at stake in "maternal" plotting and nuance the gender binary that, as with Hirsch, still thoroughly dominates her work.

In what sense, then, does Hirsch's theory of maternal plotting illuminate Barker's call upon the body as social resource? We can anticipate that it will be no idealistic vision of mothers as political vanguard in a "soft" feminist revolution. Rather, it lies in Barker's dramatic exploitation of birth and the life cycle as plot structure in a way that positions the nurturing and nurtured body as crucial to people in danger. This is not political in any conventional sense, and indeed, in her early work, can be read as a symptom of the failure of both masculinized socialist *and* middle-class feminist forms of both narrative and social organizing. Nevertheless, Hirsch's proposal that maternal plotting is a new stage in the gendered history of narrative can illuminate the intricate plots for which Barker is well known, and indeed suggest that they may be more formally innovative than her reputation as a proficient, but conservative realist usually allows.

Barker's first novel *Union Street* presents a "maternal" form of narrative as her most minimal political hope. Here, the otherwise only loosely related women's stories are tightly ordered along the axis of ascending age, thus offering not only a view of the street but a picture of a female life cycle defined through childhood, youth, childbirth, maternity, old age and death. This story of aging intersects with the fatalistic aspects of the women's prospects for escape from their doomed society. At the same time, it cannot be reduced to it, for it also functions as a metanarrative that contains implicit resurrection in birth. Women's position as birth-givers, enhanced by their emotional and social work of reproduction, is established as a circular order of quiet hope. Joanne's story, for example, ends with a moment of unity in which "the baby, which all day long she had 'felt' as a hard nodule of fear, seemed to melt away inside her, to float and merge with her into the peace and safety of [Joss's] room" (*Union Street*, 106). The story is followed by that of Lisa Goddard, a young mother, battered by her husband and unhappily pregnant with her third child: a picture of Joanne's likely fate. Yet, in turn, this story ends with Lisa gaining a mystical sense of the future through identifying with her daughter's body:

> Now she held her daughter in her arms. And the thought that inside that tiny body was a womb like hers with eggs waiting to be released, caused the same fear, the same *wonder* [as when she watched a hatching chrysalis as a child]. *She walked across to the window holding the child in her arms.* (*Union Street*, 139; emphasis added)

The following story, in which Muriel Scaife loses her husband to a lung disease, again, ends with a turn from mourning to the life of caring for her children. This pointedly contrasted with her husband's fate as a man of unforgiving stoicism made harder by sickness and unemployment. His graphically described death from an oral hemorrhage reads as an inversion of female birth, Muriel frantically pulling at an umbilical "rope" of blood from the "black hole" of his mouth, in an attempt to deliver him from the clot that suffocates him. This feminizes the male stoic as more mute and passive than the laboring mother he so ironically resembles, the body into which time more truly disappears (*Union Street*, 163). In contrast to this barren male death, the ability of the maternal body to give birth is a reversal of the *unheimlich*, a border of inside and outside that can, however briefly, exceed the repressive social inscription that kills John Scaife.

These reproductive moments symbolically join women otherwise strikingly divided, and enact a principle of maternal transmission at the level of narrative form itself. This becomes obvious at the end of the novel, where the character of the first story, Kelly, appears in that of the elderly, dying Alice, whom we now also recognize as having appeared in Kelly's story. The narrative is thus unified with a meeting from two ends of the female life cycle, and the double effect of closure and continuity is symbolically emphasized by the women's joining hands as they sit on the bench, under a symbolic tree of life. Auguring merely survival, not social change, maternity signifies a loss of political vision metonymically embodied in the circularity rather than the linearity of its narrative. Yet this ending attributes an integral harmony and unity to the life cycle heightened by its contrast with the fractured social geography of the ironically named Union Street. On this level of physical stoicism and the material reproduction of the community, a "maternal" plot is posed as the structure of survival that has silently supported the male working class, and now persists despite the disintegration of its trade unions.

The emphasis on female reproduction as narrative and political solution can be seen as a troubling essentialism. Ian Haywood has objected to *Union Street* in these terms:

> The preponderance of female bodily "essences" in the stories . . . creates the strong impression that these working-class women inhabit an elemental world of feminine experience, though there is always a danger that such an approach reinforces biological reductionism.[11]

This underestimates the extent to which that "feminine experience" of the body is problematized through its performance of unconscious social desires of class and sexuality. In other words, we must accept Barker's analysis as reductive to the same extent as psychoanalysis itself: what one loses in social context, one gains in psychological precision. A critique of "biological reductionism" also ignores the fact that within the societies in crisis that Barker explores, *biological* questions of physical survival—"stoicism," recovery, or simply birth itself—are fundamentals that must not be underestimated. For the poor, ill, or war-torn, the birth of new life and physical resistance are not necessarily "reductive" so much as astonishing. Here, I would argue, Barker modifies and qualifies Hirsch's psychoanalytic schema as much as Haywood's socialist one in foregrounding the survival of the body as the basis for *class* as much as maternal plotting. It is on this level that we must understand Barker's emphasis on women as mothers in her early novels, for they are the literal and emotional progenitors of class communities that have been given little means for social or cultural reproduction on a larger scale. Working-class and feminist interests do not, in fact, easily resolve, as we see in the harassed Liza and Brenda, distracted Viv, or the frankly cruel Louise. While Haywood points out the fact that the women are "unable to control their bodies (except in Kelly's demonic form) in the 'social[ly] backward' and 'deeply regressive' 'social milieu,'"[12] Barker is surely deliberately showing women's unconscious self-sacrifice—precisely the *unwanted* pregnancy—to be the (worrying) condition of continuity and possibly change, for themselves and even for their communities. On one level, this returns to Simone de Beauvoir's view of women's "immanence" as reproducers, from the ironic perspective of an epoch in which both class and female emancipation has supposedly already been achieved. On another level, it asserts birth as a narrative concern in its own right, the first condition for a future both material and literary.

The relationship between maternal and working-class interests is less ironic and contradictory in Barker's other most explicitly "maternal" plot, *Liza's England*. Here, indeed, it is suggested that a maternal perspective may be the key to any regeneration of working-class culture and politics post-Thatcher. A young social worker, Steven, is sent to convince eighty-year-old Liza to leave her home for sheltered accommodation. His visit precipitates a healing review of her life, from the moment of her birth on the stroke of midnight, 1900, and in turn, he is provoked to confront his own working-class family and his hopes for the future of the violent estate on which he works. As the original title of the novel, "The Century's Daughter" suggests, Liza's life provides the measure for English national history through the decades. However, this is not merely articulated as a history of private rather than public event, but as a different temporality defined through the physical rhythm of the body, the life cycle and the medium of memory. Reworking the traditional position of the mother as the stultification of plot, the female generations sustain a history precisely through the ability to endure rather than change with time. Liza's mother, cruel and unloving to her daughter, nevertheless proves a model of physical and emotional survival that Liza inherits and passes on to her own, equally unmaternal daughter. In Liza's case, endurance takes a more benign and heroic form. Stephen reflects that "Like a rock that wind and sea have worked on since the beginning of time, she needed to apologize for nothing, explain nothing," and her life story is clearly suggested as resource for the regeneration of her dying community as well as her descendants.[13] Female endurance is thus structured into the narrative as counterpoint to the chronological narrative of a masculinized national history. It is no accident that at almost exactly each quarter of the book a new birth is described, and symbolic circles permeate the novel, from dancing the clog dance or cakewalk or revolving on the coal heap while scavenging for coal, to the decorations on Liza's box of family documents.[14] While the male characters are introduced only to die or disappear, in depression, unemployment, or war, female childbirth and rearing, women's solidarity in pleasure or labor is made the basis of an iterative, spiraling narrative of class survival.

The class story at stake in Barker's maternal narrative is driven home in Liza's death, a moment when the distinctive temporality of maternal identification that Hirsch identifies is also obvious. Despite her gift for survival, Liza's extraordinary resistance is finally outdone by the male youths on her estate, who mug her believing her box of family documents contains money (as, it must be said, Stephen did originally). Under the blows of the youths, her hallucinated regression through her past to her childhood and mother is presented as a merciful escape from historical time itself, as she turns *into* rather than out of the circular time of the body:

> The clock on the mantelpiece ticked, but a louder ticking had started inside her.
> She beat time, not with hands and mind alone, but with every cell of her body.
> Not a tick really, more like a pulse, it might even be her heartbeat; but no, it was
> too loud and strong for that. It shook the bones of her shoulders and chest as if

this pendulum might shatter the case. Pounding and stamping, louder and faster, and then again more slowly as the music ebbed, and she turned away from the circling dancers, from the lamplight and the spinning rope, and looked across the street to where her mother stood in the shadows holding out her hand. . . . It was late, later than she'd ever been before, the clock on the stairs was striking midnight; but she noticed, as she ran towards the shadows, that her mother stood in front of an open door and smiled as she beckoned her in. (*Liza's England*, 276–77)

This dramatic splitting off of history from the body, male violence from maternal embrace, protects Liza from knowing the pain of her cruel death. Yet the reader is fully aware of the ironic reality of her murder by "young men" like those who have paved the way with their own deaths in war. Barker's characteristic use of free indirect speech, here emphasizing the dissonance between reader and Liza's comprehension, and the synchrony of clock, heartbeat, and blows, insists we relate inner to outer time, narrative death to the sacrificial logic of class history. The maternal legacy, despite its fragility (pointedly demonstrated in this misapprehension of the box's value), is one that Barker suggests must be brought out of the body and its quiescence into history for any hope of working-class regeneration.

We can thus see that the transmission of women's memories to a larger political sphere—and particularly to men—is crucial to Barker's view of the maternal as agent of social transformation. Again, the narrative's dominant construction as "female" life plot allows for a particularly obvious feminization of the archetypal theme of intergenerational transmission. This is literally imaged in the box of family documents that Liza received from her mother and into which she delves to begin her story. This box functions as the condensed metaphor for the plot that the narrative metonymically unpacks, decorated (so as to make sure we get the point) with a circle of female dancers clasping hands and an androgynous figure handing over a gift to a young man.[15] The box is a metaphorical womb that can both preserve time as memory and also precipitate new life, and as such, we are clearly asked to see the novel itself as the working out of a maternal narration or aesthetic in the context of a mother-child—specifically, mother-son—relationship. While Liza imagines that Stephen resembles her dead son, Stephen feels Liza's stories nourish him in equally primitive terms: "Sometimes [he] felt he was draining her, squeezing her dry, though he knew too, that she looked forward to his visits" (*Liza's England*, 15).

The function of the novel as regenerative national memory must be read through this passionate transference between the two. This is more than the symptom of entrapment in patriarchal and child-centered language and logic that Hirsch suggests conditions any maternal narration, and goes beyond the paternal genealogy or erotic seduction of "tales within tales" enumerated by Peter Brooks as the template for narrative transmission. Indeed, Stephen as son and model reader reverses the logic of narrative as the journey away from the mother. Furthermore, his own "maternal" position, as social worker and the inheritor of Liza's story, bridges both masculine and feminine time (in which his homosexuality is a facilitating factor). He represents the caring male body through which, paradoxically, maternal life must be reproduced for political hope.

Clearly, the fate of the working class, and England, by extension, is linked to men's ability to enter the maternal space, *not as dutiful or even feminized sons, but as birth-givers themselves.* Barker's shift from female- to male-centered scenarios has often been defended as an extension rather than abandonment of her feminist vision, but nobody has yet suggested this most novel aspect of her interest in masculinity.[16] Rejecting the more obvious solution of reconstructing fatherhood or male sexuality, Barker explores male stoicism and caring as it can encompass bodily nurturing and even generation, and the liminal, maternally identified space of bodily, subjective time outside of conventional, narratives of desire and death. The increasing emphasis on this "masculine maternal" as her work progresses gradually erodes the fatalistic biologism of female reproduction in *Union Street,* paradoxically turning the body into the scene of greatest social hope. Important markers in this evolution are Joss's cooking for Joanne in *Union Street,* the epiphanic scene where Bill undresses and dries his wife Maggie at the end of *Blow Your House Down,* Stephen's social work and nursing of his father in *Liza's England,* and Colin's fantasies of gender change in *The Man Who Wasn't There.*[17] *Another World* shows no flagging of such interest: Fran's pregnancy is paralleled by her partner Nick's palliative care for his uncle, while in *Border Crossing* psychotherapist Tom Seymour gets passionately involved in helping child murderer Danny.

The most spectacular exploration of the masculine maternal is of course to be found in the *Regeneration* trilogy, in which the male-run military hospital and battalion provide the framework for its most ironic working out as answer to male, class, and national violence. Furthermore, as in *Union Street* and *Liza's England,* its extremely complex architecture itself can fruitfully be read as a "masculine" maternal plot, in which narration itself is turned toward the problematic of birth as much as death. The title of both the first novel and the trilogy, *Regeneration* establishes birth as its encompassing concern. How, Barker suggests, could and did people survive the First World War? As a national, gender, and class crisis as well as literal apocalypse, a social, symbolic, emotional, as well as physical regeneration of the most fundamental order was necessary. I have posited that her assessment is pessimistic: the mechanisms for political change (soldiers' strikes like Sassoon's; the pacifist anarchism of Beattie Roper; a questioning psychoanalytic practice) were too slight, and the vested interests, psychological as much as material, in war were too strong. Prior's logic of sadism ultimately wins out. Yet an alternative story of possible rebirth or redemption is proffered at a symbolic level in men's physical and emotional care for each other, a story itself situated symbolically in the subtextual position of the female life cycle in her earlier work. More encompassing of contradiction than Rivers's belief in rational "enlightenment," yet more ambitious than the merely physical reproduction of future as pregnancy in *Union Street,* we are reassured here that the body has its own "reason."

The need for the impossible of male birth to counter male death is signaled in the most literal discussion of "regeneration" in the text: the extraordinary real-life research into the nervous system, performed by Rivers and his mentor the surgeon Henry Head at Cambridge before the war. There, Rivers assisted in severing and suturing the nerve in Head's arm, then tested its regrowth over five years. They observed two stages in the redevelopment of sensitivity, the protopathic, a crude all-or-nothing nervous response, followed by the epicritic, sensation that could be graded in both location and intensity. Barker develops this in relation to Rivers's wartime psychoanalytic practice as an equally dangerous experiment into feeling. What is the point of teaching men to feel if they remain only objects of war, rather than subjects that can escape? Rivers is all too aware that his method encourages a sensitivity that may be suicidal in wartime, and more, that it attacks the founding of English masculinity on emotional repression (a protopathic sensibility) in ways that he cannot contemplate addressing personally. To make sure we understand this, Rivers is given a nightmare in which Head asks why he does not submit *himself* to the experiment, and cuts Rivers's arm with a scalpel. Yet, the experiment demonstrates that the psychological cannot be separated from the physical. As Rivers muses again on the experiment in *The Eye in the Door*, "the epicritic system carried out two functions: one, to help the organism adapt to its environment by supplying it with accurate information: the other, to suppress the protopathic, to keep the animal within leashed" (*The Eye in the Door*, 327). Thus Rivers's metaphorical interpretation of the nerve regeneration experiment can also be read in reverse: men's *emotional* reconstruction will also require a *physical*, embedded one, not only in epicritic growth but in relationship with other men. His physical "testing" of Head, heightened by its sexual undertones, is, in this sense, a scene of men's rebirth through each other.

This kind of "epicritic" maternal relationship is what Rivers offers his patients. As a stimulant for emotional (re)growth that we have seen linked to a literal development of the nerves, Rivers's treatments can be read as birth scenes. He rescues Anderson, who has a phobia of blood, from a fetal position in the bathroom (*Regeneration*, 121) brings back Burns from nightmare by "coaxing, rocking" a body with the "ragdoll floppiness of the newborn" (160). In a scene reminiscent of the regeneration of Head's nerves, he tests the return of sensation in Moffet's legs with a pin, encouraging him out of hysterical paralysis purely through suggestion.[18] Even Prior, as the limit case for therapeutic treatment is, to an extent, emotionally reborn by Rivers, regaining his memory in *Regeneration* after a hypnosis session that finds him "butting" Rivers like a "suckling kid" with a "blind and slobbery face" at the end of it. In *The Eye in the Door*, Rivers' is confronted with Prior in a dissociated state, in which his sadistic unconscious has taken complete hold. Yet here too, he unites him with his conscious self through analysis in which his father's brutality is shown as the central cause of his trauma. Prior's return to the front in *The Ghost Road* is motivated, as for Sassoon and Owen, as much by his own sense of "maternal" responsibility toward his "men" as by his cynicism, a responsibility upon which Rivers plays.[19]

Thus Rivers, at one point literally surrounded by hatching chicks, is both model and disseminator of male mothering (*Regeneration*, 136). Yet, remembering one patient's flirtatious comment that "I don't see you as a *father*, you know ... more a sort of ... *male mother*," he is uncomfortable (97). Are only women capable of nurturing then, he asks himself, "as if [when done by a man] the ability were in some way borrowed, or even stolen, from women—a sort of moral equivalent of the *couvade*. If that were true, then there was really very little hope" (97). Here, Rivers becomes the spokesperson for the paradox inherent in Barker's own imaging of reconstructive masculinity in feminine terms. Barker has said that of the year the real Rivers spent at Craiglockhart War Hospital: "He learned to integrate his nurturing side. I don't like to call it feminine, but what you have really is a sense of mothering the men, not fathering."[20] At stake in this identification is an obvious doubt that the terms of "fathering" can express the change involved. Yet it also raises precisely her fictional Rivers's question as to how nurturing can become as deeply a masculine as feminine identification. I would suggest that the "maternal" is preserved as metaphor not because of any great female virtue, which Barker clearly dismisses, but because of its ability to express a bodily relationship to which Barker attributes the "hope" of cheating humanly caused mortality. Rivers, as both psychoanalyst and physician, understands this bodily logic.[21] At the same time, his quasi-magical power to "regenerate" cannot provide even the miserable narrative future that Joanne Wilson creates in unwanted pregnancy.

Barker's basic materialism thus returns her to the binary of gender that she sets out to undo both fictionally and historically. This is borne out by the ambiguous wielding of a "masculine" maternal as a narrative principle in ways we saw used in *Union Street* and *Liza's England*. The three books of the *Regeneration* trilogy take us through 1917–18, a chronology aligned both with historical record and the disaster of the war, from Sassoon's failed protest against the war in July 1917 to Owen and Prior's deaths attempting to cross the Sambre-Oise canal in November 1918. Yet this journey toward death is counterpointed by a principle of stability and renewal, structurally and thematically articulated in Rivers's therapy and hospital sessions. These domestic, private spaces of memory and the unconscious, dialogue, and nurture, establish an alternative temporality to that of the war. If Prior, like her earlier male characters, acts as the protagonist of the narrative of desire that must end in death, Rivers, like Liza, personifies the "rock" that can resist time. Again, as in her earlier novels, these two narrative structures are made to impact on each other to suggest that justice in England depends upon developing a maternal perspective. Rivers at the end of *Regeneration,* reflects on how he himself has been politicized by caring for the shell-shocked in terms that evoke his own "fertilization":

> A society that devours its own young deserves no automatic or unquestioning allegiance. Perhaps the rebellion of the old might count for more than the rebellion of the young. Certainly poor Siegfried's rebellion hadn't counted for much, though he reminded himself that he couldn't *know* that. It had been a completely honest action and such actions are seeds carried on the wind. Nobody can tell where, or in what circumstances, they will bear fruit. (*Regeneration*, 218–19)

The end of the trilogy as a whole returns us to the hospital scene with which it opens, a return that also symbolically marks Rivers's outliving of the dead and Prior's end a page earlier. Barker's maternal plotting through men's relationships with each other, across class and sexuality, posits her greatest vision of national regeneration.[22]

It is impossible to talk about the presence of the body in Barker's work without acknowledging its other: the hallucination or ghost. The combination of the raw and the refined, the material and the mystical is one of her hallmarks: bloody guts but also crowds of starlings in the sunset; wartime pubs but also whispering ghosts; computer games but also the longhaired girl-ghost at the window. Like Barker's bodies, these haunting figures speak of a world in which reason, logic, order are continually threatened by trauma, injustice, and desire. In *The Man Who Wasn't There*, her most sustained early experiment with the fantastic, Colin is frightened by a mysterious apparition whom he discovers is not his absent father but his own future alienated self. In her most explicit ghost story, *Another World*, a nineties family of liberal ideals and modern comforts finds itself repeating the murderous jealousies of a Victorian family they discover painted on their sitting room wall. But if Barker's supernatural intrusions confirm her representation of life as divided between inner and outer, unconscious and conscious, psychic and historical, how do they relate to the maternal principle of regeneration and renewal? I suggest that even as they enhance the sense of a world out of human control, they confirm her biological materialist vision of an underlying organic order marked by the life span. Like the maternal body, spirits in this schema augur the hope of (re)birth as much as the unresolved and irrational death.

Critics have been divided over Barker's startling combination of realism with the supernatural. While to some it has appeared as a peculiar inconsistency and sentimentality in an otherwise solidly "social realist" writer, others have seen it as her claim to postmodernist status.[23] I will attempt to show that these two elements do resolve if her biological materialism is confronted, through comparison with Anne Whitehead's excellent, yet one-sided argument for Barker as postmodernist. Whitehead concentrates on Barker's figuring of the supernatural in *Regeneration* as a play with temporality and interpretation that disrupts stable meaning and authority. She shows how Barker milks the implications of the real Rivers's theory that shell shock was belated remembering to mount an attack on linear time, memory, and authority, indeed, exaggerating this aspect of her sources to challenge her *own* narrative's invocation of historical temporality. If Barker thus uses Rivers to show that psychic health involves a necessary "fictionalizing" or composing of the past, she plays with her own narrative contract to unsettle the boundaries of history and fiction. This denies the reader a simple "therapeutic" literary experience of explanation just as Rivers shows his patients that therapy provides no simple access to the past. In Whitehead's terms, "the detective story, or the mastery of the past through a process of interpretation, has become a ghost story, in which the specters of the past persistently haunt the present."[24] The most obvious of these techniques is Barker's hinting that "real" ghosts walk among those explained as the patients' "projections," while Prior is used to undermine Rivers's attempts to provide a "sense of mastery over the past."

Whitehead thus shows Barker as postmodernist antiauthoritarian, allowing competing models of authority to coexist, even as she displays her mastery of the line between historical material and fiction.

Whitehead's teasing apart a "modernist" and "postmodernist" relation to the past and to authority is compelling and echoes many features of what I have articulated as a shift away from a linear to a "spiral" model of narrative. However her schema does not allow for the existence of a third temporality that is figured through the body, that of a cyclical exploration of birth and death. Given the political investments I have shown are made in this bodily materialism, this leaves out both the gendered and classed marking of the unreason that returns. If there is any doubt by now that both time and narrative are thus marked, we might note that in precisely the paragraph following Prior's rejection of Rivers's "solution" to his amnesia, Prior turns to Rivers as a suckling kid to its mother (*Regeneration*, 95). The destabilization of a modernist paradigm of history is thus *also an assertion of bodily knowledge.*

Once Barker's interest in "matter and mortality" is taken on board, the continuities with Barker's earlier work as a materialist exploration of survival and the life cycle come into focus. Prior may be a postmodern spirit of cynical (un)reason and fluid identity, but he is also a man of flesh and omnivorous physical appetite. Rivers may be a proto-postmodernist clinging to modernist hopes of truth, but he is also a mother managing the purpose of that flesh. In this light, I would argue that Barker's persistent use of ghosts and haunting is less the figure of a postmodern relativizing of time and reason than the completion of a cosmological view that has far more in common with the premodern sensibility of the Polynesian headhunters of *The Ghost Road.* Here mind, body, and spirit are equally present as components of a holistic perception of human life defined explicitly as an attempt to reconnect death with birth.[25] Allan Young's analysis of "bodily" memory in the context of post-traumatic stress disorder sheds further light on how Barker makes this a platform for a more ethical perspective on human violence. Young contends that the body possesses a sense of time and reason quite distinct from mental memory:

> Bodily memory's particularity is that it gets traumatic time to run unequivocally in one direction, from trauma to syndromal effects. Mental memory, at home in the brain's cortex, is notoriously revisable and permits time to move in two directions; bodily memory, locked into the limbic and sympathetic systems, is revisable only through evolutionary mechanisms. . . . Beneath this mental memory, the bodily memory installs a second narrative and also a second system of accounting—one whose elements are reduced to fear, anger, and pain; whose highest value is defined as survival rather than virtue; and whose bio-logic may, in the right hands, challenge the mental memory's moral logic.[26]

Barker, like Young, would seem to propose that the body's very amorality in pursuing survival beyond virtue, ironically, can sometimes be more moral than a naive idealism. As I have tried to show, in Barker's hands "bio-logic" becomes an argument not for Darwinian fatalism but for feminist and working-class investment in a bodily future.[27]

Although her later novel *Another World* does not make this case nearly so elegantly as the *Regeneration* trilogy, it does make her thinking more obvious, and I will conclude with its consideration. The most overt of her ghost stories *Another World* is also a story of pregnancy and the death of a 101-year-old Somme veteran, who is convinced that his ancient bayonet wound is bleeding him to death. The similarity between the ghost and the hysteric body is obvious here as they both disrupt chronological time and reason through parallel unresolved traumas of fratricide. Yet unlike the ghost, the body measures an alternative time in the relationship between birth and death. In this sense, the veteran's death is more similar to Fran's pregnancy. It is no surprise that Barker portrays the pregnancy in witheringly unromantic terms: ugly, painful, even morbid, her stomach "a bag of drowning kittens" (42). Yet both acts retain an absolute significance as the terms of human plot. Significantly, the one difference between the uncanny mural of the Victorian family and their modern-day counterparts is that the ghostly mother is *not* pregnant. Barker even builds in an academic argument with a "postmodern" perspective in the form of Nick's debates with Helen, an oral historian who views the veteran Geordie's memories as "rema[de] to fit in with public perceptions" (*Another World*, 83). While her views are initially supported, in the end Nick rejects it for its overclinical *disembodiment* of memory and hallucination:

> He hears again Geordie say: "I am in hell." Present tense, the tense in which his memories of the war went on happening. A recognized symptom of post-traumatic stress disorder, a term Geordie probably never knew. Though he knew the symptoms well enough, he knew what it did to the perception of time. . . . But suppose, Nick wants to shout at rows of faceless white-coats, suppose you're wrong and he was right. Suppose time can slow down. Suppose it's not an ever rolling stream, but something altogether more viscous and unpredictable, like blood. Suppose it coagulates around terrible events, clots over them, stops the flow. . . . It's nonsense, of course. And just as well, because if true, it would be a far more terrible truth than anything the passage of time can deliver. Recovery, rehabilitation, regeneration, redemption, resurrection, remembrance itself, all meaningless, because they all depend on that constantly flowing stream. But then Geordie's truth had been terrible. Ultimately, for him, all those big words had meant nothing. Neither speech nor silence has saved him. *I am in hell.*
> (271)

While the fact that trauma points to the ultimate collapse of the past tense seems to support Whitehead's thesis of Barker's postmodern relativity, the image of time as a flow of blood returns us to it in the more primitive form of the life span. This is both more worrying and more hopeful. On the one hand, it suggests the deeper level of trauma that Nick here articulates, in which "recovery, rehabilitation, regeneration, redemption, resurrection, remembrance itself" are meaningless in their conventional historiographical interpretation. On the other hand, physical birth and nurturing remain as possible means by which precisely those terms of return can become those of a future. It is just so in the ending of the novel, where Geordie's funeral anticipates

Fran's birth of a new child, the disappearance of the ghost, and the resolution of the family's traumas.

Barker shows us a world of division and displacement, in which bodies and spirits as well as speech must be interpreted to understand English history and its peculiar psychology of class and gender. Psychoanalytic models of the self, bound as much by inner as outer struggle, the sub and supernatural alongside historical fact, reinvigorate the tradition of social realist working-class fictional tradition on which she draws. As we have seen, these are as much formal as thematic revisions, in setting up quests for total explanation through detective stories and case histories that are then left half-answered; in invoking historical chronologies that are undermined through memory and relativized through bodily time. Barker shows that there is still much to discover about familiar landscapes of national memory. Yet if we can see her work as itself a kind of therapy working on that tradition, in which the specters of unreason are released, no cathartic cure, either political or literary, is on offer. The collective narratives of class or gender emancipation, as much as that of national imperialism, are set up as hollow and disintegrating structures, tragically unavailable to those who need them most.

At the same time, manifested through circular plotting, dialogue, and third-person omniscience, a collective and unifying time remains available. This is the human life span itself, where plots of birth articulate the material future of second chance. Even in her later male-centered novels, this bodily narrative is explored as the effect of a feminized, or "maternal" perspective that implicitly challenges a patriarchal historical narrative of desire and death. Does this provide an alternative basis for political agency and social regeneration? Barker clearly makes the regeneration of working-class culture as much as women's liberation contingent upon the development of a masculine maternal, and ultimately the dissolution of gender as it is expressed through the binaries of sadism and masochism, violence and nurture. Her exploration of men as well as women's ability to regenerate the body certainly argues for a more political understanding of this apparently biological view of redemption. Reproduction, precisely because it is private, semiconscious, even essential, becomes the place of optimism, the term that can continue to unite across social divisions in a shared condition of struggle. In this, she differs considerably from current notions of the body as flexible to the point of dissolution (whether advanced by queer theory or genetic science). Despite their permeation with psychological needs and social controls, Barker's hysteric bodies are always returned to the body that is born, gives birth, and dies, just as ultimately she splits mind, body, and spirit only to suggest the need for their unification. This representation of biological order offers little hope for the revival of older narratives of socialist or feminist emancipation in the context of working-class fiction. But in the context of postmodern dematerialized fragmentation it powerfully asserts the continuing need for collective forms of interpretation and accountability. As she has Owen say to Sassoon, "There's a point beyond which you can't press the meaninglessness." In this sense, the reproductive body as narrative principle continues to open up both a social perspective and an aesthetic with which we are still only coming to terms.

NOTES

1. Pat Barker, *Union Street* (London: Virago, 1997), 2; Pat Barker, *Another World* (London: Penguin, 1999), 40. All subsequent references will be included in the text.

2. Pat Barker, *Blow Your House Down* (London: Virago, 1996), 47. All subsequent references will be included in the text.

3. Pat Barker, *Regeneration* (London: Viking, 1991); *The Eye in the Door* (London: Viking, 1993); *The Ghost Road* (London: Viking, 1995). All subsequent references will be included in the text.

4. Blake Morrison, "War Stories: What Booker Prize Winner Pat Barker Sees in Soldiers," *New Yorker,* January 22, 1996, 78–82.

5. See Juliet Mitchell, "Feminism and Psychoanalysis at the Millennium," *Women: A Cultural Review* 10, no, 2 (1999): 185–91, for an excellent assessment of the political efficacy of psychoanalysis after thirty years of feminist appropriation.

6. Blake Morrison, "War Stories," 82.

7. See Ann Ardis's essay, "Political Attentiveness vs. Political Correctness: Teaching Pat Barker's *Blow Your House Down,*" in this volume.

8. Donna Perry, "Going Home Again: An Interview with Pat Barker," *Literary Review* 34 (1991): 236.

9. Marianne Hirsch, *The Mother/Daughter Plot: Narrative, Psychoanalysis, Feminism* (Bloomington: Indiana University Press, 1989).

10. Ibid., 163.

11. Ian Haywood, *Working-Class Fiction: From Chartism to Trainspotting* (London: Northcote House, 1997), 146.

12. Ibid., 145–47.

13. Pat Barker, *Liza's England* (London: Virago, 1996), 6. All subsequent references will be included in the text.

14. Liza gives birth to Tom (80), to Eileen (141); Eileen gives birth to Kath (211).

15. See Peter Brooks, *Reading for the Plot: Design and Intention in Narrative* (Cambridge: Harvard University Press, 1998), 26, for a discussion of how the archetypal motive of transmission in the narrative is figured metonymically in plotting as "unpacking," often of an original condensed metaphor such as Liza's box.

16. It is significant that Barker does not develop sexual relationships between women as a possible means of healing. She does represent one lesbian relationship, between Jean and Carol in *Blow Your House Down,* but although convincingly developed and given the status of a refuge from exploitation, there is no equivalent of the symbolic regeneration suggested in maternal men.

17. Tracing of Barker's repeated use of the male hemorrhage through her novels reveals this increasing confidence in a masculine maternal. Compared to Muriel Scaife's futile attempt to save her husband in *Union Street,* it is Stephen who does the same for his father in *Liza's England*—holding his father as a "new-born child." Similarly in having the nephew Nick clean up his uncle after an anal hemorrhage in *Another World,* Barker shows us a new generation of men whose mothering of each other alone will break down the doomed and stifling model of working-class male stoicism and violence. In *Regeneration,* hemorrhaging once again makes an appearance, where an army doctor witnesses a young soldier die from a hemorrhage he did not see quick enough for its coating of mud. This failure to preserve life, however, is measured by the doctor's intense guilt, and subsequent phobia about blood.

18. Interestingly Henry Head tempts Rivers down to Central Hospital in London so he can deal "with physical trauma and war neurosis in the same hospital" (*Regeneration*, 147).

19. In this context, homosexual relationships are represented in terms of the facilitation of men's mutual nurturing rather than sexual desire, as in *Liza's England*. (Prior's sadistic [homo]sexual experiences as the exception to this are contained within his bisexual omniverousness.)

20. Samuel Hynes, "Among Damaged Men," *New York Times Book Review*, March 29, 1992, 1–2.

21. While on the ward, Rivers muses at one point, "All those bodily transformations causing all those problems. *But they solved them too.* Alice in Hysterialand." *The Ghost Road*, 442.

22. The originality of Barker's working-class maternal aesthetics in the trilogy is striking compared to another First World War novel that came out the same year as *The Eye in the Door*, Sebastian Faulks's *Birdsong* (London: Hutchinson, 1993). In this also hugely acclaimed novel, many of the same themes are visible: a vulnerable yet stoic masculinity driven mad more by enforced passivity than action; the interweaving of home and front; the importance for England in remembering the war in the 1990s. As Elizabeth uncovers the story of her grandfather's doomed affair with a married woman before the war and his subsequent hardened but courageous military experience, she realizes her need to "repay the debt," to "complete the circle" (417). Most strikingly, the novel ends with a kind of redemption through Elizabeth's delivery of a baby boy, that she names John after her grandfather's promise to "have children" for a man who died next to him in the tunnel (452, 490). Yet the difference between Faulks and Barker is the heterosexual plotting of the war and of birth. For Faulks, the gendered division of labor that sustains war and is encoded in the archetypes of both narrative and myth remains untouched. The final image of Elizabeth's partner being sent outside the house after the birth is telling, in physically separating father from child, his overwhelming joy a spiritual and abstract moment.

23. Ruth Rendell described "the appearance of . . . ghostly visitants" in *Another World* as the "powerful novel's" only flaw in *Sunday Times*, October 18, 1998, 8, and Alison Pearson criticized the development of the narrative into a "spectral whodunit," asserting that Barker's depiction of the supernatural is superfluous to her evocative representation of human conflict in *The Electronic Telegraph: booksonline*, October 26, 1998, at http://www.electronictelegraph.com.uk. I am grateful to Charlotte Jones for pointing out these references.

24. See Anne Whitehead's essay, "Open to Suggestion: Hypnosis and History in the *Regeneration* Trilogy," in this volume.

25. See Frank Kermode, *The Sense of an Ending: Studies in the Theory of Fiction* (New York: Oxford University Press, 1966) for a general comparison of "premodern" cosmological "circular" perceptions of time as seasonal versus the premise that modern linear plotting makes of an apocalyptic end to an otherwise endless history.

26. Allan Young, "Bodily Memory and Traumatic Memory," in *Tense Past: Cultural Essays in Trauma and Memory*, ed. Paul Antze and Michael Lambek, 98–99 (New York: Routledge, 1996).

27. Barker tellingly defined happiness as "having grandchildren" in an interview on *Another World*. Susannah Simons, "Mistress of Her Art: Interview with Pat Barker," London, August 28, 1999, Classic FM Radio.

HEATHER NUNN AND ANITA BIRESSI

In the Shadow of Monstrosities
Memory, Violence, and Childhood in *Another World*

As the title *Another World* (1998) suggests, Pat Barker's most recent work explores multiple dimensions of time and place. In this novel Barker produces complex interrogations of class, gender, and family relationships. Trauma lies at the core of this text. The roots of trauma are located in both the public monstrosity of the First World War and in a private dilemma that takes place in the aftermath of war in which distinctions between reality and fantasy cannot hold and an old soldier's testimony conceals a personal distress and grief that resists public expression. The novel is also an exploration of contemporary fears: of risk taking, of the loss of childhood, of random violence and unspeakable horrors. At a time when the specter of legitimized state-sanctioned violence (especially war) and the public grieving associated with it seems to have receded in the English imaginary, individual but publicly mediated horrors, or as Barker calls them "monstrosities," take center stage in media culture.[1]

Another World operates as a dialogue with these horrors, these events that violently disturb the cultural order. As Alison Young argues, in the public imagination of crime, such crises are "an occasion for storytelling, for the generation of narratives which describe, respond to, or displace a critical rupture in the cultural order."[2] The specters of the murderer, the abducted child, the violent child, and the aberrant family haunt the text, not always explicitly stated but often implied in asides or motifs that rely on the reader's recognition of a contemporary sense of continuous vulnerability and the recurrent fantasy of unprovoked attack that characterizes current fears for the self in the social world. Characters live in the "shadow of monstrosities":

> Peter Sutcliffe's bearded face, the number plate of a house in Cromwell Street
> [inhabited by the Wests], three figures smudged on a video surveillance screen,
> an older boy taking a toddler by the hand while his companion strides ahead,
> eager for the atrocity to come.[3]

The worlds of Fred and Rose West, Peter Sutcliffe, Mary Bell, Jon Venables, and Robert Thompson, which seem in media coverage so different from and incomprehensible to the world of Barker's mainly middle-class protagonists in *Another World,* are persistently present and obtrusive. These iconic figures—Bell, the young girl who killed two small boys in 1968; Sutcliffe, the serial killer of women in the 1970s and early 1980s; the boys Venables and Thompson, who were filmed leading two-year-old

James Bulger to his death in the early 1990s; and the Wests, whose systematic sexual abuse and serial killing of young women came to light in the early 1990s—have become ciphers of "evil" reproduced across the pages of newspapers and on TV screens. Collectively they have come to represent the hidden aberrance at the heart of the modern family or child. They are seen as individuals who eluded and obscenely transgressed the contours of safe acceptable family life. Sexual assault, physical brutality, and emotional abuse are embodied in these figures: they reside in the popular cultural imaginary as the monstrosities that we not only fear but may become.

Another World tracks the relationships between individual and collective guilt, personal and social history, violence and the memory of violence, public and private life, loss and silence. The book features Geordie, an elderly man who, as he begins to die, struggles to come to terms with his experience of the First World War and of the loss of his brother Harry on the front line. Geordie claims a terrible burden of responsibility for his brother's death. "All Geordie's words . . . orbit round a central silence, a dark star. . . . It's Harry's name he shouts in the night" (158). Eventually, we learn that Geordie killed Harry on the front line as he lay dying in agony, snagged on barbed wire. Geordie's taped, almost hallucinogenic, recollections of his crawl from the trenches to his injured brother in the muddy battlefield are played back for his grandson Nick after his death:

> Just as I'm crawling the last few feet a flare goes up, he's screaming, all I can see is
> the mouth, little blue slitty eyes, and his guts are hanging out . . . all I can see is
> the open mouth, and my fingers are digging into his chest, finding the right place
> and then I ram the knife in and the screaming stops. (263–64)

This traumatic personal memory, with its painful indeterminacy, its slippage between accuracy and distortion, real event and fantasy, is the "hell" that Geordie imparts to Helen, the oral historian. As with many serious traumas, the truth of the event eludes him and others:

> You see, when I'm remembering all this, it's like falling through a trapdoor into
> another room, and it's still all going on. I don't remember the mud on my face, I
> feel it, it's cold, gritty. And I see everything like that until I get to Harry's wounds.
> And then what I see in my mind's eye is something like fatty meat coming out
> of a mincing machine. . . . It's . . . I know that what I remember seeing is false, It
> can't have been like that, and so the one thing I need to remember clearly, I can't.
> . . . So how do I *know* I couldn't have got him back? (264–65)

Throughout the novel and even at the end the possibility is left open that Geordie simply seized the opportunity to brutally fulfill a childhood fantasy of sibling rivalry and murdered his brother. Harry, in a sense, becomes a doppelganger, a fully formed but ghostly figure that haunts his brother's memories of the war and personifies his inexpressible grief and trauma. The secret Geordie bears and passes on through loaded silence to his grandson Nick—the "dark star"—is this shameful or unspeakable experience which is barred from conscious memory. Harry is the phantom come back from the unconscious to persist into the next generation. Locating this kind of transgenerational haunting of the family line, Nicholas Abraham and Maria Torok have noted:

> Grief that cannot be expressed builds a secret vault within the subject. In this crypt reposes—alive, reconstituted from the memories of words, images and feeling—the objective counterpart of the loss, as a complete person with his own topography, as well as the traumatic incidents—real or imagined. . . . [4]

In this notion of transgenerational haunting the "buried speech" and unspeakable experiences of earlier generations—parents, grandparents—are transmitted as symptoms or pockets of repressed memory to those that follow. Here, the persistent social trauma of war is connected to individual trauma and the violence of sibling rivalry. Harry is Geordie's "objective counterpart," a figure formed from memory, guilt, and trauma that will not go away. The unreal or the supernatural becomes the only way to translate the dead gap in recollection. Harry is a foreign body from the past who breaches the present. For example, Geordie recalls the "The Great Family Portrait," taken in 1919 by a spiritualist at his mother's insistence, which showed this "thing" in the background, a thing that might be Harry: "You couldn't make out the features, but you could just about see it was a face" (153–54). Geordie seems still to be linked to his invisible "counterpart," a double who invokes the uncanny. He is himself, therefore, also a figure of connection between past and present as memories resurface and he increasingly fails to distinguish between then and now. His present-tense exclamation "I am in hell" interrupts and challenges others' self-reassuring perceptions that past traumas remain in the past rather than bleeding into present time. His disembodied voice, captured and preserved on Helen's tape recorder, survives his death, inhabiting a space akin to photographs, of presence and absence, the familiar and strange.

In this novel different temporal worlds overlap like the circles in Venn diagrams producing strange spaces of convergence, echo, and repetition. As Geordie fades away, he seems to be "living to the tick of a different clock" (148), reliving experiences of the war. But as his grandson Nick quickly learns, Geordie's multitemporal existence is not so difficult to grasp or rather it is not so easy to avoid. In the dead of night Geordie loses his grasp on time and crawls through the local streets as if through the trenches, "slithering away into the shadow of the trees." Nick, appalled, follows him as he hides behind telegraph poles and crawls along the cobbled road through the dirt. At nighttime his grandfather's fantasy becomes irresistible and Nick's grasp on the situation starts to slip. "His day-time self vanishes. . . . It's too insubstantial an identity to survive in the dark wood at night" (160). Later Nick glimpses this world of imaginative embodiment once again in a highly refracted form. His own stepson Gareth has run away from home and darkness has fallen. He discovers him lying in the lane with his toy sniper in the old armaments factory area surrounded by debris and barbed wire. When discovered Gareth begins to cry, "behind him the little soldier, face blank and resolute, crawls out of the circle of light into the dark" (211–12).

Barker's remarkable achievement here is to layer imagery and perspective with a subtlety that provokes readers to consider the almost inexpressible connections and tensions between cause and effect, determinism and individual agency, and contingency and predestination. The articulation of connections between generations of men in particular, and their positioning as violent/guilty subjects, is one to which we will return in the conclusion. The importance of remembering and the transmission of knowledge through *experience* is fundamental here.

Memory has gained in value as a subject of public fascination and as a means to interpret broader public social events. As Thomas Elsaesser has noted, for instance, "history has become the very signifier of the inauthentic, merely designating what is left when the site of memory has been vacated by the living."[5] On one level, *Another World* is concerned with the horror, violence, and loss experienced by young men in the trenches of the First World War; this is a focus for the contemporary fascination with personal recollection and subjective experience of traumatic history. At a second level these reopened wounds are crosscut with the contemporary fear of the violent and potentially murderous child (epitomized most clearly through the figure of Gareth, Geordie's great-grandson). The state-sanctioned slaughter of the enemy by young men barely out of boyhood is juxtaposed with the claustrophobic and damaging battleground of the family. Both scenarios of violence confront the reader, in dramatically different ways, with the suspense and arousal of fear that accompanies experiences and fantasies of oppression, violence, and conflict.

The call for Geordie to tell his story of the horror of war to public audiences and his ready focusing on contemporary audiences' demands for stories of the trenches partly reveals a deference to and a shaping by public taste. As the text reveals, social forces obliged Geordie's memories to be repressed in the immediate aftermath of the war. The culture had no place for masculine vulnerability, for disorder from the memories of the ranks with their potential disruption and invalidation of national myths of heroic battle and triumph. Geordie's unthinkable, unspeakable experiences remained outside, excluded from the level of public speech and, consequently, the public commemoration and ritual of Armistice Day provided no avenue for his grief and distress. Helen, the historian who records Geordie's recollections, provides one perspective on the potential malleability of private memory to public form. Generations freed from personal experience of the war demand a different response from Geordie. His public talks on the experience of the war are valued in a contemporary therapy culture where confession, personal revelation, and the public display of intimacy are accorded the status of truth. His past is rearticulated for a generation interested in the subjective story and importantly in the truth that is believed to lie concealed below the level of language, revealed in the faltering sentence or display of emotion, in the revelation of "fear, pain etc. The horror, the horror" (82–83). *Another World* tracks different attempts to plot or capture the experience and memory of these events. And, in addition, highlights the personal, sometimes questionable, investment of the listener or reader in Geordie's narration of his past.

The different texts that feature in the narrative reveal what is now a commonplace for many cultural analysts—that the past is only accessible through re-presentation. Geordie's grandson Nick compares traumatic memory to the cinema—a "hallucinatory" process of immediate fragments of image. Barker's story exposes other texts as ciphers or clues open to interpretation and routes into different but always incomplete knowledge or experience of the past. Films and classical music, Geordie's autobiography, his taped interviews, and postcards from the front reveal the manipulation of events through representation; their editorial potential as truth, propaganda, satire, or censored message. Moreover the York Time travel experience, visited by Nick's family, reveals history reduced to spectacle. Here, the abstraction of the past as "shots" or tableaux is disclosed—"an air-raid warden from the Blitz, an unemployed man in a cloth cap, a First World war officer, his arm raised, cheering, a lady in a crinoline" (231). However, even these technologically transformed events are presented in Barker's text as potentially resonant material, ready for individual reuse. As Nick's daughter, Miranda, watches the video of digital reconstruction of a Viking face she becomes frighteningly aware of the "skull beneath the skin" (234). Instead of marveling at the transformation, at the ability to look "at the face of the past," the uncanny computerized transformation of the skull invokes her own personal trauma and transformation by invisible anger. Nick's desertion of Miranda's mentally ill mother for a new family and the expectation that she bonds with them are the basis of her brooding resentment that she, nonetheless, conceals beneath a mask of compliance. As in Barker's *Regeneration* trilogy, a fictional and indeed metafictional comment on the textuality of history as story reveals that storytelling can become a process close to therapeutic practice. In this sense the author knowingly reveals *Another World* as a text immersed in the contemporary fascination with "acts of retelling, re-membering, and repeating all pointing in the direction of obsession, fantasy, trauma."[6] Private grief, unspoken fears and extreme distress "speak" through physical symptoms, memory fragments, and eruptions of violent resentment in Nick's extended family who are seemingly branded, as well as fused together, through the legacy of their bloodline.

In *Another World* the family is depicted as a space of potential violence, abuse, and seething malevolence. In a second narrative thread, the monstrosities of both war and familial violence cast a shadow over the new family home as Nick moves with his family into an imposing Victorian house on Lob's Hill in Newcastle-upon-Tyne. Here he, his pregnant partner Fran and their little boy Jasper, together with two children from earlier relationships—Gareth and Miranda—come to realize that the house has a terrible past. A shockingly explicit painting of the earlier occupants, the Victorian Fanshawe family, is revealed as Nick and his quarrelsome family strip back the old wallpaper in preparation for redecoration. A grotesque family portrait of the Victorian paterfamilias, his wife, and three children depicts the father with an exposed penis that "springs from the unbuttoned flies," the mother with breasts exposed as "great, lard-white footballs" and two boys and a girl who appear both sinister and tense (40). Through present-tense description the inanimate fresco takes on a life of its own. Its animation suggests the lurid figures or sentinels who, with genitals exposed, guard forbidden places or exude apotropaic powers of warding off danger. These figures verge on the absurd, they are monsters in many senses of the word: their abnormality both "shows" and "warns" those who gaze upon them.[7]

This scene parallels an autobiographical moment recalled by Andrew O'Hagan in his book *The Missing* (1995), which was also serialized in the *Guardian* in September 1995. O'Hagan's critically acclaimed book is both a memoir of childhood and lost paternity and an exploration of "Westworld," a space inhabited by murderers such as the Wests, where missing people go unremarked and seemingly unmourned. This mixture of reminiscences of "childish violence" and adult atrocities begins with a formative moment in O'Hagan's childhood. He recalls as a little boy the eerie discovery of a framed photograph of his dead grandfather, who went missing at sea during the First World War, lodged behind the gas boiler:

> There was something there; I knew there was; it had been there for ages. . . . In the end I squeezed my body halfway round, and pulled hard until it loosened and fell into the middle of the room with me underneath. . . . The grandfather was covered in dust and damp patches dried in . . . he had the darkest eyes I'd ever seen. His hair was slick, combed up to a glistening ridge; the lips were thin, the cheeks were white.[8]

Both Barker's and O'Hagan's portraits seem to represent a lost but still feared patriarchal authority. O'Hagan's phallic and adamantine grandfather with ridged hair and "a forehead fit to launch ships with" glowers out of the past. In Barker's picture the horror of the sexualized patriarchal family haunts the contemporary nuclear family already fraught with the uneasy alliances of second relationships, step and half siblings. The portrait presents the father's "phallus as weapon, pure and simple" (42) and indicates the uncanny threat at the heart of the home and the family. While not overtly spoken at the outset of the book the implied taint of past incest and certainly patriarchal domination haunts the house.[9]

Appositely, in "The 'Uncanny'" (1919) Freud analyzes the convergence of two apparently opposite words *heimlich* (the familiar, the homely) and *unheimlich* (the strange, ghostly, unfamiliar). These words meet in the sense of something uncanny that should remain hidden and secret but that has come to light.[10] What is frightening, then, about the uncanny is not the new experience but the return of repressed knowledge, particularly sexual knowledge. Lob's Hill is constructed as a site where what is unspeakable in the past rises through the wallpaper to disrupt the present inhabitants and also to offer a monstrous double of the family: "The living stand and gaze at the dead. Probably the same thought occurs to all of them, but it's Miranda, her voice edging up into hysteria, who finally says what they're all thinking. 'It's us'" (41).

Reading a popular true crime history book, *Mary Anne Cotton's Teapot and Other Notable Northern Murders,* in the gift shop of the Fanshawe's second home, Fleete House, Nick discovers another layer to the monstrous secret of the Fanshawe portrait: the daughter and older son were accused of the murder of their two-year-old brother James. He chooses not to disclose this story to his family. On November 5, 1904, little James is found to be missing. There is no sign of a forced entry into the house. His brother Robert and sister Muriel claim they have heard nothing. Later a truant child discovers his body in the heart of an unlit bonfire, "The guy's mask had been placed over his face, perhaps to hide the terrible injuries underneath, but blood had seeped through" (108).

The fictional Fanshawe case operates in dialogue with the now notorious murder in Liverpool, Britain of two-year-old James Bulger. On February 12, 1993, James slipped away from his mother as she paid for her purchases in a shopping mall in Bootle on Merseyside. CCTV recorded boys Jon Venables and Robert Thompson luring him away. Together they dragged James for two miles, encouraging him to fall into a canal. When he failed to do so they dropped him on his head and finally hauled him along busy roads until they reached a railway line. Here they poured blue paint into his eyes and kicked and beat him with bricks and an iron bar. Finally they removed his lower clothing and left him on the train tracks. More than thirty people had witnessed James's rough journey with his abductors; only one had tried to intervene.

It has become a commonplace that the Bulger case was not only a private tragedy but also a public event. The frequently repeated footage resonated with a public already entering a new era of peculiar and paradoxical television intimacy, arriving at a time when personal revelation, agonized press conference appeals, and tabloid exclusives seem to "reveal all." QC (Queen's Counsel) Alan Levy was quoted as saying, "The video will be seen as being as important as the film of President Kennedy's assassination. It touched a nerve with the public and still does."[11] A glimpse on the video of the shop Mothercare underlined the poignancy of the case and chimed with concerns that family disintegration had been the catalyst of the crime. The two murderers were demonized as "nonchildren," as misfits who not simply failed the ideal of childhood but murdered it.[12]

A series of coincidences link the Fanshawes, the Bulger case, and the contemporary dwellers of Lob's Hill. The ages of the Fanshawes and Nick and Fran's older children coincide—a girl of thirteen, a boy of eleven. Both have a young brother whose name begins with "J" (the murdered boy James also anticipating James Bulger). Here the monstrosities that Nick locates in present crimes—Peter Sutcliffe, the Wests, Jon Thompson, and Robert Venables—are shown to have a longer trajectory. The real-life child murderer Mary Bell (who also lived near Lob's Hill) is included in the *Mary Anne Cotton* book alongside the fictional Fanshawe murder of two-year-old James. The nightmarish description of Robert and Muriel Fanshawe's murder and disposal of their brother James rivals the now infamous journey toward death made by Bulger. As with Bulger, James Fanshawe's final journey, wheeled by his brother and sister to his resting place, was witnessed by a bystander and represented to a horrified public: The children were seen: "The creaking trolley, with its grotesquely masked burden, haunted the imagination. People had nightmares about it" (110).

The echoes and repetitions of names, events, and crimes in the text returns us to Freud's essay on the uncanny. In his discussion of a story by E. T. A. Hoffmann, Freud tracks uncanny themes of doubling and identity:

This relation accentuated by mental processes leaping from one of these characters to another—by what we should call telepathy—so that one possesses knowledge, feelings and experiences in common with the other. . . . And finally there is the constant recurrence of the same thing—the repetition of the same features or character-traits or vicissitudes, of the same crimes, or even the same names through several consecutive generations.[13]

Here names, personal traits, and even crimes echo across time and place creating the disturbing familiar/unfamiliar sensations associated with the uncanny. The ghost of the Fanshawe daughter Muriel is encountered by all of the family except the mother Fran, who is denied by Barker the insight afforded to the other characters. Her maternal body, discursively equated with the monstrous feminine, with mutation and bodily fluids, seems to preclude her identification with less tangible horrors and the emotional space that they occupy. Only Fran refuses to identify with the Fanshawe portrait, pointing out that Mrs. Fanshawe was not pregnant. Pointedly, the ghost represents not the victim but one of the perpetrators of child murder. These encounters with Muriel are arguably nothing more than an unconscious projection of the unspoken anger, aggression, desire, and malevolence that all the family members feel at different times for each other, but refuse to articulate or recognize in themselves. Death haunts the family: Geordie's imminent death, the death of the soldiers supplied by arms from Fanshawe's armament factory in the Great War, the death of Fanshawe's sons—James murdered, Robert killed in the Somme—the death of Geordie's brother Harry. The ghost then is not only a signifier of displaced sexual anxiety and family aggression—the culturally invisible—but also an uncanny encounter with death.[14] *Another World* refers to taboo subjects normally silenced and rather than the threat of mortality reveals the artificiality of cultural distinctions between proper and improper responses, "real" life and fantasy, past time and present. As with Geordie's belief that his old bayonet wound is killing him, the ghost reveals that "the power of old wounds to leak into the present was not so easily dismissed" (75).

True crime and the cultural mythology that surrounds such cases as the Bulger murder intersect with Barker's text in such a way as to add suspense and a dreadful anticipation to the encounters between the children Miranda, Gareth, and their baby stepbrother Jasper. Gareth, feeling neglected and anxious about his new and rather rough school, resents Jasper and gradually heaps small and incremental cruelties upon him. The implication is that it might only be a matter of time before Gareth will remove him from the scene just as James Fanshawe was removed. The family's day out at the beach toward the end of the novel brings events to a climax, leading the reader into a convincing scenario of how child murders might occur. As his parents sleep Jasper wanders into a rocky stream closely observed by his brother from above. Gareth begins to throw stones at Jasper who cannot work out where they are coming from: "It's like playing with an ant, it's so easy to make him do stupid things. The stones start to get bigger" (190). Jasper is seriously hurt. Gareth's emotional estrangement is starkly drawn:

Nick runs faster than Mum. . . . They don't look like real people, Gareth thinks, they look like actors on the telly. . . . He can't understand why Jasper's crying. From the moment the first stone hit his head Gareth's known he was dead . . .

it's just that he wouldn't lie down. He'd thrown the other stones out of despair
because he wouldn't stay down. He'd wanted it to be over quickly. (191–92)

Barker's text contradicts the notion that childhood crimes are rare anomalies: care-
less violence, small offenses, and fantasies of aggression and retribution seem to be
everywhere present. For Gareth is not simply an aggressor he is also a victim of physical fear. Class difference cuts across his future as he moves to a school populated with
children from the local estate who are depicted as truants and troublemakers. When
he vindictively kicks a small boy as he passes through the estate, a gang of four girls
retaliate, punching him and sexually embarrassing him (170–74). His later attack on
Jasper is consequently part of a cycle of aggression and a riposte to his earlier sexualized humiliation.

Power relations and obligations at the micro level of the family and within smaller
groups and institutions—the gang, the neighborhood, and the school—are clearly
central to *Another World*. Integral to these power relations is the child's ability to
resist adult power revealed both in the Victorian children who escape judicial justice
(perhaps because of their facility in matching the ideal of Romantic childhood and
certainly because of their class affiliation) and in Gareth's seething resistance. Gareth
embodies childish recalcitrance. The child, as Charles Jenks has pointed out, is
"obliged by the adult world to be happy" and yet Gareth is moody and withdrawn,
anxious about beginning the term in a new school, resentful of his baby brother,
grimly determined to hate his stepfather Nick. The child, as Anne Higonnet explains,
must also be innocent to be desirable to adults yet Gareth is neither innocent nor
desirable. His mother consciously shrinks from physical contact with him since his
very presence seems to operate as a rebuke: "Fran becomes aware that Gareth has
come into the room behind her. He moves quietly, and his eyes wince behind his
glasses, no more than an exaggerated blink, but it tweaks her nerves, says: You're a
lousy mother" (4).[15]

Although Nick and Fran try to prevent their son's obsession with violent computer games they also welcome his absence from family life as he spends the school
holidays mesmerized by games such as *Crash, Fighting Force, Mortal Kombat* [*sic*],
Shock, Riot, Alien Trilogy, Rage, and so on. Gareth is a symbol of a generation that
perceives and decodes the world through media that arguably erode the differences
between childhood and adulthood, and between fantasy and reality. The flow of television, its accessibility, and its location at the heart of the family means that it reveals
what were formerly cultural secrets to everyone simultaneously and indiscriminately;
secrets about sex and reproduction, about death and decay and about family dissolution.[16] And children like Gareth seem to be left alone to make sense of these knowl-
edges. For example, Fran's pregnancy does not seem to have been discussed with
Gareth despite the liberal ethos of the family. Early in the novel he tries to comprehend his mother's pregnancy within the generic conventions of the horror movie:

Gareth's thinking how ugly she looks, with her great big bulge sticking out. He
wonders what the baby looks like. Is it a proper baby with eyes and things or is it
just a blob? He'd watched a brill video at Digger's house, when his mam and

Teddy were still in bed. A woman gave birth to a maggot because her boyfriend had turned into a fly or something like that, he never really got the hang of it because Digger kept fast-forwarding to the good bits. And the maggot was all squashy when it came out, and they kept looking at each other to see who'd be the first to barf but nobody did. (6)

Moreover, the only shared moment of intimacy between mother and son occurs on another occasion when they discuss their viewing of the violent science fiction film *Terminator,* a movie that is very much about the relations between paternity, maternity, and violence. In horror movies and violent computer games the violation of taboo and violation itself are both repetitive and repeatable through new media technology. Gareth can spend forty hours a week watching highly similar acts of digital violence or repeat the same scene on a video recording. Media repetition becomes both a warning and a motif of an obsession with and distancing from violence and aggression.

As Jenks notes, murder is inconceivable within the conceptual space of childhood but that space has been reconfigured within media and professional discourses as the "death" or "crisis" of childhood.[17] Gareth invokes contemporary fears of the child and of childhood corrupted, as narrative insight into his inner resentments and revengeful fantasies contests adult notions of childhood innocence. He invokes the possibility that children can be brutal, cruel, and violent. But he is also a class-bound figure and this alters the ways in which readers are asked to understand his dilemma.[18] The novel opens with class-bound images of the monstrous child, as the middle-class academic Nick drives to collect his daughter through the run-down working-class estate that contrasts with his highly disciplined childhood at his father's school. He encounters an animalistic "pack" of youths who are described through brute behavior and repulsive physicality: "a glimpse of furred yellow tongue, spit trapped in bubbles between bared teeth, noses squashed against glass . . . like a pack of flies" (3).

This encounter at the beginning of the novel coincides with Nick's fears for his teenage daughter's vulnerability to attack on public transport and his growing realization that she is a sexual subject. As he collects Miranda from the train station he is aware that she is changing, her legs longer and thinner, her shoulders curved to hide her developing breasts. She arrives telling crude jokes told to her by a drunken stranger on a train. The text opens, then, with images of adult uncertainty about childhood in the late modern era and the child appears throughout the novel as focus of adult fears and fantasies. Through Gareth's violence toward his young brother and his experiences of beatings and humiliation at the hands of other children and through Miranda's nascent sexuality and precocious seriousness, *Another World* reveals children as ambivalent figures, increasingly straddling the child and adult worlds.

Distinctions between reality and fantasy, past and present, real and fictional violence are collapsed in *Another World.* Geordie's reliving of the Somme and his refusal to speak of his brother's death operates as one structuring absence in the text. The elision between the past familial murder and the present danger to Jasper fuses public and private trauma and suggest this ghost story as a tale of "transgenerational haunting." The narrative then is about silences, guilt, and complicity at both an individual and a collective level.

Endangered *masculine* subjectivity and male power and experience are also pivotal in this text. The childhood fascination with the ritual of watching a man shave signifies the act as emblematic of masculine adulthood. Geordie's trench shaving mirror, into which Nick looks after Geordie's death, failing to recognize his own reflection, is a motif of the transmission of masculine pride, guilt, and vulnerability. Geordie's steel mirror is unbreakable but it also returns a blurry reflection. It seems that the story of Geordie's death is also the story of his struggle against the emasculation that accompanies death in the modern world. In hospital and postoperative he is denuded of hair, Nick notices that "The groin is hairless, infantile" (55).

Like the nocturnal hallucination of trench warfare that Nick mimics as he follows the demented Geordie on his crawl across back alleys, the sins (real or imagined) of the fathers intrude upon the sons. Essentially, as in many of Barker's novels, this is a tale of masculine shame, anxiety, and discontent. The women in *Another World* lack the complexity of consciousness and depth accorded Nick, Geordie, and Gareth. Fran and Miranda, as well as the absent and mentally ill first wife Barbara, are entrenched in the conventional physical and emotional signs of femininity: maternity, illness, fraught pregnancy, menstruation, nascent sexuality. The final haunting phrase "I am in Hell" that Geordie mutters, and which keeps rupturing Nick's thoughts as he mourns, signifies that male loss, pride, power and pain are the powerfully shameful and unsayable phantoms "that persist through generations and determine the fate of an entire family line."[19] It is this hidden, unspoken presence that is a subterranean force throughout the book.

Nonetheless the resolution of *Another World* attempts to refute any deterministic model of familial betrayal and violence, insisting on individual autonomy and the adoption of personal responsibility for actions undertaken. Gareth's growing sympathy for his stepfather and the promise of a better future for him within the family is indicative of something far more complex than predestination. As Nick revisits the church where Geordie's funeral service was held and where the graves of the Fanshawe family remain "the innocent and the guilty . . . side by side," he is grateful that he never revealed the Fanshawe murder to his family. Despite the burden of history and the threat of contemporary horrors Nick's story ends on a hopeful note. Nick thinks to himself, "It's easy to let oneself be dazzled by false analogies—the past never threatens anything as simple, or as avoidable, as repetition" (277). Finally then, although Nick's family and especially the children must live under the "shadow of monstrosities" of both familial and social violence their future seems to remain, partly at least, in their own hands.

NOTES

1. This book, then, like others by Barker such as *The Eye in the Door* (London: Viking, 1993), shows up a "complex circulation of emotion" and how ostensibly unconnected "public events can and do cover for each other" (Jacqueline Rose, "The Cult of Celebrity," *London Review of Books* 20, no. 16 (August 20, 1998.) In Martin Amis's autobiography, *Experience*

(London: Vintage, 2000), 62, which includes an account of the loss of his cousin Lucy Partington at the hands of the Wests, he provides an apposite example of how this works. Here Amis explicitly links the grieving for the war dead of the First World War with the inexpressible grief and very public loss of Partington.

2. Alison Young, *Imagining Crime* (London: Sage, 1996), 79.

3. Pat Barker, *Another World* (London: Viking, 1998), 3. All subsequent references will be included in the text.

4. Abraham and Torok are discussed in Ann Scott, *Real Events Revisited: Fantasy, Memory, and Psychoanalysis* (London: Virago, 1996), 88.

5. Thomas Elsaesser, "Subject positions, speaking positions: from *Holocaust, Our Hitler,* and *Heimat* to *Shoah* and *Schindler's List,*" in *The Persistence of History: Cinema, Television and the Modern Event,* ed. Vivian Sobchack, 145 (London: Routledge, 1996).

6. Elsaesser, "Subject Positions," 146. These acts are also scrutinized relentlessly in Barker's subsequent book *Border Crossing* (London: Viking, 2001).

7. The symbolic power of these figures is addressed by Marina Warner in *No Go the Bogeyman: Scaring, Lulling, and Making Mock* (London: Pimlico, 1998), 240–42.

8. Andrew O'Hagan, *The Missing* (London: Picador, 1995), 4.

9. The possibility of paternal sexual misdemeanor is also implied in relation to Geordie who on several occasions refers to Nick not as his grandson but as his son.

10. Sigmund Freud, "The 'Uncanny,'" in *Art and Literature, The Penguin Freud Library,* vol. 14 (Harmondsworth: Penguin, 1919/1985), 363–64.

11. R. Ford, "How the Bulger Killing Became a Media Event," *Times,* June 4, 2001, 4.

12. Diana Gittens, *The Child in Question* (London: Macmillan, 1998), 8, 39.

13. Freud, "The 'Uncanny,'" 356.

14. Rosemary Jackson *Fantasy: The Literature of Subversion* (London: Methuen, 1981), 68.

15. Chris Jenks, *Childhood* (London: Routledge, 1996), 122; Anne Higonnet, *Pictures of Innocence: The History and Crisis of Ideal Childhood* (London: Thames and Hudson, 1998), 132.

16. Neil Postman, in *Out of the Garden: Toys and Children's Culture in the Age of TV Marketing,* ed. Stephen Kline, 71 (London: Verso, 1993).

17. Jenks, *Childhood,* 118. For discussions of the "death" or "erosion" or "crisis" of childhood see, for example, Christine Clegg, Vicky Lebeau, and Paul Myerscough, ed. *New Formations* 42, special issue "Ruins of Childhood"; Anne Higonnet, *Pictures of Innocence: The History and Crisis of Ideal Childhood* (London: Thames and Hudson, 1998); Neil Postman, *The Disappearance of Childhood* (London: W. H. Allen, 1983); and David Buckingham, *After the Death of Childhood: Growing Up in the Age of Electronic Media* (Cambridge: Polity Press, 2000).

18. This is also true of the Fanshawe children. It is implied that they were not convicted because the only person to identify them was a working-class former employee of their father, whose credibility was questioned. Also, images of the ideal child of the period would have been bound up with notions of innocence and respectability rooted in imagery of the middle class.

19. Scott, *Real Events Revisited,* 86.

Family at War

Memory, Sibling Rivalry, and the Nation in *Border Crossing* and *Another World*

Memory, who remembers for you?
Patrick Chamoiseau, *Childhood*

The disaster takes care of everything.
Maurice Blanchot, *The Writing of the Disaster*

In the decades spanned by her literary career Pat Barker has become a writer for whom liminality has proved a paradoxically enduring concern. Her novels are marked, on the one hand, by their clear-sighted evocation of distinctive social and historical milieux (the backstreets of 1950s northern England, the gradually attenuating heroics of the First World War), and on the other by an acute interest in the psychologically opaque and intransigent. Barker has managed to avoid descriptive encapsulation almost as successfully as the heroes and heroines of her fictions do.[1] With reference to the feminism of her work, for instance, she has declared the reduced valency of a sexual politics that is restrictive rather than exploratory and redefining, and has taken care to explain that what compels her is what men and women lose, in human terms, as they go about the challenging task of acquiring a gendered, which is to say social, identity.[2]

In *Another World* (1998) and *Border Crossing* (2001) a further zone of liminality is as central to the composition of the nation as to the work of the novelist.[3] Barker questions what separates childhood from adulthood. It is perhaps an inevitable move for Barker for whom the relation of the workings of memory to history is always central precisely *as* a question. As a condition of affective unbelonging or subjective homelessness that troubles received fictions of origin, particularly families, hysteria appears most noticeably in a repeated scene: in *Another World* a child, and in *Border Crossing* three children, self-consciously engage(s) in physical violence towards another, younger child or infant. By locating acts of sibling violence within a past that continues to disturb the lives of the characters and their families, both novels, like Barker's earlier work, show the past/present distinction to be one that we habitually use to manage the traumatic impact of certain events.

Both novels are set in contemporary England, and both have haunting acts of murderous violence at their centers. In transposing her earlier concerns of war and (sexual) trauma into the English present, Barker pushes the realist form further than has been her custom—relying in *Border Crossing* on what at first appears to be coincidence, and in *Another World* on supernatural elements—which some reviewers have reacted against.[4] But I do not think these books renege on Barker's historical interests. On the contrary, their focus on sibling violence and their experimentation with the realist form enable her to proceed with the challenging task of elaborating a history of the vanishing present.

Another World and *Border Crossing* are tales of dysfunctional, recognizably modern, families, and both turn on violent crimes committed in the past, in the former case during wartime, and in the latter during a time of relative peace. These crimes are shown to be caused by the dynamics of the family and the pressures with which it is faced. Nick, the middle-aged protagonist of *Another World*, is watching his grandfather Geordie, a veteran of two world wars, die of cancer, while his second wife Fran, in the final months of pregnancy, struggles with the conflicting demands of a boisterous toddler, a recalcitrant eleven-year-old son from a former relationship, and the visit of Nick's thirteen-year-old daughter Miranda, necessitated by her mother's admission to a hospital psychiatric ward. Nick and Fran have moved from a small flat to a large Victorian house which awaits renovation. One of their desperate attempts to reconstitute their ailing family involves stripping wallpaper from the waiting-to-be-renovated living room, in the course of which they uncover a luridly obscene painting depicting the Fanshawes, the original nineteenth-century owners of the house.

Nick gradually uncovers the story of the Fanshawes' bitter past with the aid of a book of local history, deciding eventually not to share his findings with Fran. The reader learns that the two elder Fanshawe children were accused of the murder of their younger sibling, the outcome of the case remaining, in many people's minds at least, uncertain. The Fanshawes' history bizarrely parallels that of the family of Nick and Fran, since Fran's son Gareth is eventually discovered to be violently bullying Jasper, his toddler brother. These two stories are interwoven with that of Geordie, who, in the final weeks of illness, is visited by traumatic nightmares that place him back at the scene of his first experience fighting, as a teenager, at the front. Geordie claims to believe that it is his ancient bayonet wound, received in the First World War, and not his cancer, that is killing him, but as death approaches and the nightmares worsen, Nick and the reader discover that the real wound is in Geordie's memory. He is haunted by the figure of his brother Harry, who died at the front, and whom, he fears and believes, he murdered under cover of wartime fighting.

By contrast *Border Crossing* centers on the relationship of Tom Seymour, a psychiatrist who specializes in children's conduct disorder, and Danny Miller, whose life Tom saves one September afternoon by pulling the drowning young man from a river. To his horror and fascination Tom discovers that Danny, now Ian Wilkinson, is the former ten-year-old on whose case he worked when Danny was on trial, thirteen years earlier, for the murder of seventy-eight-year-old Lizzie Parks. Tom's task was to report on Danny's degree of knowledge of the finality of death, evidence of which, he later comes to believe, crucially influenced the jury's verdict. Against his own better judgment Tom enters into a pseudoprofessional dialogue with Danny who is out of prison on parole, ostensibly motivated by Danny's desire to revisit the traumatic event of Lizzie's death. As Tom's and Danny's excavations take them closer to the killing, Tom's relationship with his wife Lauren, already under strain, crumbles. Events take a dramatic turn when breaking news of two young boys charged with the murder of an old woman leads the press to angrily pursue Danny, who flees to begin another pseudonymous episode of his life.

Where *Another World* puts the Fanshawes at the troubled center of the novel's modern family—sex and death in the living room, a sinister original—*Border Crossing* develops a kind of narrative version of the primal scene of psychoanalysis. Danny brings his suffering to Tom, as the seductive hysteric brings her suffering to the analyst and out of (Freud's) dialogue with which the science of memory is birthed. Hysteria is a disturbance of memory that opens onto the field of trauma where inexplicable physical symptoms create an impasse in social life and personal experience. Indeed, questioning the effects of trauma on the hysteric is the means by which Freud develops the key psychoanalytic concepts of the symptom, repression and the unconscious mind.[5] In *Border Crossing* the portrayal of Tom's therapeutic relationship with Danny is the narrative means of uncovering the trauma of the murder. In the course of their conversations Tom becomes increasingly uncertain as to his professional relation to, and his own culpability for, Danny's suffering, as Danny effectively relives the trauma in the effort to recall the extent of his crime.

The question of borders in the relationship between Tom and Danny is the central figure for other kinds of liminality powerfully engaged by the novel. Tom's earlier requirement to pass judgment on the child Danny's degree of mortal (and thus moral) understanding—Question: what is the difference between life and death? Answer: the dead don't come back—is overdetermined by present reality (Danny's dead do come back, and to Tom in particular). From the moment Tom agrees to allow Danny to talk with him about his past, the past/present distinction, like the child/adult distinction with which it is imbricated, comes under increasing pressure. Tom's reasons for engaging in the excavatory journey are suspect from the first, so that the border between patient and therapist is also in question. "If you have the slightest suspicion that I need . . . anything out of this," Tom says to Danny early on in their therapeutic journey, "you should run a mile." Danny responds with an admission of his own "permeability" that is greeted with dour recognition by Tom (*Border Crossing*, 58).

Tom seems to be a deliberately pathetic character, while Danny is the (formerly) quintessential knowing child. Tom's and Lauren's marriage breakdown is largely due to Tom's sexual inadequacy in the face of his and Lauren's efforts to conceive, and one of Tom's fears is that he himself will relapse into childishness, "that people who remain childless never really grow up." He envies his colleague Roddy, who has three children, because

> at least he knew where he was in the generations. . . . When he thought of the
> childless marriages he knew, it seemed to him that, in almost every instance, one

of the partners had become the child. Somewhere, in the distance, was a vision of total selfishness, that dreadful, terminal boyishness of men who can't stop thinking of themselves as young. (*Border Crossing*, 26)

From one point of view Danny is the hysteric in *Border Crossing*, or as some current therapeutic parlance has it, the borderline personality. His is the violent trauma, in which he plays, initially at least, an unclear role, his the seductive maneuvers, years of suffering and parasitic energy, the lucky, last-minute escape to a tantalizing future others envy. But as Freud found and Lacan reiterated, hysteria becomes legible through its effects on others; its suffering registered in the body at the arcane place where basic drive material becomes social, subdued, albeit always insufficiently, by symbolic demand.

As Claire Pajaczkowska observes, "gender needs to be understood in relation to both sexual difference," the assumed differences between men and women, "and the difference between the generations, the two components of Oedipal reality."[6] Without a sense of the vertical, the horizontal can seem overwhelming, which is not unlike the sense of invasion of indecipherable signs visited on the subject by a trauma, or a nation by a war. In the course of the novel Tom's and Danny's roles reverse so that, instead of the image of a strong father and an innocent infant—what we might describe as a properly patriarchal myth—we have the opposite: Danny is the strong or enduring one but he is not innocent; Tom is the weak one although he is the adult who should know best. In war time they might be merely soldiers on opposite sides, but because there is no war they seem like ordinary sibling rivals, at a loss for lack of a standard to fight by whether true or false. If war makes things both more and less real, as there is some evidence to suggest,[7] then we might see the portrayal in the novel of a morally dystopian reality as showing us the cultural fantasies that, without the cover of war, lose their own cover and wind up running scared.

In fearing a premature return to childhood, Tom articulates an anxiety that goes to the secret heart of contemporary Western cultural fantasies of masculinity, where self-reliance, lacking a differential term (a child, or, we might speculate, a mother) can turn to crippling dependency ("can't stop thinking") and sterile self-delusion, a fate explored to somewhat different ends in Ian McEwan's novel *The Child in Time*.[8] Yet Barker makes us feel Tom's discomfort in the way the narrative seems curiously centerless, as though a void with centrifugal force is gradually opening up between Tom and Danny. While on one level, Danny is moving backward in time, Tom is moving forward, filling in the gaps in his knowledge of Danny's thirteen years at school in prison. But on another level, Tom himself is regressing. One by one he loses, out of apparent lack of interest, the trappings of adulthood: his wife (the loss also entailing a painful retrospective postmortem of the marriage), his professional self-regard and, finally, his home. Even so, during the course of their sessions, Tom is learning Danny (Tom is, after all, writing a book about juvenile delinquency). Danny is Tom's instructive cipher, around whom he comes to organize his life, and by whom it is found in disarray. His final lesson places him in the passive, childlike place he fears inhabiting in the future—in a sense, a prison—as he discovers that his only real decisive, manly or heroic act (which is also his right to be read as hero of this story), his rescue of Danny, was engineered *by* Danny and was to a large extent not Tom's decision at all. Tom's future, as it happens, is out of his hands, bizarrely taken care of by the disastrous return, the return to disaster, that detonates in his and Danny's past.

One of the novel's climactic scenes has Danny arrive unscheduled at Tom's house to find Lauren, as prearranged in view of her and Tom's separation, packing up some of her furniture as Tom is still returning from a writers' weekend led by Danny's former English teacher and alleged lover, Angus (part of Tom's increasingly frenetic researches into Danny's former life). Tom arrives home to a house in a state of defamiliarization, with "gray ghost squares" on the walls where pictures, painted by Lauren, once hung, and furniture stands in the middle of a room. This is the point at which Danny literally and figuratively enters Tom's private world—"Danny was inside, now" (*Border Crossing*, 164)—intruding on "the intensely private trauma" of Tom's and Lauren's breakup. But it also turns out to be the moment of revelation that precipitates Danny out of Tom's future, as Danny tells Tom the news of another recent child murder (*Border Crossing*, 163–64). Danny, terrified that public outrage over the new case will stir up interest in his own, is paralyzed by an extreme, suffocating sense of a past repeating itself that is by now also deeply affecting Tom:

> "It's going to open up again," Danny said, his voice strangled with misery and fear. Already he'd seen on television all the things that had happened to him: fists beating on the sides of a police van, shouted threats, the blaze of publicity, nowhere to run, nowhere to hide. (*Border Crossing*, 165)

In the exchange that follows, Danny voices his fears of recognition in terms that are "an entirely accurate description of the way Tom's memory worked," but what disturbs Tom most is that he "couldn't recall any conversation in which he and Danny had talked about the different ways people recall the past" (*Border Crossing*, 165).

Psychoanalyst Juliet Mitchell claims that "the relationship between hysteria and psychoanalysis has been haunted since its inception by [the] crucial omission" of sibling relationships.[9] She connects this omission with the repression of male hysteria in favor of psychoanalytic constructions of "femininity in general," in particular the British object relations tradition's focus on the mother and child.[10] In part, this amounts to reading psychoanalysis as its own kind of post-traumatic stress disorder, unable to deal with the sibling rivalries of its founder or those later found within its ranks. But if we bear in mind that those social processes which arguably infantilize contemporary citizens—to quote Carol Watts: "flexible labor markets, radical transformations in the relation between public and private, post-Fordist production, consumption as citizenship"[11]—are also feminizing, then Mitchell's claim has more modern resonance. Hysteria is the condition of an excess of desire that manifests as a refusal of gendered, familiar norms for its management, pointing instead to the trauma or irrecuperability that is sexuality, beyond all templates for experience. It is associated with femininity because it is mimetic, and the feminine in Western culture has the task of screening or standing in for sex and death, the real, unknowable parameters of existence. Thus hysteria takes a recognized feminine behavior, such as dieting, to extremes, troubling and provoking the social body where its rules for gendered behavior mask real uncertainties. But what happens to hysteria when the populace at large begins to undertake this function, when it is men such as Tom who express the desire for a desire characteristic of hysteria as the central question of their masculinity? A key way to describe the impact of the late capitalist or postmodern period, the historical scene of both novels, is as a process of infantilization resulting in a feeling of powerlessness, expressed, for example, in the characterization of the late 1990s as the time of victim or trauma culture. Here, childhood, femininity, and citizenship achieve a bizarre coincidence.[12] If femininity has become the cover story of sibling rivalry, psychoanalytically speaking, is hysteria more or less present now that the two have come to appear indistinguishable?

Danny and Tom are metaphorical or modern sibling rivals with contestable claims to memory, but *Another World*'s Geordie and Nick also find their respective familial roles changed. As the nearest and most capable grownup, Nick, attending Geordie's bedside and physical nighttime wanderings, discovers the true nature of his grandfather's memories. These involve infantile regression to the rivalry with brother Harry, and, like the ghost plot of sibling murder attested to on the walls of Nick's and Fran's home, horribly reenacted in Fran's son Gareth's bullying of baby Jasper, have a literally haunting quality. As traumatic events Geordie's memories escape historical frameworks and commonsense understanding, but, precisely because of their traumatic or world-breaking nature, repeat themselves through history, never over and done with.

Thus, Geordie's traumatic memories elude the grasp of historian Helen's constructionist frameworks. As a historian Helen is interested in the ways public perceptions, changing over time, alter the meanings of memory and how memory in turn affects historical perception. So for her Geordie, having spent the years of his life immediately following the First World War not speaking of the war, only to become a kind of war veteran celebrity who could not stop speaking of it, is the fascinating historical source, the talismanic real of history. And while Geordie is more than willing to fit most of his memories into the spaces where listeners seem to need to put them, his traumatic memories remain beneath, protected by these memories, which are not memories at all so much as living screens.[13]

This is why Geordie cannot agree with Helen, who wants to know how his memories have altered to accommodate public attitudes to the war. While for Helen, as Nick observes, "memories are infinitely malleable," they are not so for Geordie, whose "past isn't over. It isn't even the past" (*Another World*, 255). Geordie's final words, "I am in hell," delivered at the end of his seemingly endless illness, reveal the fantastical nature of screen memories, personalized but culturally constructed images. Nick, who reads the transcripts of Geordie's and Helen's interviews, discovers the "wordless, hallucinatory filmic quality" of Geordie's memories: "A flare goes up, illuminating bleached sandbags and tangled wire, but the trembling light never falls. A scream begins and never ends" (*Another World*, 241). This, Nick later learns, is the mere deadened screen time of late twentieth-century movie iconography of the war. The relation of such imagery and recollections to real trauma is one of masking, not revelation. When trauma is reencountered, it shatters conscious memory, the imaginary stasis of secondhand loss. As the chasm beneath the screen memories of the war that have also been unconsciously working to manage Nick's own troubles opens, he meets the same sinister enemy as Geordie. Where on the outside is Geordie's nightmare foreigner or a foreign history and under the skin a brother, Nick's ambush is his own family enclosed within the Fanshawe home, its traumas summoned by the ghosts that jar the realist narrative of *Another World*.

Barker does not give the reader any clues as to how to read the supernatural elements in the novel, just as she does not give any clues as to who is ultimately responsible for the treatment and reentry into society of Danny in *Border Crossing*, despite the claims of some reviewers.[14] But like Jolly, who sees Billy Prior's diaries which feature at the close of *The Ghost Road* as a defamiliarizing novelistic trace, I am inclined to regard the indigestibility of these moments as an attempt to get readers to observe ourselves taking things for granted, being taken too easily in.[15] One reader of *Another World* sees Nick's relationship to the family's haunted house as "a lost narrative thread that has never quite worked its way into the fabric of the plot" and concludes that, as a result, "some overriding connection seems missing" in the book, making it "smaller than the sum of its parts."[16] But I think this obvious missed connection, like the play with the idea of the border in *Border Crossing* rather than, as is more typical, using it as the invisible support of the narrative by sustaining the imaginary border between two worlds, can also be seen as a genuine experiment Barker is making within the terms of the realist tradition.[17]

By questioning fashionable notions of collective memory represented by Helen in *Another World* and Tom in *Border Crossing*, Barker stages a subtle inquiry into the relation between public and private forms of memory. How can something (memory), she seems to ask, be culturally constructed whose only raison d'etre is to enable other constructions—for instance history, or literature—by serving as their medium, their equivocal (now you see it, now you don't), enabling means? Can a public memory (yours and mine, a monument to visit, a photograph to cherish, a book in which to read and write; in short, a stand-in for an earlier disappearance) and a private memory (mine alone, the fragile screen beyond which childhood simply *is not there for loss or finding*) ever come together when their mode of operation is to be, for each other, full of loss?[18] We must remember the First World War, we are enjoined, *lest we forget*; which is almost an injunction to remember memory instead.

On the one hand, what is so disturbing about the sibling violence that is virtually repeated in both novels is the way the incidents morph childhood into adulthood as eerily and smoothly as Gareth's blitzed-out warriors respond to his fingers on the keyboard, on the screen.[19] And yet, at the very point where childhood and adulthood blend, there is an inexplicable act of violence accompanied by a resistance to knowledge. What if childhood is indescribably violent, and we just fail to remember? What if crime, once it is out there enjoying itself, can never be brought safely home? When Tom remembers himself as a child, accompanied by a friend, cruelly tormenting four-year-old Neil, "because he was a problem they couldn't solve," what interests him as an adult is

> how little responsibility he felt now. If somebody had asked him about that after-
> noon, he'd have said something like, "Kids can be very cruel." Not, "I was very
> cruel." "Kids can be very cruel." He knew he'd done it, he remembered it clearly,
> he'd known then, and accepted now, that it was wrong, but the sense of moral
> responsibility was missing. In spite of the connecting thread of memory, the per-
> son who'd done that was not sufficiently like his present self for him to feel guilt.
> (*Border Crossing*, 48)

As Adam Phillips notes, this holding or connective function is part of the work we expect childhood to do for us, usually without knowing it. And he suggests we consider what childhood might be like if as adults we no longer needed to use it to link us back, through deadening repetitions, to the positing of world-shattering traumas in the past.[20] One of the strengths of *Border Crossing*, in my reading, is Barker's account of trauma, which manages while still in realist mode to be performative: she disables the reader from easily identifying with either Tom or Danny, giving primacy rather to their dramatic situation at the heart of which is lodged a perpetually retreat-ing event. Yet this is also, I suspect, at the heart of the negative reception of the book by some reviewers. A repeated strain of criticism from American readers—which to me reads like a kind of baffled culture shock—is the charge that Barker is here "too polite," "proper," even "correct" for her material.[21] One reviewer even mentions her "admirably liberal instincts" and the "coziness" of the novel,[22] which makes me think we must have read a different book. In order to try and understand this reaction and its relation to what I have been arguing is Barker's singular project of opening received accounts of history up to the space of the intimate workings of their terms, I will need to turn back, briefly, to an earlier moment in English history where fic-tions of childhood, the novel, and the nation conjoin.

The birth of the novel as its own version of a haven in an increasingly hostile world is by now itself a well documented tale but one that, in England, was subject to a par-ticularly strange dislocation of its own. As Simon During writes, after the French Revolution—itself a kind of mythical beginning for accounts of nationalism—when other European nations undergo consequent change centering around new defini-tions of freedom, England makes liberty a product of history, or better, makes history into its own reward, its own freedom, in the guise of a proud, unmatchable national heritage.[23] The organicism of Scott and Austen becomes, in During's reading, not only the beginning of the tradition of social realism but a Burkean labor of *counter-revolution*, which is to say, in my own addition, an imaginative task that, in creating other or adjacent worlds, quietens or plays a part in meeting and otherwise diverting the needs of England's own.

Thus history, in English post-Enlightenment tradition, absorbs revolutionary fer-vor by first using it to create, and then forgetting that it has created, a parallel story of the past, named English history or heritage. In this way nostalgia, in reality a turning around of the past as lost object, a disorienting experience in the present, is given a fallback linear framework that assuages fears of revolution as fraternal uprising—an excess of sibling rivalry without a familial stopgap—and loss of imperial power that accompany modernity. Those uncertainties that militate around new definitions of fraternity and freedom are transferred to the image of a perfect, which is to say lost, past. In this way a conservative move, one whose energies are directed backward, where to salvage is to make a show of strength, draws to itself the energies of revolution. This partly explains why a nation can cling so tenaciously to myths of a past it never knew: it was as a defense against what it hoped to avoid knowing—bloody revolution and rioting at home—that such myths became necessary to its identity.

During cites a fascinating instance of what he calls English "literature's encounter with nationalism" in De Quincey's 1849 piece *The English Mailcoach*, the mailcoach that uncannily carries news of British victories functioning as an early form of the postal technology that will become, with time, an important disciplinary arm of the state.[24] De Quincey, as During notes, is naturally not writing a simple tale of English victory and instead tells of an incident in which he, being opiated, is unable to prevent the coach, driven by a momentarily sleeping coachman, from crashing into and killing a girl (not so different from the episode in *Another World* where Nick, driving slightly drunkenly home from Geordie's house, encounters the girl who haunts the former Fanshawe home, believing his car to have struck her). De Quincey and the coachman, as During writes, "fail to display exactly that male trait central to the formation of militarized nationalism," although their guilt is somewhat mitigated by the superior, mechanized power of the speeding coach. "Action may be the quality of Englishmen," he observes, and "English bodies may beat with one heart, but discipline, inertia, and a tolerance for destruction are now required by the British state."[25]

During admits that the indictment represented by these comments has "not reached the core of de Quincey's text," and they are instead articulated in the form of accounts of his drugged dreams. In these, passivity takes on a new and deadly kind of violence, as the dreamer is carried into the alien territories of imagined colonial islands in which he finds, "housed in himself, some separate chamber in his brain," a "horrid, alien nature. What if it were his own nature repeated? How if the alien nature contradicts his own, fights with it, perplexes it and confounds it. How again, if not one alien member but two, three, four, within what he once thought the inviolable sanctity of himself?"[26]

Such gothic ruminations, of course, return with psychoanalysis, but with a difference. Children, novels, and nations, particularly those subject to colonial rule, are all depicted as being close to the unconscious, the longed-for home place that recedes further from us the more we seek, but it is childhood that has borne the symbolic brunt of this post-Enlightenment burden.[27] For psychoanalysis, hysterical symptoms are the means by which childhood becomes simultaneously devoid of innocence and an unknown, and thus readily romanticized, region. Yet hysteria also functions like the speeding mailcoach of de Quincey's dream, damaging the family in such a way as to question it as a place of origin, returning it to its basic conditions of sibling rivalry or aggression. When, in the late eighteenth century, the nuclear family becomes privileged as "the most active site of sexuality" it is simultaneously required to mask this truth.[28] Modern, domesticated sexuality, like the nation, is a fantasy whose role is to manage a potentially revolutionary force. In the world of Barker's latest novels, the English family and English history may each simply fail to find an imaginary framework in each other, but one could argue that this failure of coherence is the real story, as Jacques Lacan would say, of any history. It is simply not amenable to being remembered or written down.

With regard to English national fantasy and to the history of psychoanalysis, the trauma of revolution, being constitutive, has already happened, which makes a degree of conservatism appear innate, a habit that cannot be done without. One way to read the project of the novels under discussion is as a demonstration of the dream work that childhood so often performs for adulthood, or fantasies of English history for the English nation: a looking back that is a means of managing anxiety about the future in the present but one that, if unchecked, can threaten to overturn or annihilate all meanings. As Barker reminds us, and it is a psychoanalytic insight that also belongs to or rather insistently troubles the later Freud, "the past never threatens anything as simple, or as avoidable, as repetition" (Another World, 278).

"Analysts make progress," as Julia Kristeva writes in New Maladies of the Soul, "by identifying with hysterical discourse. . . . Such is the foundation of psychoanalytic treatment, which joins together the shared fates of hysteria and interpretation."[29] Fates, and sharing, are apt words because hysteria and psychoanalysis both force, or, in the latter case, allow, others to feel what might be common about the mutually exclusive, where an alleged difference—that between the sexes, say, or Oedipal reality —is maintained by the fear of replacement, a more primal ambivalence that manifests as sibling rivalry. A version of the question Danny puts to Tom ("can people change?") was also the one Freud was asking himself in 1920 when he wrote "Beyond the Pleasure Principle," in part as an effort to understand the curiously detemporalizing effects of the First World War. This was also inevitably a question about the human psyche's innate conservatism. Max Hernandez remarks how psychoanalysis itself can be read as a post-traumatic theory in this way, the framework of the Oedipus complex having served as a placeholder for a question that, in his earlier years, Freud lacked the means to ask yet, a kind of hypothetical domestication of havoc so to speak. Thus Hernandez describes the Oedipus complex as a "normative" or "nuclear structuring trauma,"[30] a kind of provisional history making, which, when faced with the therapeutic exigencies of the war—an increase in traumatic neuroses in returning soldiers—is forced to breaking point by an excess of contradictory tasks. Wartime trauma, that is to say, in both theoretical and therapeutic contexts, is the storm that blows the house built of psychoanalytic principles apart.[31]

Hysteria, like psychoanalysis, does not so much make an environment happen (because from another viewpoint this is exactly what it does do) as get us thinking about the parts we are always unwittingly playing in making one happen at this instant. Another way to put the question of the hysterical aspect of English literary history, then, is to ask in what ways reading a realist novel, such as Barker writes, is, not only like, but also a way of participating in, the life of a nation. Alison Lee's reminder—after Wallace Stevens—that "realism has little to do with reality,"[32] recalls us to the fact that the realist novel came into being, in large part, as a performative necessity or correlative of the Enlightenment requirement that certain European regions bring themselves together in collective, yet at the same time apparently deeply idiosyncratic groupings.[33]

It is not especially original to read the period following the European Enlightenment as the elaboration of a post-traumatic symptom; after all for those not safeguarded by the enabling framework of emergent myths of nationhood the era was in many ways progenitively traumatic. But to do so could help us understand how conservatism does not only shore up fictions of the nation through their emergence in realist fiction but can also be a mode of measured exploration of their ends. What would it mean to attempt a hysterical view of English novelistic history? From a psychoanalytic, or more particularly an object relations perspective, this is also a version of the question: what does English literature, in canonical novelistic terms, use beliefs about history to do, and what might be the role therein of hysteria's peculiarly frame-breaking mode of action? What would history look like if we read the novel alongside it, not only, as we are more used to doing, in historicist terms as engaging in a generative, two-way conversation with various disruptions, surprises, and procedures there arising but in what I am tempted to call hystericist terms instead? That is, reading for the leftovers of meetings of things that could never encounter, never go into, each other (as arguably memory and history cannot and do not go). Barker's treatment of contemporary subjectivity as sibling rivalry in the context of a challenge to historical realism is, I think, an excursion into this sort of territory.

If we read Barker's pushing the form of the realist novel toward its definitional limits in *Another World* and *Border Crossing* with During's citation of de Quincey in mind, we can see a subtle critique of what is made invisible but remains powerful in received accounts of English history. I have suggested that conservatism may be its own kind of revolution, or turning around of the lost objects that propel its history, while at the same time appearing not to being do so. This could explain Alison Light's claim that conservatism "of the lower-case variety" has been "largely unaccounted for; as one of the great unexamined assumptions of British cultural life its history is all but non-existent."[34] Its history is all but nonexistent because it is constitutive; the history we think we know, made up of dates and wars and places, is fantasy or second-order history, as a family frames the unknown of sexuality. If conservatism can be a revolutionary mode of trauma management, as we have more willingly come to accept of psychoanalysis than of English history, then postrealist novels such as Barker's *Another World* and *Border Crossing* can be read as endeavors to discover how history works when its reliable revolutions no longer comfort, when our status as citizen sibling rivals threatens to flatten or annul it altogether.

In indicating commitment to the form of the realist novel, along with her enduring interest in trauma, Barker seems to be questioning the received wisdom of a severing of past from present in addressing the question of the nation's future. As Roger

Luckhurst and Peter Marks observe, it seems that we suffer nowadays not so much from the ways "capitalized and technologised accelerations of modernity . . . *abolish time*," as some have claimed, so much as the ways they "confront us with an urgent need to recognize a number of temporalities in various relations" that together swarm upon and rapidly impel forth the present.[35] In England in particular, the Thatcherite legacy of governmental nonliability and individual and fiscal self-reliance has been seen, on repeated occasions, to have produced a crisis of responsibility manifested in the ironic call for a return to family (and in a particularly bitter strain, Victorian) values. As Jacqueline Rose has argued, this may reveal the inherent poverty of conservatism's historical vision, its need to circumvent the question of being behind the times by deferring the question of its ends.[36] Still, in Barker's hands, we might ask what a sustained look at conservatism through the lens of historical trauma might offer, too.

Novels with buried crimes at their heart(h)s, these are also tales about modern English families and their relation to children's violence. What role do families, in their multifarious and changeful current forms, play with regard to the troubling phenomenon of children who break the law? To the child who kills? To what extent is the proliferation of new temporal and spatial reconfigurings of the family responsible for children's (allegedly increasing) lawlessness, and how can we tell?[37] And how should modern families care for children who, born in an age of hypermediatization, grow into adults amidst technologies that appear to offer not so much satisfaction as an ever-increasing restlessness, whose demand seems simply that there be more and more demand, offering from one point of view a kind of death not only to history but to the present? How should families, in such times, best look out for *themselves*?[38]

And this is really the heart of the matter. If hysteria is still with us—and both hysteria and psychoanalysis arise amidst the problematics of the family—then it is because for us, perhaps, sibling rivalry is the dominant mode of existence. Trauma now is in the body social rather than the nuclear family, and is just as elusive and painful and creative as it ever was. Time has compressed our lives, making the generational patterns of the nineteenth century and the 1940s, on which psychoanalytic practice was based, first for Freud and then for the various English schools, almost completely reconfigured now. One way to read contemporary trauma or post-traumatic culture is as a need to (re)find and maintain the productive meanings of ambivalence when time and space seem to change their meanings so quickly and so dramatically. Arguably, our lives in the twenty-first century are about having to make, not laterality, because we have too much of that, but *verticality*, what Lacan calls the Father's name, the embargo on original bliss that dictates the use we will make of the sufferings imposed by language.

If hysteria has gone global today, as Slavoj Zizek suggests,[39] then history and trauma will have a changed relationship. Somewhere between childhood and adulthood, we join the nation, the ranks of those who undertake to uphold the law in return for having ideally been protected by it. Yet the question of the difference between childhood and adulthood only seems to arise for real when there is danger.[40] Fear and anxiety join children and adults together, as can war and other kinds of traumatic violence, and it is often forgotten in debates over children's lawlessness the extent to which democratic privilege is, if not exactly infantilizing, then at least hystericizing, in so far as its comforts are in the realm of the impossible: each citizen's vote counts *for itself* while its power effectively resides within the greater number (which is another way to say, you cannot have your childhood and remember it properly, too).[41]

We do not know anything of our own history (or laterality), the everydayness of our lives, in other words, until we forget to frame our questions with qualifying disclaimers, as Nick comes to see through Helen's cultural constructionism and as Tom, through Danny, revisits his traumatic past. Psychoanalysis suggests that history, as the mode of action by which we ordinarily narrativize the present, can only be found in a kind of parallel present, unknowable except in moments that resist immediate analysis and register in temporally disjunctive and spatially estranging effects. Precisely because Barker is reading the English articulation of history as a symptom, something that cannot stop giving itself away through its very means of imaginative regulation or containment, *Another World* and *Border Crossing* border on what critics have not quite found the courage to call, in the work of a Booker Prize–winning author, a sort of realist failure. But the present moment, when the wishfully retrospective tone of many kinds of nationalism and the myths it tries to anxiously recover or make good are under pressure, might be a good time, in my view, to consider how a novel manages to "carry the incommensurable to extremes in the representation of human life," as Walter Benjamin characterized the impossible profession of the novelist.

"In the midst of life's fullness," Benjamin writes, "and through the representation of this fullness, the novel gives evidence of the profound perplexity of the living."[42] To give evidence of profound perplexity as Barker's latest novels, in my reading, try to do, might be to do hysterical work in a psychoanalytically curative or creative way. In Lacanian terms the cure is anything but redemptively exciting: to the contrary, it is what we are left with when the symptom, the peculiar uses to which a person, or a nation, has put the incorporable elements of its history, has stopped drawing attention to itself. Then, and only then, might one find oneself in a position to think, not only nationhood but its closeted cousin, childhood, in a way that might offer any real access to it. The dream of access to childhood being a mythic belief, one that adults (or postnationalist cultures?) use to make things happen, we might expect to find, if we read such complex, postrealist novels hysterically that the future is both nearer, less terrifying and more expandable than of literary postmodernity, as a method of anxiety management has led us to expect.

There is no time like the present for getting away on us, as Lacan might have said, for hiding the costs of its labors of forgetting, nor for seeming to be the most violent of times in history either. Psychoanalysis suggests that history, as the mode of action by which, unconsciously, we try to manage present losses, is something that is difficult to count on. There is no place like the family for making home, in retrospect, unhomely, as Barker's uncanny fictions of contemporary families show. Precisely because they are haunted by their histories, these familial fictions indicate how families and fictions are, beyond their imaginary functions—that is, what we think they're there for—also histories of the real. And it is the real of history that insists in every story as its unassimilable element, from which we will sooner or later have to learn the uses and abuses of history.

NOTES

1. Margaretta Jolly describes the resistance to categorization of Barker's work in terms of her writing, "on the one hand . . . from a strongly feminist perspective about the crushing effects of male sexual violence and the sexual division of labor." Later works, on the other hand, display a "shift to male protagonists, a favoring of the masculinized spheres of pub, battlefield, hospital or government, and a leaning towards the epic rather than domestic scale." "After Feminism: Pat Barker, Penelope Lively, and the Contemporary Novel," in *British Culture of the Postwar: An Introduction to Literature and Society, 1945–1999,* ed. Alistair Davies and Alan Sinfield, 59 (London and New York: Routledge, 2000).

2. While discussing her book *The Man Who Wasn't There* in an interview, Barker says that "I suppose everybody thinks, 'What would my life have been like if I had been born the other sex?'" Donna Perry, "Going Home Again: An Interview with Pat Barker," *Literary Review* 34, no. 2 (1991): 240. She suggests, feminism "is about the way in which gender stereotypes distort the personal development of both sexes and makes people less creative and happy than they otherwise might be" (244). To the same interviewer in 1993, she claims that "you can't deal with one gender in isolation from the other." Donna Perry, "Interview with Pat Barker," in *Backtalk: Women Writers Speak Out,* ed. Donna Perry, 51 (New Brunswick: Rutgers University Press, 1993). The point is well made by Sharon Monteith, who argues that "Barker is much more energized by the ways in which gender stereotyping may distort and repress the personal development of individuals of both sexes" than in exploring typically male or female preoccupations. "Warring Fictions: Reading Pat Barker," *Moderna Språk* 91, no. 2 (1997): 127.

3. Pat Barker, *Another World* (London: Viking, 1999); *Border Crossing,* (London: Viking, 2001). All subsequent references will be included in the text.

4. See Chris Barsanti, "*Border Crossing,*" *Book* 81 (March); Richard Eder, "Shades of Gray," *New York Times Book Review,* May 16, 2001, 1; Nan Goldberg, "Review of *Another World*" (1999) at http://www.salon.com/books/review/1999/05/17/barker; Malcolm Jones, "All Starch, No Cheese: Barker's Proper Thriller," *Newsweek,* March 5, 2001, 58. However, Sharon Monteith in her essay in this volume argues that *The Man Who Wasn't There* is an example of Barker breaking open the realist form.

5. See Sigmund Freud and Josef Breuer, *Studies on Hysteria: The Standard Edition of the Complete Psychological Works of Sigmund Freud,* vol. 2., ed. and trans. James Strachey (London: Hogarth Press, 1955); Sigmund Freud, *Introductory Lectures on Psycho-Analysis,* trans. James Strachey, ed. James Strachey and Angela Richards, *The Penguin Freud Library,* vol. 1 (Harmondsworth: Penguin, 1963). See also Max Hernandez, "Winnicott's 'Fear of Breakdown': On and Beyond Trauma," *Diacritics* 28, no. 4 (1998): 134–41.

6. Claire Pajaczkowska, "Art as a Symptom of Not Dying," *New Formations* 26 ("Psychoanalysis and Culture" issue, 1995): 82.

7. See Jacqueline Rose, *Why War? Psychoanalysis, Politics, and the Return to Melanie Klein* (Oxford and Cambridge, Mass.: Blackwell, 1993), 15–40; Steven Connor, "The War in Truth" (1997) at http://www.bbk.ac.uk/Departments/English/Staff/wartruth.htm

8. Ian McEwan, *The Child in Time* (London: Vintage, 1997)

9. Juliet Mitchell, *Mad Men and Medusas: Reclaiming Hysteria and the Effects of Sibling Relations on the Human Condition* (London: Penguin, 2000), 19.

10. Ibid.

11. Carol Watts, "Back to the Future: Revisiting Kristeva's 'Women's Time,'" in *Literature and the Contemporary: Fictions and Theories of the Present,* ed. Roger Luckhurst and Peter Marks, 157 (London: Longman, 1999).

12. See Kirby Farrell, *Post-Traumatic Culture: Injury and Interpretation in the Nineties* (Baltimore and London: Johns Hopkins University Press, 1998); Mark Seltzer, *Serial Killers: Death and Life in America's Wound Culture* (New York and London: Routledge, 1998); Eluned Summers-Bremner, "Post-Traumatic Woundings: Sexual Anxiety in Patricia Cornwell's Fiction," *New Formations* 43 (2001): 130–47; Oliver Bennett, *Cultural Pessimism: Narratives of Decline in the Postmodern World* (Edinburgh: Edinburgh University Press, 2001).

13. Serge Leclaire, following Freud ("Screen Memories," in *The Freud Reader,* ed. Peter Gay, 117–26 [London: Vintage, 1899, 1995]), points out that "the practice of analysis forces us to recognize that *all* the recollections registered in what we commonly call memory always create . . . a limit or a screen, beyond which unfolds the scene of *another memory,*" and that Freud, "from the beginning of his discovery . . . only acknowledged memory insofar as it is unconscious, denying to consciousness even the capacity of memory" "Unconscious Inscription: Another Memory," in *Psychoanalysis and Literature: A French-American Inquiry,* ed. Alan Roland, 76 (New York: Columbia University Press, 1978).

14. See Anon., "The Easy Way Out; British Fiction; Pat Barker's *Border Crossing,*" *Economist,* March 10, 2001, 7; Richard Eder, "Shades of Gray," *New York Times Book Review,* May 16, 2001, 1.

15. Jolly, "After Feminism: Pat Barker, Penelope Lively and the Contemporary Novel," 75–76.

16. Nan Goldberg, review of *Another World.*

17. For an account of realism that stresses the heterogeneity of the term's reference see Andrej Gasiorek, *Post-War British Fiction: Realism and After* (London and New York: Edward Arnold, 1995). See also Mark Greif, "Crime and Rehabilitation," *American Prospect,* April 9, 2001, 36–39, on the ghost story as family story in *Another World.*

18. Writing of the overdetermined nature of adult reconstructions of childhood, Adam Phillips notes that "one's own childhood, in which one acquired and developed a capacity for representation, can seem more like a dream than a documentary, with its odd highlights and its persistent fadings. It is as though there is childhood, but not for us; that much of our so-called childhood was the experience of our parents, of the adults, who looked after us. They, as it were, told us about it in their own way, as it was going on, but it was like a commentary on a programme we ourselves couldn't see." "Children Again," *New Formations* 42, no. 16 (Winter 2000): 16.

19. Barker has said that in *Another World* the reader is meant "to be comparing Geordie's fantastic memory, his belief in remembering the past and using the past as a guide to the present, with Gareth's total ability to reinvent the past, even down to what happened the previous day." Quoted in Alida Becker, "Old War Wounds," *New York Times Book Review,* May 16, 1999, 1.

20. Adam Phillips, "Children Again," 13–17.

21. Anon., "The Easy Way Out," 7; Malcolm Jones, "All Starch, No Cheese: Barker's Proper Thriller," 58.

22. Anon, "The Easy Way Out," 7

23. Simon During, "Literature: Nationalism's Other?" in *Nation and Narration,* ed. Homi K. Bhabha, 145 (London and New York: Routledge, 1990). See also Patrick Wright, *On Living in an Old Country: The National Past in Contemporary Britain* (London and New York: Verso, 1985).

24. See Bernhard Siegert, *Relays: Literature as an Epoch of the Postal System,* trans. Kevin Repp (Stanford: Stanford University Press, 1999).

25. Simon During, "Literature: Nationalism's Other?" 150.

26. Thomas De Quincey, *Collected Writings,* vol. 12, ed. David Masson (London: A. and C. Black, 1897). Quoted in During, "Literature: Nationalism's Other?" 150–51.

27. See Christine Clegg, Vicky Lebeau, and Paul Myerscough, "Editorial," *New Formations* 42 (Winter 2001): 5–17; Lebeau, "Another Child of Violence," ibid., 19–29.

28. Michel Foucault, *The History of Sexuality,* vol. 1. *An Introduction.* Trans. Robert Hurley (New York: Vintage Books, 1976), 109. Cited in Elisabeth Bronfen, *The Knotted Subject: Hysteria and Its Discontents* (Princeton: Princeton University Press, 1998), 119.

29. Julia Kristeva, *New Maladies of the Soul,* trans. Leon S. Roudiez (New York: Columbia University Press (1993) 1995); Hélène Cixous and Catherine Clément, *The Newly Born Woman,* trans. Betsy Wing (Minneapolis: University of Minnesota Press 1975, 1986); Jean-Pierre Klotz, "The Passionate Dimension of Transference," in Richard Feldstein et al., *Reading Seminar XI: Lacan's Four Fundamental Concepts of Psychoanalysis* (Albany: State University of New York Press, 1995), 91–97.

30. Max Hernandez, "Winnicott's 'Fear of Breakdown,'" 135.

31. Sigmund Freud, "Beyond the Pleasure Principle," *The Standard Edition of the Complete Psychological Works of Sigmund Freud,* vol. 18, ed. and trans. James Strachey (London: Hogarth Press, 1920), 1–164. See also "Freud: Frontier Concepts, Jewishness, and Interpretation," in *Trauma: Explorations in Memory,* ed. Cathy Caruth, 113–27 (Baltimore and London: Johns Hopkins University Press, 1995): Samuel Weber, "Wartime," in *Violence, Identity, and Self-Determination,* ed. Hent de Vries and Samuel Weber, 80–105 (Stanford: Stanford University Press, 1997).

32. Alison Lee, *Realism and Power: Postmodern British Fiction* (London and New York: Routledge, 1990), 5.

33. See Homi K. Bhabha, "Introduction: Narrating the Nation," and Timothy Brennan, "The National Longing for Form," in *Nation and Narration,* ed. Homi K. Bhabha, 1–6, 44–70; Benedict Anderson, *Imagined Communities: Reflections on the Origin and Spread of Nationalism* (London and New York: Verso, 1991); Jacqueline Rose, *States of Fantasy* (Oxford: Clarendon Press, 1996).

34. Alison Light, *Forever England: Femininity, Literature, and Conservatism between the Wars* (London and New York: Routledge, 1991), 14.

35. Roger Luckhurst and Peter Marks, "Hurry up Please It's Time: Literature and the Contemporary," in *Literature and the Contemporary: Fictions and Theories of the Present,* ed. Roger Luckhurst and Peter Marks, 3 (London: Longman, 1999). See also Peter Osborne, *The Politics of Time: Modernity and Avant-Garde* (London and New York: Verso, 1995); Carol Watts, "Back to the Future: Revisiting Kristeva's 'Women's Time,'" in *Literature and the Contemporary,* 156–78; Wendy Wheeler, *A New Modernity? Change in Science, Literature, and Politics* (London: Lawrence and Wishart, 1999).

36. See Jacqueline Rose, *States of Fantasy,* 56–77.

37. See Oliver Bennett, *Cultural Pessimism: Narratives of Decline in the Postmodern World,* 78–95.

38. See Michael Neve, "Nuclear Fallout: Anxiety and the Family," in *The Age of Anxiety,* ed. Sarah Dunant and Roy Porter, 107–23 (London: Virago, 1997).

39. Slavoj Zizek, *The Plague of Fantasies* (London and New York: Verso, 1997), 136.

40. See Christine Clegg, Vicky Lebeau, and Paul Myerscough, "Editorial," 5–6; Adam Phillips, "Children Again," 13–17.

41. See Ian Hacking, "Biopower and the Avalanche of Printed Numbers," *Humanities in Society* 5 (1982): 3–4. Cited in Joan Copjec, *Read My Desire: Lacan against the Historicists* (Cambridge, Mass., and London: MIT Press, 1994), 150. See also Claude Lefort, *The Political Forms of Modern Society: Bureaucracy, Democracy, Totalitarianism,* ed. John B. Thompson (Cambridge, Mass.: MIT Press, 1981, 1986); Homi K. Bhabha, "DissemiNation: Time, Narrative, and the Margins of the Modern Nation," in *Nation and Narration,* ed. Homi K. Bhabha, 291–321.

42. Walter Benjamin, "The Storyteller," in *Illuminations,* trans. Harry Zohn (London: Jonathan Cape, 1970); quoted in Homi K. Bhabha, "DissemiNation: Time, Narrative, and the Margins of the Modern Nation," 311.

Double Vision
Regenerative or Traumatized Pastoral?

> A generation that had gone to school on a horse-drawn streetcar now stood
> under the open sky in a countryside in which nothing remained unchanged but
> the clouds and, and, beneath these clouds, in a field of force of destructive tor-
> rents and explosions, was the tiny, fragile human body.
>
> Walter Benjamin, "The Storyteller"

> Strange how the savage England lingers in patches: as here, amid these
> shaggy gorse commons, and marshy, snake infested places. . . . The spirit of
> the place lingering on primeval, as when the Saxons came, so long ago.
>
> D. H. Lawrence, "England, My England"

In Pat Barker's short story "Subsidence," written and set in the summer of 2003 as American and British politicians sought to justify the (second) war on Iraq, an ordinary marriage collapses. Ruth discovers that her husband has been having an affair as the TV rolls out continual war bulletins, "filmed minute by minute yet failing to connect with reality at any point."[1] The journalists covering the conflict have the content of their reports constrained by a set protocol:

> No corpses. Apparently corpses were forbidden. Plenty of shots of journalists
> shouting gas! Gas! Gas! Fumbling to fit masks, floundering through the green sea
> of night-vision lenses. Gas! Gas!
> No gas appeared.[2]

The allusion to the First World War, and specifically to Wilfred Owen's "Dulce et Decorum Est," is as unmistakable as it is tightly bound into Barker's own *Regeneration* trilogy in which the effects of war and war neuroses are explored. Equally pointed is the age-old tension between what the war photographer on the "inside" should show to the viewers on the "outside" and what they should be protected from seeing, a tension that is central to the novel Barker published two months after "Subsidence." In *Double Vision* Barker explores some of her signature themes and tackles new and topical issues: the novel is at once a departure and a return.

In her later work—*Another World* and *Border Crossing*—marriage is an institution that has caught Barker's imagination and, tellingly, in his screenplay of *Border Crossing* Andrew Bovell focuses on this most strained of relationships, developing Tom and Lauren's marriage beyond the source novel.[3] In "Subsidence" Ruth has been decorating the new family home, slowly and methodically papering over the cracks in the ceilings that persist as a result of subsidence: the house is built on the former Durham coalfield and it "creaks and sighs" around her. Where the short story distills anxieties over loss and change in its layered images of a crumbling home life, the pace of the novel while slower evokes similar if stronger emotions. At the close of the story, Ruth has made a decision that she can no longer ignore the cracks in her marriage: "No more lies, she thought, turning away from him." The tension between the personal trauma that precipitates a new start for Ruth and the hope a new start engenders also speaks to the double structuring of *Double Vision*.[4]

Most reviewers have acknowledged the alternating perspectives of Kate and Stephen as they coincide in dealing with loss—in death and in marriage—the impact of global and local traumatic events and the slow progress toward personal recovery from such events. But they have failed to acknowledge previous "doublings" of character and of text: Liza and Stephen in *Liza's England;* Rivers and Njiru in *The Ghost Road; The Eye in the Door* with *The Strange Case of Dr. Jekyll and Mr. Hyde,* and that in the dialogic exchanges there is a telling ambivalence. Reviewing *Double Vision,* Douglas Hurd, formerly Margaret Thatcher's foreign secretary, expected a "trumpet call" to sound out "fully argued through" themes: "I was waiting for a blast of trumpet, for some conclusive link between the difficulties of describing the truth of war and the intricate fears and loves of the characters."[5] But Barker typically does not deliver easy equations and balks at the idea of writing a "novel of ideas."[6]

Very early in her work, for example, Barker drew attention to correlations between the local and the global, and between experiences traditionally gendered male or female in her application of the term "trench dialogue" to the working-class women characters in *Union Street* and *Blow Your House Down* who survive domestic violence. She equated poor women's communities in postindustrial Britain with the camaraderie of men in the trenches of the First World War in the *Regeneration* trilogy and described their powerlessness in domestic terms: "The war that had promised so much in the way of 'manly' activity had actually delivered 'feminine' passivity, and on a scale that their mothers and sisters had scarcely known."[7] In *Trauma and Recovery* Judith Lewis Herman argues that "the most common post-traumatic disorders are those not of men in war but of women in civilian life."[8] Barker does not make such a claim in feminist terminology. However, she employs the word "domesticate" three times in *Double Vision,* each time in direct relation to a traumatic event. She describes the September 2001 attack on the World Trade Center in New York as "domesticated" by TV coverage; she uses the word in counterpoint: to describe Peter's nocturnal mime of sculpting the Christ as "imitating" Kate is to "domesticate" an act Kate finds much more frightening; and, finally, with regard to the assault on Stephen's girlfriend Justine by two burglars, "domesticate" describes a natural reaction whereby fear and violence are located within a discourse that makes them manageable—and not only media-made. "To domesticate" is a verb that holds connotations of home and the familiar and in Barker's fiction the loss of safety demands a studied return to the quotidian (as in her domestication of the supernatural in *The Man Who Wasn't There*). Rural havens can be as unsafe as anywhere else but a violent event may also be an epiphany. In the case of the attack on Justine, Stephen recognizes how much this young woman means in a deeper sense than the sex that has brought them together.

In *Double Vision*, by juxtaposing the characters of Kate—a sculptor coming to terms with her husband's murder while herself recovering from a serious road accident—and Stephen—a war correspondent suffering the traumatic effects of covering conflicts in Bosnia and Afghanistan as well as from the fallout of his divorce—she tests her domestic analogy on new ground. Stephen leaves his job abroad and his base in London to regenerate personally and professionally in the rural Northeast, close to his brother. He is contracted to write a book he would have coauthored with Kate's husband Ben; the war photographer Ben Frobisher was his closest colleague and friend. In the aftermath of life-changing decisions, anxiety is Stephen's predominant feeling: "At the station he lugged his cases on to the platform and stood with them, one on either side, like inverted commas, he thought, drawing attention to the possible invalidity of the statement they enclosed. Invalid, or invalid, whichever way you cared to pronounce it, that was how he felt" (35). Stephen, like Siegfried Sassoon or Wilfred Owen, or Barker's other neurasthenic soldier characters, has been invalided out of the war zone and his homecoming is fraught with similar psychological unrest. Barker raises the martial term post-traumatic stress disorder (PTSD) by name with regard to Stephen's behavior. The term was formally recognized in 1980 and when she tackled the term in *Another World*, it was to demonstrate that the neologisms that we find to preserve for the future our definitions of human trauma may be new but the ideas that underpin them are not, as in "shell shock" or "battle fatigue."[9] Alongside the usual defining symptoms of PTSD (a delayed response to the trauma itself, nightmares, and emotional numbing), Cathy Caruth notes a further effect, "possibly also increased arousal to (and avoidance of) stimuli recalling the event."[10] The focal image of Stephen's nightmares is of a raped girl in a stairwell in Sarajevo, despite the fact that, as he consciously reminds himself, she does not constitute the most horrific image he has seen on his travels. He dreams she is in bed with him, that "when he rolled over on his stomach, trying to get away from her, he found her body underneath him, as dry and insatiable as sand" (55).

The soldier-poet of *Regeneration* has developed into the war correspondent in *Double Vision*: the lone journalist or photographer recording images and scenes that will come to epitomize the tragedy of war and the role of the media in reporting that tragedy to the outside world. The war correspondent is not new to British fiction: in 1937, for example, Evelyn Waugh's *Scoop* satirized lazy drunkards in far-off places. A newspaper editor sends a country feature writer with no previous foreign affairs experience to cover a nonexistent war in "Ishmaelia" in East Africa. Waugh is scathing: his character William Boot writes on nature for the *Daily Beast* and Ishmaelia is a cruel twist on Fleet Street's wandering outcast "witness."[11] Barker critiqued the press at its most predatory in *Border Crossing*[12] but in *Double Vision* she is gentle.

Stephen and Ben are seasoned professionals having clocked up many "tours of duty," they take risks, and there is no evidence that their ideals have been corrupted by cynicism. Ben even sustains a loving marriage while the general expectation is that the job will overwhelm domestic happiness, as in Stephen's case. In Ben, Barker represents the war photographer at the very moment that the role seems most under threat: few newspapers or magazines continue to maintain full-time photographers on the staff or to commission them to immerse themselves in a war zone for months on end to produce a photo essay. In 1990 Don McCullin, a British photojournalist whose work Barker admires, writes with lucidity of the moment that the *Sunday Times,* his employer for some eighteen years, sacked "the old war-horse" when it changed, he argues, from a newspaper to a "consumer magazine" so that "I stand around in the office, and don't know why I'm there."[13] At around the same time, new digital technology also impacted the photographer's craft and allowed for "expert" technical manipulation and enhancement of images. It is not the first time that Barker has explored an important social role on the verge of extinction in its most "authentic" form. In *Another World* her portrait of the centenarian Geordie draws attention to a vanishing generation of First World War veterans, witnesses whose testimony is fast turning to history. During the Armistice Day commemorative ceremony of 2003, for example, commentator David Dimbleby paused to ponder for a moment on how only a handful of veterans are still living nine decades after the guns fell silent. Barker's preoccupation with memory and history across the *Regeneration* trilogy and *Another World* in particular, is brought into sharp focus when allied with the ethical and aesthetic problems around representation in *Double Vision.*

While some contemporary commentators descend into nostalgic editorials declaring that war reporting can never be as good as it used to be (William Russell and Robert Fenton in the Crimean War, Matthew Brady in the American Civil War, Martha Gelhorn and Robert Capa in the Second World War, McCullin or Michael Herr and David Halberstam in Vietnam), the contemporary photojournalist is more than a synonym for a postmodern downturn in Barker's novel. While the role may be more regulated, there have always been "embedded" journalists (Richard Harding Davis and Stephen Crane in Cuba in 1898 for the Spanish-American War, the former assigned by William Randolph Hearst to act the part of the dashing correspondent), and censorship has often allowed only cursory coverage (the Falklands War as controlled by the British government). The potential for foreign correspondents being killed has increased, though, in recent years and in this sense they are literally an endangered species. Thirty journalists died in Bosnia in the early 1990s and when *Double Vision* was at press it had already been reported that five months in to the war in Iraq around twenty had been killed, a number of them by coalition forces. John Simpson of the BBC returned from Iraq on crutches. Journalist Declan Hill feels that "expectations have changed. Now we expect our cameramen to be in the first convoy into Baghdad."[14] In this sense, journalists have come to function as martyrs for the truth.

On the one hand, Owen's mantra "The Poetry is in the Pity," so maligned by W. B. Yeats, still tugs at Barker's literary imagination but, on the other, it tussles with Susan Sontag's recognition that war is "the most irresistible—and picturesque—news" and that unlike the soldier-poet, the correspondent stands outside of the fighting and watches.[15] As reporters and recorders Ben and Stephen work cooperatively in the way that Barthes describes in "The Photographic Message," Stephen's words complementing Ben's "lines, surfaces, shades." But in Barthes's analysis the traumatic photograph is a sort of negative epiphany in which the trauma is a "suspension of language, a blocking of meaning" whereby "the more direct the trauma, the more difficult is connotation."[16] Stephen is not blocked except with regard to a single image—that of the raped, murdered girl in whom sex and death meet as spectacle and Barker does not turn to Barthes (or to Umberto Eco's contention that the photograph is an argument) but to Sontag in *Regarding the Pain of Others*, listing it among the books she found thought-provoking and useful alongside McCullin's in her author's note for *Double Vision*. Sontag is Barthes's disciple and his popularizer but she can be distinguished from him in her emphasis that we feel and experience art immediately before we analyze its wider effects. Goya epitomizes this dual focus in which the emotive shock therapy is privileged over the larger conceptual field. Goya's own art was a product of personal suffering as well as a response to larger social forces; painted for himself (he expected no other observer of the "black" paintings, murals he painted straight on to the walls of his home in his old age).

Barker turns to Goya, arguably in *Los desastres de la guerra* the archetypal visual recorder of war and the effects of war in the eighteenth century and, in *Pinturas negras*, of pain and suffering in the nineteenth. Goya's art is very much of its time but Goya is often claimed as modern; Robert Hughes describes him as morally urgent, having his face "pressed to the glass of our terrible century, mouthing to make his warnings understood."[17] His most telling warning in Barker's context is rendered in the captions beneath the cumulative images of *Disasters of War*: "No se puede mirar" (One cannot look), "Yo lo vi" (I saw this) and "Esto es lo verdadero" (It is the truth). She takes these as her epigraph, a reminder that Goya was a tragic social critic as well as a court artist and creator of the Black Paintings. Barker refers to Goya self-consciously through Stephen, the "Yo" or "I" who saw the raped and murdered girl, an emotive indictment of the West's failure in Bosnia. Similarly, while writing his book on war reporting Stephen remembers Goya via another recorder of pain and suffering, Jules Naudet who turned off his camera during the aerial attacks on the World Trade Center at the moment he came across two burning bodies with the statement "No one should see this." While the analogy hits home, the topical reference to the redoubtable 9/11 is the weakest moment in the novel though it is, fortunately, also its most fleeting image. The Naudet brothers, filming a documentary about a "rookie" New York City firefighter, kept their cameras rolling on September 11, 2001, and each image that they did not censor is fixed by Jules's quiet proclamation that "There is always a witness for history . . . on that day I was chosen to be that witness."[18] Representing September 11, 2001, is fast becoming an uncomfortable vogue for writers[19]—and the power of *Double Vision* resides in the ethical quandary that Naudet's words stir up. But much more effectively, the novel is grounded in memories of Bosnia, of Milosevic's subsequent trial for war crimes and of the war in Afghanistan during which Ben dies.

Barker has begun to deploy artists and art more widely in her fiction. In *Liza's England,* she draws on Renaissance painting, in *Blow Your House Down* and *Regeneration* on church murals and stained glass windows and in *The Man Who Wasn't There* Colin is an artist-in-the-making who is visually dominant as a result of his obsession with cinema. More recently, in *Border Crossing,* Lauren is an artist who leaves a painting as her parting gift for her husband Tom. It is an abstract, almost apocalyptic study of the River Tyne:

> The sun hung over the water, a dull red without rays and without heat, as it
> might look in the last days of the planet. Beneath was an almost abstract swirl of
> greys and browns, and in the bottom right-hand corner, barely in the picture, a
> dark figure, himself, looking out over the water.[20]

Tom is the silent witness at the edge of the frame, the "tiny fragile human body" to borrow Benjamin's words from the epigraph to this essay, against which a vast landscape and the "force of destructive torrents and explosions" may be measured. The artist's composition renders the human figure in direct relation to the landscape, an idea to which this essay will return in reading *Double Vision* alongside *To the Lighthouse.* However, as Susan Sontag notes, in the photographic composition, "We want the photographer to be a spy in the house of love and death, and those being photographed to be unaware of the camera, 'off guard.'"[21] It is an expectation that Barker turns on its head more than once in *Double Vision.*

After Ben's death, Kate chooses a series of his pictures to mount as a private art exhibition for herself in which Ben is a significant living presence at the edge of the frame. Barker describes the prints through Stephen's eyes when Kate invites him to look at them. They are technically flawed and therefore all the more interesting for his study of the ways in which war is represented:

> One showed a group of boys on the border between Afghanistan and Pakistan,
> ragged, thin, peering out at the camera from behind a fence, and flashing mirrors
> into the sun to blind the photographer. A flash of light had whited out the face
> of the boy holding the glass, so in the narrow technical sense the picture was a
> failure. Further along, a man's face, distorted with anger, one hand half covering
> the lens. Another was of an execution. A man on his knees staring up at the men
> who are preparing to kill him. But Ben had included his own shadow in the shot,
> reaching out across the dusty road. The shadow say's I'm here. I'm holding a
> camera and that will determine what happens next. In the next shot the man lies
> dead in the road, and the shadow of the photographer, the shadow of a man with
> a deformed head has moved closer. (123)

The usually invisible photographer is present as endangered eyewitness and the fact of his presence with the camera changes the scene. But, Ben has also "exploded" the convention of the war photographer's stock-in-trade. His shadow at the edge of the frame is at once a signature and, for those who mourn a husband or friend, an emotional fingerprint, a trace of the artist and the man at work and in his work. The shadow is an image that gains imaginative force with each mention in the novel.

The final photograph of those Kate has chosen is unusual for its lack of a human subject. It is a tableau of rotting Soviet tanks left behind after the invasion of Afghanistan: the detritus of war. It is also, Stephen is painfully aware, the last shot Ben took before being shot and killed; it records the moment before Stephen comes upon the body of his friend in a bomb crater on a quiet road. Barker defers the scene of Ben's death until almost the end of the novel, as she defers representing scenes of actual war until the final novel in the *Regeneration* trilogy. In death Ben looks steadfastly at the sun, "his open eyes stare[d] into the white sun without wincing" (305). He is held in a war-traumatized landscape in which his artist's eye has discovered an ugly beauty. Stephen is initially surprised at why Ben should have scrambled down into the bomb crater—they have passed along this deserted road many times before —but then he realizes that "he hadn't spotted what Ben saw. From the bottom of the crater they [the tanks] looked like a wave breaking. A sun so white it might have been the moon hung in the sky behind them. All the time he was talking to Ben, saying, 'You fucking idiot. You stupid, fucking fool. Your life—*for that*?'" (305). When they work together as on the day they discover the dead raped girl in Sarajevo, they follow each other so closely that one shadows the other, or they almost fuse into one body: "Their joined shadow on the snow.... They stayed still for five minutes, their breathing becoming gradually less painful, their eyeballs less congested, fingertips no longer shaken by the beating of their hearts" (54–55). Without Stephen shadowing him, Ben dies alone and Stephen is unable to cry for the part of himself that is lost.

Tension between the importance of presenting atrocities and protecting victims, of looking closely or turning away, and returning to look again, is epitomized in the problem of Ben's composition of the picture of the raped girl in the stairwell. When Ben and Stephen first come across her corpse in a bombed-out building, her skirt is bunched up around her waist, "her splayed thighs enclosing a blackness of blood and pain" (52). Stephen's immediate reaction is to cover her up in order to "protect" her but when Ben returns to photograph her, he returns the dead girl to her original state of disarray to reveal the misogyny at the heart of the crime. In so doing, he makes an explicitly ethical statement that responds to Stephen's guilt: "She was waiting for him, that's the way it felt. She had something to say to him, but he's never managed to listen, or not in the right way" (55). Ben bears witness to the horror where Stephen's impulse is to cover up the evidence of a hate crime. Barker complicates the scene even further by throwing into doubt whether what has been committed is a war crime or a civil crime ("Increasingly war and crime shade into each other," 53) and whether the victim should be viewed in the same way in each case. In this she recalls Goya, whose graphic images of the Spanish war against Napoleon include a soldier about to commit rape. The implication is that Stephen feels the girl is not the war correspondent's subject; that Ben clearly thinks she is an important subject for a photograph is underlined by the risk he takes in returning to the scene of the crime alone. For Avishai Margalit, "witness-risk" is a form of "victim-risk": "The moral witness should himself be at personal risk, whether he is a sufferer or just an observer of the suffering that comes from evil-doing. An utterly sheltered witness is no moral witness."[22] Rape is, of course, a war crime when situated within the larger context of civil war and Ben's testimony to the fact reinforces his symbolic presence at the center of a novel exploring trauma and recovery.

In the *Regeneration* trilogy it is a crucial element of the "cure" that Rivers administers that soldiers succeed in locating their trauma within a wider perspective on suffering: to make it describable. Burns, perhaps the most distressed of Rivers's patients, having been forced to imbibe the innards of a horrifically blown corpse, finally begins to apprehend his previously indescribable torment through the asphyxiation of Christ and the idea that death by suffocation had first to be imagined as suitably horrific torture. In *Liza's England* Frank finds solace in Piero della Francesca's *Resurrezione* which epitomizes his tortured memory of the First World War. Kate's monumental Christ looms over *Double Vision*. Like the resurrection, it is a canonical image of Judeo-Christian martyrdom but the norm is changed. The Christ is never described in detail but demands attention even in a culture of spectacle because he disturbs and fascinates. These two facets underpin the images Barker creates. In *Border Crossing* Tom Seymour is drawn into a crowd watching a street act in which a young boy performs a Houdini-like escape from a sack in which a large tattooed man has tied him. He is at once fascinated and profoundly disturbed by the performance. The spectacle of war also involves a seduction and fascination, as Barker explored in earlier fiction and the tortured or endangered body can function similarly.[23] Throughout the first half of *Double Vision*, Kate drags her broken body through physiotherapy, regenerative exercises that painfully restore her body to its previous elasticity. Again, this recalls Goya. Robert Hughes believes Goya was "one of the few great describers of physical pain, outrage, insult to the body," a statement that derives in part from Hughes's own near-fatal car crash in 1999 in the aftermath of which he dreamed of Goya.[24] However, Barker also includes the burning carcasses of animals sacrificed to foot-and-mouth; Kate's loss of her husband Ben is described as an amputation; and Justine describes Peter finishing their relationship as "he cut my head off" (168). The body and images of its death and desperation proliferate in this quiet country village on the edge of rolling moors. The Green Man, traditionally a signifier of renewal in English mythology, is shown to be a spurious symbol, for example. Barker reminds the reader that gargoyles of green men found in churches like the one where Alec is vicar, are choking on leaves. Such images are more reminiscent of soldiers choking to death with gas-filled lungs in Owen's "Dulce et Decorum Est" than of spring and rebirth.

Double Vision is not set in a war zone but takes place in a traumatized English landscape, the rural Northeast recovering from the effects of the foot-and-mouth crisis that decimated the area in 2001. Two years later climbing a hill near his sixteenth-century cottage, Stephen is shocked to see scorched earth so close to the pastoral scene in which he is beginning to find peace. The reader may be surprised and prickled by the rural retreat that is the setting of *Double Vision* since this is Barker's first foray into village life and its sedimented history: Kate's house is five hundred years old and the "dragon's teeth" on the beach further north are tank traps, a holdover from the Second World War. Barker shows that seismic shifts are taking place in ways that may not be immediately apparent beyond the symbolic—Kate's house may be ancient but the roots of her life's foundations have been rocked by her husband's violent death in war. Barker's characters seek an emotional foothold in a wounded landscape as she explores what is repressed in the social.

Barker has a long tradition of demythologizing: she undercuts the myth of an English working-class continuity in *Union Street* and *Liza's England* and gives the lie to the vernacular of stoic silence that has surrounded working-class women; she disrupts easy ideas of patriotism and heroism in war and, as Ron Paul's essay in this collection shows, reverses the messages of classical war novels in the *Regeneration* trilogy. The village has been the most heavily mythologized symbol of traditional English culture and Barker explores a traditional community in which membership has become discrepant. She imagines her most atomized characters in the closest and most insular community she has so far created. In *Union Street* characters may appear hermetically sealed in separate stories and in Craiglockhart they suffer in separate rooms along a dark corridor, yet stories overlap and characters often share aspirations as readily as they reinforce each other's nightmares. In *Double Vision*, people live in each others' houses: Alec has had Peter Wingrave stay at the vicarage and now he is courting Angela she stays regularly; Justine stays overnight with Stephen and both Stephen and Justine live in Robert and Beth's house when they go away on holiday, Stephen renting their garden cottage the rest of the time. Kate allows both Peter Wingrave who works for her and Stephen keys to the outbuildings on her property. Yet, despite the apparent closeness of the rural community, much is left uncommunicated.

The historical—or traditional—is waning as the place turns into a commuter village populated by "weekenders" who attend church "as if . . . God was thrown in as a job lot with Labradors and waxed jackets" (27). It has, of course, been waning for a very long time. Philip Larkin's poem "Going, Going" bemoaning the loss of English meadows and lanes in favor of new roads was itself commissioned by the Department of the Environment in 1972 and influenced by John Betjeman. The village as the focus for a critique of consumerism is hardly new: John Lucas dates it back to the 1680s and most particularly the Glorious Revolution of 1689, and we find another key critique in Oliver Goldsmith's *Deserted Village* of 1770.[25] In *Double Vision*, Barker unsettles the binary of city and country in which life amidst the "green-wellied Christians" is comfortably contrasted with urban centers where city kids are "off their heads on crack" (27). There is little that is safe here and the image of rural England as "the moral heartland," commented on obliquely in *Border Crossing*, receives detailed exploration. The village is a place in which cruel and random violence can strike. The burglars' attack on Justine takes place on a beautiful daffodil-filled, sunny day, and Wordsworthian regenerative images of spring are blasted open with the first blow to her head and reintroduced when Stephen visits her with simple daffodils. Peter Wingrave, on the other hand, leaves her red roses with wire wrapped around the stems and buds to pin the petals closed; Justine had been "rejoicing in the unsubtlety" of the daffodils in the moments before she suffered the attack and she is disturbed by the imprisoned beauty of the rose, that most "English" of flowers. Barker maintains a precarious balance between the sensuality inherent in the pastoral and its dissolution.

If in Paul Fussell's view, war is the "ultimate anti-pastoral" it is perhaps not surprising that the most antipastoral image is of the soldier from the wars returning.[26] It is an image Barker has twisted and turned in *Another World* in her gentle critique of historian Helen's refusal to disturb her initial hypothesis for the book she is writing, titled *Soldier, from the Wars Returning*. When a primary source, First World War veteran Geordie Lucas, suggests that his memories of war are too raw to be contained within the paradigms she seeks to inscribe ("late twentieth-century preoccupations. Gender. Definitions of masculinity. Homoeroticism"),[27] she refuses to unsettle the smooth lines of her thesis to accommodate him. In *Double Vision* the returning soldier is presented as a cultural discontinuity: "It's part of English mythology, that image of the soldier returning, but it depends for its power on the existence of an unchanging countryside. Perhaps it had never been true, had only ever been a sentimental urban fantasy, or perhaps something deeper—some memory of the great forest. Sherwood. Arden. Certainly Stephen had returned to find a countryside in crisis" (201). As Barker fuses Stephen with the returning soldier, she acknowledges the pull of such myths. Stephen has hung up his flak jacket and left London in search of a new start in a new year but his rural retreat is itself barely natural: the forest is cultivated and what is most noticeable as he drives toward the cottage in which he will live, is not "Nature" but roadkill, or "carnage" as his brother Robert refers to the "crushed bundles of flesh and fur" (39). The first thing his young nephew informs him is that he has found a dead badger and he hopes his surgeon father will cut its head off in order for him to look at "the secret structure underneath":

> "Can you cut his head off, Dad?"
>
> "I don't think so. It's not that easy, cutting off heads. The neck ligaments are very strong."
>
> A machete would do it easily enough, Stephen thought, blinking the images away. Suddenly he wanted to be indoors, somewhere safe, away from the memories of long grass and skulls you trip over in the dark. (41)

Again, Stephen's experience is made to recall Wilfred Owen's in *Regeneration*, a novel in which skulls seem to multiply like mushrooms and images of Golgotha proliferate: "Armageddon, Golgotha, there were no words, a place of desolation so complete no imagination could have invented it."[28]

Stephen has sought out what he feels sure will be a quiet place but to retreat geographically is, it becomes clear, a poor substitute for addressing the psychological turmoil that colors Stephen's day-to-day life. In the remote cottage, far from anything except his brother's smallholding, he dismisses the possibility of writing at a desk by the window: "Flying glass. He'd always felt bizarrely safe in the Holiday Inn in Sarajevo because the glass in the windows was long gone" (48). In case the reader assumes a correlation between safety and the countryside, Barker shows that Nature is just as unpredictably dangerous: tree branches thrust through the windscreen of Kate's car in the crash and seem to claw at her face; Alec fears that similar branches will encroach on him through the vicarage windows (229). The land itself is traumatized, fields are violently cut open to become funeral pyres for dead animals giving off acrid black smoke. While the landscape has symbolic weight, the mental geography that overlays the rural descriptions seems to contradict the pastoral. This was true of the trilogy as when Billy Prior dismisses the English pastoral as a middle-class fantasy and when Burns walks out of Craiglockhart hospital into the countryside and comes upon a tree laden with dead animals. He lays the corpses on the ground ("Now they could dissolve into the earth as they were meant to do") and lays with them, naked to feel closer to the forest dead. The scene is given mythic proportions as he recalls it: "A shaft of sunlight filtered through leaves, found one of the magpies, and its feathers shone sapphire, emerald, amethyst. . . . He could stay here forever."[29] The primeval scene could be described as Lawrentian and it has been argued that Barker reorients Lawrence and facets of a masculine British literary tradition in fictions that are earthy and sexually explicit.[30] As Barker has herself pointed out, to assume shared subject matter between Northern working-class writers almost a century apart is to acknowledge that certain working-class scenes may be archetypal rather than the imaginative property of one writer. Following Robert Pogue Harrison, for example, Jonathan Bate points out the historically overarching metaphor that is the pastoral: "In the beginning man's shadow was the forest." For Harrison it is a "sylvan fringe of darkness" that defines the limits of cities and institutions "but also the extravagance of the imagination."[31] Barker compares dark natural places with the dark places in the psyche, as Lawrence criticized psychoanalysis for its failure to account for the dark places in the individual and the social. But in this she may be as usefully compared to Virginia Woolf as Lawrence for the psychological depth each writer achieves.[32]

Woolf's *Three Guineas* would have been an obvious text for Barker to return to as intertext in *Double Vision*. In fact, Sontag begins her discussion of images of war atrocities in *Regarding the Pain of Others* by recalling Woolf's antiwar polemic. But, it is more elucidating to read *Double Vision* alongside a novel in which the central images are also of marriage and family but in which the characters remain atomized and traumatized by death, a novel that is influenced by a painter and her painting (Woolf's sister Vanessa Bell's impressionism). Virginia Woolf's *To the Lighthouse* is a novel riven in two by war and loss. Barker has alluded to Woolf previously—Septimus Smith in *Mrs. Dalloway* was an early literary incarnation of Sassoon and in *Liza's England* Frank, like Smith, hallucinates that he is stepping on the faces of his dead comrades as he walks the streets after the war. In *Double Vision*, the intertextuality serves to strengthen Barker's artistic vision (Woolf's novel closes with Lily Briscoe "laying down her brush in extreme fatigue, I have had my vision")[33], and to underline the insatiability of neurosis through the intervention of Peter Wingrave in search of another host in Kate. A reading of chapter 27 reveals Barker's double structuring at its most symbolic and allusive. While it does not form the novel's conclusion—the final chapter serving as an epilogue that returns the novel to its pastoral theme with the lovers walking on the sand—Kate's "vision" of Christ is completed as Stephen and

Justine cross to an island off the Northeast coast. In this *Double Vision* comes as close to a resolution as Barker will allow. Lily Briscoe completes her painting once the First World War is over; Kate Frobisher her sculpture in the aftermath of the war in Bosnia and in the wake of Ben's death in Afghanistan. Crossing the water and reaching the shore is a metaphor for hope in both novels and in each Lily and Kate act as mediums, curiously divided between the prospect of completing an artistic project and their focus on a journey being undertaken by their emotional alter egos.

In *To the Lighthouse,* the trip has been mooted for some time and finally Mr. Ramsay, Cam and James set out as Lily paints at the edge of the lawn looking out to sea. Her thoughts linger on the war dead and mourn Mrs. Ramsay as she strains to envisage the boat reaching the lighthouse across the bay until "'He has landed,' she said aloud. 'It is finished.' . . . There it was her picture."[34] In *Double Vision* Stephen and Justine set out for the Farne Islands the day following the violent attack to help Justine convalesce and to gain some perspective on the event. The night before in a tranquilizer-induced sleep, Justine dreams of being unable to make such a journey: she is walking on the thin ice of a frozen lake, a long way from the safety of land; the weather is nefarious—the wind slashes her face and the dark frightens her—and in panic, unable to find her way to the shore, she wakes (266–67). As they set off for the north coast, Stephen and Justine retrace a journey that Ben and Kate used to make regularly at the same time of year, as if they are a living proxy for the couple. Throughout this chapter, like Woolf, Barker slips in and out of the conscious thoughts of each character, so that they are maintained in parenthetical relationship. There is a fragility and vulnerability at the heart of the scene that derives from the aftershock of assault, from Justine's dream, and the thick white mist that closes in as they drive. Stephen is navigating through a "dense damp whiteness"—"blankness" and "white-outs," much like Justine's dreamscape—that temporarily clears to reveal the border country of Ben's photographs. Seeing the landscape for the first time, Stephen suddenly understands its meaning for his friend, "a place where every blade of grass had been fought over, time and time again, for centuries and now the shouts and cries, the clash of swords on shields had faded into silence, leaving only sunlight heaving on acres of grass, and a curlew crying" (282). More than any other scene in *Double Vision,* this empties the pastoral of green and pleasant connotations: death and desolation, vulnerability and despair form part of Barker's traumatized pastoral. Don McCullin's collection of photographs of England titled *Homecoming* is perhaps the closest analogy to Barker's rendition of Ben's aesthetics. Recalling the two years in which he traveled around England, photographing poverty, urban decay, and the "desolate beauty" of some Northern cities, he confides, "I was still seeing the dead bodies I had crawled past and touched in other people's countries. Burning stubble at evening time in English fields reminded me of scorched-earth strategies, and that is how they came out in my photographs. Mallards rising in the mist from marshes looked like formations of B-52 bombers."[35]

As the land accrues meaning for Stephen, who has shared Ben's traumatic experiences, he reaches for Justine's hand because violence is the catalyst for the change in their lives also. As Kate enters her studio for the final creative burst that will render her sculpture finished, she pauses to glance at the misty hills and hopes that the weather clears for Stephen and Justine's "crossing": "So many times she and Ben had set out to go to the Farnes and nearly always at this time of year. Her heart felt full. A distinct, entirely physical sensation. Possess, as I possessed a season, like countries I resign" (284). In recalling A. E. Housman's line from "Last Poems," Kate recaptures his lyric to a lost pastoral ("For nature, heartless, witless nature / Will neither care nor know / What stranger's feet may find the meadow / And trespass there and go") in the very moment she creates a bridge between her own experience and theirs. "Setting out" for the Farnes is not the same as reaching the islands, and one is reminded in the phrasing of how James Ramsay's pleas to go to the lighthouse are dependent on the weather (The novel opens with "Yes, of course, if it's fine tomorrow") as well as the agreement of his parents. When Stephen and Justine arrive at the point of the crossing, the land is veiled in mist, so that the boat, like the car, "had become its own world." Kate seems to acknowledge as Lily Briscoe does that "so much depends . . . upon distance: whether people are near us or far from us . . . coming back from a journey, or after an illness, before habits had spun themselves across the surface, one felt that same unreality, which was so startling; felt something emerge. Life was most vivid then."[36]

As Kate pauses in her work, Peter Wingrave intrudes on a purely pastoral moment, just as the burglars shattered Justine's rejoicing in the coming of spring. Kate is momentarily entranced by a moorhen and her chicks "and thought of nothing, only the pleasure of seeing them" (289). Peter's appearance at her side is unlike the presence of miserable Mr. Carmichael who appears as Lily finishes her painting in *To the Lighthouse*; he is instead reminiscent of the "shadow of monstrosities" cast across *Another World* and *Border Crossing* that continues to adumbrate Barker's vision and underpins her excavation of popular psychiatry. Peter's opening remark is telling, "I was just passing" (289). He is the consummate "passer" and yet he remains a traumatizing presence for many of the characters. At the end of *Border Crossing* psychiatrist Tom Seymour stares after Peter as he was then in his incarnation as a student and Tom's senses are assaulted by a smell of lilacs. Monteith has argued that the scene purposefully recalls T. S. Eliot's classic opening image to *The Waste Land* where in the spring lilacs emerge, "breeding . . . out of the dead land, mixing memory and desire," portending an anti-pastoral unease in which images of regeneration ("Dull roots with spring rain") are overwhelmed with ambivalence.[37] It is that unease that finds its apogee in *Double Vision*. But, Peter is rebuffed; Kate disallows him any entry into her personal life by disdaining to ask about his. She acknowledges his contribution to her sculpture of Christ—he made the armature after all—but the vision is hers, she assures herself.

Turning away from Peter, Kate turns back to her sculpture which is at once a concluding triumph and a self-actualization: evidence of her own regeneration. Kate stands back to survey her work because, like Lily Briscoe, she knows instinctively that when she has "finished" she will have created a fresh perspective on a traditional

subject, a nonrepresentational piece of art: "The secret was to put the critical intelligence to sleep, peel off the hard outer rind and work from the core" (288). Barker
does not describe the sculpture in detail but the reader is aware that this Christ could
not be further from the "gooey" pictures of Christ that the prisoners paint in Peter
Wingrave's short story (161). It is closer to the indeterminate image "enclosed in a
double helix of barbed wire" (161) that exudes the horror of torture as well as beati-
fication. The nonrepresentational allows for a plethora of perspectives, not just the
artist's own. In *To the Lighthouse,* Mrs. Ramsay describes herself as a "wedge-shaped
core of darkness" just as the painter Lily Briscoe predicates her vision of her subject
as a dark wedge, "a triangular purple shape."[38] Mrs. Ramsey is a shadow that remains
over the text after her character's death and in a novel filled with shadows the most
shadowy presence is Peter Wingrave, the shadow of Danny Miller / Ian Wilkinson—
the character who has crossed over from *Border Crossing* into *Double Vision* and
whom Barker has tellingly described as "a dark patch in an overall picture."[39]

By the close of the novel, key characters have gained distance and perspective on
themselves and on the events that have shaken them. Finally, it is not redemption or
regeneration but self-preservation and adaptation that count in *Double Vision.* Kate
adapts to life without Ben. At the same time she preserves herself against Peter
Wingrave's incursion into her life, if not into her art. Stephen discovers sexual regeneration: "He noticed every woman he passed. The sensation was almost painful, like
blood flowing back into a numbed limb" (141), and his relationship with Justine
revives his interest in life following Ben's death. When deliverance comes, in Barker's
work it is often through passionate sex and Barker agrees that it is "the real redemptive force" in her writing and wonders whether in many ways it remains taboo, "not
the mechanics of sex but the emotions it gives rise to."[40] Such difficult feelings are
captured in Kate's Christ—a symbol *and* a man—and in Peter Wingrave's grotesque
short stories. While the representations are differently skewed toward timeless
trauma or regeneration in the present, they share a conflict of opposites: the refusal
to split off good from evil—as in the doubling of Dr. Jekyll and Mr. Hyde—creation
from destruction, life from death, or self from other. Kate's Christ survives the contradictory images heaped upon it and, Barker hopes, it is "a rougher, harsher Christ
than she sets out to create since through Peter she has taken something into the
Christ that she may not have intended."[41] Peter makes the armature and mixes the
plaster and the Christ incorporates his residual memories of killing Lizzie Parkes in
Border Crossing: "Betrayal, torture. Murder" (292). Kate naturally correlates his words
with the betrayal and murder of Christ, unwittingly combining the "sacred" with the
"profane." It becomes clear that Peter's search for a new host is also the urge to con-
fess to his crime that Kate—purposely or otherwise—deflects; he may be present in
the artistic "mix" but he is only the source of one of a melée of feelings Kate has
mined in the Christ. Barker also imbues the sculpture with Kate's own profound
sense of loss following Ben's murder.

If the authority of the moral witness comes from, among other things, provoking
an immediate response through their ability to "describe *this,*" as Margalit attests,[42] in

chapter 27 of *Double Vision* Barker shifts that authority from the war correspondent to the artist, Kate. She is a resilient artist struggling against pain and in her sculpture she conveys a visceral response, not only to murder but to resurrection and regeneration through her own trauma. The sculpture is cathartic. She and Stephen have ridden out their survivors' guilt as they integrate pain and regret with hope and desire, an idea that Lawrence captures in "The Novel and Feelings":

> Unless we proceed to connect ourselves up with our primeval sources, we shall degenerate. And degenerating we shall break up into a strange orgy of feelings. They will be decomposition feelings like the colours of autumn. And they will precede whole storms of death like leaves in the wind.[43]

Lawrence was writing during the First World War and he differentiates between emotions that can be named and contained and the "chaos of feelings" that retains something of the soldier-poet's ability to witness hope in the misery of war. As Kate looks at Goya's picture of the seven prisoners in the Bowes Museum she feels simultaneously the depths of despair and joy in his creation. The dialectic is carried over in the war photographer's facility for standing both inside and outside a moment to extrapolate meaning from it, an aesthetic awareness that both Kate and Stephen admire in Ben.

A deepening perspective on the closeness of hope and despair in self-actualization is what the reader takes away from this novel; Stephen and Kate both choose Goya over therapy. She needs to feel Ben's loss as an injury, an amputation with its connotations of a war wound and of traumatic separation, just as when hospitalized with a head wound in *Regeneration* Sassoon feels "amputated" from his men at the front. Stephen acknowledges that he may be suffering from PTSD but resists the "talking cure," opting instead for what Barker herself has called "a sort of secular or aesthetic equivalent for healing" inspired by Goya's representation of the carnage of war and the painter's successful management of his own deafness.[44] In returning to Goya, Barker asks by extension whether getting close to traumatic images or events—the raped girl in the stairwell, Ben's corpse, the crime Peter committed in childhood, or the Christ—equates with gaining any moral proximity. In the description of Stephen attending Milosevic's trial, Barker makes clear that the thinnest barrier of glass distorts his vision of the man and his crimes. The images of Milosevic generated on the TV screens in The Hague seem more real to Stephen than the man sitting across from him in the courtroom; and clambering down in to the bomb crater where Ben's body lies, Stephen thinks he is still alive simply because there is no visual evidence of the bullet having penetrated. Both Stephen and Kate are inspired by Goya's "steady and compassionate eye" and his sloughing off of despair (153), recognizing that "It's not true that images lose their power with repetition, or not automatically true anyway" (155). When she turns to Nature, Barker engages with a constant feature of the pastoral in its traditional mode: it contains within it contradictions that are presented allegorically rather than mythically. Appearance (the pastoral as regenerative) and reality (the pastoral as traumatized) are neither mutually exclusive nor simply the result of a heartless, savage nature, but infused with human tragedy.

NOTES

1. Pat Barker, "Subsidence," *Guardian Review*, July 19, 2003, 26–27.

2. Ibid., 26.

3. Andrew Bovell, *Border Crossing* (2003), an unpublished manuscript in Barker's possession. Read and referenced with permission from the author.

4. Barker, "Subsidence," 27. Barker, *Double Vision* (London: Viking, 2003). All subsequent references will be included in the text.

5. Douglas Hurd, "Sunset over Tanks," *Financial Times*, August 30, 2003, 32.

6. See Sharon Monteith, "Pat Barker," in Sharon Monteith, Jenny Newman, and Pat Wheeler, *Contemporary British and Irish Fiction: An Introduction through Interview* (London: Arnold, 2004), 31–32.

7. Pat Barker, *Regeneration* (London: Viking, 1991), 107–8.

8. Judith Lewis Herman, *Trauma and Recovery* (New York: Basic Books, 1992), 28.

9. See Monteith, *Pat Barker*, 81–85.

10. Cathy Caruth, *Trauma: Explorations in Memory* (Baltimore: Johns Hopkins University Press, 1995), 4.

11. Other fictions that take foreign correspondents as characters include Graham Greene's *The Quiet American* with the cynical Thomas Fowler. Since Barker published *Double Vision*, there has been a spate of British fictions in which they feature: Mark Lee's *The Canal House* (2003), Alan Cowell's *A Walking Guide: A Novel* (2003) and Maggie Helwig's *Between Mountains* (2004).

12. Tom Seymour is interviewed about children who commit murder and afterwards the journalist continues to chat to him informally but "looking down into her open bag, Tom saw the red light on her tape recorder still lit." Pat Barker, *Border Crossing* (London: Viking, 2001), 188. In this novel the press is a mob of baying hounds hunting down Danny Miller: "A storm of blue flashes. Blurred hands, clicks, whirs, questions, voices calling his name, this way, that way, an outdoor microphone like a dead animal hanging over his head" (200).

13. Don McCullin, *Unreasonable Behaviour: An Autobiography* (London: Vintage, 1990), 270.

14. See "War Correspondents Seek Answers to Mounting Toll," *Age*, August 25, 2003. See also recent autobiographies by foreign correspondents, Kate Adie, *The Kindness of Strangers* (London: Headline, 2002), and John Simpson, *Strange Places, Questionable People* (London: Pan, 1999).

15. W. B. Yeats dismissed soldier-poets by omitting them from *The Oxford Book of Modern Verse* (1936) because in his view "passive suffering is not a theme for poetry." Yeats's "Introduction" reprinted in *Modern Poetry: Essays in Criticism*, ed. J. Hollander, 83–104 (Oxford: Oxford University Press, 1969); Susan Sontag, *Regarding the Pain of Others* (New York: Farrar, Straus and Giroux, 2003), 43.

16. Roland Barthes, *Image, Music, Text*, trans. Stephen Heath (London: Fontana, 1977), 16, 30–31.

17. Robert Hughes, "A Despairing Assault on Terminal Evil," *Time*, January 30, 1989, 70.

18. *9/11*, directed by Jules and Gedeon Naudet and James Hanlon (Goldfish Pictures, 2001).

19. Since September 11, 2001, various writers approached the topic but wary of reception in the United States. Many of those that have been published are crime novels (by Sara Paretsky, Michael Connelly, Jim Fusilli, and Lawrence Block). See Elsbeth Lindner, "Avoiding the

Disaster," *Evening Standard,* September 1, 2003, A35. Janette Turner Hospital's *Due Preparations for the Plague* (2003) was revised after the attack in order to close with it. More recently S. J. Rozan's *Absent Friends* (2004) covers similar ground.

20. Barker, *Border Crossing,* 167.

21. Sontag, *Regarding the Pain of Others,* 50.

22. Avishai Margalit, *The Ethics of Memory* (Cambridge, Mass.: Harvard University Press, 2002), 150.

23. For a wider discussion and exemplification through photographs, see, for example, Chris Hedges, *War is a Force that Gives Us Meaning* (New York: Anchor, 2003); Philip Knightley and Sir John Keegan, *The Eye of War: Words and Photographs from the Front Line* (London: Weidenfeld Nicolson, 2003).

24. Robert Hughes, *Goya* (London: The Harvill Press, 2003), 8–10. Barker's novel was published in August 2003 and Robert Hughes's *Goya* later the same year.

25. John Lucas, *England and Englishness: Ideas of Nationhood in English Poetry, 1688–1900* (London: Hogarth Press, 1990). See also Dennis Brown, "The Last of England," in *John Betjeman* (Plymouth: Northcote House, 1999), 36–50.

26. Paul Fussell, *The Great War and Modern Memory* (Oxford: Oxford University Press, 1975), 231.

27. Pat Barker, *Another World* (London: Viking, 1998), 83.

28. Barker, *Regeneration,* 44.

29. Ibid., 38–40.

30. See, for example, Michael Ross, "Acts of Revision: Lawrence as Intertext in the Novels of Pat Barker," *D. H. Lawrence Review* 26, nos. 1–3 (1995): 51–63. Ross provides a close reading of particular moments in *Sons and Lovers* and *The Rainbow* comparatively with scenes in *Union Street* and *Liza's England.*

31. Jonathan Bate, *The Song of the Earth* (London: Picador, 2000), 88.

32. Monteith, *Pat Barker,* 57–58.

33. Virginia Woolf, *To the Lighthouse* (London: Granada, 1977), 192.

34. Ibid., 191.

35. McCullin, *Unreasonable Behaviour,* 224–25.

36. Woolf, *To the Lighthouse,* 177.

37. Monteith, *Pat Barker,* 105.

38. Woolf, *To the Lighthouse,* 60.

39. Monteith, "Pat Barker," 30.

40. Authors' interview with Pat Barker, August 2003.

41. Ibid.

42. Margalit, *The Ethics of Memory,* 168.

43. D. H. Lawrence, "The Novel and Feelings" (1914), in *Study of Thomas Hardy and Other Essays* (London: Grafton, 1986), 175–76

44. Monteith, "Pat Barker," 23.

Contributors

ANN ARDIS is professor of English and associate dean for arts and humanities in the College of Arts and Science at the University of Delaware. She is the author of *Modernism and Cultural Conflict, 1880–1922* (Cambridge: Cambridge University Press, 2002) and *New Women, New Novels: Feminism and Early Modernism* (New Brunswick: Rutgers University Press, 1990) and co-editor (with Leslie W. Lewis) of *Women's Experience of Modernity, 1875–1945* (Baltimore: Johns Hopkins University Press, 2002) and (with Bonnie Kime Scott) of *Virginia Woolf Turning the Centuries: The Proceedings of the Ninth Annual Virginia Woolf Conference* (New York: Pace University Press, 2000).

CARINA BARTLEET read biological sciences at Oxford before going on to study for a doctorate in drama, on the intertextual dimension of Sarah Daniels's plays, at the University of Exeter. She has been a lecturer in drama at the University of Glamorgan and, currently, teaches at the University of Reading.

ANITA BIRESSI is senior lecturer in cultural and media studies at Roehampton University of Surrey. She researches discourses of law and order and crime in the media and is the author of *Crime, Fear, and the Law in True Crime Stories* (New York: Palgrave, 2001).

JOHN BRANNIGAN is college lecturer in English at University College Dublin. His publications are *Orwell to the Present: Literature in England, 1945–2000* (London: Palgrave, 2003), *Brendan Behan: Cultural Nationalism and the Revisionist Writer* (Dublin: Four Courts Press, 2002), and *Literature, Culture, and Society in Postwar England, 1945–1965* (Lewiston, N.Y.: Edwin Mellen, 2002). He is currently at work on a book on Pat Barker.

SARAH BROPHY is assistant professor in the English department at McMaster University in Canada. She works on contemporary autobiography and memoir, representations of health and illness, cultural studies, and gender theory. Her book *Witnessing AIDS: Writing, Testimony, and the Work of Mourning* is forthcoming.

DENNIS BROWN is the author of numerous articles, and his books include *The Modernist Self in Twentieth-Century English Literature: A Study of Self-Fragmentation* (London: Macmillan, 1989), *Intertextual Dynamics within the Literary Group: Joyce,*

Lewis, Pound, and Eliot (London: Macmillan, 1990), *The Poetry of Postmodernity* (London: Macmillan, 1994) and *John Betjeman* (Plymouth: Northcote House, 1999). He is Emeritus Professor of Modern Literature at the University of Hertfordshire.

SARAH DANIELS is an award-winning playwright who also writes for television and radio. Her plays have premiered at the Royal Court Theatre, London, the Royal National Theatre London, The Crucible Theatre in Sheffield, the Manchester Royal Exchange, and The Albany Theatre, London and have gone on to have subsequent productions around the world. Her play *Masterpieces* was named as one of the best plays of the twentieth century by the Royal National Theatre.

MARGARETTA JOLLY is a lecturer in the School of English, University of Exeter. She is the editor of *The Encyclopaedia of Life Writing* (London: Fitzroy Dearborn, 2001) and *Dear Laughing Motorbyke: Letters from Women Welders of the Second World War* (London: Scarlet Press, 1997). She is currently writing a book on letter writing in the second wave women's movement.

SHARON MONTEITH is reader in American Studies at the University of Nottingham. She writes on American and British fiction and film. She is the author of *Advancing Sisterhood? Interracial Friendships in Southern Fiction* (Athens: University of Georgia Press, 2000), and the first book on Barker, *Pat Barker* (Plymouth: Northcote House, 2002). She is the co-editor (with Peter Ling) of *Gender and the Civil Rights Movement* (New Brunswick: Rutgers University Press, 2004) and (with Suzanne Jones) of *South to a New Place: Region, Literature, Culture* (Baton Rouge: Louisiana State University Press, 2002). Her *American Culture in the 1960s* is forthcoming. She is writing a book on the civil rights movement in popular cinema.

JENNY NEWMAN is reader in creative writing at Liverpool John Moores University. Her novels are *Going In* (London: Hamish Hamilton, 1994) and *Life Class* (London: Chatto & Windus, 1999), and her short fiction has appeared in *This Is, Pool*, and *The London Magazine*. She is the editor of *The Faber Book of Seductions* (London: Faber and Faber, 1988), and co-editor of *Women Talk Sex: Autobiographical Writing on Sex, Sexuality, and Sexual Identity* (London: Scarlet Press, 1992) and *The Writer's Workbook* (London: Arnold, 2000). With Sharon Monteith and Pat Wheeler she published *Contemporary British and Irish Fiction: An Introduction through Interview* (London: Arnold, 2004).

HEATHER NUNN is a senior lecturer in cultural studies at the University of Surrey Roehampton. Her research interests include gender and political communications; violence, trauma, and media representations. She is the author of *Thatcher, Politics, and Fantasy: The Political Culture of Gender and Nation* (London: Lawrence and Wishart, 2002). She is currently completing a co-authored book with Anita Biressi on factual TV programming and reality TV.

RONALD PAUL is associate professor at the University of Gothenberg in Sweden. His publications are *Fire in Our Hearts: A Study of the Portrayal of Youth in Post-War*

British Working-Class Fiction (Göteborg: Acta Universitatis Gothoburgensis, 1983); *Unruly Nations: A People's History of Britain* (Malmö: Akademiförlaget, 1996) and *Dissonant Voices: Literature and Society in Britain from Chaucer to the Present Day* (Malmö: Akademiförlaget, 1999).

SHERYL STEVENSON teaches at the University of Akron, where she is associate professor of English. Her published research has concentrated on twentieth-century women's writing, first in the area of feminist dialogics, and more recently in connection with theories of psychological trauma. She is currently at work on a book on violation, terror, and survival in Pat Barker's fiction.

ELUNED SUMMERS-BREMNER is lecturer in women's studies at the University of Auckland, New Zealand, where she teaches on gender and sexuality in the arts and media. Her research interests are psychoanalysis, cultural memory, literature, and performance. She has published articles in *New Formations, Hypatia,* and *Feminist Studies,* and is at work on two book-length projects, one on the function of memory in the imagination of home and exile and the other on the contemporary function of the fantasy of childhood in photographic, literary, and televisual texts.

KARIN E. WESTMAN is an assistant professor of English at Kansas State University. Her research and teaching interests include modernism, contemporary British literature and culture, and women's literature. She has published essays on Virginia Woolf, A. S. Byatt, Georgette Heyer, and J. K. Rowling, as well as *Pat Barker's "Regeneration": A Reader's Guide* (New York: Continuum 2001). She is currently completing a book on contemporary British women novelists and realism.

PAT WHEELER is a senior lecturer in literature at the University of Hertfordshire in the UK. She publishes on British fiction, science fiction and contemporary women's writing. Her articles have appeared in *Critical Survey* and *Foundation.* She is the author of *Sebastian Faulks's "Birdsong": A Reader's Guide* (New York: Continuum, 2002) and (with Sharon Monteith and Jenny Newman), *Contemporary British and Irish Fiction: An Introduction through Interview* (London: Arnold, 2004). She is currently at work on a book on science fiction.

ANNE WHITEHEAD is lecturer in contemporary literature and theory at the University of Newcastle upon Tyne in the UK. She has published numerous articles on trauma theory and modern fiction. She has two books forthcoming, *Trauma Fiction* and *W. G. Sebald: A Critical Companion* (co-edited with J. J. Long).

NAHEM YOUSAF is senior lecturer at Nottingham Trent University in the UK. He writes on contemporary British and American literatures with an emphasis on the postcolonial. His books include *Alex La Guma: Politics and Resistance* (Portsmouth, N.H.: Heinemann, 2001), *Chinua Achebe* (Plymouth: Northcote House, 2003), *Hanif Kureishi's The Buddha of Suburbia* (New York: Continuum, 2001) and *Apartheid Narratives* (Amsterdam and Atlanta, Ga.: Rodopi 2001). He is currently at work on a book on new immigrants in the American South.

Index